# World Traveler's Guide to Disney

# World Traveler's Guide to Disney

How to Visit Mickey's Kingdoms around the Globe

MICHAEL FRIDGEN

ISBN-13: 9780996857420
ISBN-10: 0996857427
Library of Congress Control Number: 2017900804
Dreamlly Books, Minneapolis, MINNESOTA

Disclaimer: This book is the opinion of the author and is not endorsed by, or associated with, any division of the Walt Disney Company. All places, attractions, and characters mentioned in this book are copyrighted by the Walt Disney Company and are used by the author under the Fair Use Doctrine. The cover photographs were taken by the author.

*For Jesse and Dottie, who gave me my very own Donald Duck*

World Traveler's Guide to Disney: How to Visit Mickey's Kingdoms around the Globe

MICHAEL FRIDGEN

# Table of Contents

# 1

## An Introduction to Mickey's World

### Why Visit a Disney Park?

**D**URING THE SIXTEENTH century, it was often noted that the sun never set on the Spanish Empire. With many territories spread around the globe, the sun was always shining on some piece of land that was controlled by Spain. As with most things, the tides eventually changed. During the nineteenth and twentieth centuries, the sun rarely set on the British Empire. Then, in 1997, the British handed its control of Hong Kong back to China. Thus ended the reign of global empires—or so it seemed.

With theme parks in five time zones, a resort in the middle of the Pacific Ocean, and cruise ships in constant motion, it can be said that the sun never sets on Mickey Mouse's global territory. It's a magical empire that runs on dreams instead of oil. The lands of this empire are built as much from imagination as they are from concrete, and their only armament is the power of determination. These kingdoms have their roots in one man's tenacity and courage, but they also required the work and belief of countless others.

Does the previous paragraph sound sweet and idealistic? It should. Mickey Mouse is sweet, idealistic, optimistic, friendly, trustworthy, dependable—and about two hundred other adjectives that describe the best in all of us. Sure, there will be a bit of greed, corruption, and debt discussed in the history sections of each chapter. But those negative shortcomings make us remember why we need Mickey Mouse: we yearn for constant reminders that there are a lot of good things in this flawed world of ours.

Yet, with all that said, some questions occur:

- Why should a traveler devote precious time and money to visiting a Disney park?
- Why would anyone include Tokyo Disneyland on an itinerary of this already unbelievable city?
- How can Disneyland Paris possibly be worthy of a city where you can also visit the Eiffel Tower, Versailles, and the *Mona Lisa*?
- Isn't Disneyland just for kids?
- Does the experience of visiting Walt Disney World justify the expense?
- Why visit Disney's parks in Hong Kong and Shanghai when there is a local amusement park near my home?

For several years, I was the director of international programs for a coordinate campus of the University of Minnesota. This job required me to travel and interact with many academic-type people. I'm ashamed to admit that I often hid my theme-park-loving side from my colleagues.

"Michael," they'd ask me, "what are you going to do on the day off in Tokyo?"

I'd answer, "Oh, I'm just going to hang out with some friends that I have in the city."

I didn't feel the need to tell them that my friends were Donald Duck, Pinocchio, and Ariel. I'd grab my Suica card (see chapter 4) and take the train to spend an unforgettable day at Tokyo DisneySea. The rest of them would tour some sort of shrine or museum. I was embarrassed about my obsession with Disney.

Then, as I grew older and more confident, I realized that I did not have an obsession. I had a passion—a passion for quality and creativity. I was on a quest to have fun and to watch others having fun. I had an intense desire to experience incredible storytelling. I had a yearning for a sense of nostalgia and belonging. Mostly, I had a passion to seek out the things that I was passionate about.

One day, once I was more comfortable with myself, I returned and bumped into a colleague. She showed me some pictures on her phone of a shrine she had seen. I grabbed my phone and displayed a few photographs of Tokyo Disneyland's World Bazaar. She met my glance with a bit of a sneer.

She asked, "You wasted a whole day in Japan at an American amusement park?"

"Well, [insert an academic-sounding name of your choosing here], I wanted to relax and have fun on my day off."

"Well, Michael, I wanted to spend my time in Japan doing the things that the Japanese do. That's what all good travelers should experience."

"Wait a second. Look at your pictures. Who do you see at that shrine you were visiting? All I see is other tourists; I see very few Japanese people. But did you know that ninety-nine-point-seven percent of all visitors to Tokyo Disneyland are Japanese? I saw maybe just one other white person the whole time I was there. Look at my pictures for proof. Also, an amusement park is a place with a collection of rides. I went to a Disney park—an immersive experience of themed environments full of creativity and imagination."

Since that day, I've become much more assertive in defending my love of theme parks and why I choose to visit them. I fully realize that Disney parks are not for everyone—but they are for me. If someone doesn't judge me for visiting them, then I won't judge that person for neglecting them. (OK, I might judge a little.)

The fact is that Disney parks offer an unparalleled opportunity to observe culture because that's where a part of the current culture is vacationing. Viewing art is beautiful and historical, but viewing other people viewing art is fascinating. That's why you should visit a Disney park while traveling: observing others interacting with Disney's well-known brand provides insight into their culture.

Observe a crowd of kids as they watch Mickey and the Magical Map, a show at Disneyland in California. Five thousand miles away, observe a different crowd of kids as they watch a similar show at Disneyland Paris. The difference in these audiences will be striking. Spoiler alert: the European kids are way better behaved as they sit silently and motionlessly during the entire show. You will begin to question American culture and its ability to raise children. You may also question French culture and wonder if silent children are adequately prepared to become adults. Neither approach to parenting is better than the other, but your effort to think about these things will have given you the insight to accomplish a major goal of traveling: to observe and learn from other cultures.

Trains were extremely important to Walt Disney and are a fixture of Disney parks. Yet there is no railroad circling Tokyo Disneyland. When you learn the reason for its absence, you will also learn about an interesting historical phenomenon that occurred in Tokyo during American-occupied post–World War II Japan (see chapter 4). There is an important cultural reason there aren't haunted mansions in Hong Kong and Shanghai (see chapter 6). You could visit every museum in Paris and have little interaction with French workers. However, any visit to a Disney park will include many opportunities to interact with cast members ("Disneyspeak" for employees). Notice that the cast members at Disneyland Paris are fewer than and not as comprehensive as those in Shanghai. To explain this difference, you will need to understand French labor laws (see chapter 5). Consider this difference and you will learn about complicated human systems; you will wonder how these systems impact workers' rights in your own town.

People drive on the left side of the road in Hong Kong and on the right side in Shanghai, even though these cities are both in the same country. Guests arrive fifteen minutes late for a show at Disneyland in California and are seated. At Tokyo Disneyland, guests even twenty seconds late are told that, out of respect for those who arrived on time, they must leave and try again later. In order to learn from an experiment, you must observe the constant and the variables. Think of visiting Disney parks like a great social experiment: the parks are the constant, and the cultures are the variables.

By all means, visit the museums of Paris. But don't overlook Disneyland Paris Resort; after all, it is the most-visited attraction in all of Europe. See the beautiful temples and shrines of Asia—then enjoy the amazing Asian cuisine at one of Disney's restaurants in Tokyo, Hong Kong, or Shanghai. Go to the beaches of Florida and California. They are incredible. But if you really want to observe American families and learn how they interact, you must visit Disneyland and Walt Disney World.

Perhaps all this talk of magic and culture still hasn't convinced you of Disney's appeal as a destination. Maybe you are a person who is interested in the numbers from a business sense. Let me assure you: Cinderella and Snow White are well off. In 2015, Mickey Mouse's net income was $8.38 billion. He has $88.18 billion in assets; after considering for debt, Mickey is worth $48.65 billion. In 2015, 137,902,000 people passed through a Disney turnstile somewhere on the planet. That's 75,002,000 more people than their nearest competitor: Britain's Merlin Entertainments Group. Disney's nearest US competitor, Universal Studios Recreation Group, had a total attendance of 44,884,000 at their parks worldwide—that's only one-third of Disney's visitors.

The highest-revenue-producing single-site restaurant in the United States is not in New York City or San Francisco. It's Cosmic Ray's Starlight Café in Tomorrowland at the Magic Kingdom in Florida. Visit this eatery any day between 11:30 a.m. and 1:00 p.m. if you doubt this fact.

Japan is a country that embraces capitalism. Every major city is full of department stores, shops, and markets. But the highest-revenue-producing single-site store in the entire country of Japan is the World Bazaar Confectionary at the entrance of Tokyo Disneyland. This shop has more checkout lanes than your local Walmart, and the lines of guests waiting to pay can rival anything America's Black Friday may offer. The largest single-site employer in the United States is not Boeing or General Motors. With just over sixty-two thousand cast members, Walt Disney World is the largest single-site employer in the United States.

People all over the globe are willing to support Disney with their precious time and hard-earned money. They don't do this because they have no other option or are somehow stupid. People choose to partake in a Disney experience because they want quality, enjoyment, nostalgia, and a lot of magic. For many people, memories are worth the expense.

I've learned that the best way to approach life is the way a child does—through wonder, optimism, and curiosity. If I want to live this way, then I want to travel this way too. I'm not ashamed that my best friends include a frustrated duck, a puppet who moves without strings, and a princess from under the sea. I hope you aren't ashamed of those things either.

## Why Read This Book?

This book is a comprehensive guide to Disney's six resorts around the world and Disney's expanding line of cruise ships. Each chapter includes sections about transportation, money, history, accommodations, and sights to see outside the Disney parks. It's easy to skip the sections you don't want to read. If you're already familiar with Hong Kong, then skip the sections about transportation and accommodations. If you're not interested in the history of a particular location, you can skip that section as well. I promise that there won't be a quiz at the end; however, your conscience will know if you are a lazy reader (and Jiminy Cricket can be quite persistent—you might as well just read the whole thing before he gets on your case).

The heart of each chapter is, of course, the descriptions of the parks themselves. I've attempted to break each park into "lands" and provide details on the attractions located within. I've also written about the major restaurants and larger quick-service options. Please know that I haven't discussed every square inch of every park—you'd never be able to carry this book if I had! Use this book as a guide, but if your eyes lead you elsewhere in a park, just go with it. You may find your own cherished spots that you'll want to write about when you get home.

As with all travel books, there are a few points of notice that we need to get out of the way. By reading the notices, you will get to know me better, and that will help you understand this travel guide.

**Notice #1: How I Pay the Piper.** I've never received any compensation from the Disney Company, including free nights in hotels or complimentary tickets to the parks. I've been several times to each of the Disney parks and boarded Disney Cruise Ships for many voyages. This has all been accomplished at my own expense. Sometimes I was on a business trip. In these instances, the airfare was paid by my employer, but my visits to Disney parks were taken on my own time and at my own expense.

You may wonder how I have the means to do all this traveling. We probably all know that these parks aren't cheap (hey—Mickey didn't become a billionaire by giving away free tickets). For twelve years, I was a public elementary school music teacher. After that, I worked for a coordinate campus of the University of Minnesota for five years. Now I'm a full-time writer. I consider myself middle class. I finance these journeys through a combination of smart choices and structured priorities. (See Notice #4 to learn about one of my priorities.)

**Notice #2: Things Change.** Walt Disney famously remarked that Disneyland will never be complete; as long as there was imagination and innovation left in the world, Disneyland would continue to expand and change. Today, this is truer than ever. Construction of Star Wars Land at Disneyland in California and the development of Avatar Land at Disney's Animal Kingdom in Florida are but two examples of projects you may notice on your vacation. Construction walls can turn up in any land at any time.

On top of all the new construction, theme parks are places that need regular maintenance. Disney parks require even extra maintenance to keep them in the pristine condition that we have become accustomed to. Cinderella Castle at the Magic Kingdom in Florida is the most photographed building in the world. But even the most photographed building needs fresh paint and a new roof from time to time. (Yes, Cinderella Castle is the correct name of this building—never Cinderella's Castle.) The presidents inside Liberty Square's Hall of

Presidents need to have their suits dry-cleaned every so often. Cinderella may not actually be scrubbing the floors of her castle anymore, but somebody is. When that scrubbing occurs, you may be directed elsewhere in the park.

The guide you are reading was completely accurate at the time of publication. But, unfortunately, all travel guides are a bit out-of-date even one week later. To combat this discrepancy and discover the most recent knowledge, the Disney parks websites are your best sources of updated information. The official website for each park contains the most up-to-date park hours and schedules of attractions that are under refurbishment. These are also the sites where you can purchase tickets, reserve Disney hotel rooms, view ride wait times, and, in the case of Walt Disney World, reserve your FastPass+ selections (see chapter 3).

Disneyland: disneyland.disney.go.com

Walt Disney World: disneyworld.disney.go.com

Tokyo Disney Resort: tokyodisneyresort.jp (Choose the small globe in the upper right to change language.)

Disneyland Paris Resort: disneylandparis.com (Choose the small globe to change language.)

Hong Kong Disney Resort: hongkongdisneyland.com (English is normally the default language.)

Shanghai Disney Resort: shanghaidisneyresort.com (Choose the menu on the upper left, look for the small globe, and select it to change language.)

Disney Cruise Line: disneycruise.disney.go.com

In addition to the websites, Disney parks apps offer a plethora of information. After a much-needed technology integration plan, the apps finally look like each other and offer similar features. The best part of the apps is the ability to get instant access to a map that shows the current wait times for attractions. If you are traveling to Florida, the My Disney Experience app is an absolute must. This is where you can choose your FastPass+ selections and manage them throughout your stay. Your dining reservations will also show up on this app. The other parks don't currently offer the same features, but they may in the near future.

Please note: Tokyo Disney Resort is the only location that is not even partially owned by the Walt Disney Company (see chapter 4.) Consequently, there is no official Tokyo Disney Resort app. There are, however, several third-party apps that are free and will give you maps and ride times. My favorite is TokyoDMap.

*Dreamlly's Disney Direction*

This is Dreamlly. He is a narwhal. Narwhals are whales that are close cousins to the belugas. They live in the far north and retreat under ice for protection. Their most distinctive feature is a long horn that started the myth of unicorns back in medieval times. However, the horn is technically a tusk as it is an elongated tooth that protrudes through the narwhal's upper lip. Narwhals are my personal symbol because they cannot be captured. Even though belugas can be found in aquariums all over the planet, no narwhal has ever survived even a few days in captivity. They would simply rather die than live in a cage—I like that about them. Dreamlly is named after two of my favorite things: "Dream" comes from the Disney Dream cruise ship, the most relaxing place on earth. The "lly" is the last three letters of the name Dolly. Dolly Parton has inspired me for years through her music and philanthropy, plus she owns her own theme park! (Check out my guide to Dollywood, available at amazon.com.)

Dreamlly is going to pop up from time to time during this book. He'll offer a few words of advice that will help with your vacation planning.

This installment of Dreamlly's Disney Direction is all about managing expectations. I was an elementary school teacher for twelve years, and I learned that most meltdowns occur when children are not having their expectations met. Of course, this is inevitable when embarking on such an all-encompassing vacation as Disney offers. Your favorite princess might not show up for work that day. The Yeti at Expedition Everest may be down for repairs. It may rain the entire time you are in Tokyo. In my experience, the best thing you can do to prepare children for disappointment is to have open dialogues with them as you prepare for your journey. Talk to them about the possibility of attractions being broken. Talk about how to respond to that situation.

Children love to role play. Ask one of the kids to pretend to be the ride operator at Space Mountain. One of the parents can pretend to be a guest. When the kid (ride operator) tells the parent (rider) that the ride is down, have that parent role play with the biggest pretend tantrum of all tantrums that there ever was. Make it absurd and funny. Later, while in the parks, when some sort of disappointment occurs, remind each other of your role play. Hopefully they will remember the humor and that will help to alleviate some of the unpleasantness.

▲ ▲ ▲

**Notice #3: Do your homework.** While I was a teacher, like a lot of my colleagues, I assigned homework. However, I never used homework as part of a grade; I allowed the students to live with the natural consequences of doing or not doing their assignments. You won't get an F if you fail to do the homework involved in making dining reservations for Walt Disney World in Florida. But you will suffer the natural consequence, which is, in this case, the impossibility of finding anyplace to eat dinner without a two-hour wait. An hour or two of homework before you leave home will result in a much more pleasant Disney experience—no matter which of the destinations you choose. Even if you use a travel agent, you are not off the hook. Do your homework and double check that everything is confirmed as you want it to be.

Nowhere is homework more important than when it comes to budget. You should always start saving for your next vacation by making smart choices during the planning phase of your current journey. Run the numbers, look at the bottom line, and then run the numbers again. Do all this unpleasant math before your departure so that you can truly enjoy, and afford, your entire vacation.

**Notice #4: Eat cheap.** Please understand that notice #4 is my own personal choice, and I am in no way advocating that you travel the same way. I eat cheaply when I travel. It's no secret among my friends that I can spend less than fifteen dollars per day in Manhattan eating pizza, pretzels, and fruit. I make this choice because I'm always on a budget, and I'd rather spend my money on a better-located hotel. I've visited grocery stores all over the world to stock my hotel room with bread, fruit, and Diet Coke.

In the Disney parks, I don't mind spending money on theme-park-type dining experiences. These include character brunches and evening show dining packages. I view these as more a part of an attraction than they are a way to get a meal. I write about these experiences in this book. However, I am not able to offer comprehensive reviews of any of the expensive sit-down restaurants in the resorts. It's just not my priority to spend a lot of money on food.

Please know that this is not a judgment of anyone. I have plenty of friends who consider themselves connoisseurs of good food and wine. More power to them! I enjoy hearing about their experiences, and I'm quite happy to help them arrange a reservation and transportation. By all means, go to Victoria and Albert's at the Grand Floridian and enjoy your duck confit. There's a turkey sandwich back at the All-Star Music Resort with my name on it!

**Notice #5: For Disneyphiles.** If you've spent any time on a Disney blog or in a chat forum, please read this notice. If you didn't know that there are Disney blogs and chat forums, please skip ahead. (Pausing for a few seconds.) OK, now that all the amateurs have left, I can make an appeal directly to the ultimate Disney lovers among us: please be nice. I know how passionate you all are—it's one of the reasons I love Disney so much. No other theme park fan base can even come close to your level of dedication, knowledge, and passion. However, along with those attributes, there sometimes also appear a bit of enmity and borderline bullying.

I was once ridiculed in a chat forum for posting my opinion in a discussion thread. I expressed my view of the Disney Dining Plan at Walt Disney World in Florida. I've done the math many times using several different scenarios, and I can't find a way that the Disney Dining Plan makes financial sense—even if it's offered free. (Spoiler alert: Nothing is free. In order to get the dining plan free, you must purchase a resort room at the rack rate that will be 25 percent higher than the regular Internet rate.) In the online forums, I never said that nobody should get the Disney Dining Plan. I never stated that the dining plan was a big mistake. All I said was that the math does not work for me and the way my family travels. However, the level of outrage waged against me was so bad that I had to remove myself from the entire forum.

To make a very long story short, Dear Disneyphiles: I love your passion. I love how you wear costumes to the Halloween parties. I love the excitement you show every time you board a Disney cruise ship. I love how you can spot a hidden Mickey ten miles away. You won't agree with everything I write in this book. Heck, many of you could write sections of this book better than I could ever hope to do. Some of you have forgotten more about Disney than I will ever know. Just please be nice. Channel that inner Thumper and subdue your internal Maleficent for a bit. And thank you for being you.

**Notice #6: Which ocean is that?** Please listen to these words and take them to heart. Repeat them at least four times each day. *Disneyland is in Anaheim, California. Walt Disney World is in Orlando, Florida.* There is a famous episode of the ABC sitcom *The Middle* where the Heck family arrives in Florida with tickets to Disneyland. Chaos ensues. Don't make this same mistake.

You may think this must be a rare occurrence that happens only to stupid people on sitcoms. You would be wrong. This situation occurs more than you'd think—it's much easier to make this mistake than you might imagine. The ticketing websites look identical. Mickey looks the same no matter the location. Yes, Disneyland's castle is smaller, but that's a detail that many don't pay attention to when they purchase tickets online. I have a friend who used to work for the Walt Disney Travel Company. She often tells about the times she had booked a complete vacation, including airfare and resort rooms, only to have to redo the entire booking when she simply mentioned the word "California" at the end of the confirmation. The guests wanted to go to Florida.

Just to clarify, Disneyland is in California. It has Sleeping Beauty Castle and the Grand Californian Resort. Walt Disney World is in Florida. It has Cinderella Castle and the Grand Floridian Resort. Disneyland Resort includes two theme parks and uses a Fastpass system based on a paper coupon. Walt Disney World Resort includes four theme parks and uses the FastPass+ system that is based on a MagicBand that you wear around your wrist (see chapter 3).

**Notice #7: Dollars and sense.** All prices quoted in this book are based on the most current information as of January 2017. Since Disney is notorious for lowering prices, many of the figures will change. (That was a joke just to make sure that you're still paying attention. Disney hasn't lowered a price since they displayed a rack of discounted *The Black Cauldron* merchandise after the failed 1985 film.)

Prices for Disneyland and Walt Disney World will be given in US dollars ($). The Disneyland Paris chapter will include prices in both euros (€) and dollars. Japanese yen (¥) and US dollars will accompany text about Tokyo Disney Resort. Please note that even though Hong Kong is technically in China, the city remains a special administration region (see chapter 5). Consequently, Hong Kong uses different currency than mainland China. The Hong Kong Disneyland prices will be given in both Hong Kong dollars (HK$) and US dollars. Shanghai Disney Resort will have its prices displayed in both Chinese renminbi, also called yuan (¥), and dollars.

Conversions among the different currencies were calculated in January 2017 using google.com. Remember, conversion rates fluctuate hourly. Always check the latest rate before you purchase foreign currency. Each chapter of this book will include information about the best way to use currency at the local parks.

**Notice #8: Consistent meal prices.** You may be shocked by this one. You won't find a lot of dining prices quoted in this book. This is because Disney's prices are surprisingly consistent across levels and locations. As you read, keep in mind these general guidelines:

- A quick-service meal inside a theme park or Disney hotel is normally around $8 for a kid's meal and $14 for an adult. This includes one side but no beverage. It doesn't really matter which park you're at; even internationally, quick-service restaurants like to stay around this price point.

- A table-service entrée is going to be about $12 for a child and $20 for an adult. This is again without a beverage. Also, remember to tip your hardworking wait staff in the United States. (Just round up the bill in Europe, and don't tip in Asia.)
- A character meal will be around $25 for a child and $60 for an adult. This most often includes a beverage and dessert.
- The big exceptions to these guidelines are the premier dining establishments inside the resorts. Cinderella's Royal Table at the Magic Kingdom is going to cost more; so is filet mignon at the more upscale hotel restaurants. Disney is transparent with all their prices on their websites.

**Notice #9: No "must dos" here.** Most Disney guidebooks will point out which attractions the author(s) considers as must dos—things that should not be missed on your visit to a Disney park. Don't look for these in this book because I haven't included any. Everyone has different tastes, and nobody knows what you will like better than you. In Florida, Country Bear Jamboree is an absolutely must do for me. However, I know people who believe this attraction was the longest twenty minutes of their lives. Some people love the spinning teacups and would never think of skipping them. For me, they are a blurry pukefest that should be included as one of Dante's levels of hell. For my parents, sitting on a bench and watching families walk past is their must do. Get the point? Make your own list of must- dos no matter what anyone else may think.

You should destroy this book. Yes, it's true—and I may be the only author ever to encourage the destruction of the written word. But I pack light, and I encourage you to do the same. Don't carry this whole book with you to Hong Kong; just cut the binding apart with an X-Acto knife and take only the Hong Kong Disneyland chapter when you travel. I am the king of torn-apart travel books. If you ever see a very handsome man walking around the streets of Tokyo with a bunch of book pages duct-taped together, that's me! Stop and say hi.

▲ ▲ ▲

## Consider the Source

In this age of Wikipedia and corporate publishing, it is important to carefully consider the author's expertise, especially while reading a book about travel. Teams of people assigned through a publisher write many bestselling guides and tour books. Sometimes these writers have not even visited the places they are offering advice about. So if you're wondering who wrote this book and why you should read it, I'm about to tell you. If you are not wondering or are anxious to get to the details, go ahead and skip to the next section.

When I was five years old, I received a map of Disney World's Magic Kingdom for Christmas. Today, if a kid gets a map of Disney World as a present, he or she can probably assume that the real gift is an actual trip to the famous park. But I knew that my family did not have the means to make such a journey. I also knew that my parents realized how much I loved looking at maps. Regardless, I can credit my many hours of staring at that map, and using it to drive my Matchbox cars on, as the beginning of my love of theme parks.

I liked maps of real places too, but these were usually messy with mountains, rivers, and lakes to navigate. The Magic Kingdom map was beautifully drawn and instantly made sense to me. I took my little car and easily planned how to get from the entrance gate to the moat around Cinderella Castle. Many nights I dreamed that someday I would spend one day at that magical place. But back then, I had no idea how my life would develop, and I couldn't imagine the numerous theme park visits I would one day make.

I grew up in Minnesota, and every year we took the two-hour journey by station wagon to spend one day at what I thought was the happiest place on earth, Valleyfair in Shakopee, Minnesota. I vividly remember getting little sleep the night before because of all the anticipation. I also remember saying a prayer because I was afraid that if our house burned down during the night, we wouldn't be able to go there.

They called Valleyfair a theme park, but even today I'm unsure what the theme was. Back then, a large patriotic man called Colonel John Phillips Oom-pa-pa roamed the asphalt with his girlfriend, Chocolate Moose. She was a furry brown moose that wore a frilly dress and straw hat; I always thought she looked like Minnie Pearl from the television show *Hee Haw*. Valleyfair had these ladybugs that went around in a circle and an enormous green chair where the Jolly Green Giant supposedly sat, although we never saw him.

I'm unsure how that one glorious day each summer and my Disney World map turned into a lifelong obsession with theme parks. I'd probably need to employ a psychiatrist with deep analytical skills to determine what from my childhood made me crave the fantasy realness of a themed land. But when it comes down to it, I guess I don't care why or how I got this way because it's a good way to be. Hey, there are a lot of other worse obsessions I could have.

I believe that theme parks are truly magical places because they force us to forget the real world and pause for reflection. Each year, it's where we kids measured our progress toward adulthood. Nothing marks time better than the ride attendant holding up a painted wood pole next to you and stating that you can go on the High Roller. That pole measured both our physical growth and inner bravery. Every summer, our parents saw the changes in us, and we saw the difference in ourselves. I didn't grow up in the age of box socials and cotillions. Our annual trip to Valleyfair is how we generation Xers marked time.

I was twenty-one years old the first time I stepped foot inside a Disney park. (Yep, I was a late bloomer.) My parents, sister, grandparents, and I drove from Central Minnesota to Orlando. We didn't have many resources at the time, and we packed all of our food into a small trailer that we pulled behind our vehicle. We stayed, all of us in one room, at a motel in Kissimmee, Florida. I'm not sure which motel it was, but I think the name was something like the Cockroach/Drug Dealer/Mass Murderer Motel. (Thankfully, the budget hotel market has improved greatly in the past twenty years. There are now many options that are safer and cleaner. Even Disney offers several value choices in Orlando.)

I was beyond excited. Remember, I'd had a map of the place since I was five. But, alas, sometimes travel throws you a curve. Even though Orlando is in Florida, it is very rare for a hurricane to directly impact the area. Walt Disney World is in the central part of the Florida peninsula; hurricanes tend to hit the coasts and the southern tip. Regardless, 1995 Hurricane Erin hit the Murder Motel the first night of our arrival. This storm crossed the entire peninsula, hitting both coasts, Orlando, and the panhandle. It was windy. And rainy. And thundering. And very, very windy. Seriously, it was windy.

The next morning, there was no electricity in the motel, and most of the windows had been broken. The worst news, as heard on our emergency travel radio, was that the Disney theme parks were temporarily closed. I was heartbroken. My grandma got bored and decided to wash all our clothes in the bathtub. (Yes, we really were that cheap.) She didn't figure that the electricity would be out for days, rendering the motel dryers useless. So Grandpa, in all his Depression-era glory, got some rope from our food trailer and strung up our wet underwear between a couple of palm trees. And then, in the middle of the afternoon, the Blue Fairy must have heard my wish. The radio announced that the Magic Kingdom was open!

We left our hanging clothes, thinking that drug dealers had more money than us and probably wouldn't want anything we had. Orlando was a mess of branches, paper, and yard furniture. We doubted the radio's news of an open Magic Kingdom when we saw that nobody in the city had any power. But then we took an exit off the highway and saw our first Disney road signs. They had their own road signs! I jumped out of my skin.

Believe it or not, the sun was shining. The entire Walt Disney Resort had electricity because they make their own and channel it underground. I saw the gates—those wonderful, magical gates that still send a shiver through my body. My nineteen-year-old sister screamed with joy. At that moment, we weren't hurricane-ravaged adults carrying our own food from the Murder Motel, where our underwear currently hung. Magically, we were all kids.

I remember each detail of that wonderful afternoon and evening: the monorail, the castle, ghosts, pirates, country bears, presidents, happy dolls, Donald Duck. I grasped as much of it as I could because I thought I'd probably never travel back there. I bought a Mickey Mouse mug. Little did I know the kind of life that I would have one day.

Through some smart decisions and hard work, I've obtained a life where I am fortunate enough to be able to travel to the places I love. I've been to many theme parks in the United States and abroad. I've been multiple times to each of the Disney parks around the globe. I count among my favorite places Dollywood in Tennessee, Ocean Park in Hong Kong, Tivoli Gardens in Copenhagen, EuropaPark in Germany, and DisneySea in Tokyo.

All of us take many roles in life. In order for any one place to be considered a true lifelong destination, it must be able to appeal to you during all those changing roles. Theme parks have not disappointed me in this regard. As my own life has changed, I've experienced Disney parks in new and different ways.

I have been to theme parks as:

- a small kid being pushed around by his parents
- a preteen trying to be brave with friends

- a high schooler on a marching band trip
- a college student traveling with family
- a working adult traveling with family
- an uncle with a ten-month-old nephew
- a grandson with elderly grandparents
- a single person who just wanted to get away
- an adult traveling with other adult friends who I coerced into going
- an uncle with preteen and toddler nephews
- part of a couple on our honeymoon
- a person in a wheelchair after having ankle surgery
- an uncle with a teenage nephew, preteen nephew, and a third kid, my niece
- part of a couple still choosing to spend vacation time in a fantasy realness

In the 1970s, my grandma chased after me at Valleyfair when I wanted to ride the little boats instead of eating. Thirty years later, I ran around that same park trying to find which shop she had gone to. I hope in thirty more years my nephews and niece will be able to push me around the attractions as I now push them around the play areas.

And that brings me back to my original point: theme parks are magical places because they give us pause to mark the progress we make as people. It's my hope that you will travel to your own Valleyfair and use the fantasy realness to mark your own life. Mostly, I hope you've learned from this section that you can trust me to write this guidebook.

### *All I Really Needed to Know I Learned in Theme Parks*

- A good map is essential to find your way.
- If you want to eat dinner, you can't spend all of your money on games.
- Waiting in line is dull, but it gets better if you can occupy your own brain for a while.
- Respecting other people's space is a good thing to do.
- Facing a fear can be extremely difficult, but the reward is amazing.
- You may be disappointed at times. Just deal with it.
- Like the weather, things will happen that you can't control. Just deal with it.
- Planning ahead makes your day a lot easier.
- Keep track of your stuff because nobody else will.
- Prioritize what you want to do, and make choices that lead in that direction.
- Taking care of your body is important if you want to fit on all the rides.

- If your group splits up, always make a plan to find each other again.
- Cleanliness is a good thing, and if you keep things clean, others will too.
- An active fantasy life inspires you to make your real life even better.
- Creativity still means something on this planet.
- A healthy human always has something to look forward to.
- Be nice to all those who are doing their jobs because tomorrow that will be you.
- As you get older, sitting on a bench and watching a roller coaster can be as much fun as riding it yourself.
- Laughter and having fun are essential parts of life worthy of your time and money.

▲ ▲ ▲

## Developing a Travel Philosophy

I've heard this strange rumor that some people don't like theme parks. As hard as it is to believe, I've also heard that some people don't like Disney theme parks. I've met some of these people. Some of them are even productive, law-abiding citizens.

All kidding aside, when I ask people why they didn't have a magical time on their Disney vacations, it's usually because they pursued a side of Disney that didn't meet their purpose. One of my colleagues wanted a relaxing time creating memories with her kids. However, while at Walt Disney World, she wanted everyone to see everything. Consequently, her family drove each other nuts as they forced themselves to run through each park for days. Another couple I know desired a very active theme park vacation and was dismayed when they had to spend a lot of time stuck in traffic. They all came away hating Disney—but that wasn't necessarily Mickey's fault.

My colleague made the mistake of forcing activity when so many lovely Disney pools would have been better. The couple I mentioned made the mistake of not staying at a hotel close to the theme parks. But, in both cases, they made the crucial mistake of traveling without a philosophy. We don't often ask ourselves, "Why do I want to travel, and how can my destination support that purpose?"

I have a good friend who knows that in addition to theme parks, I also love Las Vegas. (I guess Las Vegas is kind of like one big theme park for adults.) One winter, she thought she'd vacation in Sin City. She hated it and wasn't afraid to share that with me. "Everything was so fake—not just the buildings but also the people. Everything is about money there, and I just couldn't stand all the superficial people running around. The whole town was about status, money, and how trashy you could look."

Now I know what some of you are thinking. What in the world was she expecting? What did she think Las Vegas was—a Tibetan monastery? Well, in this case, the destination was not the problem. The destination is rarely the problem. The problem was that my friend didn't consider what kind of experience she wanted on vacation. Why did she want to travel, and how could Las Vegas support that purpose?

There are plenty of authentic experiences to be had in Las Vegas. She could have visited the superb cactus gardens at Ethel M's Chocolate Factory. Both Grand Canyon and Zion national parks are easy drives away. A tour of Zappo's corporate headquarters gives great insight into the workings of a socially responsible company. The Neon Graveyard is fascinating from both a historical and design perspective.

My friend fell into the trap of doing what she thought she had to do in Las Vegas. She was stuck in casinos on the Strip because that's the Las Vegas she saw on television. She should have crafted a more tailored itinerary. However, this is easier said than done due to societal pressure.

As soon as you tell someone that you're going to Las Vegas, you will get all sorts of advice and stories about how to go crazy on Las Vegas Boulevard. You'll hear all about the hotels and bars that you *must* go to because so and so had an epic night there. When you return home, it gets even worse. You will have to face the barrage of "Did you see that? No? Oh, you really missed out." My advice: don't let other people's expectations of your trip have an impact on your journey.

When it becomes known that your family has chosen a Disney vacation, former Disney travelers will come out of the woodwork. They will each have a list of things you must do or else your trip will not be nearly as good as theirs was. There are also 12,258 blogs telling you how to vacation with Disney. Of course, it's fine to seek guidance and learn from others who have experience. But, again, don't let other people's expectations of your trip have an impact on your journey.

I've been on trips to Walt Disney World when I've never set foot in a theme park. This may sound very strange, but it's true. The Disney resorts in Florida are huge with lots of activities and amenities. Outside of the resorts, Disney Springs is an entertainment district that is as large as a theme park and doesn't require any admission to enter. There are watercraft activities on Disney's Bay Lake and the Seven Seas Lagoon. Sometimes this is the kind of vacation that I want.

To summarize this section, remember these three things:

- Spend some time before your departure considering what kind of experience you want to have on vacation.
- Take advice from others, but don't let them dictate your journey.
- It's OK to do things that are atypical for your destination.

So go ahead and vacation the way you want. After all, it's your time and money. I'm giving you permission to go to Hawaii and skip the beach. Go to Rome and pass on the pasta. Go to Japan and eat at McDonald's. Go to Disneyland and sleep in, or get up early because you love theme parks in the morning, or avoid the park and spend the day by the pool. Be brave, and travel according to your philosophy.

# 2

## Disneyland Resort

**M**ANY REFER TO any Disney park as "the happiest place on earth." However, there is only one official happiest place on earth—the original Disneyland, which is one part of the Disneyland Resort in Anaheim, California. This is the property that started it all. It's the world's first theme park with multiple lands and a single entry. It's the only park that Walt personally designed and walked down Main Street, USA. It's adorable and magical—truly an American creation.

Disneyland Resort includes two theme parks: the original Disneyland and Disney California Adventure. There are three hotels: Disney's Grand Californian Hotel and Spa, Disneyland Hotel, and Disney's Paradise Pier Hotel. A large shopping and dining district, Downtown Disney, connects the theme parks to the hotels. In addition, the resort holds several sprawling parking lots and the largest indoor parking ramp on the planet.

### Disneyland Resort Pros

- It's the most historical park, where Walt Disney practically lived for the last eleven years of his life.
- It's small and manageable. You can easily walk from one park to the other and to all the hotels.
- Disneyland still holds the most classic rides of any Disney park.
- Like Mary Poppins, the weather in Southern California is practically perfect in every way.
- A large number of inexpensive non-Disney hotels are just a few minutes' walk or ride away.

### Disneyland Resort Cons

- Of all the Disney parks worldwide, this one has the least amount of "Disney bubble." The outside world is quite visible.
- Millions of Californians treat Disneyland as their personal playground. This creates a fun

environment that can also be a bit annoying at times.

- Disneyland's on-property hotels are outrageously expensive.
- Because residential neighborhoods are so close, the famous Disney fireworks are canceled at any sign of wind. This occurs more frequently than you (or Disney) would like.
- With little room to expand, a new attraction almost always means the destruction of an old one.

▲ ▲ ▲

## History

More lore and speculation surround the history of Disneyland than any other theme park on earth—and many of these rumors were probably created by Walt Disney himself. Walt was first and foremost a storyteller. He fully realized the incredible power of a story to get attention. Some people believe that Disneyland was entirely a realization of Walt's fatherly dreams. Others think it was a calculated business decision. I think it's probably a bit of both.

Walt often told a story that when his two daughters were young, he'd take them to Griffith Park in Los Angeles on Saturdays. He'd put the girls on the carousel and sit on a bench to watch. Now, Walt was a very smart man, and I doubt his brain was ever idle for long. Consequently, he was bored to tears and desired a place where kids and adults could have fun together. The dreamer in him saw the chance to do something with his daughters. The brilliant futurist in him saw the chance to offer something for the first families in human history to have disposable income.

This was post WWII in the early 1950s. America had a middle class with lots of children and the means to spend money on entertainment. The automobile was king, and highways connected the country. There was a fairly new industry of air travel that began to grow. Walt, ever fascinated by human progress, noticed all these things.

Families started showing up to vacation in Hollywood. Those who lived and worked in the famous neighborhood thought this was quite bizarre because there was nothing to see. Everything that occurred in Hollywood happened behind a gate on a closed sound stage. But what Hollywood didn't anticipate was that practically every television show and movie in the entire nation was one big advertisement for the glitz and glamour of a place that didn't really exist.

Walt saw all this and began plans to create a park in Burbank, right next to Disney Studios. He envisioned a piece of land with a carousel and a few other rides. He thought it would be great if the craftsmen at Disney Studios could build the rides to feature characters from his films. He planned to call it Mickey Mouse Park.

Lillian Disney, his wife, hated the idea. She had been to amusement parks all over the country and saw how dirty they were. She also noticed that they attracted criminals and were mostly run by swindlers. Walt heard all this and promptly told her that his park would be different because Mickey Mouse was not a criminal or a swindler.

In modern America, CEOs are judged by two things: how much money the company made in the previous quarter and how much personal wealth the CEO can stash into private accounts. Walt was not of today's era. I doubt that Walt Disney ever cared about the previous quarter as he was much more occupied with long-range plans. He was a visionary who was creating for decades to come, and he'd sacrifice much to reach those goals.

Although extremely famous, Walt was never a wealthy man. He was often broke and had a habit of taking out mortgages on his personal property to finance the studio's next venture. (Lillian must have been an extraordinary person to support this practice.) Can you imagine what achievements airlines and automobile manufacturers might attain today if the CEOs thought as Walt did?

But it wasn't just Lillian who had some reservations about an amusement park. Walt's brother Roy, the financial boss of the company, was also quite skeptical. So were most banks. However, Walt persisted and sent a proposal to the Burbank City Council to rezone the land next to the studio for entertainment purposes. The proposal lost by one vote. (I wonder who the poor guy was that kept a multi-billion-dollar enterprise out of his town!)

Of course, in true Mickey Mouse style, nothing was going to stop a great idea. By 1953, Walt was ready to make a theme park his top priority. He was calling it Disneylandia. He even had a napkin where he'd drawn the famous "hub and spoke" design—since copied by many other parks.

Walt hired a couple of guys to scout the area and find a good location for Disneylandia. He was looking for a specific piece of land that was large enough, cheap enough, close to the then-under-construction Santa Ana Freeway, and not too far from the Los Angeles metropolitan area. After a few months, the men suggested a suitable location in Anaheim, a town that nobody had heard of, about forty miles southwest of the Disney Studios in Burbank. Walt agreed and purchased the land, which was an orange grove at the time.

Of course, in true Walt Disney style, he had already mortgaged everything, including the studio, to finance the project. He needed more funds to begin construction and sent brother Roy to tap into any source he could find. Nobody was interested; the idea was too risky. Then the brothers formed a connection with the relatively new television network ABC. Mickey Mouse and his companions were extremely popular, and ABC knew that American children would likely watch a weekly television show starring these characters. They also knew that no home in the United States had more than one television, so whatever the kids were watching, the parents had to watch too.

Walt agreed to create a series for ABC, and they, in turn, financed the rest of Walt's park in Anaheim.

However, they didn't like the name Disneylandia and convinced Walt to call both the television show and the park simply Disneyland. By this time, excavation of the site had been completed, and structural construction began on July 16, 1954.

The park needed a hotel since there were none in the area. Still strapped for cash, Walt approached his friend Jack Wrather, a wealthy Texan. Wrather agreed to build a hotel next to the park provided that the Wrather Corporation retained full ownership of the hotel forever. Walt agreed, and construction soon began on the Disneyland Hotel. (This partnership becomes quite important to the future of both Disneyland and Tokyo Disneyland. Stay tuned.)

Walt also created partnerships with businesses to operate real shops inside the park. He was so hard up for cash that he'd sign a lease with anyone. Believe it or not, the Hollywood-Maxwell Brassiere Company was one of those businesses. Yep, on Main Street, USA, the Wizard of Bras sold corsets and other undergarments right in Disneyland! (Can you imagine the outcry if Victoria's Secret opened today right next to the Mad Hatter?)

One year and one day later, Disneyland opened to the public on July 17, 1955. The total price tag was $17 million. This is fairly astounding in today's climate when a typical suburban high school requires $60 million and about thirty-six years of construction.

Yes, there were some minor problems that first day, like a lack of toilets and several unfinished buildings. But for the most part, the publicity received during the ABC show worked, and thousands were curious to see this wonderful place. The business community of the time thought that a good measure of success would be Disneyland's ability to attract one million guests within five years. Pretty much the entire state of California, including Walt, was shocked when Disneyland welcomed its millionth guest in October 1955—just three months after opening.

Seemingly overnight, every piece of land surrounding the park was purchased and developed. Disneyland was soon landlocked with all sorts of motels and tourist traps sprawling across the area. Walt finally had money, but there was nothing left to purchase. Even Jack Wrather refused to sell the Disneyland Hotel to him. So Walt set his focus on a different coast (see the next chapter).

Disneyland continued to thrive and develop even after Walt's death in 1966. The whole thing had been an unprecedented success, but lack of land kept the park within its bounds. In 1982, a couple thousand miles away, EPCOT Center opened at Walt Disney World in Florida. This had an enormous impact on Disneyland in California. The benefits of having a second park, or "gate" in Disneyspeak, were extraordinary. A second gate increased attendance and revenue in all areas, including hotels, dining, merchandise, and tickets. A second gate meant that families could spend an entire week with Disney instead of two or three days. Disneyland was desperate to find a way to add a second gate in land-strapped Anaheim.

This was the mid-1980s, when Michael Eisner was Mickey's top business partner at the Disney Company. Eisner, in a move to get the Disneyland Hotel under Disney ownership, purchased the entire Wrather Corporation. Disney sold off a bunch of the company that they had no interest in, but they were quite happy to finally control the hotel that bore the name of their famous park. Then things got interesting.

The Wrather Corporation owned and operated a large piece of oceanfront property in Long Beach, California. This property, about twenty miles from Disneyland, was right on the ocean. *The Queen Mary*, a decommissioned ocean liner, was anchored on the property and in use as a hotel. Two ideas soon emerged for this new Disney land.

One, perhaps a copy of Florida's successful EPCOT would work in California. This idea was dubbed the WESTCOT project. Second, since the land was right on the ocean, maybe an ocean-themed park might work. This concept was called DisneySea and would contain themed harbors as Disneyland contained themed lands. Soon, the entire property in Long Beach was being referred to as Port Disney.

As you can imagine, the folks over in Anaheim were getting a bit nervous hearing all this stuff about Long Beach. Their concern was that Disney would build a new park and several themed resorts at Port Disney. Their great fear was that Disney would find a way to offer easy and quick transportation between Disneyland and Port Disney. Tourists would have no reason to stay and spend their money in Anaheim if it was newer and better to stay in Long Beach—and then just hop on a monorail to Disneyland for the day.

The business community in Anaheim made plans quickly. The stakes were too high for any one business owner to get in the way. Eventually, Anaheim made Disney an offer they couldn't refuse. A parcel of land adjacent to Disneyland, formerly containing motels and such, was sold to Disney at a bargain price. Eisner jumped at this opportunity and began construction on the world's largest parking structure, the Mickey and Friends parking ramp. This freed the former Disneyland parking lot to be developed.

Part of the new development called for an entertainment district of shops and restaurants. This area would not require an admission ticket and would serve as a way for Disney hotel guests to walk to the parks. Yep, that's "parks"—plural. The other part of the new development was dedicated to a theme park and luxury resort. The entertainment area became Downtown Disney.

Although successful, EPCOT Center had been extremely expensive to build, and Eisner was not interested in assuming more debt for the company. It was also decided that the amazingly themed DisneySea would not work this far inland. (Are you sad that DisneySea was scrapped? Stay tuned—California's loss will eventually be Tokyo's gain.)

When Disney succeeds, they really succeed. When they fail, they really fail. In 1995, it was decided that

Disney would pursue a California-themed park as a sister for Disneyland. Construction began in 1998, and Disney California Adventure opened on February 8, 2001. A resort, Disney's Grand Californian Hotel and Spa, opened as well.

The park was met with lackluster enthusiasm, and attendance was not great. There were really two problems. One, people go to a Disney park because they want to step into a story. There just wasn't a story being told at Disney California Adventure. Two, as famous as it is, Disneyland Resort still draws heavily from the local area. Californians just weren't that interested in visiting a park about California. Simply put, nobody wanted to drive from San Francisco to see a replica of the Golden Gate Bridge.

However, to Disney's credit, they didn't simply abandon Disney California Adventure. In 2007, a massive billion-dollar renovation began that was completed in 2012. The Golden Gate Bridge was dismantled and replaced with a new entrance and entertainment plaza, Buena Vista Street. Cars Land opened and gave guests the opportunity to step into the various stories of the Cars franchise of films. A nighttime show, World of Color, debuted to rave reviews and has attained legendary status.

Disneyland recently celebrated its sixtieth birthday. Sleeping Beauty Castle sparkled with diamond turrets for the entire year, and the rest of the park shined as well. A major expansion, Star Wars Land, is under construction at Disneyland, and parts of Disney California

Adventure are getting new stories from Disney-acquired Marvel Comics. As Walt himself said, Disneyland will never be complete. But for many of us, Disneyland is as much about the past as it is about the future. No other park has this level of nostalgia, and for Disney fans, Disneyland will always be the park where Walt walked.

## Travel Knowledge

### Arrival

Disneyland Resort may be the only Disney location where most people arrive by car. The resort is located right off Interstate 5, which is also called the Santa Ana Freeway; it is the main highway connecting Los Angeles and San Diego. If you've ever watched any television show or seen any movie, then you know that traffic in Los Angeles is legendary. Some of this is a bit exaggerated. Still, use Google Maps to plan the best route to the resort. As you approach the property, keep your eyes peeled for signs directing you to your destination. Whether your goal is a theme park, hotel, or Downtown Disney, the roads that bring you there can change with the use of electronic signs. For example, many ramps that connect I-5 to the property will use one direction in the morning and reverse for the afternoon. This is how Disney dedicates more lanes going toward the resort in the morning and away from the resort in the evening.

For those flying, Los Angeles International Airport (LAX) is thirty-five miles northwest of Disneyland Resort.

This is the main sprawling airport of the area that offers the most direct flights at more competitive prices. This airport is huge with several terminals. All the amenities associated with a world-class airport are available. However, it seems to be constantly under construction—keep that in mind while planning your journey.

If you are flying into LAX and Disneyland Resort is your only destination, I highly recommend you avoid renting a car. Driving in the area is just not fun, especially when there are great alternatives. Disneyland Resort Express (graylineanaheim.com) is a fantastic service that costs $48 round trip per adult. You can easily purchase your ticket online before your journey. The express buses are modern, clean, and staffed with friendly drivers who will peacefully deliver you from LAX to hotels in the Anaheim resort area. Check online to see if your hotel is serviced. The Disneyland Resort Express stops at all terminals of the airport right outside the arrival doors. Just look for the large Disney-themed buses. I've found them to be prompt and capable of quickly navigating traffic conditions. When you board the bus, the driver will give you a card detailing how to arrange your ride back to the airport.

Taxis are readily available at LAX, but they are not economical. Expect to pay around $115 for a one-way journey. If you are a user of Uber or Lyft, you can easily get an estimate on their apps. An off-peak fare is usually around $45. The pick-up points for ride-sharing services can change; the apps will let you know the correct location.

For some reason, we tend to think that Los Angeles just has the one airport. We can all name New York's three airports, but LAX is often portrayed as the only LA airport. That's quite incorrect; if you're flying to Disneyland, there are other options.

Orange County John Wayne Airport (SNA) is fourteen miles from Disneyland Resort. This great airport offers fewer direct flights but has much easier access to Disneyland. The same Disneyland Resort Express (greylineanaheim.com) operates from SNA and will cost $35 round trip per adult. A taxi will run you around $51 one way; an Uber is around $27 off-peak.

Only seventeen miles from Disneyland is Long Beach Airport (LGB). This small airport offers the fewest direct flights, but it will provide the quickest security lines for your return home. There is no resort express, and a taxi will cost around $55 one way. UberX is currently not available for this airport; UberBLACK is around $87.

Don't forget that San Diego, one of the most beautiful cities in the United States, is only ninety-five miles south of Disneyland Resort. San Diego International Airport (SAN) can be a convenient airport to use, but you will need to rent a car. It's a beautiful coastal drive between San Diego and Disneyland.

### *Entry Requirements*

Although some places in the United States can seem like another country (I'm talking about you, Florida), US citizens do not need a passport to travel to Southern

California. A driver's license will do for most domestic travel.

Foreign visitors will need a valid passport from their home countries. Travelers from Europe, the United Kingdom, Canada, Australia, New Zealand, and Japan do not need a separate visa to gain entry into the United States. Travelers from other countries may or may not require a visa, depending upon the specifics of your travel. All foreign visitors should check their specific entry requirements by visiting the official US Department of State Travel website (travel.state.gov).

Upon arrival in the United States, expect to proceed through both a passport control and customs check. At most major entry airports, including LAX, the customs forms are now automated for return travelers and require a stop at a kiosk before proceeding to a border control agent. The kiosk will ask a few questions about your possessions and print a small paper for you to hand to the agent. If it's your first time as a foreign visitor to the United States, you'll be given a blue form on the airplane to complete during the flight. In this case, you bypass the kiosks and give the form directly to the customs agent.

The good news is that once you have been admitted to the United States, you may travel anywhere within the country without stopping for border control. You will still need to show your passport to fly from one location to another, but as long as you stay within the fifty states, you will not need to perform a customs check.

## *Time*

The Disneyland Resort is located in the Pacific Time Zone. This time zone is three hours behind New York and nine hours behind Paris. California does observe daylight saving time. Clocks are moved back one hour during November and ahead one hour in March. Daylight saving time in the United States does not occur during the same weekends as it does in Europe. This can be confusing, so check a calendar if you are traveling during these months.

Asia does not observe daylight saving time. In the summer, Disneyland is sixteen hours behind Tokyo and fifteen hours behind China. In the winter, Disneyland is seventeen hours behind Tokyo, sixteen behind China.

## *Language*

The predominant language of most of the United States is English. Those from Britain may want to point out that it is specifically American English. Those from the other states may also call it specifically California American English. Nevertheless, English is by far the dominant language. But don't worry if you don't speak English (although it does make me wonder how you're reading this book). Disneyland Resort is quite accustomed to visitors from other countries. If you have a problem, ask any cast member, and he or she will be able to assist you; they will know how to obtain a translator if required. Most signs around the resort are in English and Spanish. In addition, Disney does a great job of using pictures to communicate with guests.

## Weather

Southern California is known for beautiful weather. Typically, there is little or no humidity, and the temperatures range from the midseventies to the mideighties (that's twenty-one to twenty-eight for you metric folks). However, please note that Disneyland Resort is far enough inland that it has a bit more heat than areas closer to the shore. It can get quite hot in the summer.

Everyone who knows me will tell you that I am a sunscreen fanatic. I have seen the damaging and deadly impact that skin cancer causes. Even though some very cool breezes may be blowing, you *must* wear sunscreen during the daytime in Southern California. You simply must. If anyone in your party is too cool for sunscreen, Google "melanoma" and show that person the disfiguring effects of this terrible disease. A Disney vacation is not cheap. Don't ruin it by being in pain from a bad sunburn.

## Money

Disneyland used to have its own currency. Disney Dollars, printed with the images of various characters, were actual currency with an exchange rate of one to one with the US dollar. Sadly, Disney Dollars have been discontinued. So that leaves the good old dollar as the only official currency of the happiest place on earth.

Most Americans carry very little cash; credit cards are used frequently. Writing a check is often frowned upon (especially if I'm behind you at the grocery store), and travelers' checks are mostly a thing of legend.

ATMs (automated teller machines) are available throughout Disneyland Resort. This includes both theme parks, Downtown Disney, and all the hotels in the area. You can exchange most any currency at LAX, and many hotels can exchange the more popular currencies of Canada, Mexico, Europe, the United Kingdom, China, and Japan.

Visitors from other counties should note that prices in the United States never include tax. The sales tax in Anaheim, California, is 8 percent. That means you must add 8 percent to all purchases, including merchandise, tickets, and food. The lodging tax in Anaheim is 15 percent; this tax applies to the rate per night of lodging, not on hotel purchases or services.

Also, in the United States, it's customary to tip 15 percent for service at any table-service restaurant or bar. You can adjust the percentage up or down for better or worse service. You should calculate the tip based on the pretax total of the bill. Unlike across the rest of the world, the amount for an item listed on the menu will not be the final amount. Remember to add tax and tip.

### *Tickets*

Tickets for Disneyland Resort theme parks are more complicated than tickets to your local amusement park.

But they are simpler to understand than tickets for Walt Disney World (where you must have an advanced degree in mathematics to even visit for a single day).

At Disneyland Resort, children are anyone between the ages of three and nine. Those older than nine are adults (even though they may not act like it—heck, many adults don't act like adults, and they also have to pay full price). Those younger than three are free. A one-day ticket to *one* of the two parks is $89 to $119 for adults and children. Why is there a range? Well, Disneyland recently introduced a variable ticket system that depends on the date you plan to visit.

There are three types of days: value, regular, and peak. Check the calendar at disneyland.disney.go.com to discover which type of day you need a ticket for. Typically, value days are weekdays during the fall and winter. Weekends during these periods are considered regular. Most days in the summer and around Christmas are peak, as are days during spring break season. A calendar/calculator on the website will tell you the cost of admission based on your date and if you are an adult or a child. For reference, a value day for a child is $89, $95 for adults. Regular days are $99 for children and $105 for adults. Peak days cost $113 and $119.

If you want to visit both parks on one day, you will need a hopper. A one-day hopper is $50, in addition to your ticket, for both children and adults. Remember, once you enter a park on a one-day ticket, you may only visit that park on that day unless you purchase the hopper option. Also, the one-day hopper option does not give you one day at each park; it means that you have one day to hop between both parks.

Thankfully, there isn't a variable day system for multiday tickets—yet. A two-day pass (allowing entry to one park per day—they can be the same park if you want, but you must choose one park for each day) is $195 per adult, $183 per child. A two-day hopper (where you can access both parks for two days) is $235 per adult, $223 per children. Three days without hopping cost $255 per adult, $243 per child. A three-day hopper will set you back $295 per adult, $283 per children. Four days of hopping cost $320 for an adult, $305 for children. There are many different types of annual passes (yearlong) available. Depending upon how many blackout dates you want to deal with, they range from $549 to $1,099.

It's also worthwhile to mention that three-day passes come with the ability to attend Magic Morning at one of the parks. Each day, one of the two theme parks opens an hour early for guests of Disney hotels and those with passes good for three or more days. You can check the website to see which park is open early on which day.

Tickets can be purchased online (disneyland.disney.go.com) and printed on your home printer. There is no discount for prepurchasing tickets. Tickets can be purchased by phone (714-781-4400), but there is a $10 charge to mail them to you. You can also buy tickets directly at the park or at any of the hotels in the area.

Be very careful of counterfeit tickets. This is an increasing problem with all the Disney parks. When you purchase a discounted ticket online, always remember that if a deal is too good to be true, it's probably too good to be true. Each ticket is scanned at the entrance, and counterfeit tickets can ruin your vacation. To be safe, purchase tickets directly from Disney, from your hotel, or from someone who you can easily locate if there is a problem.

And, because you can never be reminded of this enough, Disneyland is in California, and Walt Disney World is in Florida. Their websites look quite similar. Make sure you are purchasing tickets for the correct coast.

*Dreamlly's Disney Direction*

Yes, it's all very expensive. I'm not denying that, and I fully realize what happens when you multiply the admission price by the number of people in your travel party. Like most everyone, I live and travel on a budget, and I know how many pounds of ground beef and physician copays can be covered by a trip to any Disney park. But just oblige me for a minute and consider the tremendous value—because when you think about it, admission to a Disney park is quite a value.

Where I live, it costs $12 to see a first-run movie on a Friday night. It costs about eight times more than that to visit Disneyland. Does Disneyland give you at least eight times the entertainment? Absolutely! There is unlimited entertainment in the form of shows, fireworks, and parades. I can spend over twelve hours at Disneyland as opposed to a two-hour movie. The attractions and people-watching at a Disney park are things you can never get in a dark theater. I would like to argue that even the food at Disneyland is cheaper than it is at your local cineplex. Also, you must remember that while you may go to the movies a couple times a month, most people visit a Disney park sporadically. It's definitely worth the sacrifice.

But don't just stop with a movie. Compare Disney to other entertainment choices, and you will still see a value. How much does it cost to bring a family to one of those big sports bars with all the arcade games? How much does it cost to treat your entire clan to a steak dinner? And—here's the big one—how much does it cost to attend an NFL game? You'll soon see that Disney is quite a value.

The local theme park I wrote about earlier, Minnesota's Valleyfair, is $52 per day for one adult. It's a good park with coasters and all the other rides you'd expect. Is a day at Disneyland worth at least twice as much? Absolutely! While Valleyfair is fun, it doesn't come near to offering the level of immersive, detailed theming as a Disney park. There is one show at Valleyfair; there are hundreds at

Disneyland. Aside from all the attractions, Disneyland is much cleaner. Its cast members wear elaborate costumes themed to wherever it is they work. The restrooms at a Disney park are spotless and themed. The trash cans are themed! I'm not stating that you should skip your local amusement park entirely; they're not Disney, and they probably don't even want to be. Your local park provides unlimited memories and a place where whole families can be entertained. I'm simply saying that one day at Disneyland is a better value than two days at Valleyfair.

I guess what it all comes down to is that budgets are about priorities and choices. In the case of a Disney park, I'm advocating for a choice of quality because it's worth the sacrifice.

▲ ▲ ▲

### Parking

Parking at the Disneyland Resort costs $18 per day per vehicle. This applies to those staying at Disney hotels ($18 per night) as well. However, if you're parking at one of the hotels or Downtown Disney and you eat in one of their restaurants, you can get reduced parking. Dining at a hotel will get you three hours of free parking in that hotel's lot. Visiting Downtown Disney gives you two hours of free parking in their lot even if you don't shop or eat. The Downtown Disney lot is $12 per hour after your two free hours are over. Follow the signs for your specific destination, and a parking attendant will explain the fee.

If you park at Downtown Disney or any of the hotels, you can walk from the parking lots to your destination. Those who park in the Mickey and Friends parking ramp are directed to efficient trams that will whisk you away to the entrance plaza for the theme parks. Don't worry about having to take a tram back to your car at the end of a long day; Disney is well organized and has this system down to a science. You won't wait long.

### Park Hours

Depending upon the season and even day of the week, theme park hours at the Disneyland Resort can fluctuate. The parks may open as early as 8:00 a.m. and stay open as late as midnight. But, then again, they can also close as early as 7:00 p.m. Also, quite often, Disneyland and Disney California Adventure have different operating hours. You must check disneyland.disney.go.com to discover the hours for your visit.

All guests staying at a Disney hotel are granted special early access to one of the two parks each morning. Some guests purchasing a three-day pass can also use this benefit. Again, disneyland.disney.go.com is the best place to learn which park will be open early for these types of guests.

## Accommodations

### Disney Hotels

There are three Disney-owned hotels at the Disneyland Resort. They will be more expensive than other hotels in the area, but you are paying for fantastic Disney theming and legendary Disney service. At Walt Disney World in Florida, if you want to stay close to the parks, you must choose a Disney hotel. That's not the case in California. In fact, some of the non-Disney hotels are closer to the action than either the Disneyland Hotel or Disney's Paradise Pier Hotel. Still, staying at a Disney hotel comes with certain benefits:

- Expect over-the-top theming around every corner. While staying at a Disney hotel, you will be immersed in the design and theme of that property.
- Disney hotel guests can use a private entrance into Disney California Adventure; you must show your room key at this entrance, located within Disney's Grand Californian Hotel and Spa.
- One park is open one hour early every morning for guests of Disney hotels. This Extra Magic Hour requires a ticket, and the schedule for which park is open which day is posted at disneyland.disney. go.com. However, this benefit is not exclusive to Disney hotel guests. The Magic Morning option gives the same benefit to holders of certain multi-day passes. (Extra Magic Hour is often promoted as a Disney hotel exclusive. I guess it is if you really like the name Extra Magic Hour. The exact benefit is available to non-Disney guests under the name Magic Morning.)

- Disney hotel guests are guaranteed entrance to the parks with a ticket even if the parks are closed due to capacity. Yes, when the parks reach a threshold of visitors, they will temporarily stop admitting people—even if they have tickets. This almost never occurs except during the week between Christmas and New Year's Day.
- If you stay at a Disney hotel, you can charge all your purchases, including food and merchandise, to your room. While shopping in the parks, you can have your purchases delivered to your hotel.
- Guests at any Disney hotel can access the services of Pinocchio's Workshop, a licensed childcare facility inside Disney's Grand Californian Hotel and Spa.
- You can get a wake-up call from Mickey Mouse himself!

### Disney's Grand Californian Hotel and Spa

This is Disneyland Resort's premier luxury hotel—and, boy, is it ever. Built in the craftsman style of the early twentieth century, the soaring lobby is worth a look even if you're not staying there. Think about lots of wood with warm colors, and you can imagine the look of this hotel. It's really quite stunning.

The hotel has the most varied types of rooms at the resort. There are standard rooms with either one or two beds, family rooms with bunk beds and trundles, and multiple bedroom suites. Some of the larger suites have kitchens and hot tubs. This is also the only hotel on the property where every room has a balcony of some type.

The best aspect of Disney's Grand Californian is the view. Rooms here offer unique views that can't be found anywhere else in the area. Some rooms look directly into Disney California Adventure; it's pretty amazing to be able to sit on your balcony and watch guests enjoying the park below. Other rooms look onto the busy shoppers and diners of Downtown Disney. Still other rooms offer views of the incredible pool area. The monorail (which links Disneyland's Tomorrowland and Downtown Disney) runs right through the hotel. You might be lucky enough to have a room with a view of the sleek monorail as it quietly races past.

The pools are extraordinary, though not the best at the resort (stay tuned for the incredible pools of the Disneyland Hotel.) At Disney's Grand Californian, the Redwood Pool is well themed—kids will enjoy the waterslide as it wraps around a giant redwood tree trunk. Nearby, mostly adults enjoy the tranquility of the Fountain Pool.

There is a very nice gift shop in the lobby as well as **Pinocchio's Workshop**. The workshop is a licensed child-care facility that is open to guests of all Disney hotels. For the adults, there is the luxurious Mandara Spa with all the services you would expect.

One of my favorite places to eat in California is the **Storytellers Café**. It's well themed with murals depicting famous stories that are set in California. The café always offers a buffet that changes for breakfast, lunch, and dinner, plus there is a standard menu. Breakfast offers a character buffet featuring Chip and Dale. Prices range from $8 for a child's entree to $32 for an adult dinner buffet. I've never had a bad meal at this place.

The hotel's signature restaurant is **Napa Rose**. It's won a ton of awards and features California cuisine. Of course, wine is important at this establishment. Entrees range from $25 to $60+. The **Hearthstone Lounge** is a great place to get a nice cocktail or cup of coffee in the morning.

**White Water Snacks** is the hotel's quick-service eatery. Prices are cheaper than anywhere else at the hotel, and the food is just as good. I find that you can't ever go wrong if you start the day with a Mickey waffle—and this is the place to get it. There are salads, sandwiches, pizza, and all sorts of snacks.

Overall, Disney's Grand Californian Hotel and Spa is beautiful and luxurious. A standard room, with parking lot view during low season, will cost $394 per night. That same room will be $630 with a better view during high season. Suites can run to $900 or more per night. Believe it or not, a multibedroom villa will set you back as much as $7,200—per night! But like I said before, do your homework. Only you can make the choice that is best for your budget.

What's a character meal? Well, I've found that most people see these events one of two ways: they are a delightful heaven with food, or they are about as much fun as being a prisoner of war. There is no middle ground here; you will either love them or hate them. I love them.

Character meals can be a buffet or a standard restaurant experience. But they will always be well organized as Disney has this whole thing down to a science. As you dine, Disney's famous characters will make the rounds and visit each table. A cast member with an iPad makes sure that no table is forgotten. And, yes, there will certainly be a lot of loud children and adults in the room. I'm not normally someone who likes to eat in loud atmospheres, but for some reason the character experience works for me. It's just so much darn fun watching kids and adults interact with Disney's famous folks.

Photographs are encouraged. Many of the best photos in my collection are from a character meal. The characters will not be rushed. Of course, some characters are more talkative than others. Mickey, Donald, and friends like to act cheery and pose for pictures without much conversation. The less costumed characters, like the princesses, are charming as ever as they greet each guest. Remember, these are not actors and actresses playing a part—these are the real people themselves. Belle is the real Belle who will talk and act like Belle. Even the most skeptical adult can't help but become immersed in her charm. On the other hand, Cinderella's stepsisters are not charming. They are loud, obnoxious, and will take food off your plate—it's happened to me more than once. (I'm not ashamed to admit that I loved it each time.)

The characters present at each meal are posted on the Disney websites. Reservations are highly recommended for these very popular events and can be made online or using the specific app for the park you are visiting. If you stay at a Disney hotel, you can make reservations 120 days before you arrive. (Cinderella's Royal Table, inside the castle at the Magic Kingdom in Florida, is the hottest reservation to get in all of Disney; you must be online 120 days before your arrival to secure a place.) Prices will vary depending upon location and type of meal, but expect to pay $50 per adult and slightly less for children.

▲ ▲ ▲

### Disneyland Hotel

OK, I'll try to stay calm, but I love this hotel. I've stayed at most of the Disney hotels around the world, and the Disneyland Hotel in California is my favorite. It's just the perfect combination of history, theming, location, and facilities. This is the famous hotel that opened alongside Disneyland in 1955. It's the inn that was built by Jack Wrather and wasn't owned by Disney until the 1980s. Of course, it's been through many changes over the years, but recent renovations have made it modern with a heavy nod toward its heritage.

Rooms here are in one of three towers: Adventure Tower, Fantasy Tower, and Frontier Tower. Notice how the landscaping around the hotel changes as you approach each tower. The Adventure Tower is surrounded by lush palm trees. Topiaries of the Disney characters line the walks toward the Fantasy Tower. You'll know you're near the Frontier Tower when you see towering pines and shooting geysers.

Not to be left out, Tomorrowland also has a huge presence at the hotel in the form of the amazing pools. Recently renovated, the Disneyland Hotel's E-ticket Pools are extraordinary. The waterslides are shaped like authentic monorails and the iconic Disneyland entrance sign sits high above it all. In the early days of Disneyland, guests purchased a park ticket depending upon what type of attraction they wanted to visit. An E-ticket was required to ride the most elaborate and popular rides, like the Haunted Mansion and Space Mountain. Here, the hotel's pools pay homage to this as E-tickets are embedded in the tile work surrounding the pools.

There are historical displays all over the hotel. I highly recommend the free Disneyland Hotel History Walking Tour. It's offered most days; check the resort schedule and reserve a place with the concierge if you're interested. Remember, for many years this was the choice hotel for dignitaries visiting Disneyland. Kings and queens have literally slept in these beds.

Most of the rooms here are standard with two beds. They all have incredible theming. Each room contains salutes to Mickey. Above the beds, a giant headboard is carved with an image of Sleeping Beauty Castle. And to make it even better, just flick a switch and watch the castle come to life with fiber-optic fireworks and soft music. (You can also turn the music off and let the fireworks run all night. I guess you could also just leave the fireworks off, but I wouldn't know because I'm not one to pass up the opportunity to sleep under fiber-optic fireworks.)

**Goofy's Kitchen** is the most popular restaurant here. It's a character buffet for breakfast, lunch, and dinner. This is the place to go to meet Mickey and his entourage. It will be loud but lots of fun. You are guaranteed to get great photos during this experience.

The premier dining establishment at the Disneyland Hotel is **Steakhouse 55**. It's themed in that Golden Age of Hollywood that probably never really existed style. This is the place to go for steak and seafood. Entrees range from $25 to $60. The attached lounge is quite nice and a fantastic place to get the perfect martini.

My favorite place to eat at the Disneyland Hotel is the **Tangaroa Terrace**. It's a retro-Hawaiian themed restaurant located near the Adventure Tower. There are great views of the pools and all the tiki-themed ambiance. The food is great and reasonably priced.

Located on the backside of Tangaroa Terrace is one of the most famous places in the whole resort. **Trader Sam's Enchanted Tiki Bar** is a must to visit even if you just peek inside and leave. This is where you step into 1950s Waikiki with all the music and kitsch you can imagine. There are frequent thunderstorms inside. The drinks are fantastically themed, and most are flaming or smoking in some fashion.

There are two shops on the first floor of the Fantasy Tower. One stocks travel necessities, and the other is full of Disneyland merchandise.

Overall, the Disneyland Hotel is where you want to stay if you grew up looking at photos of Disneyland through your View-Master. It's a bit cheaper than Disney's Grand Californian, but it still comes with a price. Standard rooms range from $300 to $600, depending upon the season and view. If you have the Disney Chase Visa credit card, keep your eye out for special promotions in your e-mail. I've often used a Disney Visa "stay two nights and get one free" deal at this hotel—especially during the off seasons.

### Disney's Paradise Pier Hotel

This is a newer Disney hotel in an older building that has had many names. The structure opened in 1984 as the Emerald Hotel of Anaheim. It changed to the Pan Pacific Hotel Anaheim in 1989. Disney purchased the building in 1995 and renamed it the Disneyland Pacific Hotel. In 2000, its name was changed again to Disney's Paradise Pier Hotel. This last name makes the most sense as the hotel is located near the Paradise Pier land of Disney California Adventure.

The theme is Mickey and Friends at an oceanfront amusement pier in the early twentieth century. There are beach ball pillows in all the rooms as well as lots of other nods to the characters as they frolic in the sand.

Disney's Paradise Pier Hotel is comprised of two towers that are connected by a three-story lobby atrium. Above the atrium structure is the pool and recreation area. The beach theme continues into this area. The pool is large but nothing like those at the other two Disney hotels.

Most of the rooms are standard with either one or two beds. However, many rooms come with a twin day bed and a sitting area that is great for larger families. The rooms are nice but nothing extraordinary.

There is a coffee bar in the lobby but only one real restaurant. **Disney's PCH Grill** is also located on the ground level. The PCH stands for Pacific Coast Highway, and the theming of the establishment reflects that. Breakfast offers the Surf's Up with Mickey and Friends character brunch. This option is served buffet style while your favorite Disney friends in their beach attire stop by your table to chat and pose for photographs. Lunch and dinner at the grill are á la carte.

Disney's Paradise Pier hotel is the farthest from Downtown Disney and the entrances to the theme parks. Expect at least a fifteen-minute walk to Disneyland. Disney California Adventure is a bit quicker to access as guests can take a ten-minute walk and use the private entrance through Disney's Grand Californian Hotel and Spa.

Depending upon season and view, standard rooms range from $225 to $420. Some of the rooms look directly into Disney California Adventure. These offer a great chance to sit and people watch, although there are no balconies.

As you may tell from my description, I'm not all that enthusiastic about this property. I can't really think why anyone would pay these prices to stay at this hotel considering that cheaper, non-Disney options are even closer to the action. Many of these non-Disney options have better pools and rooms. Maybe you really like the private entrance to Disney California Adventure through Disney's Grand Californian Hotel and Spa. If not, stay elsewhere and visit the hotel for the character breakfast if you want to see the beach theme.

### Non-Disney Hotels

Around the globe, Disneyland Resort and Tokyo Disney Resort are the only locations with conveniently located non-Disney hotels. In Florida, Hong Kong, Paris, and Shanghai, there are definite location advantages gained by staying in a Disney property.

At Disneyland Resort in Anaheim, there are more than forty hotels in the area. Some are within walking distance, and many others offer shuttles. Most of these hotels carry the Disneyland Good Neighbor Hotels seal. This doesn't mean that they have met any certain standard, but it does mean that they offer packages that bundle accommodations and theme park tickets together. Good Neighbor Hotels are also bookable directly through Disney either using disneyland.disney.

go.com or by calling the Walt Disney Travel Company at 714-520-5060.

If you choose a non-Disney hotel, the main thing to remember is that you must do your homework. First, consider your budget. These hotels range from economy options all the way to luxury choices of suites and spas. Please note that most of these hotels will have hidden charges you must recognize, including parking, additional occupancy fee, cost of the shuttle to Disneyland Resort, and possibly resort fees.

After budget, consider location. Use maps.google.com to determine the extract distance from the hotel to the gates for Disneyland. There is a lot of personal preference in this regard. Some of you may treasure the ability to be able to walk to the parks and avoid a wait for a shuttle. Others might love climbing into a van and saving your feet after an already exhausting day. Only you can do the homework and make the decision that is best.

Then consider the kinds of amenities you like. Do you want a free breakfast? Is it important that there is an onsite restaurant? What do you need for a pool? To this day, I'll never figure out why my mother loves to do laundry on vacation. Seriously, you could say, "Mom, they just announced that they are giving away free diamond necklaces at Disneyland to celebrate their anniversary jubilee! The necklaces will be handed to you by Mickey himself, and they will come wrapped in rare Chinese silk. They will also include a lifetime admission to any Disney park and free flights on Delta Airlines for life. But we have to go now!" She will reply, "Oh, I really need to do laundry. So you go ahead." For my mom, guest laundry is at the top of her list. For me, it's not.

The last piece of homework you must do, and it's the most difficult and time-consuming, is to research the Good Neighbor Hotel reviews online. I still find that tripadvisor.com is the best site to determine the quality of a hotel. Read through the most recent ten reviews. Forget about the two best and two worst reviews you read. Then, when you look at the remaining six reviews, you will have a pretty good idea of what the hotel is like. Remember to look at other travelers' photographs with a grain of salt. A piece of dirt on a tile may look horrendous when it's the entire focus of a picture when, in reality, the room is quite clean.

I'm not in the business of rating non-Disney hotels. There are just too many of them, and they change frequently. This is where the teacher inside of me assigns the work to you. Embrace it, and enjoy the options you have surrounding Disneyland Resort. When we travel to Florida for the next chapter, you will wish you had something to do homework on.

## Disneyland

Congratulations, you've made it to the happiest place on earth! You've navigated transportation, hotels, budgets, and ticketing options. Now take a deep breath and savor the moment of standing before the famous gates and the giant floral shape of Mickey Mouse that Walt Disney planted himself. Above you is the iconic Disneyland Railroad Station, which millions upon millions have glanced before you. Groups of families run past you to get in line to meet Peter Pan as he stands under the station, signing autographs and posing for photos. On the train platform above you, Donald and Daisy Duck wave enthusiastically to the cheering crowds below. As a steam engine charges into view with a nostalgic whistle, you start to cry. Whether it's your first visit or your twelfth, you will cry. If you're not crying, then there is something wrong, and you need to see either a doctor or a baker. Welcome to the original Disneyland—it's your land.

Walt is ever-present at Disneyland, but nowhere is there a greater reminder of that than the firehouse in Town Square. As you pass under the train tracks and enter Town Square, which is the beginning of Main Street, USA, look to your left. Next to City Hall is the Main Street Fire Department. There will be a lamp burning in the second-story window.

As you can imagine, Disneyland consumed an awful lot of Walt's time. The park is forty miles from Disney studios and even farther from Walt and Lillian's home. To save time, Walt built and furnished an apartment above the fire station. He often slept there, sometimes joined by his wife and daughters. Above the fire station, Walt could oversee the daily operation of the park. But I think that was just one reason for building the apartment. If you could live in your very own dream world that you suffered to build, wouldn't you? I believe that Walt built his apartment because he wanted to. It was fun for him to see the guests enjoying the park and to wake up every morning in his kingdom. (Dolly Parton has a similar apartment above Apple Jack's Restaurant inside Dollywood. I'm going to do the same thing when I build Michael's World.)

Anyway, the early cast members of Disneyland always wanted to be on their best behavior when Walt was around. After all, he wasn't just their boss; he was also one of the most famous humans on the entire planet. They soon learned that if a light was on in the firehouse, it meant that Walt was in the park. Each morning, cast members would look to see if the light was on, and they would spread the word to the others.

Walt Disney died from lung cancer on December 15, 1966. An unknown cast member came up with the thought that the fire department lamp should be turned on. It was his or her idea that without Walt, it was up to all cast members to keep his spirit alive by performing their duties as if the boss were watching. The lamp is a reminder to keep the park spotless, friendly, and spectacular.

Through the years, the lamp was only ever turned off when Lillian Disney or one of Walt's daughters was in the park—as a sign of respect. Now that those three women have joined Walt in a different kingdom, the lamp is never turned off.

▲ ▲ ▲

## Main Street, USA

Walt often said that Main Street was a reaction of his time growing up in Marceline, Missouri. However, if you've ever been to Marceline, Missouri, you will notice very few similarities. Here, Main Street is immersive, detailed, and full of the sights and sounds of early 1900s America.

Designed and constructed by movie set designers, Main Street uses forced perspective to make the guests feel like they are walking into a story. The first floor of each building is the typical size. The second stories are five-eighths scale to the first. The third floors are only half scale. This gives the visitors the illusion that the buildings are much taller than they are. It also makes the whole street seem intimate and inviting. (Even better uses of forced perspective can be found at the Magic Kingdom in Florida—stay tuned.)

This land also gives you your first glimpse of the iconic Sleeping Beauty Castle. A royal residence shouldn't belong on an American street, but somehow it all works and looks quite normal. We'll talk more about the castle when we get to Fantasyland.

There is a lot happening on Main Street, USA. Take some time to enjoy the scene. The gaslights along the street are real and used to shine in the cities of St. Louis and Baltimore. Remember, you will have to pass this way again to exit the park.

### Disneyland Railroad

Walt Disney was obsessed with trains. He simply loved them, and it's no surprise that he had to have one circle his park. There are four stations along the Disneyland Railroad: Main Street, New Orleans Square, Mickey's Toontown, and Tomorrowland. Main Street, USA is the station where most people get off, so it's the easiest station to find a vacant seat. However, Main Street is the only station that is not accessible to those in wheelchairs.

An entire round trip takes about twenty minutes and is highly recommended. You will pass through most of the various lands of Disneyland, and a narrator will describe the sights. While on the train, you must wave to all those you pass. This is a general theme park rule. If you don't follow the waving rule, the theme-park gods will surely punish you—most likely by making all your lines extra long that day.

Between the Tomorrowland and Main Street stations, the train passes through two unique scenes. The first, a recreation of the Grand Canyon, was added in 1958. This diorama was painstakingly created with all the scenery and animals you'd expect to find in Arizona. The second scene is Primeval World. Dinosaurs and prehistoric foliage surround the train as it chugs past. Primeval World was part of the Ford Automobile Pavilion at the 1964–65 New York World's Fair. (More information about this famous fair and its impact on Disneyland can be found under the Fantasyland section.)

### Main Street Vehicles

Several types of vehicles make the journey down Main Street, from the train station to far-off Sleeping Beauty Castle. Guests are welcome to ride on these vehicles—just look for the signs posted in Town Square and line up near them. Some of the vehicles have motors, and others are pulled by horse. As you ride up and down the street, keep an eye out for the Dapper Dans barbershop quartet and the Mayor of Main Street.

### The Disneyland Story, Presenting Great Moments with Mr. Lincoln

Located inside the Disneyland Opera House, the first part of this attraction is a wonderful museum devoted to the creation of Disneyland. Here you can see an enormous model for what was then Disneylandia. There are other artifacts, including a bench from Griffith Park, where Walt Disney watched his daughters and conceived the idea for the park. There is a historical film starring comedian Steve Martin and Donald Duck.

The best part of this attraction occurs well inside, in the opera house itself. For the 1964–65 New York World's Fair, Walt created his first human audio-animatronic figure. The state of Illinois asked Walt to create an attraction that paid homage to their favorite son, sixteenth president Abraham Lincoln. What they got far exceeded their expectations, and Great Moments with Mr. Lincoln was a star of the World's Fair. In fact, the figure was so lifelike that the 1960s brain couldn't quite comprehend it; many fairgoers fainted.

Here at Disneyland, after a brief film on Lincoln's life, you will see the original presentation as it was during the fair. Lincoln stands and talks as if John Wilkes Booth never succeeded. It's amazing even today, and I can't imagine what they thought of it over sixty years ago.

### Main Street Cinema

Halfway down the street, on the right-hand side as you walk toward the castle, you can watch several vintage films in the Main Street Cinema. The films feature an early Mickey Mouse and his friends. Of course, Steamboat Willie, the first animated film with sound, is always playing. The films run concurrently on several screens, and there is a raised platform for good viewing.

### Shops of Main Street, USA

Main Street is the commercial heart of Disneyland. The street is lined with shops, and you can take as much (or as little) time as you want to browse. **The Emporium** is the largest shop in the park. You will also find candy shops, a bakery, specialty clothing shops, hat shops, and expensive stores that sell jewelry. **Disneyana** sells original artwork and other valuable artifacts. Of course, what Main Street in America would be complete without a Starbuck's? Remember, Walt himself courted businesses and asked them to open shops on Main Street—even the Wizard of Bras! (Knowing this fact makes the Starbuck's seem more appropriate.)

### Dining in Main Street, USA

**Carnation Café:** Table service for breakfast, lunch, and dinner. Good food at reasonable prices with fantastic views of all the activity on Main Street.

**Market House:** Freshly made treats and snacks with Starbuck's coffee.

**Jolly Holiday Bakery Café:** Quick-service option with hot and cold food and the best sandwiches in the park. You can decide which of the items Mary Poppins would approve of.

**Plaza Inn:** Table service for lunch and dinner in a gorgeous setting. Indoor and outdoor seating with full Victorian decor. For breakfast, this is the home of the Minnie and Friends character meal. Reservations are highly encouraged.

**Refreshment Corner Café:** Quick-service option at the end of Main Street. This is the place for hot dogs and Mickey pretzels.

### Central Hub

Many believe that the castle is the center of Disneyland. That's incorrect and not how Walt envisioned the park.

Sleeping Beauty Castle is meant to be the entrance to Fantasyland and not a structure in the middle of it all. That honor belongs to the central hub and its wonderful statue.

The central hub is where all the spokes of the wheel come together. Standing here and rotating, you can see some of Disneyland's famous lands. In the exact center is the touching sculpture called *Partners*. I won't describe it now; it's better for you to discover it on your own.

**Adventureland**

As you exit Main Street, USA, the first land to your left is Adventureland. This is that bizarre combination of retro Hawaii, the Amazon rainforest, Southeast Asia, and a touch of the African savannah. It all goes together quite well, and like everything else in Disneyland, the juxtaposition just works.

The foliage here is lusher than any other place in the park. It's gorgeous, and the soothing sounds of the tropical music add to the ambiance.

*Jungle Cruise*

One of the original attractions of Disneyland when it opened in 1955, this is the legendary boat trip that defined the concept of a Disney attraction to the world. You will sit in a steam boat named for one of the planet's great rivers and float through several different types of environments. Leave your passport at home—you won't need one here to visit South America, Asia, and Africa.

Many animatronic animals line the tour, and your skipper/guide will point them out to you.

Speaking of the skipper, this is one attraction where cast members are encouraged to let their personalities shine. In the early history of the park, guests bought tickets for each attraction. To financial-minded Roy Disney's dismay, once guests had ridden a ride, they didn't often pay for a second trip. Then Walt noticed that one of the Jungle Cruise skippers was interjecting some corny jokes into the tour, and his boat was packed with return guests. Walt began to encourage all the skippers to do the same. Still today, the embellishment and corniness change with each boat skipper, and no two journeys on the Jungle Cruise are the same.

I'll be very frank with you: I find this attraction just OK during the day. It can be hot, crowded, and even annoying. However, for me, darkness brings out the legendary status of this attraction. Riding the Jungle Cruise during a nighttime parade is a delightful adventure. You will have lots of space in the boat to experience the shadows and subtle glow of the animals. The skippers, perhaps feeling less inhibited in the dark, will exhibit an even drier sense of humor than they do during the day.

One of the questions I'm asked the most is, "Aren't all the parks the same? Isn't Hong Kong Disneyland exactly like the one in California?" My answer: definitely not!

Studying the differences in parks that are supposed to be seemingly similar is a fascinating and educational activity. The Jungle Cruises in California and Florida are fairly similar. The version in Tokyo is remarkably different. Still, nothing compares to the amazing journey that is the Jungle Cruise of Hong Kong Disneyland. There isn't a Jungle Cruise in Paris, and the version in Shanghai is a thrill ride with a drop. Throughout this book, I'll point out these variations—many times they result from differences in the home cultures and how these rides are perceived.

▲ ▲ ▲

### Walt Disney's Enchanted Tiki Room

This wonderful show will always have Walt Disney's name on it because it belonged to him—literally. Sure, the entire park sort of belonged to him, but it did require a lot of financing and organization from all sorts of partners. Each attraction, shop, and restaurant had to somehow be financed, whether by Disneyland, Disney Studios, ABC Television, some corporate sponsor, or the like. However, Walt Disney's Enchanted Tiki Room was Walt's. He personally paid for it.

Walt always had a fascination with mechanical clones. His office and home were filled with all sorts of wind-up trinkets and things that moved on their own. In 1963, he developed Walt Disney's Enchanted Tiki Room; it was the first audio-animatronic attraction in the world. Yep, all those pirates, ghosts, presidents, and happy, singing, worldly children owe their existence to these birds.

Again, there is a lot going on here. It's a fifteen-minute show where the audience sits around a tropical fountain. Soon the four emcees will come to glorious life. Spanish José, German Fritz, French Pierre, and Irish Michael will guide you through the show. There are around 225 audio-animatronics in this attraction. The birds sing, the flowers sing, the tikis sing, the masks sing, the audience sings—everyone sings until a huge thunderstorm shuts down the festivities. While you could take a nap in the air-conditioned comfort of Mr. Lincoln's presence, you probably won't be able to actually fall asleep in the midst of this tiki-run-amok atmosphere.

### Tarzan's Treehouse

Originally the Swiss Family Treehouse from the 1960 film, this luxurious elevated abode was sold to Tarzan in 1999. Anytime Disney makes even the smallest change at Disneyland, diehard fans go absolutely crazy and swear they will never return. But they do. In this case, it's a good change as Disney's 1999 animated version of Tarzan is an amazing film with some of Disney's best music, thanks to Phil Collins.

The classification of this tree is Disneyodendron Semperflorens Granis, which is Latin for "a big Disney tree that always has flowers on it." This is a walk-through attraction; you experience it at your own pace. There are no boats or omni-moving vehicles carrying you around. It's a nice respite and a good way to get some exercise.

You will see all the jungle amenities you'd expect from a man who grew up with apes. Of course, Jane has definitely made her presence and London style known.

### Indiana Jones Adventure

*Fastpass*   What would Adventureland be without Indiana Jones? He epitomizes everything we love about adventure: exploration, bravery, intellect, humor, and a fear of snakes. The Indiana Jones Adventure is a major thrill ride. Consequently, you should know what you're getting yourself into. A special note to grandparents: don't let your grandchildren con you onto a ride that you're not sure about. Many a grandma has lost her cookies because some smiling twelve-year-old told her, "It's not any worse than Pirates of the Caribbean, Grandma!"

This experience is Disney at its immersive finest. After a long queue that is well themed, you will board a transport vehicle for your trip through the world of Indiana Jones. Yes, you will need to wear a safety restraint as there are numerous twists and turns.

The world of Mr. Jones is full of mummies, volcanoes, jewels, artifacts, and snakes. Lots and lots of snakes. They are animatronic, but they are snakes nonetheless. Seriously, there are a lot of snakes here.

In true Disney style, there is a story being told during the entire ride. You can pay as little or as much attention to the story as you want. The Disney imagineers designed a ride system that can change as the story develops. No two rides are ever exactly the same, especially at the ride's climax in the Temple of the Forbidden Eye.

Nowadays, every theme park has some sort of line-skipping advantage. Some of these advantages come with hefty price tags, especially at Universal Studios and Six Flags. You can expect to pay well over $100 to skip lines at these parks. To the enormous credit of Disney, their Fastpass system is free—mostly (keep reading).

Each Disney park has its own version of Fastpass. Here at Disneyland, the attractions that accept Fastpass will have an area of themed kiosks near the ride entrance. Approach the kiosk and insert your park ticket. You will get a small printed coupon in return. The coupon will have an hour written on it. That's the hour you may return to the ride and skip the line. You can insert the park tickets of anyone you want to ride with and get the same window of opportunity to return.

When your hour arrives, use the special Fastpass entrance for the attraction you've chosen. You must ride within the hour specified on your coupon. There can sometimes be over a three-hour wait to ride Indiana Jones Adventure, but with a Fastpass, that wait will be under ten minutes. You can only have one Fastpass at a time; a computer system will make sure of that. However, after you've ridden your ride, you can immediately get another Fastpass. Also, two hours after you've printed a Fastpass coupon, you can get a Fastpass coupon for another ride in the park even if you haven't ridden the first one yet.

Fastpass coupons are not just for rides. Some parades, shows, and fireworks also use this system. In these cases, a Fastpass gets you access to a priority area to view the experience without having to arrive an hour earlier to stake out your seat.

Not every attraction uses this system, and the whole thing can change at any time. Still, it's a reliable way to make your time at Disneyland much more efficient. I've mentioned *"Fastpass"* in the description of each attraction where it's recommended. At other Disney parks around the globe, the Fastpass system can be different and much more complex. (Again, I'm looking at you, Florida.)

Starting sometime in 2017, both parks at the Disneyland Resort will begin a second Fastpass system called Maxpass. Maxpass will cost $10 per person per day. It won't give you any faster access to the rides, but it will electronically obtain and manage your Fastpasses via a smartphone app. Essentially, you're paying not to have a paper coupon and not to waste time walking to an attraction to get one. However, Maxpass will also give you all your photopass photos, including those taken during rides. Depending upon the number of people in your party, this could be an excellent deal. But be advised: if Maxpass is successful, the $10 charge will likely increase.

▲ ▲ ▲

### Shops of Adventureland

Most shops here sell safari-type merchandise such as hats, jackets, and shorts with lots of pockets. Adventureland is also the place to purchase any kind of plush animal you can imagine. **The Indiana Jones Adventure Outpost** offers items specially based on the Indiana Jones franchise.

### Dining in Adventureland

**Tiki Juice Bar:** This is a piece of Oahu in Anaheim. Pineapple is the star of pretty much every item. The biggest seller, by far, is the legendary Dole Whip. It's sort of a nondairy pineapple soft-serve ice cream. There are often long lines.

**Bengal Barbecue:** A quick-service café that offers skewers of chicken, beef, and bacon-wrapped vegetables. (That's one way to get your veggies!)

### New Orleans Square

New Orleans Square is the most immersive land in the park. I love how the streets twist, leading you farther into the city. It's not only the location of two legendary rides, but it's also home to arguably the best restaurant at Disneyland Resort. New Orleans Square is by far the finest version of New Orleans on the planet (and I'm including the one in Louisiana).

### Pirates of the Caribbean

Here is the one legendary attraction that built a film empire and earned Disney about twenty gazillion dollars. While he didn't live to see it completed, Pirates of the Caribbean was the last Disneyland attraction designed under the supervision of Walt Disney.

It takes sixteen minutes for your boat to discover the tale of swashbuckling pirates and their mischievous antics. Does it glorify some really bad behavior? Yep. This is definitely one time you'll want to tell your kids, "Don't try this at home."

The special effects and audio-animatronics are superb. Again, this is Disney at its best. You'll start in New Orleans and peacefully float through the bayou to the strains of an old man and his banjo. The crickets chirp, and the night is full of fireflies. Then suddenly you're plummeted into the Caribbean villages where pirates are up to their dastardly deeds. This ride inspired the films, and the films returned the favor. Look for Captain Jack Sparrow and his enemy Captain Barbossa.

This version of Pirates includes some nice surprises that make it better than its cousins in Florida and Tokyo. The version at Disneyland Paris is a bit creepier, which makes me like it better, but it also scares quite a few kids. However, nothing can compare to the new over-the-top Pirates of the Caribbean attraction inside Shanghai Disneyland.

### Haunted Mansion

*Fastpass* Look for a stately plantation home on the outskirts of New Orleans Square. It's elegant and inviting. It's easy to imagine some southern belle hosting a charming garden party without a care in the world. As you get closer, you'll see that there is a party of sorts going on in the mansion, but the southern belle looks less like Scarlett O'Hara and more like something out of *The Walking Dead.* This is the Haunted Mansion in all its creepy and silly glory.

If the line is long, use a Fastpass and come back later. The Haunted Mansion is much more fun than it is scary, and most kids over the age of five shouldn't have a problem venturing forth. Still, only you know your own kids and what will keep them up at night.

After a visit to the famous stretching room, your Ghost Host will load you into a Doom Buggy for a tour of the mansion. You'll see the library, dining room, ballroom, attic, and other abodes haunted by the 999 resident ghosts. Of course, no visit would be complete without a tour of the graveyard. As you enter the graveyard, look for the caretaker and his dog. They are the only characters that are alive on your tour.

During the Halloween and Christmas seasons, which run from the first week of September through the second week of January, the Haunted Mansion welcomes a bunch of new haunts on its tour. Jack Skellington, Sally, and the rest of *The Nightmare Before Christmas* gang are featured here. It's a nice twist on a classic ride—a must visit for those who are fans of the movie. Tim Burton pulled off the amazing juxtaposition of Halloween and Christmas quite well in the film, and the Haunted Mansion does justice to the experience.

### Shops in New Orleans Square

The quaint streets of New Orleans Square were made for shopping. There are several shops with French-sounding names that sell everything from perfume to high-end jewelry. **Pieces of Eight** is a pirate shop that is actually the exit for Pirates of the Caribbean. **Port Royal Curios and Curiosities** sells Haunted Mansion-themed merchandise.

### Dining in New Orleans Square

**Café Orleans:** Table-service Cajun café. Gumbo, vegetable ragout, and Mickey-shaped beignets are offered. There is both indoor and outdoor dining. Entrees are $25 to $50 per adult.

**French Market:** Quick-service version of Café Orleans near the New Orleans Square Railroad Station.

**Mint Julep Bar:** Stop at this window, also near the train station, for Mickey-shaped beignets.

**Royal Street Veranda:** Always very popular, this outdoor quick-service café features spicy soups in delicious bread bowls.

**Blue Bayou:** The most famous, and best, place to eat inside Disneyland. The atmosphere is amazing as you sit inside the darkness, surrounded by old New Orleans trees and Spanish moss. At this table-service restaurant, boats of people enjoying Pirates of the Caribbean float by in the quiet darkness. It's always busy, and you must make a reservation. To secure a table right along the water (without a doubt the best view), make a lunch reservation for 11:00 a.m., the time when the restaurant opens. Be there at 10:40 a.m. and be one of the first to enter when the door opens. You'll just have to take your chances to get a waterside table for dinner. Kids' meals are around $15, and adults can expect to pay up to $60 for an entree.

### Frontierland

Here is a beautiful version of the Old West, with towering pines replacing bandits. There is some activity here, but mostly this land takes it slow. The inhabitants of Frontierland like to sit by the river or float gently on the Mark Twain Riverboat.

### *Big Thunder Mountain Railroad*

*Fastpass* Hold on to yer hat! Another on Disneyland's long list of iconic rides, these runaway mine trains twist and turn around the beautiful formations of Monument Valley. This ride is an exception to the otherwise slower-paced Frontierland.

The queue is as much an attraction as the ride. Meander through an old mining town complete with hotels, saloon, newspaper office, and mercantile. As always, Disney's attention to detail is astounding, so take your time to look at everything as you slowly wait in line.

Big Thunder Mountain is not the most extreme coaster on the planet. Heck, you probably get more action on the parking lot tram. Still, it's so immersive in theming that you'll be glad you waited. The rocks are colorful, the geysers spray on cue, and you will giggle your way around the stone formations.

Like the Jungle Cruise, this is another ride that is much better at night. Above each Fastpass collection of kiosks, you'll see an electronic sign that tells what your current return time will be. Glance at this sign whenever you pass this way, and try to get a Fastpass for sometime after sunset. Darkness makes this ride much more intense.

### Mark Twain Riverboat and Sailing Ship Columbia

The large waterway in Frontierland is dubbed the Rivers of America. The Mark Twain Riverboat is always making its rounds on the river. On days of high park attendance, the Sailing Ship Columbia also provides a fifteen-minute tour.

The Mark Twain was present at the opening of Disneyland. It's a complete paddle wheeler constructed in a five-eighth scale compared to traditional Mississippi riverboats. There are a few seats in the front of the vessel, but most guests lean against the railings or wander around to enjoy the scenery. It's a nice, calm tour and a great way to get away from the crowds on a busy day. You'll pass landscapes reminiscent of the Mississippi and Missouri frontiers long ago lost. Keep an eye out for wildlife as you'll see a lot of it. You can decide which animals are real and which are brought to you through Disney magic.

Even when the Sailing Ship Columbia is not sailing, you'll still be able to see it moored near the Haunted Mansion. It's a replica of an actual ship that was built in 1787 and was the first American ship to sail completely around the globe. This Columbia was built in 1958. It's a stunning vessel and makes an excellent backdrop for photos.

### Tom Sawyer Island

Tom Sawyer Island is an actual island surrounded on all sides by the Rivers of America. Consequently, the only way to reach the island is on a raft. Don't let a small wait for the raft scare you away; there is a lot to do here.

Fans of Mark Twain's famous novel will find hundreds of references to the Missouri-based story. But even if you're not familiar with Tom and Huck, you can literally explore the place for well over an hour and not get bored. There's a lot to investigate, and marked trails will guide you to the various points of interest.

Tom Sawyer Island is a lifesaver for any parent of a kid who just can't wait in one more line. Once on the island, there are no lines, and kids have the freedom to explore.

### Golden Horseshoe Saloon

Throughout the park, you can pick up a copy of the daily Times Guide. This schedule lists all the show times for everything around the park, including the presentations inside the Golden Horseshoe Saloon.

There's plenty of good seating, and the saloon makes a nice, air-conditioned escape on a hot day. The shows vary in content, but all fit well within the Frontierland theme. Expect music and lots of dry humor.

Unlike on the real frontier, there is no alcohol served in Frontierland—or anywhere else in Disneyland Park. But the Golden Horseshoe does serve soft drinks, ice cream, and excellent chili in a bread bowl.

### Shops in Frontierland

Expect to find a lot of denim and plaid sold in mercantile-type stores. **Westward Ho Trading Company** is the place to go if you want to start a Disney pin-collecting habit.

### Dining in Frontierland

**Golden Horseshoe Saloon**: Quick service with a show (see description above).

**Rancho Del Zocalo:** A quick-service Mexican-inspired eatery. Tacos and burritos are available as well as flan and chocolate cake for dessert.

**Big Thunder Ranch Barbecue:** Reservations are recommended for this table-service buffet restaurant. Everything is all-you-can-eat priced for lunch and dinner.

The seating is entirely outdoors on long tables, so you may be sitting family style with other guests. The food includes all the things you'd expect at a barbecue, like chicken, ribs, and coleslaw. Depending upon your age and the time of day, prices range from $15 to $29.

**River Belle Terrace:** This quick-service café has both indoor and outdoor seating. Breakfast, lunch, and dinner are available at reasonable prices. However, note that for dinner the River Belle Terrace turns into a table-service restaurant that is a bit pricier. Expect to pay around $12 per entree during quick service and $25 during dinner.

## Critter Country

This small land is a natural offspring of Frontierland. In fact, you may not even know you're in a new land until you see the ultra-cute woodland creatures of Splash Mountain. Originally called Bear Country, this land opened in 1972 as a home for Big Al and the other players of the Country Bear Jamboree. But the bears were kicked out in 1989 to make room for Brer Rabbit. (Don't worry about the bears though. They have other homes in both Florida and Tokyo.)

### *The Many Adventures of Winnie the Pooh*

Who doesn't love Winnie the Pooh? This bear's heart is always in the right place, even if that place is his stomach. Guests embark on a journey through the Hundred Acre Wood by riding in beehives. Along the way, you'll meet

Piglet, Owl, Rabbit, and the rest. Of course, Tigger is heavily featured as your beehive bounces along with him.

Though full of brightly painted scenes, this is still a dark ride. Some small children may be a little apprehensive, but most will be too excited to mind.

### Davy Crockett's Explorer Canoes

These thirty-five-foot fiberglass canoes are real boats that glide along the Rivers of America. They are not on a track, as you'll soon find out if you choose to ride them. The canoes do not operate every day; there is a sign posted on Davy Crockett's Landing that will state when the next excursion is scheduled.

Two cast members, one in back and one in front, guide the canoe. There is no motor on these vessels. So who provides the power? You do. Yep, in a park famous for its cutting-edge technology and magical movement everywhere, these are real canoes that rely on paddling guests. Think of it as the workout you missed or the chance to burn off some of those Mickey-shaped beignets.

### Splash Mountain

*Fastpass* Another example of Disney at its best, you must use a Fastpass for this ride, especially on a warm day. This is Disneyland's answer to the traditional log flume found in your local amusement park.

The imagineers went all out when designing Splash Mountain, and it's still quite impressive today. One hundred and three audio-animatronic characters tell the tale of Brer Rabbit, Brer Fox, and the rest of the gang from the 1946 film *Song of the South*. If you're not familiar with this film, I'm willing to bet you're familiar with its theme song: the Academy Award-winning "Zip-a-Dee-Doo-Dah."

You will ride with six other people in a hollowed-out tree. There is a lot of water on this ride, and you will get wet. You could possibly get quite soaked. But it's worth it to see the over-the-top animatronic climax that occurs at the bottom of the drop.

Speaking of the drop, it's not the height that's concerning; Splash Mountain is only fifty-two feet tall. It's the angle of the drop that scares the brer crap out of most people. At a forty-seven-degree angle, it's the steepest log flume in the world. There is a true genius of design at the bottom of the mountain. Spectators only see the riders falling into a mass of briar—we never get to see the log safely reach the bottom.

*Dreamlly's Disney Direction*

If you're like me, you detest getting wet—even on a warm day. I just don't like sopping around in soaked underwear while my T-shirt sticks to me. That's why I always have at least one disposable rain poncho in my theme-park satchel.

I'm not talking about the rain ponchos that you can buy inside the park. Those are too thick, hot, and expensive. Go to your local dollar store or amazon.com to purchase a few cheap rain ponchos that are just about as thick as plastic food wrap. I wouldn't want to rely on one of these in a hurricane, but they're great for theme parks because they are so lightweight. Just put one of these on, ride Splash Mountain, and throw it away. Or, if you want to reuse the poncho, carry a small plastic sandwich bag in your satchel and stuff the poncho in there until you can dry it out at home.

What else do I have in my theme-park bag? Not much. Nobody wants to carry around a heavy sack all day, and I'm no different. But I do want to always have a few things with me. In addition to the disposable poncho, I usually have a small tube of sunscreen that I refill, Band-Aids, pen and paper (I'm a writer), hand sanitizer, napkins, and a small container of Advil. At Disneyland Paris, I carry a few packets of ketchup because...well, I'm a Minnesotan, and I just need to have them. At Tokyo Disneyland, I also pack a few packets of salt. (In the land of soy sauce, you can't find salt to save your life—go figure.) And at Hong Kong Disneyland, I always add an umbrella—not because of rain but because if you don't shield yourself from the sun, you will combust in under ten seconds (see chapter 6).

▲ ▲ ▲

### Shops of Critter Country

The two shops in this land focus on the two rides found here. **Briar Patch** sells Splash Mountain merchandise, and **Pooh Corner** sells Star Wars items. (Just checking that you're awake; Pooh Corner, of course, sells Winnie the Pooh souvenirs. I'm sure that, when completed, the nearby Star Wars Land will have plenty of shopping opportunities.)

### Dining in Critter Country

**Harbour Galley:** Located near the docked Sailing Ship Columbia, this quick-service café offers soups, salads, and lobster rolls.

### Fantasyland

Beneath the jagged peaks of the Matterhorn and the sparkling spires of a castle lies the best-known land in all the realm. Fantasyland is almost synonymous with Disneyland itself. It's the land of princesses, stringless puppets, and kids who refuse to grow up. It's also full of witches, evil queens, and other terrible villains. Despite its name, for me Fantasyland has always been the most real land in the park. My life has been full of heroes and villains; I suspect yours has been the same. For now, step inside the iconic stories we all loved and feared as children.

### Sleeping Beauty Castle

According to Kodak, Sleeping Beauty Castle is the second-most-photographed building in the world. (See

chapter 3 to learn about the most-photographed building in the world.) On your first visit, you will find that
the castle is much smaller than you thought it would be.
It's seventy-seven feet tall, not even half the height of
Cinderella Castle in Florida.

Walt admitted that he never imagined the castle
would become as big a deal as it did. He thought of it as
a gateway into Fantasyland and a visual beacon to draw
people down Main Street. But soon, Sleeping Beauty
Castle became not only the symbol of Disneyland but
also the symbol of the entire Disney Company. Walt
was even surprised to learn that guests wanted to go inside and tour the place. Unbelievably, when Disneyland
opened in 1955, the second floor of the castle contained
a bunch of offices. This mistake was quickly fixed, and all
future Disney castles, with the exception of Hong Kong,
are much larger. (But when Hong Kong Disneyland's
new castle opens in 2019, Anaheim will again have the
smallest.)

When designing the structure, Walt instructed the
imagineers to closely consider King Ludwig II's castle
of Neuschwanstein in Bavaria (Southern Germany).
Ludwig II, the most famous Bavarian king, and one of
my personal heroes, used a theatrical designer instead of
an architect for the design of Neuschwanstein. How does
Disneyland's castle seem so perfectly romantic, historical, graceful, and charming? Because it's modeled after a
real castle that was modeled after a theatrical castle that
never really existed!

Walt was famous for "plussing" his projects. He used that term when he wanted to make something seemingly perfect even better. Everything, from animation to Disneyland, could become even more over the top—that's what the guests would remember. However, plussing was always expensive. Walt wanted Sleeping Beauty Castle's turrets covered in gold. Not gold paint—real gold. But brother Roy held the purse strings tightly and refused. Walt always found a way. When Roy left Hollywood for a business trip to New York, Walt found some money, and it only took one week for twenty-two-karat gold to appear above Fantasyland.

Today, you can go inside the castle—and you should. On the castle's opposite side from Main Street, you'll find a sign directing you to the Sleeping Beauty Castle Walk-through. A small spiral staircase will lead you up inside the famous structure. It's beautifully done. You'll see amazing stained glass and a series of dioramas that tell the tale of Princess Aurora, aka Briar Rose, aka Sleeping Beauty. You'll also meet Prince Phillip and the evil, misunderstood Maleficent. Unfortunately, you must be able to climb stairs in order to see the attraction. However, on the ground floor, there is a virtual experience for those who are unable to navigate the stairs and narrow passages.

### Fantasy Faire
Beside the Frontierland side of the castle, you'll find the best place to hang out with the various royal families that

live harmoniously together. It's all quite charming and well themed. This fantasy village includes two sections: the Royal Hall and the Royal Theatre.

**The Royal Hall,** with its unbelievably beautiful interior, is the place to go to meet the royal folks. Remember, these people are all very busy running kingdoms, going to balls, slaying dragons, and such. Consequently, they take turns meeting guests in the hall and posing for photographs. You can find out specifically who is scheduled to appear on the Disneyland app.

**The Royal Theatre** hosts several performances of resident Renaissance bards retelling Disney stories. Check the daily Times Guide for the performance schedule. The shows are a lot of fun, and adults will appreciate the inside humor of these talented bards.

### Pixie Hollow

On the opposite side of the castle, find Pixie Hollow. This is the home of Tinker Bell and other Disney fairies. As you enter, everything gets much larger to make you feel like you've shrunk to the size of Tink and her friends. Even if you're not interested in meeting the fairies, the area is beautiful, and you'll appreciate this nod to creativity.

Between Pixie Hollow and Sleeping Beauty Castle, you'll find Snow White's Wishing Well and Grotto. It's cute and worth a glance. It's also a great example of forced perspective. You see, the original sculptor didn't quite understand the concept of Snow White and the

Seven Dwarfs. He made each sculpture the same size. Rather than redoing Snow White to make her taller, Walt just placed her farther away from the dwarfs, and your brain does the rest.

### Peter Pan's Flight

Behind the castle, in the heart of Fantasyland, you'll find the first of many dark rides for children—and adults like me. This is what sets Disneyland apart from all its cousins around the globe. The original and extremely nostalgic dark rides are still here.

Peter Pan's Flight is beautiful. You will board a vessel and fly around the Darlings' bedroom. Suddenly, you're whisked out of the window, and you'll gracefully glide above London. Of course, your final destination is Never Land. Here you'll discover all the fantasy of the second star to the right. You'll watch Peter Pan defend Wendy from the nefarious Captain Hook and be brought back to current-day Anaheim.

The line can be long, and there is no Fastpass option. Get here early in the day or ride during a parade.

### Mr. Toad's Wild Ride

*The Adventures of Ichabod and Mr. Toad* (1949) isn't the best-known of Disney's films. But it did inspire one crazy ride. Mr. Toad's Wild Ride is arguably the most cherished dark ride in the park. I suspect that any plan to change the ride would result in mass hysteria and open revolution from many Disney fans.

You'll get into a taxi cab for a wacky drive through Toad's house and London. As you may imagine, Toad, Badger, and all his wildlife friends are not the best drivers. You'll crash into lots of stuff, including a warehouse full of dynamite and a locomotive. You'll have to face a judge who will sentence you to...well, just take the ride to discover the bizarre ending.

### Snow White's Scary Adventures

This is the film that started it all: Walt Disney's *Snow White and the Seven Dwarfs*. Walt bet the farm on this one, and it provided a big payoff. Released in December 1937, the animated classic became the highest-grossing film of 1938. Adjusted for inflation, it's still one of the ten biggest-earning films of all time.

So it's appropriate that Snow and her tale get a prime spot at Disneyland. During this dark ride, you will see the story from Ms. White's perspective. You'll travel through the quaint home of the seven dwarfs and through a frightening forest as you dodge the Evil Queen.

Please note that the name Snow White's Scary Adventures is *very* fitting. The ride is terrifying—even for some adults. You will witness the Evil Queen turn into the Old Hag about six inches from your face. She also pops out at you from behind trees and tries hard to tempt you with one of her delicious apples.

Of course, in the end, everything comes out OK, and Snow White lives happily ever after with her seven dwarf friends and prince.

### *Pinocchio's Daring Journey*

There are many cats in the Disney universe but none as adorable as Figaro. This is reason enough to ride Pinocchio's Daring Journey. Here, you'll board a hand-carved cart and follow Jiminy Cricket through the Italian Alps-inspired world of Pinocchio. You'll see Geppetto's Workshop—a light sleeper's nightmare—and follow the story all the way to Pleasure Island. Monstro the whale is present but not that scary.

The Blue Fairy ensures that everything turns out all right in the end. Yes, when you actually sit down and think about the story of Pinocchio, it doesn't really make that much sense. But remember, this is one of those old folktales where the lessons of morality are more important than the plausibility of practically anything that occurs.

### *King Arthur Carrousel*

What's a theme park without a carousel? Absolutely nothing, in my opinion. This carousel is gorgeous and meticulously cared for by cast members. Built in 1875, it's much older than Disneyland and was imported from Germany. Every horse moves up and down—Walt insisted on that.

Each horse is different, and that's real silver and gold leaf making them sparkle. Beautiful murals around the top tell the story of Sleeping Beauty.

Before you send me an email correcting my grammar, please note that for some reason unknown to anyone in the universe, Disney changes the spelling of the word *carousel* from park to park. Here, it has two r's. Mary Poppins would not put up with this malarkey!

### Dumbo the Flying Elephant

Almost as iconic as Sleeping Beauty Castle, Dumbo soars around as Timothy Mouse watches all the action. You can control the height of your elephant, but you'll want to spend most of the time at the very top, where you get the best view of Fantasyland.

This is one of the few attractions that's pretty much the same at every Disney park. It's also the only Disney attraction to be on display at the Smithsonian Institution in Washington, DC.

### Alice in Wonderland

The only double-decker dark ride at Disneyland, Alice has been entertaining guests for over fifty years. You'll see all the famous characters, including the awful Queen of Hearts. Kids of all ages can celebrate their un-birthdays at the conclusion of the ride.

### Mad Tea Party

Another iconic Fantasyland installation, the Mad Tea Party has been quickly spinning guests at Disneyland since opening day. It's quite fun to watch. Some people enjoy riding it; I'm not one of them. The ninety-second ride seems to last for ten minutes as I desperately try to keep a Mickey-shaped waffle inside my stomach. Looping roller coasters? Not a problem. Mad Tea Party? Heck, no!

### Storybook Land Canal Boats

I love this ride. It's the most peaceful seven minutes you'll experience at Disneyland Resort. Climb aboard a cute little canal boat and float through miniature recreations of your favorite Disney films. A guide will accompany you and point out the various scenes.

Storybook Land is detail gone crazy. Nothing was overlooked in creating exact 3-D renditions of what you see on the screen. After cruising through Monstro the whale, you'll visit Peter Pan's London, Geppetto's village, Prince Eric and Ariel's castle, Arendelle (if you don't know which film Arendelle is from, then you're probably dead), the home of the seven dwarfs, Alice's English village, and the exact spot where Aladdin first met Jasmine. You'll even see Ariel's former castle, where her father, King Triton, lives under the sea.

### Casey Jr. Circus Train

Themed as the train that carries Dumbo and his mom in the film, this ride provides another way to view Storybook Land. It's just OK. A ride on the canal boats and a trip on the Disneyland Railroad give a better experience.

### "it's a small world"

How many iconic attractions can one land hold? A lot. And here is one more. Depending upon your mood, you may find this ride way more terrifying than the Haunted Mansion. Many have made fun of the singing dolls and that song that is impossible to forget. But all kidding aside, there is a reason "it's a small world" is legendary—it's a well-crafted, imaginative, and optimistic look at how the world should be.

Created for the 1964–65 New York World's Fair, the design and overall concept for the boat ride was the brainchild of the brilliant Mary Blair. Mary worked closely with Walt on several projects, including the film *Sleeping Beauty*. Her artwork is amazing and worth your time to Google.

There are over three hundred audio-animatronic dolls representing children from all over the world. They sing the famous theme song in English and in their home languages. You could ride it hundreds of times and still notice new details. There is something to see everywhere you look.

During the Christmas season, "it's a small world" changes just a bit. The dolls add traditional holiday garb from their various cultures. They also sing "Jingle Bells" in their home languages. This yuletide version of the ride only occurs in California and Tokyo.

For the remainder of the year, Disneyland contains the original version—shipped from New York at the conclusion of the fair. More than any of its cousins, this version has a definite 1960s feel. It's great nostalgic fun.

There will always be a link between Disney parks and the 1964–65 New York World's Fair. Robert Moses, the superintendent of the fair, enlisted Walt Disney to help plan several pavilions. It didn't take Walt long to figure out that he could use the fair to finance some amazing ideas that he lacked the funds to create.

The 1964–65 New York World's Fair was boycotted by the official World's Fair authority in Paris. They required that a fair run only one summer, and Robert Moses insisted on a two-summer fair as a more efficient use of resources. Consequently, many countries would not participate in the fair. But Robert Moses didn't let that stop him. If he couldn't count on countries to create pavilions, he'd ask corporations to do it. That's when Walt Disney entered the picture.

Corporations had money, and they liked being tied to the most famous name in the entertainment industry. Various companies approached Walt and asked him to create attractions for their pavilions. Each time, Walt agreed—with the understanding that the corporation would finance the attraction and Walt would get to move it to Disneyland when the fair closed. It was a brilliant move for Walt.

Pepsi commissioned "it's a small world" as a salute to Unicef. Great Moments with Mr. Lincoln was paid for by the state of Illinois. Primeval World, seen on the Disneyland Railroad, was a part of Ford's Magic Highway in the Sky. General Electric commissioned the Carousel of Progress, which moved from Disneyland to Walt Disney World.

As an aside, Disneyland wasn't the only theme park to get a piece of the World's Fair. The fair's log flume was dismantled and sent to a small park in Tennessee called Goldrush Junction. That park eventually became Dollywood!

▲ ▲ ▲

### Matterhorn Bobsleds

*Fastpass* Disneyland's Matterhorn is one-one-hundredth the size of the actual mountain in Switzerland. But notice how the use of smaller trees higher on the hill gives the illusion that the mountain is real—another use of forced perspective.

Inside, you'll hear the screams of those on the bobsleds. This was the world's first steel roller coaster when it opened in 1959. It's still a thrill today. You'll twist and turn your way up, down, and around the mountain. Watch out for giant ice crystals and the howling yeti. Darkness is used well to make you feel like you are going much faster than you actually are.

Thrill seekers may not want to spend time here because the thrill is a bit limited. But you should do it from a historical perspective. Without Walt's imagineers discovering the use of curved steel track, there wouldn't be any of those giga-coasters you love so much at other parks around the world.

### Fantasyland Theatre

Currently, this theater is home to the show "Mickey and the Magical Map." It's an outdoor venue, so no air-conditioning, but the audience is protected from the sun by a roof. The twenty-minute show features Mickey and his attempts to control a magical map. He finds himself stuck inside several scenes from famous Disney movies.

Shows at any Disney park are fantastic, and this is no exception. Expect a large cast, full costumes, creative sets, classic Disney music, and a good lesson to be learned from it all. Check the Times Guide for show times; the show normally plays at least five times each day.

### Shops of Fantasyland

There are a lot of shops in Fantasyland. These are the best places to find merchandise themed to classic Disney films. While the extremely popular *Frozen* franchise has a greater presence at Disney California Adventure, the two famous sisters are heavily featured in Fantasyland shops. The most-crowded store in this land is the **Bibbidi Bobbidi Boutique.** It's inside the castle and is where young girls and boys are transformed into princesses and knights.

### Dining in Fantasyland

**Village Haus:** The largest restaurant in Fantasyland, this Pinocchio-inspired establishment is quick service. Pizza, hamburgers, and salads are available for lunch and dinner. The atmosphere, especially the Alpine music, is well themed.

**Troubadour Tavern:** A quick-service café option located near the Fantasyland Theatre. It's open for breakfast, lunch, and dinner.

**Edelweiss Snacks:** This Swiss chalet near the Matterhorn offers those gigantic turkey legs that have become a staple of the theme-park diet.

## Mickey's Toontown

Toontown is the bustling city where Mickey and all of his friends live. This colorful land has no straight lines and is as zany as you would expect. Keep in mind that Toontown always closes early so that the park can prepare the evening's fireworks.

### Roger Rabbit's Car Toon Spin

*Fastpass* This is one of only two actual rides in Toontown. It offers the Fastpass, but check the line first to see if it's necessary. As the name suggests, you will spin your way around the world of *Who Framed Roger Rabbit?* In my opinion, it's as bad as the teacups and should be avoided if you get dizzy easily.

Just outside of Roger Rabbit's, look for the Toontown Post Office. Spend some time here attempting to locate the mailbox for your favorite Disney character.

### Toon Square

Wander around the business district of Toontown, and discover what this thriving metropolis has to offer. You'll find a bank, school (or skool, as the sign states), restaurants, Goofy's Gas Stations, and the town hall.

## *Mickey's Neighborhood*

Mickey Mouse lives in the vicinity of all his friends on this charming residential street. Take your time to notice all the incredible details that went into each building. This is also the easiest place to find the characters for photos and autographs. As always, check the Disneyland app to discover when your favorites will appear.

**Minnie's House:** Minnie lives in this comfortable little house, and you are welcome to see what she is up to. Look into her Cheesemore-brand refrigerator and notice the cake she is baking. You'll find that she has some messages from Mickey on her answering machine and that she's reading two magazines in the living room: *Mademouselle* and *Cosmousepolitan*.

**Mickey's House:** There is often a line to visit Mickey's House because many people want to meet the famous mouse—and he is always home. You'll see his trademark shape and colors as you tour each room. Look for his baby shoes and a photograph of him with his best friend, Walt Disney. Out in the backyard, you'll find Pluto's Doghouse, a garden, and a barn where Mickey makes movies. It's in this barn that you'll usually find him hard at work.

**Chip 'n Dale Treehouse:** Those two naughty chipmunks have taken a break from taunting Donald to welcome you to their house. This is a good place for kids to climb and get a good view of Toontown.

**Goofy's Playhouse:** Another fantastic play area for children, Goofy has opened his home and garden for you to enjoy. Go ahead and explore; you never know what crazy noises all the items in Goofy's house can make.

**Donald's Boat:** Donald Duck lives in this boat, the Miss Daisy. You can't miss it because the vessel looks like Donald and his trademark sailor outfit. The boat is moored in Toon Lake, and everyone is welcome to climb inside and explore. You'll find all sorts of wonderful things in Donald's World. (One thing you won't find—pants!)

### Gadget's Go Coaster

Gadget, from *Chip 'n Dale's Rescue Rangers*, invented this kids' coaster out of paper clips, pencils, and other stuff he found lying around. It's a fun time and a great introductory roller coaster for children. Just note: you must be at least three years old to ride, and those younger than seven must be accompanied by an adult.

### Shops in Mickey's Toontown

One shop, **Gag Factory**, sells all the Fab Five merchandise you could ever want. Who are the Fab Five? Mickey, Minnie, Donald, Goofy, and Pluto. (Don't despair if you're a fan of Daisy. She has some merchandise too.)

### Dining in Mickey's Toontown

**Clarabelle's:** Frozen drinks, sandwiches, and soft drinks served quick service by the first Disney cow.

**Daisy's Diner:** Donald's favorite gal sells pizza and cookies for lunch and dinner in this diner.

**Pluto's Dog House:** Naturally, Pluto runs this hot dog stand that also offers soft drinks and sliced apples.

## Tomorrowland

When Disneyland opened in 1955, Walt designed Tomorrowland to offer a vision of the future in far-off 1987! Just thirty years later, people started to refer to this land as Yesterdayland. A complete renovation was planned, and a new Tomorrowland opened again in 1998. This version is a vision of the future as seen from the past. Think of the writings of Jules Verne and you'll get the picture.

While Disney-owned Star Wars and Marvel Comics are becoming increasingly popular, this land changes often to include them. Attractions in this land can, and will, change.

### *Space Mountain*

*Fastpass* Another of Disneyland's nostalgic attractions, Space Mountain opened in 1977. It's actually the type of roller coaster known as a "wild mouse," but its indoor darkness increases the thrill.

You'll want to get a Fastpass for Space Mountain as the lines can be rather long. It's worth it—the visual and audio effects are outstanding. You will absolutely feel immersed and as if you're hurdling through space.

### Buzz Lightyear Astro Blasters

This attraction is different every time you ride because you're in control. You and a buddy will board a space vehicle equipped with a steering mechanism and your own ray gun. As you journey through space, you'll help Buzz Lightyear defeat the evil Emperor Zurg by shooting at targets with your ray gun. When you hit a target, you'll be rewarded with a special effect and some points added to your score. (Your score is displayed on a small screen in front of you.)

You can use the control mechanism, a joystick, to turn your vehicle. You'll need to do this a lot as the targets are all over the place. At the end of the ride, you can see your score and discover how well you did against your buddy. (Special note to big brothers: please try to be nice and let someone else win for once.)

### Star Tours—The Adventures Continue

*Fastpass* Get a Fastpass and travel to the galaxy far, far, away. In this 3-D simulator ride, you'll wear 3-D glasses and board a StarSpeeder. There are multiple stories and versions of this ride. Diehard fans will want to ride more than once.

Be advised that even though it's a simulator, it's quite turbulent. You'll be tossed around in your seatbelt, and those prone to motion sickness may wish the force wasn't with them. As a disclaimer, I'm not a fan of simulator rides. I prefer the full construction of the Indiana Jones experience over in Adventureland. But that's just me.

### Autopia

*Fastpass* One of the original rides from opening day, Autopia gives everyone the chance to drive—even those who are too young to have their license. One driver and one passenger can fit in each car that travels up to seven miles an hour. Make sure to follow all the rules of the road (and all the directions of the cast members, who tell you not to bump into other cars).

Fastpass is available for this attraction and may be necessary. Long lines have been known to form.

### Disneyland Monorail

Remember that whole section in chapter one about how you should vacation the way you want to vacation? I told you not to let people bully you into doing the things that they think you should do. Well, that doesn't apply to monorails. You must always ride a monorail whenever you get the chance; they are that awesome.

Of Disney parks around the globe, three have monorails: California, Florida, and Tokyo. They're all the best. Disneyland's is the oldest and opened in 1959. It was the first operating monorail in the Western hemisphere. The first passenger was then-Vice President Richard M. Nixon and his family. (Is that why the track is so crooked?) When it first opened, the Disneyland Monorail was a ride entirely contained in Tomorrowland. Now, the monorail is also a transportation option that can bring you to Downtown Disney and the Disneyland Resort Hotels.

After boarding in Tomorrowland, you'll see a bit of the outside world as you cruise along Harbor Boulevard. Then you'll soar above Disney California Adventure and pass through part of Disney's Grand Californian Resort and Spa. Soon, you'll pull into the Downtown Disney station. You may now return to Tomorrowland or get off to enter Downtown Disney. But remember, you must have a valid park ticket, and a hand stamp, to get back on the monorail. When riding Disneyland's Monorail, you are entering the park, and they are not going to let you in for free.

On your return trip, you'll fly along Downtown Disney, over the Disneyland Park entrance, and enter the far side of Tomorrowland. You'll wind around a bit (that's the crooked part of the monorail from 1959) and take a brief visit to Fantasyland as you soar around the Matterhorn. Finally, you'll pull into the Tomorrowland station. Altogether, the entire trip is two and a half miles long.

### Finding Nemo Submarine Voyage

Gosh, the Disney-Pixar partnership has given us some great moments. I can't even think about *Toy Story 3* without getting teary-eyed. *Finding Nemo* is another of those unbelievably magical movie experiences. Here you can take a submarine down into Nemo's world.

Everyone is here in Tomorrowland for you to see: Nemo, overprotective Marlin, delightful Dory, and totally awesome, cool dude Crush. There is a story about

Nemo wanting to visit an undersea volcano. (Yes, you do find the volcano, and it's Disneyland, so of course it erupts.)

Lines can get long for this attraction as it's suitable for all ages. There is not a Fastpass option. But please note that this is a submarine voyage. You really will climb into real submarines that are submersed in real water. I'm telling you this because the quarters are quite tight. Do not consider this ride if you are even a bit claustrophobic.

### Shops of Tomorrowland
Pixar, Star Wars, and Marvel Comics are the themes of most of Tomorrowland's merchandise. You can pretty much find anything you want with these brands featured.

### Dining in Tomorrowland
**Galactic Grill:** A quick-service option for breakfast, lunch, and dinner. There's pretty much anything you could want and a very large seating area.

**Redd Rockett's Pizza Port:** Open for lunch and dinner, this quick-service café offers pizza, salads, and pasta.

Before we leave Tomorrowland, please note that this land is subject to change more than any of the others. Expect an increased presence from the Marvel characters and perhaps a decreased presence of Star Wars. Star Wars Land is under construction on the other side of the park.

**Dreamlly's Disney Direction**

In its early years, Disneyland was closed on Mondays and Tuesdays during the winter season. Walt learned quite early that when the park was closed, no money was coming in. The park soon began daily operation.

Disneyland Park has had only one scheduled closing in its history. The park was closed on May 4, 2005, for a special media day that kicked off the park's fiftieth birthday celebration. However, Disney California Adventure was open that day.

Disneyland has been closed three times due to unscheduled events. In November of 1963, the park was closed during the national day of mourning for the assassination of President Kennedy. On January 17, 1994, a 6.7-magnitude earthquake hit the area. Disneyland was closed that day for inspections, but no damage was discovered.

The most recent unplanned closure occurred on September 11, 2001. Walt Disney World in Florida had already opened when the horrific events of the World Trade Center began to unfold. The theme parks of the Florida resort were closed and evacuated that morning. However, because of the time difference, both parks in California never opened.

▲ ▲ ▲

## Parades, Evening Shows, and Special Events
### Parades

Normally, Disney's parades are as good as you see on television. They are much more like a Broadway show and much less like the summer festival parades all over the United States. The floats are elaborate, the music is synchronized, and all the cast members are smiling wide. Everyone shows up for a Disney parade—the princesses, their princes, the Pixar buddies, and Mickey's gang. However, things in the parade department at Disneyland are a bit of a mess right now.

**Mickey's Soundsational Parade** occurs at least once each day. Check the daily Times Guide as sometimes the parade happens twice. This is a daytime parade where Mickey Mouse and his closest friends ride on floats themed to musical instruments. This whole parade is about music with a beat—it's meant to get you up and moving. The parade route is marked on the official park maps and is highlighted on the Disneyland app. Anywhere along the route is a good place to watch, but the façades of Main Street make the parade seem more special.

It's the evening parade that falls into the mess category. The absolutely amazing **Paint the Night Parade** ended its run in the fall of 2016. Disneyland announced that the nostalgic **Main Street Electrical Parade** will take its place sometime in 2017 for a limited run. Nobody knows what will happen after that. Traditionally, evening parades have been a huge event at Disneyland. We'll all have to stay tuned. For now, if there is an evening parade during your visit, claim your spot early and enjoy the magic that only darkness can provide.

### Fireworks

Fireworks and Disney go hand in hand. We've all seen the iconic photograph of a Disney castle under the glow of sparkling fireworks. Disney fireworks really are quite amazing. They often tell a story that is narrated over park speakers. The familiar melodies of classic Disney films are extremely well synchronized with the display overhead. It's a gorgeous experience that will pull at your heartstrings.

Fireworks are scheduled to occur every night at Disneyland Park. However, among all the Disney parks, this is the one where they are canceled the most. Remember, Disneyland grew up in a land-locked neighborhood as Walt just didn't have the funds to buy more land. Consequently, residential neighbors are very close to the park. You'll be surprised at, and envious of, the number of people who are next-door neighbors to Donald and Daisy. On top of that, Southern California is experiencing a record drought. Disneyland, in accordance with local fire ordinances, takes extra precaution to avoid fires. If there is any wind—and I mean *any* wind—the evening fireworks will be canceled. So, once again, manage your expectations.

### Fantasmic!

Note: Fantasmic!, the incredible water show, has been on hiatus since Star Wars Land started construction in 2015. However, park officials have announced that it will return during the summer of 2017.

*Fastpass* This amazing show lives up to all its hype. It's really good. Seriously. During these twenty-five minutes, Sorcerer Mickey battles villains on the Rivers of America in Frontierland. Anyplace you can see the water and Tom Sawyer Island is a good place to watch. You will need to claim your spot early, about an hour before the first show. If there is a second show offered, it is always less crowded.

You can also get a Fastpass that allows access to a special viewing area, but these passes are usually all claimed quite early in the day. Also, you can book a Premium Viewing Package at a participating restaurant. These packages must be booked online or via the Disneyland app. They do sell out early. For this experience, you will dine at a preassigned time. You'll pay your bill and then leave to explore the park. Your wait staff will give you a special ticket that you can present at a special viewing location prior to the start of Fantasmic!.

All the tools at Disney's disposal are on display. At one point, Maleficent will turn into a forty-five-foot fire-breathing dragon. At another point, Monstro the whale creates giant waves in the river. Along with all the pyrotechnics, water projections, and special effects, both the Mark Twin Riverboat and the Sailing Ship Columbia get into the action.

### Halloween

You'll know it's fall when Disneyland is decked out with pumpkins, leaves, and a few slightly scary decorations. Mickey's Halloween Party is a separate ticketed event that occurs on select nights in September and October. This means that Disneyland Park closes at 7:00 p.m. for its normal operating day. Everyone must leave. However, if you have a ticket for Mickey's Halloween Party, you get to stay until midnight and enjoy the spooky fun.

The ticket price varies according to the date. Weekends closer to Halloween are more expensive than weekdays in September. But expect to pay around $80 per person to attend. You can enter the park as early as 4:00 p.m. with the special ticket. My advice is to not purchase a regular park ticket that day. Just find something else to do (Knott's Berry Farm) until four.

Kids can always dress up at Disneyland. But adults are strictly forbidden—unless it's during Mickey's Halloween Party. Everyone is encouraged to dress for this enormous costume ball. However, there are many restrictions, and you'll get a list of them when you book your tickets online. Part of the fun for the event is to see what everyone else is wearing. The creativity of some humans is outstanding!

The Halloween party also features a special parade that you can't see unless you attend. It's well done, and even though full of villains, nothing here will ever be too scary. There are also plenty of opportunities to meet your favorite characters in their Halloween costumes. It's fun to get your photograph with Mickey as a vampire and Donald as a pumpkin. (You have to cut Donald some slack; his shape sort of limits his costume choices. Plus he has that whole aversion to pants thing to contend with.)

What's Halloween without trick-or-treating? Absolutely nothing—and, boy, does Disneyland partake. Stations are set up all over the park where you can approach cast members with your Halloween sack (provided) and get a ton of candy. (And I do mean a ton.) You probably won't have to purchase candy to distribute at your own home—you'll get that much during Mickey's Halloween Party.

### Christmas

Christmas at a Disney park is like Christmas on steroids plus Disney on steroids. It's hard to describe in words. You may die of spirit overload—consider yourself warned.

Disneyland always looks good but never better than when Main Street is decked out with wreaths, garland, and poinsettias. Town Square features an enormous Christmas tree. Nothing about it is gaudy. It's all so tastefully accomplished that even Scrooge McDuck doesn't mind.

In addition to meeting the Disney characters in their Christmas finest, you can also meet Santa Claus himself. The children of "it's a small world" sing "Jingle Bells," and the Jungle Cruise is renamed Jingle Cruise—complete with animals in special attire and boat captains with yuletide jokes.

Throughout the entire season, from early November to early January, the **Christmas Fantasy Parade** strolls daily down Main Street, USA. It's the same parade that's broadcast every Christmas Day in the United States.

Not to miss out, the three Disneyland Resort Hotels get into the holiday action. Everything is polished and draped with greenery for this special time of year.

# Disney California Adventure

Once a huge disappointment for Disney fans everywhere, Disney California Adventure is back to doing what Disney does best: storytelling. It's still not a twin to Disneyland or even a sibling; it's more like a second cousin once removed. OK, twice removed. Still, there are some great things going on here, including immersive theming and an awesome nighttime show.

### Buena Vista Street

Welcome to California! As you pass through the entrance gates and present the proper ticket, you're stepping back in time. Buena Vista Street is designed to recreate a Los Angeles street from 1923, the year that Walt Disney arrived from Kansas City by train. (D23 is the name of the official Disney Fan Club—the "23" stands for this year.)

There are lots of shops and restaurants, just as they probably were in the golden age that never really existed.

Up ahead, the Carthay Circle Theatre provides some height and depth to this land. The Carthay Circle is a recreation of the movie theater where *Snow White and the Seven Dwarfs* made its premier in December 1937.

Also of note in this land is a charming statue of a 1923 Walt Disney arriving in California. His face is full of optimism and dreams.

### Red Car Trolley

Just like Main Street, USA, Buena Vista Street serves mostly as an entrance/exit plaza and a place to shop. The Red Car Trolley is really the only attraction in this land. Board one of these historic recreations for a journey down Buena Vista Street to Hollywood Land.

### Shops of Buena Vista Street

Since Buena Vista Street is the main shopping destination for the entire park, you'll find many stores offering pretty much anything you could want. **Elias & Company** is the largest store, where you'll find all the Disney California Adventure branded merchandise. (Elias was Walt's middle name and the first name of his father.)

Another shop of note is **Oswald's**. Here you can purchase items themed to Oswald the Lucky Rabbit. Who's that? Well, Oswald was one of Walt's early animated creations; he was conceived in Missouri and predates Mickey Mouse. However, Walt lost the rights to Oswald in an awful dispute with his distributor. That loss led Walt to move to California—and to the creation of Mickey

Mouse. Who knows what would have happened if Walt had been able to keep Oswald? I might be writing about a park called Oswaldland located in Kansas City! (Walt has posthumously had the last laugh as Disney reacquired the rights to Oswald the Lucky Rabbit. He now makes appearances across the street from his shop on Buena Vista Street.)

### Dining in Buena Vista Street

**Clarabelle's Ice Cream:** Quick-service ice cream and other treats sold by a classic cow from Disney's early films.

**Fiddler, Fifer & Practical Café:** Did you know these were the names of the famous Three Little Pigs? Yep, and in this quick-service café, they sell breakfast, lunch, and dinner. Out of respect, bacon is not on the menu.

**Mortimer's Market:** Buena Vista Street is entirely a salute to Walt's early days in Hollywood. This quick-service snack bar is named after another of Walt's early creations, Mortimer Mouse. You've never heard of him? Sure you have! Walt's wife, Lillian, didn't like the name Mortimer and told Walt to change it to Mickey. The rest is history.

**Carthay Circle Theatre:** This recreated theater is home to one of the best restaurants at Disneyland Resort. Reservations are highly recommended for lunch and dinner. Expect to pay around $40 per entree. The atmosphere is amazing and a faithful reproduction of the original theater in Hollywood.

## Hollywood Land

Some of us realize how diverse and beautiful the state of California can be. After all, it contains deserts, mountains, beaches, forests, vineyards, massive cities, and lots of country. But to most people around the world, California is just another word for Hollywood. This is not surprising. Until the Internet revolutionized entertainment, most everything we watched came from this tiny part of a huge state. Here at Disney California Adventure, you can visit the famous film industry without battling LA traffic.

### *Monsters Inc. Mike and Sully to the Rescue*

One of the few dark rides at Disney California Adventure, this attraction gives fans of the film an opportunity to visit Monstropolis. You'll board a taxi cab and be whisked around the city as you attempt to return Boo to her home. It's not scary and is pretty tame, but the theming is well done and worth a ride if the line isn't too long. Fastpass is not an option here.

### *Disney Junior Live on Stage*

If your house gets the Disney Channel and you have anyone younger than seven living there, then you will not be able to skip this show. Don't even try because you won't succeed. The stars of *Mickey Mouse Clubhouse, Jake and the Never Land Pirates, Sofia the First,* and *Doc McStuffins* perform daily. Check the Times Guide for the show schedule.

If you don't have any idea who these people are, then keep walking. The show is quite entertaining for the young ones in your party. You'll have more fun watching the reactions of your children than you will watching the actual show.

### Disney Animation Building

This large structure holds several different attractions that aim to educate and excite you about the art of animation. After all, the whole Disney Empire started with a few sketches that seemed to move when you flipped them real fast. Here, that history is celebrated.

The **Animation Courtyard** is a central atrium that welcomes you to the building. Large projections of famous animated scenes are accompanied by the beautiful strains of familiar melodies. It's a nice place to hang out and take a break from the sun. From here, you can journey to the other attractions in the building.

Demonstrate your artistic abilities in the **Animation Academy**. Here, an experienced animator will guide you through the process of drawing a Disney character. It's all done step by step and is actually much easier than you might imagine. Go ahead and surprise yourself by creating something worthy to hang on your refrigerator back home.

**Sorcerer's Workshop** is a collection of hands-on exhibits that appeal to anyone who just has to know how things are made. You can have the chance to supply your voice for an animated character and learn how personality traits are reflected in facial animation.

Next, step into a film and meet an animated character. At **Turtle Talk with Crush**, you can chat with the most totally awesome dude from *Finding Nemo*. It's extremely well done. Crush both asks and answers questions in real time. He may notice a shirt you're wearing or have a few comments about whatever state or country you're from.

For the grand finale of Disney Animation, step even further into an animated film and meet the actual living, nonanimated stars. The film you are about to step into is *Frozen*. You may have heard of it. Visit **Anna & Elsa's Royal Welcome** to meet the famous sisters. As you can imagine, they are quite popular, and the line can get long. Fastpass is no longer an option, but you can avoid the line by visiting early in the day or during a nightly performance of World of Color. Whatever you decide, the sisters are worth a visit. They are charming, to say the least, and amazingly talk like sisters as they answer questions in tandem. (If they were actresses, I'd say they were some very fine ones with fantastic improvisational skills. But since they are not actresses and actually the famous royal sisters, I won't say that.)

### Frozen: Live at the Hyperion

*Fastpass* If you've never had a chance to visit New York City to see a Broadway show, then the next best thing is the Hyperion Theatre in Hollywood Land. Actually, shows at the Hyperion may even be better. (I have a friend who preferred the Hyperion's version of *Aladdin* over the Tony winner in New York.)

The musical retelling of *Aladdin* was replaced last year with a live version of *Frozen*. It's simply awesome. The whole story is told in about an hour, complete with all the songs and characters you love. The sets and costumes are outstanding. The special effects are captivating.

However, the best part of the experience is that it's all live. We don't get to see such fine singing performed live very often. "Let It Go" is fantastic in the film, but when you hear it sung right before your ears, it's chilling and inspiring at the same time. Disney employs more musicians than any other company in the world. Some of the best are in this show.

*Frozen*: Live at the Hyperion is performed at least four times each day. Check the Times Guide for the schedule. It's extremely popular, and guests will line up an hour before each performance. However, if you arrive at the park early enough, you can get a Fastpass. With a Fastpass, you can arrive later for your specific performance and sit in a special section.

Hyperion Street, the theater's namesake, is where the first Disney Studio was located in Los Angeles. It's where Walt had his first successes with Mickey Mouse before he moved the studio to Burbank.

### The Tower of Terror or Some Other Attraction Like It

Hovering high above Hollywood Land is the former haunted hotel of the Twilight Zone Tower of Terror. The iconic attraction scared the lunch out of guests by playing with their emotions and then randomly dropping them from thirteen stories in the air. Then it did it all again. And maybe again. It was a randomly programmed masterpiece that was never the same twice.

But, alas, much to the dismay of practically every Disney fan, the Twilight Zone Tower of Terror is closed. It's being remodeled with a new theme based on Marvel's *Guardians of the Galaxy*. I will save my judgment until the new version opens. Who knows? It may be spectacular. It better be because there are a lot of disappointed fans over this attraction.

### Shops of Hollywood Land
The shops of Hollywood Land focus on animation and the glitz of Hollywood. *Frozen* fans will for sure want to visit **Wandering Oaken's Trading Post. Off the Page** specializes in all things animated, and **Gone Hollywood** is a glamorous apparel shop.

### Dining in Hollywood Land
**Fairfax Market:** Fruit, vegetables, and mostly healthy snacks are offered at this quick-service market for lunch and dinner.

**Award Wieners:** If the Fairfax Market is too healthy, then Award Wieners is your place. Many types of hot dogs and sausages are served with various toppings. It's another quick-service café.

## Grizzly Peak and Grizzly Peak Airfield
Grizzly Peak, a 110-foot bear-shaped mountain, will remind you of California's flag and the natural beauty of

the state. A forest surrounds the peak and pays homage the state's many majestic parks. Grizzly Peak Airfield is a small adjunct land connected to Grizzly Peak.

### Soarin' Around the World

*Fastpass* When the park opened in 2001, this was one attraction that became an instant Disney classic. It's since been copied in Florida and Shanghai. Originally, it was called Soarin' Over California, but now the whole world lies below your feet.

This is your chance to hang glide over the world's famous landmarks. You'll sit in a sort of swing that moves in synchronized action with the images projected on a giant dome. You'll never be suspended more than forty-five feet above the floor, but your brain may not realize that.

The experience is as immersive as Disney can provide. The wind will whip around your dangling feet. You'll smell the flowers and hear the sounds of the cities. It's all beautifully filmed and accomplished.

Soarin' just recently made the switch from scenes of California to those of the world. Consequently, lines are long again, and you should use a Fastpass.

### Grizzly River Run

*Fastpass* This is another chance to use that dollar-store rain poncho you have in your theme-park satchel. There is a strong possibility you will get soaked on this ride. Also, on a warm day, you will probably need a Fastpass to avoid a long line.

Very much like the raft ride at your local amusement park, you'll sit with eight others in a raft that's sent careening down the Grizzly River. You'll get some great views of Grizzly Peak, but the raft spins often, and your view will change as much. The whole experience is themed well.

### Redwood Creek Challenge Trail

This is an immersive attraction that you can experience at your own pace. It's a bit like Tom Sawyer Island at Disneyland but with a stronger purpose. Russell, that persistent young man from the film *Up*, would like you to help him earn some badges in his quest to become a Wilderness Explorer.

As you enter, you'll receive instructions and a chance to orientate your experience by studying a map. There are plenty of cast members around to guide you on your journey. There's a fairly high chance of success, and you, along with Russell, will be rewarded with the appropriate badges.

Also in this area, there is a small show staring Russell and other Wilderness Explorers. It's a camp ceremony that teaches the intrinsic rewards of learning about nature.

### Shops of Grizzly Peak

Expect a lot of outdoor-type merchandise in the shops of this land. You'll also find attraction specific items for Soarin' and Grizzly River Run. At **Rushin' River Outfitters**, you'll find towels, ponchos, and other things you may need to brace the rapids.

### Dining in Grizzly Peak

**Smokejumpers Grill:** Located near Soarin', this quick-service restaurant is the only food option in Grizzly Peak. Hamburgers and such are served for lunch and dinner.

## Pacific Wharf

A little bit of Cannery Row at Disneyland Resort, this small land is beautiful but holds no attractions or shops. This is, however, the dining center of Disney California Adventure.

### Dining in Pacific Wharf

**Pacific Wharf Café:** First, enter through the rear of the building and watch a demonstration of how sourdough bread is made. It's much more interesting than it sounds. Then enter the café to buy soup served in sourdough bowls. It's quick service and open for breakfast, lunch, and dinner.

**Lucky Fortune Cookery:** This Asian quick-service option offers rice, vegetables, and protein in a variety of sauces.

**Ghirardelli Soda Fountain:** This table-service establishment, direct from San Francisco, will tempt you with everything chocolate and everything ice cream—or both!

**Wine Country Trattoria:** Secure a reservation if you want to dine at this signature restaurant. What would a California adventure be without wine? Here, enjoy wine with pasta, fish, and a host of other entrees. It's table service and runs around $30 per adult entree.

**Alfresco Lounge:** Upstairs of the trattoria. It's a full bar with some appetizer-type entrees.

**Mendocino Terrace Wine Tasting:** Wine and cheese are the stars of this open-air lounge.

**Cocina Cucamonga Mexican Grill:** Quick service for lunch and dinner. Tacos, burritos, and rice are served.

### A Bug's Land

Themed after the 1998 Disney Pixar film *A Bug's Life,* this land within Disney California Adventure is aimed to please younger guests. Everything here is big; you're supposed to feel that you're the same size as a bug.

### *Flik's Fun Fair*

This mini land is filled with the types of amusement park rides that young kids love, except they're all themed to fit into A Bug's Land.

**Francis' Ladybug Boogie:** A spinning ride similar to the Mad Tea Party at Disneyland. For me, this ride proves that one can vomit in things other than teacups.

**Princess Dot Puddle Park:** A splash zone for little ones to get as wet as they want (much to their parents' chagrin).

**Heimlich's Chew Chew Train:** A small, two-minute train ride.

**Tuck and Roll's Drive 'Em Buggies:** Bumper cars with a bug theme.

**Flik's Flyers:** Made out of oversized trash and leaves, it's similar to the flying Dumbos at Disneyland.

### It's Tough to Be a Bug!

This is a 4-D show. That means you watch a 3-D movie on a screen, with the appropriate glasses, while special effects provide the fourth D. Flik, the ant star of the movie, guides guests through the wonderful world of bugs. You will see, feel, and, yes, smell the different types of bugs introduced. Of course, nothing here is real. Again, there are no real bugs inside this attraction. Just keep repeating that when the 4-D theater tries to convince you otherwise. While the rides of A Bug's Land appeal to the young guests, this show will easily frighten toddlers—and anyone else who is scared of spiders. For the few of you who are left, it's a fun time.

### Shops of A Bug's Land

There aren't any shops in this land. However, A Bug's Land merchandise is available at **Elias & Co.** on Buena Vista Street.

### Dining in A Bug's Land

There are also no dining options in A Bug's Land. But why would you want to eat here? It's all about bugs! (Don't worry if you're hungry. Many excellent options await in the nearby Cars Land.)

### Cars Land

When the park opened in 2001, it was sorely missing some type of over-the-top immersive themed land. Cars Land was part of that massive overhaul of 2012, and it succeeds. Boy, does it succeed. No detail has been spared here, and you will feel transported to Radiator Springs. Disney California Adventure finally provides a chance for guests to step inside a movie. The nostalgic main street of Radiator Springs stretches toward towering rock formations. It's like Route 66 but with cleaner bathrooms.

### Mater's Junkyard Jamboree

The official star of the *Cars* franchise is Lightning McQueen. But everyone's favorite character is lovable Tow Mater. He's that tow truck that's part vehicle and part hillbilly. He would be just at home in Dollywood as he is here at Disney California Adventure. This attraction is another one of those that look tamer than it is; don't ride if you're easily motion sick.

You'll sit in a junkyard cart and get towed around by a little tractor. The cars get whirled around—a lot. Kids seem to handle it just fine and usually beg to ride again. It's those of us who get sick on a swing set that need to be careful.

### Luigi's Rollickin' Roadsters

This new attraction is so darn cute. You have to stop and watch it. Then you have to ride it. Then you have to watch it again. It's just so darn cute!

You sit in little cars that are automatically driven around by a trackless driving system. The cars narrowly miss each other as fantastic formations are created. It's sort of like riding in bumper cars except you don't drive, and the cars never bump into each other. I guess it's more like bumper cars if they were being driven by the Rockettes.

### Radiator Springs Racers

*Fastpass* This is Disney at its best. It's an awesome combination of storytelling, animatronics, music, and thrills. The line is often long, so grab a Fastpass if you get to the park early enough. Otherwise, I recommend using the single-rider line. It will be just a fraction of the wait time as the regular line, and this ride is so good that you won't have a chance to talk to the person next to you anyway.

Six guests sit three and three in *Cars*-themed racing vehicles. You'll first meet all your favorites from the film in unbelievable animatronic glory. Then your car will suddenly find itself right next to another. The two cars begin a race down California's iconic stretch of Route 66. You'll zip past mountains, waterfalls, and vegetation. The whole thing is set to some brilliant music that makes it all feel just so real. At the conclusion, one of the cars will get to the finish line before the other. It's completely random as to which will win.

I hesitate to give any attraction "must-do" status because everyone has different taste, but Radiator Springs Racers comes about as close to a must-do as you can get.

### Shops of Cars Land

Cars, cars, cars—that's what you'll find in the shops of Radiator Springs. If you're looking for something with a car on it and you can't find it here, then it doesn't exist.

### Dining in Cars Land

**Flo's V8 Café:** This quick-service café is open for lunch and dinner. It's well themed after a classic highway diner. Flo's offers the most substantial fare in Radiator Springs with turkey sandwiches, ribs, and pie.

**Cozy Cone Motel:** One of the cutest restaurants in Disneyland Resort, this quick-service option contains several traffic cones that each offer something different. Hot dogs in one, ice cream in another, chili in another—it's all the fuel you'll need for an afternoon of fun.

**Fillmore's Taste-In:** One of the healthier options in the entire park. Quick-service snacks of fruit and vegetables are offered.

### Paradise Pier

Paradise Pier is themed like the idyllic seaside boardwalks of California and New Jersey but with cleaner sidewalks. This land is especially appealing at night, when thousands of lights outline all the buildings and attractions. Paradise Pier represents the coastal side of Disney California Adventure.

### California Screamin'

*Fastpass* You can't miss this ride as it towers over everything else in the area. It's designed to look like an old-fashioned wooden roller coaster from your local amusement park—but it's hiding a lot of technology. Riders soon learn that California Screamin' is actually a launching steel coaster. There are a couple of inversions, and the whole thing is set to music.

Fastpasses are available, but check the line to see if one is necessary.

### Mickey's Fun Wheel

Also towering over the entire park is Mickey's Fun Wheel. At 150 feet tall, it's become the symbol of Disney California Adventure. A giant retro image of Mickey sits in its center.

There is a choice to make as you get in the line. One option is to ride around the wheel in a stationary car. This makes the ride just like any other Ferris wheel you've experienced. The other option is to ride in a swinging car. These cars move on tracks as the wheel rotates. Regardless of which version you choose, you will be treated to some fantastic views of the entire Disneyland Resort.

### Jumpin' Jellyfish

Normally, jellyfish are something to avoid while at the beach. But here, guests enjoy being lifted up and gently dropped at the whims of giant jellyfish.

### Silly Symphony Swings

Walt had a string of early animated successes with a series called *Silly Symphonies*. You've probably seen a few clips from these films without realizing it. This attraction is similar to the giant swing ride you've seen elsewhere. In fact, most of Paradise Pier contains standard rides that are themed for this seaside land.

### Goofy's Sky School
*Fastpass* This is Disney's version of a family coaster. It's mild enough for kids but just wild enough to provide a little thrill for adults. You'll fly with Goofy as a crop duster while you ride. As you can imagine, Goody isn't the best pilot around, but everything will end up OK. Parents will want to use their judgment as to whether their kids are ready for this ride.

### The Little Mermaid—Ariel's Undersea Adventure
This is a rare dark ride at Disney California Adventure; sit in a clam mobile and follow Ariel on her journey. You'll drop below sea level (a great effect) and meet Flounder, Sebastian, and the evil Ursula. All the great moments and music from the film are featured. At the conclusion, you'll be brought back up to land to meet the handsome Prince Eric.

### King Triton's Carousel
There are some horses on this carousel—sea horses! All the animals on this traditional merry-go-round are from the sea. There are no two alike. You'll find dolphins, whales, seals, and lots of other fish (but no narwhal—darn!).

### Golden Zephyr
Sit in retro space-age airships and glide around in a circle, very much like Dumbo over at Disneyland.

### Toy Story Midway Mania
*Fastpass* If you're at all a fan of the *Toy Story* franchise, then you can't leave California without riding this attraction.

You'll ride through wearing 3-D glass as you attempt to shoot at various targets. All of your favorite characters from the film are featured; they will even cheer for you when certain targets are hit. As you succeed with the targets, you will receive points that are tallied on small screens in front of you.

There are some serious fans of this attraction. You'll no doubt see some of them riding over and over again, always trying to be the day's top scorer. However, the focus you put into getting a high score may come with a price—you may miss all of the amazing effects and theming. Ride this one twice if you can.

### Games
What would a seaside boardwalk be without games of skill? You'll find all of them at Paradise Pier. You'll have to purchase a prepaid Playcard as cash is not accepted at the individual games. Try to win a prize to impress the rest of the people in your party.

### Shops of Paradise Pier
Toy Story merchandise rules at Paradise Pier. You'll find lots of it in the **Midway Mercantile.**

### *Dining in Paradise Pier*

Several quick-service options fit well within the board-walk theme. The following options are located in a food-court setting with covered dining areas:

**Boardwalk Pizza and Pasta**
**Corn Dog Castle**
**Don Tomás:** turkey legs and chimichangas
**Hot Dog Hut**
**Paradise Garden Grill:** salads and healthy options
**Paradise Ice Cream Company**

**Ariel's Grotto:** A full-service restaurant that offers character meals for breakfast, lunch, and dinner. It's the only character meal in the park and features the Disney princesses. It's not a buffet—you'll pay a set price and choose from a list of entrees. Expect to pay $25 for children and $45 for adults.

**The Cove Bar:** An outdoor lounge with a full bar. Appetizer-size entrees are also served.

### Parades, Evening Shows, and Special Events

Buena Vista Street often has some sort of live entertainment. There are roving "residents" who dress in period clothes and are ready to welcome you as they welcomed Walt in 1923. **Five & Dime** is a roving singing group that travels in an old vehicle up and down the street. Fans of the Disney musical *Newsies* will want to catch the **Red Car News Boys.** They perform songs from the musical on Buena Vista Street. All entertainment times can be found in the daily Times Guide or on the Disneyland app.

### Pixar Play Parade

This is more interactive than the parades across the plaza at Disneyland. The Pixar Play Parade features favorite Pixar characters that encourage lots of dancing and participation. It's often more like a street party and less like a parade.

The Pixar Play Parade occurs at least once each day. Check the app for the starting time; the route is marked on all park maps.

### World of Color

*Fastpass* Disney California Adventure's night show is the amazing World of Color. Sometimes touching, sometimes exhilarating, and always beautiful, this show occurs in the water surrounded by Paradise Pier and Pacific Wharf. You'll want to secure a good spot as World of Color can only be seen from one direction. If you can see both the water and the front of Mickey's Fun Wheel, you are good to go.

You can get a Fastpass that allows access to a special seating area. Try to get one of these early in the day. You can also get a special seating ticket by having dinner at Ariel's Grotto. Be advised that even though the special seating areas have great views, guests seated in them are prone to getting a little wet—especially on a windy day.

World of Color uses hundreds of synchronized fountains to showcase unforgettable moments in Disney animation. It's like the Bellagio fountains in Las Vegas but with a lot more color, music, and action. World of Color uses thousands of lights to achieve the spectacular hues in the show. Often, the lights on the water are so well done that you'll swear they used a dye in the water itself.

Large screens made of misting water are used to project images from Disney films. Of course, music is a huge part of the show, and everything is constructed to make you cry. Seriously, you will probably cry.

On top of all this water stuff, lights in the Paradise Pier section of the park are also choreographed to the show. The image of Mickey Mouse above the water makes an unforgettable backdrop to the whole event. Due to the nature of the show, it's easy for imagineers to change it for different seasons and celebrations.

## Downtown Disney

Think of Downtown Disney like a large outdoor mall. It connects the theme park entrance plaza with the resort hotels and parking ramp. The many shops and restaurants can change, so I won't describe them here. But you can always find a current list on the Disneyland app.

This is a very popular district, where an admission price does not apply. You should plan ahead and make reservations at any of the table-service restaurants in Downtown Disney. The restaurants are, of course, busy during meal times. The shops, however, are extremely busy when the theme parks close for the night. It seems that everyone wants to shop for that last souvenir on the way to their car.

Downtown Disney is also home to the ginormous **World of Disney.** This is the largest store in the entire Disneyland Resort and sells everything Disney. Most of the Disney merchandise that you see in either park is available at World of Disney. So if you want something you saw inside Disneyland but don't have the time or ticket to enter the park, you can probably find it at World of Disney. However, even though this huge store sells most Disney items, it doesn't stock non-Disney items that you see in the park. For example, you will be able to purchase a Donald Duck cowboy T-shirt that you saw at the Pioneer Mercantile in Frontierland. But you won't be able to purchase a raccoon hat at World of Disney even though it was also in the Pioneer Mercantile.

**Dreamlly's Disney Direction**

Disney restaurants are diverse, and their menus change often. The dining scene will get even more intense when we get to Walt Disney World in Florida. The good news is that Disney is very good at updating their menus online. The best places to see the most current menus are each park's website and their official app. It's also quite nice that Disney lists all food prices online.

The online reservation systems for Disneyland and Walt Disney World work well. It's easy to search for open tables by date, time, and location. The international locations are not as easy. Paris, Tokyo, and Hong Kong all have online reservation systems that you will figure out—just always look for a small globe. That globe is usually the key to changing the language to English. Shanghai Disneyland does not offer online reservations yet, but that ability is supposedly coming soon.

▲ ▲ ▲

## Area Sights outside Disney

There is life outside Disneyland! Southern California is a playground with gorgeous weather all year around. There is a lot to do here, and I've listed some of my favorites. Of course, it's a bit theme park heavy because, well—that's just me.

### Knott's Berry Farm

Seven miles northwest of Disneyland is what some say was the first theme park in America. (There seems to be an ongoing argument about which was first, Knott's or Holiday World in Santa Claus, Indiana.) Knott's Berry Farm is an Old West-themed park complete with a train and stagecoach rides. There are also several coasters, and high thrill seekers will like this park better than Disneyland. Knott's water park, Soak City, is located next door. The theme park is $47 for adults and $42 for children.

Knott's Berry Farm actually began as a restaurant. The restaurant, Mrs. Knott's Chicken Dinner Restaurant, is still open, and you don't need to purchase theme park admission to eat there. I highly recommend everything on the menu, especially the boysenberry punch.

In the parking lot of Knott's Berry Farm, you'll find an exact replica of Independence Hall. The Knotts were quite taken with the building on a trip to Philadelphia and brought back the original blueprints to California. It's free to tour the hall; inform the parking attendant that you're there just to see Independence Hall, and parking will be free too.

### Universal Studios Hollywood

It won't be any surprise that there are several movie studios open for tours in the area. But none offer an experience as good as Universal Studios. It's thirty-five miles from Disneyland Resort; note that it can take over an hour to drive if there's traffic.

Universal Studios Hollywood is a combination of studio tour and theme park. The studio tour alone is worth the price of admission. It's a ninety-minute ride through the back lots of the actual Universal Studios. You'll see the exact places where many of your favorite movies and television shows are filmed. You'll also see the enormous city set. This set is amazing as it can be any city with just the change of a few signs. Some of the other sets on the tour are historical, like the motel from *Psycho*, and others are new, like a vehicle from *Jurassic World*.

In addition to the studio tour, Universal Studios Hollywood is also a major theme park. The brand-new Wizarding World of Harry Potter is complete with Hogwarts Castle and Hogsmeade Village. Step into the animated world of Springfield, USA and visit Homer Simpson, his family, and all the other iconic characters from the longest-running primetime television show in history. This immersive land is extremely well done and offers the best food in the park. (A Krusty Burger here is much better than they are portrayed on television.)

Tickets for Universal Studios Hollywood are $105 for adults and $99 for children.

### San Clemente State Beach

For an option that won't cost nearly as much admission as a theme park, think about visiting one of California's famous beaches. Keep in mind that many beaches close to the city of Los Angeles are quite developed with lots of tourist traps. If this is your thing, go for it. If not, San Clemente State Beach is thirty-eight miles south of Disneyland Resort. Since it's a state beach, it's more rustic and undeveloped. However, San Clemente State Beach gets a fair amount of wind, so swim at your own caution. In related news, it's a good place to watch surfing.

If you really want to visit a beach, the best thing you can do is ask at your hotel. The locals know the beaches.

They will know which beach is best for families and which is better for surfing. But always be safe. Never swim alone, and pay attention to all warning signs that may be posted.

### San Diego

San Diego is ninety-five miles south of Disneyland Resort. It's a great city and an even better destination for all budgets. It's free to visit Coronado Island and tour the historic Hotel Del Coronado. Coronado Island also has an excellent beach that is gorgeous and usually quite swimmable.

The world-famous San Diego Zoo is as good as its reputation. The zoo itself, located in the city, contains thirty-seven hundred animals, including the giant panda. San Diego Zoo's Safari Park is located a bit out of town. Here, large animals roam free. Many types of single and combination tickets are available at zoo.sandiegozoo.org.

SeaWorld San Diego is also located in the city. This park offers a combination of aquarium and thrill rides. Tickets start at $69.

There is a lot to do around San Diego's beautiful harbor. You can tour an aircraft carrier, visit one of several museums, take an informative city tour, visit Seaport Village for restaurants and shops, or just sit on a bench and enjoy all that blue water.

# 3

## Walt Disney World

OK, HERE IT is: the big kahuna. La gran enchilada. Die grosse wurst. Les grandes frites. The superlatives don't end, and neither does this property. Walt Disney World Resort is the most visited vacation resort in the world. In 2015, more than fifty-two million people visited the property. While Disneyland in California carries the motto "the happiest place on earth," the Magic Kingdom at Walt Disney World is called "the most magical place on earth." And, indeed, it is.

Walt Disney World contains four complete theme parks: Magic Kingdom, Epcot, Disney's Hollywood Studios, and Disney's Animal Kingdom. There are two water parks: Typhoon Lagoon and Blizzard Beach. No less than thirty-six hotels are located on resort property—twenty-seven of them owned and operated by Disney. There are multiple golf courses, a campground, and a large complex dedicated to amateur sports. In addition, Disney Springs is a dining, shopping, and entertainment district that is as large as a theme park itself.

There are over sixty thousand employees and hundreds of thousands of guests at the resort at any given time. It's always one of the larger cities in the United States. Walt Disney World uses three million eggs and two million pounds of flour every year. Nine million pounds of French fries are consumed annually. Three hundred thousand yards of ribbon are used in the Christmas decorations alone.

You won't be able to see it all in one visit. You won't be able to see it all in fifty visits. But that's kind of the whole point of it. Walt Disney World exists to make memories. Whether those memories come from spending a week visiting all parks or from a single day at Epcot, there's no doubt that each step on this property is unforgettable.

Dreamlly's
Disney
Direction

Walt Disney World Resort Pros:

- The largest resort on the planet with endless opportunities for fun.

- Good weather for most of the year, especially fall, winter, and spring.
- Free transportation from the airport to resort hotels.
- Free transportation within the entire property.
- The thickest "Disney bubble" with no need to ever interact with the outside world.
- A MagicBand as your hotel key, ticket, payment method, and Fastpass+.
- The most Disney hotel choices for all budgets.

Walt Disney World Resort Cons:

- The property is so big that priorities and choices must be made.
- Humidity in the summer is terrible.
- Planning for your vacation can be quite complicated with advance dining reservations and Fastpass+ practically required.
- Transportation between locations on the property can take hours.
- The Magic Kingdom is the most-visited theme park on earth, and there isn't really an off season anymore.
- Non-Disney hotels are far and will require a drive.

# History

I like to think that the history of Florida's Walt Disney World began on July 18, 1955. That's the morning after Disneyland opened to the public. I imagine Walt Disney woke up in his apartment above the fire station in Town Square. He stretched, put on his Mickey Mouse slippers, and looked out the window. Then he thought, *Gee, I wish that electrical pole wasn't there. If I ever do this again, I'm going to do it a bit differently.*

It wasn't that Walt was unhappy with Disneyland—quite the contrary. Both park attendance and the bottom line proved that Disneyland was an enormous success. Even more than the numbers, Walt was thrilled at all the positive guest feedback. Make no mistake about it: Walt was proud of Disneyland, and the park never lost its place at the center of his attention.

Time marched on, and the American middle class continued to thrive. The automobile industry grew as every family got a car. Television became the entertainment of choice in every home, and many of those homes tuned into the weekly *Wonderful World of Disney*. And travel, once only for the ultra wealthy, was now possible for many.

In the early 1960s, Walt learned that only 5 percent of Disneyland's guests were from east of the Mississippi. This was at a time when 75 percent of the total US population lived east of the river. It was only natural that Walt and brother Roy considered expanding Mickey's empire to reach all those families living on the East Coast.

Several ideas were floated during those years. At one time, Walt's executives pushed for a location near one of the large East Coast cities. They were used to Disneyland, with most of its guests coming from the local Los Angeles area. It was natural that they believed a park needed to be near a large city in order for it to survive.

Walt had other ideas. One of the early lessons of Disneyland was that when the park was closed, nobody was making any money. Both Disney brothers agreed that none of the large East Coast cities had weather good enough to support a year-round theme park. It didn't take long for Walt to become set on Florida. Although more humid and tropical than Southern California, Florida weather would permit for a nice winter season. Also, Florida was still quite an infant in the early 1960s, and land was cheap. Soon, the "Florida Project" became the most-secret phrase among those close to Walt. The project was only whispered about with the greatest discretion as nobody wanted land speculation to cause a price hike in Florida real estate.

By this time, Walt was aware of the location challenges a landlocked Disneyland had to contend with. All four sides of the Disneyland property had been taken by motels, restaurants, and other non-Disney businesses. It wasn't that he was against others making a profit from his park—he just didn't like how close they were doing it. Walt felt that a bit of the magic was lost when Disneyland guests could see a Hilton Hotel from inside the park. He wouldn't make that same mistake in Florida.

He wanted a lot of land that had to be near one of the planned interstate highways. Walt had also foreseen the importance of air travel to the future of the Florida Project and required property near an airport. The Disney brothers and their secret entourage of imagineers made many flights over Florida in 1963. They looked at properties and passed over most for one reason or another. Then, in November of 1963, it seemed that they'd found what they had been looking for.

Both Interstate 4 and the Florida Turnpike were under construction at the time. The Disney group saw where these highways joined near McCoy Air Force Base. The air-force base had runways for public use. The brothers Disney were interested in a nearby area of swamp and farmland. This property contained a lake called Bay Lake. It was centrally located to catch all those East Coast travelers as they took the interstate system from New York to Miami. There were just a few small towns in the area. The closest town with any sizable population was a small farming community that nobody had ever heard of. It was called Orlando.

In late 1964 and early 1965, numerous plots of land in varying sizes were purchased in central Florida. The purchases were made by a number of companies, including the Reedy Creek Ranch Corporation and Latin-American Development and Management Corporation. All of these companies were actually fake names for Disney's Florida Project. In all, 30,500 acres of Florida swamp were purchased—that's forty-eight square miles.

In May 1965, some of the land transactions were recorded in Osceola and Orange Counties (the Disney property occupies parts of both counties). A reporter from the *Orlando Sentinel* noticed and published an article on May 20, 1965. The article mentioned several rumors that were floating around the community about the large land sale. The biggest rumor was that the federal government was buying the land for the space program. There were also rumors involving Ford Motor Company and Howard Hughes. And the article noted that Walt Disney's name had been mentioned in connection with the land, but it seemed unlikely he had anything to do with it.

Nothing more was written about the land sale until Disneyland's tenth-anniversary celebration in October of 1965. A savvy reporter from the *Orlando Sentinel*, Emily Bavar, interviewed Walt and just casually mentioned the Florida land rumor as a joke. She later stated that Walt became uncharacteristically speechless. She noted his reaction and spent the rest of her time in Anaheim digging up anything she could find. On October 21, 1965, Ms. Bavar published a front-page article in the *Orlando Sentinel* under the giant headline "We Say: 'Mystery Industry' Is Disney." Four days later, the governor of Florida confirmed the headline.

Because of the article, Walt and his people moved up their big reveal. November 15, 1965, changed the future of Orlando, and all of Florida, forever. Walt Disney and Governor Hayden Burns held a news conference in

Orlando, where they officially announced the development of a Disney attraction in central Florida. But few actual details were given; no confirmation was provided as to whether this was an "East Coast Disneyland" or something else entirely.

Walt's initial plan for the Florida property centered around something he called the Experimental Prototype Community of Tomorrow, or EPCOT. This was to be a planned city where new innovations could be tried. Walt spent a lot of time dreaming about it and even had a ginormous model of the place built. (You can see part of the model if you ride the PeopleMover in the Magic Kingdom's Tomorrowland.) The city included a central business district surrounded by numerous residential neighborhoods. People would move in and out of the city using monorails, and all vehicles traveled in underground tunnels.

We will never know what EPCOT could have been because, sadly, Walt Disney died of lung cancer on December 15, 1966. The Florida Project was in limbo for about twenty seconds when Roy Disney stepped forward and made it his mission to build in Florida—as a tribute to his cherished brother. The project was now officially named Walt Disney World.

Roy knew what Walt wanted, and he wasted no time in going forward. First, the Disney property required some special legislation to secure its autonomy. Roy Disney was not stupid. He knew that the emotional legacy of Walt's recent passing would be a catalyst to get things moving in the state government.

On May 12, 1967, Florida governor Claude Kirk signed into law the Reedy Creek Improvement District. This unprecedented act, pushed by Roy and passed through the Florida legislature, created a special entity in central Florida: Reedy Creek Improvement District. The district was divided into two incorporated cities: Bay Lake and Lake Buena Vista (formerly called Reedy Creek). The cities had all the powers of local government and were exempt from future county and state land-use laws.

The impact of the Reedy Creek Improvement District on Walt Disney World cannot be stressed enough. Disney (the company), as the sole land owner of both cities, was able to issue tax-free bonds. Their ability to do this was challenged, and the 1968 Florida Supreme Court ruled in Disney's favor. (Note: during the remainder of this book, whenever I refer to Disney, I am writing about the company and not the man.)

With revenue from the bonds and the ability to avoid all red tape because they essentially owned the red tape, Disney moved forward rapidly. Drainage canals were dug and gently curved to look like natural rivers. Adjacent to the existing Bay Lake, the Seven Seas Lagoon was created. And construction started on the Magic Kingdom. Walt's dream of EPCOT had been put on the back burner for the time being. The public wanted an "East Coast Disneyland," and Roy thought it made the best financial sense.

On October 1, 1971, Walt Disney World's Magic Kingdom opened to the public. The first guest to pass through the turnstile was Mary Poppins herself, Julie Andrews. On that day, Walt Disney World consisted of the Magic Kingdom Park, the Contemporary Hotel, Polynesian Village, and Fort Wilderness Campground. A monorail quickly whisked guests around the lagoon to the various destinations. It was spectacular, and Roy Disney was deservedly proud. Mission accomplished, Roy passed away three months later, having never retired from the company he founded with his beloved brother. (Look for his statue on Main Street, USA.)

Things went well in Florida, and Orlando began to look like the familiar vacation destination we love today. For over ten years, Walt Disney World's Magic Kingdom thrived. However, Walt and Roy had groomed a group of imagineers who just couldn't forget Walt's dream of EPCOT.

Numerous ideas for what EPCOT could be were discussed. The actual residential part of the plan was deemed too involved and perhaps even risky; the focus of EPCOT evolved into the idea of adding a second theme park to Walt Disney World. Concepts were refined and eliminated until there were two left. One idea was for a park that would showcase human achievement and the advancement of technology. The other idea was for a sort of world's fair with pavilions representing countries. Both plans must have looked pretty good sitting on a table together. The two ideas were joined as one and named EPCOT Center.

EPCOT Center opened on October 1, 1982. The front of the park, Future World, was dedicated to technology and human progress. The back of the park, World Showcase, featured countries spread around the World Showcase Lagoon. The definitive symbol of EPCOT Center was Spaceship Earth—an enormous geodesic sphere that eventually became as iconic as Magic Kingdom's Cinderella Castle.

Since opening, EPCOT Center has consistently been the third-most-visited theme park in the United States—behind Disneyland and Walt Disney World's Magic Kingdom. In 1996, EPCOT Center lost its center and its acronym. Now known simply as Epcot, the park continues to educate and entertain.

But Walt Disney World wasn't just two parks for long—only about seven years. Soon after EPCOT Center opened, imagineers were busy creating new attractions for Future World. One of the new attractions was something called the Great Movie Ride and would showcase the art of film as a human achievement. Michael Eisner, then CEO of Disney, liked the idea so much that he suggested it evolve into its own park. (He was probably a bit influenced by a rumor that Universal Studios was looking to build a movie-themed park in Orlando.)

Plans and concepts for a new park moved forward. In 1985, Disney made an agreement with Metro-Goldwyn-Mayer that gave Disney the right to the MGM name as well as to certain intellectual property. The park soon became known as Disney-MGM Studios.

The entrance of the park would take visitors back to 1930s Hollywood with all the glitz and glamour of the era. The middle of the park was planned to contain several attractions based on film, television, music, and theater. The back of the park would be an actual working studio where Disney movies and television could be filmed. A large contingent of Disney animators was moved to the new location so that park guests could see them drawing the next classic film.

Disney-MGM Studios opened on May 1, 1989, and has expanded many times during its existence. Even its name has changed. Due to a complicated legal dispute with MGM over a MGM theme park in Las Vegas, the relationship between the two studios disintegrated. For a while, Disney was prohibited from using the MGM name on a national basis but was free to use the name in Florida. This meant that the park had two names in the mid-1990s. The gate still read "Disney-MGM Studios," but television commercials simply called it "The Disney Studios."

On August 9, 2007, the park officially dropped MGM and became Disney's Hollywood Studios. The name is likely to change in the near future. Stay tuned.

In 1994, *The Lion King* roared into movie theaters. It was an instant success and soon became the top-grossing animated movie of all time. (A title it held until 2010's *Toy Story 3*. Currently, the top-grossing animated film is *Frozen*.) The enormous success of *The Lion King* prompted Disney to think about adding animal attractions at its parks. They had a lot of experience with animatronic animals, but real animals would require care and reverence. Soon, it was believed that only a dedicated theme park could do the animal world justice.

Construction began in the mid 1990s. Great care was taken to design the park with an "animals first, guests second" philosophy. Disney hired the best in the business, many of them keepers at prestigious zoos, to plan the park. Construction was a monumental task. At 580 acres, it's geographically the largest theme park in the world.

Disney's Animal Kingdom opened on April 22, 1998. It was Earth Day. The Tree of Life, a 145-foot sculpted tree, soon became this park's iconic symbol.

As this theme park development and construction occurred, other things were brewing too. Numerous resorts were added over the years to provide something for every budget. There are now thirty-six separate resorts on the property.

In 1976, Disney opened one of the world's first water parks. It was called River Country and sat on the shore of Bay Lake. River Country was such a successful concept that two other water parks were eventually developed. Typhoon Lagoon opened in 1989, and Blizzard Beach began sending guests down slides in 1995. When a drop in overall attendance occurred post-9/11, River Country was closed without plans to reopen.

In 1975, a small street of shops and restaurants opened on the very edge of Disney property—along Interstate 4. The Lake Buena Vista Shopping Village mainly catered to guests at nearby non-Disney hotels. The area expanded under the name Disney Village Marketplace. At one time, it contained the Pleasure Island nightclub experience. Eventually, this commercial area grew into an East Coast version of Downtown Disney.

In 2016, Downtown Disney officially became Disney Springs. As big as a fifth theme park, Disney Springs is a giant collection of shops and restaurants surrounding beautiful waterways. There is a new parking system that makes the district much easier to visit, and crowds are bustling.

The future of Walt Disney World Resort is unknown and always changing. As the world's largest resort destination, there will always be criticism. But I find that the whole thing is still magical. Of all the Disney resorts around the world, this one provides the best Disney bubble. Here, I can be immersed in the magic in ways that are not possible anywhere else on the planet. I may *get* tired at Walt Disney World, but I never *grow* tired.

# Travel Knowledge
## Arrival

Central Florida farmers in the 1940s never imagined that, in the future, a Lufthansa 747 from Frankfurt, Germany, would land in Orlando every single day. They couldn't have begun to fathom that over forty million people would land in their fields in order to visit a mouse.

Orlando International Airport (MCO) is the largest airport in the area. Most visitors, by far, arrive at Walt Disney

World Resort via this airport. Orlando International began its life as McCoy Air Force Base. Interestingly, this was the air-force base where bombers and reconnaissance aircraft were launched during the Cuban Missile Crisis of 1962. McCoy had a civil airstrip since 1960. In 1971, it was announced that McCoy Air Force Base would close due to post–Vietnam era restructuring. The civilian airport took over all facilities in 1975. It was renamed Orlando International Airport in 1976 but kept its MCO code.

Orlando International is a large, modern airport. All the services that you'd expect from a world-class airport are present. There is an excellent Hyatt Hotel in the middle of the terminal in case you arrive late or depart early. Multiple food courts and several restaurants are conveniently placed throughout.

The airport is divided into two sides: A and B. It's quite easy to walk from one to the other if you happen to find yourself on the incorrect side. However, once you pass through security, you'll be stuck on that side of the airport. Most of the gates require a tram ride to access them. There are additional food courts and restaurants near the gates as well.

Orlando International is not just the airport of choice for travelers visiting Walt Disney World Resort. It's also the main airport for Universal Orlando, the city of Orlando, and all the cruises departing from nearby Port Canaveral. It's a busy place.

There are several options for ground transportation. If you booked a Walt Disney World Resort Hotel, you can use the free Magical Express. This is your cheapest option if you plan to stay on the Disney property during your entire trip. If you've selected to use Magical Express on your reservation, you'll receive a packet in the mail a few weeks before your journey. The packet will include luggage tags. You can put the luggage tags on your checked bags at your home airport, and you won't need to collect your bags in Orlando. They will magically appear in your hotel room.

When you arrive at Orlando International, proceed to the B side of the airport and follow the signs for Disney's Magical Express. You'll go down a couple of escalators to the large check-in area. Friendly cast members will put you into the correct line, along with all of your carry-on bags. Eventually, you'll be loaded onto a bus and whisked away to Walt Disney World. While at the resort, you'll use Disney's Resort Transportation to get to theme parks and other hotels.

The day before you return home, you'll find a Magical Express card in your room. It will give you the time and place to meet the bus that will bring you back to the airport in time for your flight. Remember, you can only use the free Magical Express if you've booked a reservation at a Disney hotel and if you've provided your flight information to Disney.

Magical Express works great for most people. But it's not for everyone. Those who want to venture off Disney property will need a car. All rental car companies are available on site at Orlando International. It takes around forty-five minutes to drive to Walt Disney World, but note that there are several toll roads. Toll roads in Florida do not take cash or coins. If you've purchased a SunPass from your rental car company, just stay in the SunPass lane and you're good to go. If you don't have a SunPass, then a camera will take a photograph of your license plate. You'll get a bill from Florida in the mail if you're driving your own car. When using a rental car, you'll get notice from your rental car company that they've billed your credit card for the toll.

Parking at all Disney hotels is free, and once you've checked in, you can use Disney transportation to get to the theme parks.

A taxi from the airport to the middle of Walt Disney World will run about $70 during normal traffic. UberBLACK costs $60 for the one-way trip. Orlando International does not allow UberX at this time. (But experienced travelers can use an Uber work-around. UberX costs $16 from the airport area to Walt Disney World.)

Speaking of Uber, it's become a huge alternative to Disney transposition within Walt Disney World. Disney transportation is fine—it's free, always air-conditioned, and easy to locate. However, Disney transportation can be time consuming. You must allow at least an hour to get from one location to another. (Disney recommends one and a half hours just to be safe.) An Uber may get you there in under ten minutes for $4. After a long day in the parks, sometimes it's nice to spend a few bucks to get back to your hotel quicker. There are a lot of people making substantial money driving Uber around Walt Disney World.

As you continue reading, you'll come across all sorts of terms like Magical Express, MagicBand, Fastpass+, Advance Dining Reservation, MyDisneyExperience, and online check-in. All these things require advance planning, and your blood pressure may start to rise—don't let it. Disney is great with communication, and they will lead you through this magical world.

About a week after you've booked a Walt Disney World Resort Vacation by phone, online, or through a travel agent, you'll receive a small book in the mail. This book is quite magical and always makes everyone in your home scream with excitement. There's a lot of fun stuff in the book and great photographs of what a wonderful time you'll have.

But what you really want to notice is the last page. Don't lose this page—seriously, just don't lose it. It will have a picture of Dumbo on it. Get it? Dumbo's an elephant and doesn't forget. You're not an elephant and will need this page as a reminder.

This page will list everything you need to do and on what date you're eligible to do it. You don't have to count 120 days before your vacation to discover when you can start making dining reservations. Just keep Dumbo on your fridge, and you'll have the date right in front of you. You can make Fastpass+ selections sixty days before your journey; Dumbo will remind you of that too. Better still, take a photo of Dumbo's reminders and carry them in your phone for easy access.

In addition to Dumbo, you'll also get e-mails from Disney when there is something you need to do for your vacation. They'll let you know when it's time to customize your MagicBands and complete online check-in.

▲ ▲ ▲

### Entry Requirements

US travelers do not need a passport to travel to Florida, although you can purchase a souvenir passport at Epcot and collect stickers for it at all the countries around World Showcase Lagoon.

Foreign visitors will need a valid passport from their home countries. Travelers from Europe, the United Kingdom, Canada, Australia, New Zealand, and Japan do not need a separate visa to gain entry into the United States. Travelers from other countries may or may not require a visa, depending upon the specifics of your travel. All foreign visitors should check their specific entry requirement by visiting the official US Department of State Travel website (travel.state.gov).

Upon arrival in the United States, expect to proceed through both a passport control and customs check. At most major entry airports, including MCO, the customs forms for return travelers are now automated and re-quire the traveler to stop at a kiosk before proceeding to a border control agent. The kiosk will ask a few questions about your possessions and print a small paper for you to hand to the agent. Those who are inside the United States for the first time will need to complete a blue form provided on their aircrafts.

### Time

Florida is in the Eastern Time Zone of the United States— the same time zone as New York City and Washington, DC. It's three hours ahead of California and six hours behind Europe. Those traveling in November and March will want to check the dates for daylight saving time, re-membering that these dates are different between Europe and the United States.

Asia does not observe daylight saving time. Walt Disney World, in the summer, is thirteen hours behind Tokyo and twelve hours behind China. In the winter, Orlando is one hour further back.

### Language

The predominant language of most of the United States is English, although Walt Disney World is very accustomed to visitors from other countries. If you have a problem, ask any cast member, and he or she will be able to assist you; cast members will know how to obtain a translator if required. Most signs around the resort are in English and Spanish. In addition, Disney does a great job of using pictures to communicate with guests.

### *Weather*

Florida has tropical weather from midspring through midfall. It's not uncommon for temperatures to be in the nineties (that's thirty-two to thirty-five for those you who live elsewhere). We've all heard the phrase, "It's not the heat; it's the humidity." You will come to rue that phrase on most summer days in Florida. Expect high humidity from March through even November. It does get considerably cooler when the sun sets, but the humidity will keep it sticky throughout the night.

Late November through March is quite pleasant. There may still be some humidity, but the temperatures will keep it in check. You may even need a jacket for some brief weeks in January, especially at night.

It will rain sometime on your vacation. It will probably rain every day. The good news is that Florida is notorious for drenching afternoon downpours that end quickly. It's rare for all-day rains to occur. It's also rare for hurricanes to hit central Florida, but they can. Hurricane season in Florida runs from June through November. (And don't forget, rain can be your best friend when you're at a theme park; it thins the crowds and makes a wonderfully blurry line between fantasy and reality.)

Everyone who knows me will tell you that I am a sunscreen fanatic. I have seen the damaging and deadly impact that skin cancer causes. Even though some very cool breezes may be blowing, you *must* wear sunscreen during the daytime in Florida, even throughout the winter. You simply must. If anyone in your party is too cool for sunscreen, Google "melanoma" and show that person the disfiguring effects of this terrible disease. A Disney vacation is not cheap. Don't ruin it by being in pain from a bad sunburn.

### *Money*

Walt Disney World used to have its own currency. Disney Dollars, printed with the images of various characters, were actually currency with an exchange rate of one to one with the US dollar. Sadly, Disney Dollars have been discontinued. So that leaves the good old dollar as the only official currency of the most magical place on earth.

Most Americans carry very little cash, and credit cards are used frequently. Writing a check is often frowned upon and may not even be accepted.

ATMS (automated teller machines) are available throughout Walt Disney World Resort. This includes the four theme parks, Disney Springs, and all the hotels in the area. You can exchange most any currency at Orlando International, and many hotels can exchange the more popular currencies of Canada, Mexico, Europe, the United Kingdom, and Japan.

Visitors from other counties should note that prices in the United States never include tax. This is made even more confusing at Walt Disney World Resort because the property straddles two different counties. (A county is a form of local government in the United States.) Most of Walt Disney World, including all the theme parks, is in Orange County. The sales tax rate in Orange County is 6.5 percent. This means that you must add 6.5 percent to the price of all merchandise and food you purchase in Orange County. Some of Walt Disney World, including the All-Star Resorts, is in Osceola County. The tax rate in Osceola County is 7.5 percent. Yes, the same Donald Duck keychain will cost you a bit more if purchased at the All-Star Music Resort than if you purchased it at Epcot.

Lodging tax is different than sales tax. This tax applies to the rate of the room, not any of the purchases you make at that hotel. Lodging tax is 12.5 percent in Orange County. In Osceola County, the lodging tax is 13.5 percent. On behalf of the entire United States of America, I'd like to apologize to all international visitors for our complicated sales and lodging tax system.

Also, in the United States, it's customary to tip 15 percent for service at any table-service restaurant or bar. You can adjust the percentage up or down for better or worse service. You should calculate the tip based on the pretax total of the bill. Unlike across the rest of the world, the amount for an item listen on the menu will not be the final amount. Remember to add tax and tip. Please don't forget to give a tip while using the Disney Dining Plan.

Tax is already included with the plan, but the wonderful servers count on tips, even when you don't directly pay the bill.

### Tickets

All right, people, it's time for homework. In order to calculate the total price of tickets for your visit, you'll need graph paper, three whiteboards, markers, a bunch of liquor, a bulletin board with multicolored pushpins, and the direct phone number for a NASA astrophysicist.

After you've gathered your supplies, you can begin purchasing tickets either online at disneyworld.disney. go.com or by calling 407-939-1866. Online, you'll find a step-by-step calculator. You'll input information such as the number of people, dates, and what you want to do, and then you'll get a price. If you call, you'll give the cast member the same information and receive a price. The problem with both experiences is that it's difficult to know what items make the price go up and down. I'll try to break it all down for you here. For the purpose of this discussion, a child is anyone aged three to nine.

Let's begin with a one-day pass. The price for a single day ticket depends upon both the date you want to visit and which park you'd like to enter. Like with Disneyland, there are three seasons: value, regular, and peak. A one-day pass to the Magic Kingdom during peak season is $124 per adult, $118 per child. A one-day pass to any other park on the property during peak season is $114 per adult, $108 per child. With this type of one-day ticket, you must declare a park at time of purchase, and you cannot hop from that park to another. (Add $40 to the Magic Kingdom price to purchase the hopper option; this allows you to visit as many parks as you want on one day.)

Just to compare, a one-day pass to the Magic Kingdom during value season is $105 per adult, $99 per child. A one-day pass to any other park during value season is $97 per adult, $91 per child. Once again, add around $40 to the Magic Kingdom price to be able to hop to multiple parks.

Thankfully, when you start to consider multiple-day tickets, you no longer have to worry about season and location. Multiple-day passes are good for any day and at any park. However, once you use the first day of the pass, you have fourteen days to complete the pass. For example, if you have a two-day pass, you can enter any park whenever you want. Then, after the first day, you have thirteen days left to enjoy the second day at any park you want. This makes it economical for families to purchase a four-day pass during a weeklong vacation and skip Disney for a few days to do other things in the area.

A two-day pass is $202 per adult, $190 per child. With this pass, you can enter one park each day for two days. In order to enter more than one park on either day of your pass, you will need to purchase a hopper for an additional $55. With a two-day hopper, you can visit all four parks as you wish for two days. The more days you add to your pass, the cheaper the per-day amount will become.

Using a two-day pass, you are paying around $100 per day. Let's look at some longer options.

A five-day pass is $340 per adult, $320 per child. Now you are down to around $70 per day. In order to hop on a five-day pass, you will need to add a $69 hopper. Let's say that you arrive early on a Saturday and are departing late on the next Saturday; you want to spend all your time in the parks. An eight-day pass is $380 per adult, $360 per child—not all that much more than a five-day pass. You're at about $48 per day. An eight-day hopper option is an additional $69. (In fact, the hopper option does not increase in price after day four.)

Now, just to complicate it a little, all the passes above are for theme parks only: Magic Kingdom, Epcot, Disney's Hollywood Studios, and Disney's Animal Kingdom. They cannot be used at either Typhoon Lagoon or Blizzard Beach. However, the ticket structure for the water parks is much easier to understand. A one-day ticket to either water park, valid from May 28 through August 28, is $60 per adult, $54 per child. The rest of the year, because the water parks aren't as popular, a one-day ticket to either water park is $55 per adult, $49 per child.

If you purchase a multiple-day theme park pass, then you can add the Waterpark Fun & More option for $64. That's $64 for the entire pass, not per day, regardless if you're adding it to a two-day pass or a ten-day pass. When you add a Waterpark Fun & More option, you get *one* visit per day to *one* of these attractions:

- Typhoon Lagoon Waterpark
- Blizzard Beach Waterpark
- ESPN Wide World of Sports (both play and watch sporting activities)
- Disney's Oak Trail Golf Course (one round of golf per visit)
- Disney's Fantasia Gardens Miniature Golf (valid before 4:00 p.m. only)
- Disney's Winter Summerland Miniature Golf (valid before 4:00 p.m. only)

A nifty benefit of the Waterpark Fun & More option is that you can save your unused visits and combine them. For example, that same family with the eight-day pass purchased Waterpark Fun & More for $64 per pass. They went to theme parks for seven days and didn't use any of their Waterpark Fun & More. This means that on the eighth day, each of the family members still has eight visits to one of the six attractions listed above. They could all play eight games of miniature golf, or they could play six games of golf and visit each water park once; the possibilities are endless. (Well, they are endless until their multiple-day passes end that day.)

If you're still with me, congratulations! We're almost through. There is just one more option that can be added to your tickets. Everywhere at Walt Disney World Resort, you'll see friendly cast members willing to take your picture. They will use their really nice camera for the best possible photo. And as another great benefit that Disney allows, their cast members will also take the same photo with your own camera. This is a great way to get some fantastic pictures right on your phone. But what about all those photos that get taken with Disney's expensive cameras?

Up until thirty days before your trip, you can purchase Memory Maker for an extra $149. It doesn't matter how many days you'll be at Walt Disney World; it will cost $149 to access all of the professional photographs taken during your stay. (If you purchase Memory Maker within thirty days of your trip, the price increases to $199.) When you return home, you have thirty days from the first day you log on to Memory Maker to download as many photos as you want. Don't underestimate the value of these professional photographers. They know exactly how to capture Cinderella Castle at the moment you're there. They know how to account for crowds and sun.

If you book a Disney hotel reservation, you can add your park tickets to that reservation by creating a Magic Your Way package. This is the most convenient way to keep track of everything in one reservation. You can create these packages either online or over the phone.

That's it! You can now drink that liquor that I mentioned earlier. What? Now you're worried about keeping track of theme park passes, water park fun crap, memory picture stuff, and hopping tickets? As Dory says, "Just keep reading!"

### MagicBands

MagicBands are a Walt Disney World Resort exclusive—they're not used at any other Disney property. MagicBands are plastic bracelets that fit securely around your wrist. They are removable with a plastic clasp. You can wear them in the swimming pool and on all attractions. Two months before your arrival date, you will get an e-mail reminding you to customize your MagicBands. You'll follow a link and use an online tool to choose the color of the MagicBand for each person in your party. You'll also enter the names they'd like personalized on the back. About a month before your vacation, a fantastic package will arrive in the mail containing all your MagicBands. It's normal for everyone in your family to start screaming with excitement when this package arrives.

MagicBands are simply a way to communicate with Disney's master computer system—no information is actually stored on the band. But through the master computer, they can serve a number of purposes. MagicBands are your key to get into your Disney hotel room. They are also your theme park passes. They contain your Waterpark Fun & More options. When you complete online check-in for your Disney hotel, you'll choose a PIN. Your MagicBand, plus the PIN, gives adults the ability to use their MagicBand as a room-charging device. They also hold all your Fastpass+ privileges. When you have your photograph taken by a Disney cast member, present your MagicBand, and it will connect all your photographs together.

The best aspect of the MagicBand is that it's extremely easy to disable. If you, or anyone in your party, lose your band, just open the Disney World MyDisneyExperience App and disable that MagicBand. This instantly turns the MagicBand into a very unmagical plastic bracelet. You can easily replace a MagicBand at any shop on the property. The free bands that come with your hotel reservation are solid in color. But the MagicBands you can buy on the property are adorable and themed to an endless array of the Disney universe. Some people have been known to lose their free MagicBands on purpose so that they can purchase a cuter one—not that I would ever think of doing such a frivolous thing.

Sometime during the spring of 2017, Walt Disney World is switching over to MagicBand2. You won't be able to choose which generation of MagicBand you're going to receive; when the switch occurs, you'll get the new version in the mail. MagicBand2s have the same function as the original MagicBand but have a removable center. This center contains the transmitter and can be pushed into a number of other accessories including key chains, necklaces, and rings. Guests who don't like wearing a wrist band will appreciate the ability to turn their MagicBand2 into something else. Just be advised—two of the smallest screws in the world make transferring the removable center quite difficult.

I do have one huge complaint about the MagicBand system. Every time you book a room reservation, you'll get a MagicBand in the mail—even if it's just for one night. My husband and I like to take a couple of smaller trips rather than one long vacation. We've collected many MagicBands, and it's a bit of a waste—not to mention that they come with an unbelievable amount of packaging. If you're listening, Mickey: please let us opt out of receiving a new MagicBand; we can just use an old one. (In exchange, you should offer us a free quick-service meal voucher.)

### *Parking*

I'm about to say something that may blow your mind, so hang on to your Mickey Ears: some of the parking options at Walt Disney World are free! That's right; it's completely free to park at either Typhoon Lagoon or Blizzard Beach as long as you have a valid ticket or pass. If you are a registered guest at a Disney hotel, it's also free to park there. And it's free to park for up to three hours at any Disney hotel where you have dining reservations. If that's not enough, it's free to park at Disney Springs.

But you do have to pay to park in the theme park lots. Standard parking in any of the four theme park lots is $20 per day. You can switch parks without having to pay again if you keep your receipt. Preferred parking, the front part of the parking lot that's closest to the entrance gate, is $35 per day.

I know what some of you more frugal readers are thinking, *Can't I just park for free at the Contemporary Resort and walk to the Magic Kingdom? How will they know I'm not staying there? Couldn't I just tell them I have a dinner reservation at the hotel?* Well, yes, you could do any of those things, but I wouldn't recommend it. Disney has been cracking down on parking violations. When you enter any of the Disney hotel lots, you will stop at a gate. A security guard may ask your name and validate your reservation on a computer. They don't ask every car that passes, so the gamble is yours to take.

### Park Hours

Among all the Disney properties, Walt Disney World Resort contains the theme parks with the most widely changing hours. Depending upon the season and capacity of the on-property hotels, hours will fluctuate. You may find that the Magic Kingdom closes at 7:00 p.m. on the first night of your visit and it's open until 3:00 a.m. on the second. Visit disneyworld.disney.go.com or use the MyDisneyExperience app to obtain the most current park hours.

Extra Magic Hours are a great benefit that allow access to a theme park either before or after it's open to the public. Unlike Disneyland, here in Florida you must be a guest of a Disney hotel in order to access Extra Magic Hours—you cannot buy this privilege. How will they know you're a hotel guest? You'll scan your MagicBand at the entrance gate to verify your hotel and ticket information.

The Extra Magic Hours calendar is posted online and on the MyDisneyExperience app. One park will open an hour or two earlier in the morning, and another park will stay open as long as four hours later in the evening. Not every attraction at the specific park will operate during Extra Magic Hours, but many will. It's a great way to experience some of the more popular attractions with shorter lines. All Disney transportation buses keep running until well after Extra Magic Hours.

A word about preplanning. Walt Disney World is the most magical place on earth—it's an entire kingdom devoted to your vacation. Even though there is a considerable amount of things to preplan, don't let it add too much stress to your life.

Everything that you preplan is changeable. And you'll be glad to know that the MyDisneyExperience app makes changes easy to accomplish. Sometime after you've booked your vacation but prior to 120 days before you arrive, make a basic itinerary of what you'd like to do during your time at Walt Disney World.

Yep, this is more of that homework I was talking about. Grab a sheet of paper for each day that you'll be on vacation. Divide each sheet into morning, afternoon, and evening. Sketch in a preliminary schedule, making sure that you consider your priorities and budget. Is eating at Cinderella's Royal Table a priority for you? If so, pencil it in. Do you want to have a lot of time to explore the different countries at Epcot? Cross out two evenings for that. Just start somewhere until you have a basic idea of how you'll spend each day. Don't forget to put down swimming and relaxation time.

Let all that sit for a few days. Then come back to it and be more specific. Pencil in other meals and list attractions that you must see. Again, let it sit and come back to get even more specific. Eventually, you'll have a nice schedule.

You will really appreciate that you've done this work when it comes time to make dining reservations and Fastpass+ selections. Remember, don't worry—this is all about vacation. You can change anything.

▲ ▲ ▲

### *Dining Reservations and the Disney Dining Plan*

I understand that it's impossible to know where you want to eat six months from now when you don't even know what's for dinner tonight. But securing some reservations will save you a lot of time waiting when you're at the resort.

One hundred and twenty days before your date of arrival, you can begin to make dining reservations for your entire trip. Refer to that Dumbo reminder card that you put on your fridge; it will have the exact date noted for you. Use your rough itinerary and make the reservations online, via the app, or by calling the resort. The app woks best for me.

Now sometimes I know that my budget isn't going to allow me to eat at table-service restaurants. That's not a problem because there are so many quality quick-service options. It also means that I don't have to take time to make any dining reservations. But if my priorities and budget allow for any character meals, then I'll make those reservations first.

The most difficult reservation to attain at Walt Disney World is Cinderella's Royal Table. It's a character meal that's served inside Cinderella Castle at the Magic Kingdom. You get to meet a bunch of Disney princesses as you dine. It's expensive ($62.95 per adult), and I avoided it for years, but once I did it, I fell in love with the awesome atmosphere. It's worth it. However, to get this reservation, you must be ready on the day your window opens. Remember that you can book for your entire stay 120 days before your first day. That means you have a bit of an advantage over the days toward the end of your stay.

Cinderella's Royal Table is the only dining experience that requires prepayment at time of reservation. You can cancel and get a refund. For all other restaurants, Disney will ask for a credit card, but they will not charge it. If you fail to show up for the reservation and don't cancel it within twenty-four hours, then you'll be charged a ten-dollar penalty. The reservation cancelation policy can change at any time. Disney does a great job of letting you know the rules before you accept the reservation.

Whenever you eat anywhere at Walt Disney World Resort, you'll be asked if you are on the Disney Dining Plan. Remember when I said that you needed to find a NASA astrophysicist in order to understand the ticket options? Well, now you need to find that person's supervisor to understand the Disney Dining Plan. First, I'll describe the plan, and then I'll share my frank opinion of it.

You purchase the Disney Dining Plan when you book a Disney hotel and ticket package (Magic My Way Package.). There are a couple of different dining plans available. Basically, the more expensive plans give you more meals than the cheaper plans. The Disney Dining Plan you purchase will come with a set number of meals per day. For example, a more expensive plan may include one breakfast, lunch, dinner, and snack per person in your party. Your MagicBand keeps track of what you have used. A cheaper plan may just include a lunch and dinner without breakfast and snack.

It gets more complicated when you learn that you can swap meals. If you don't eat at all one of your days (maybe you went to the beach), you can then have an extra breakfast, lunch, dinner, and snack on some other day. You will see people in the hotel shops using up their dining plans by buying a boatload of snacks on their last day. However, the plan can go the other way too. Some restaurants require more than one meal on the dining plan. One dinner at Cinderella's Royal Table uses two of your dining plan dinners. In this case, you'll need to skip dinner one of the other days of your trip.

The components of your meal are also dictated by the dining plans. Your plan may define lunch as an entree and beverage. Dinner may be an appetizer, entree, dessert, and beverage. You'll need to pay attention to the definition of a meal; all cast members are well aware of these. (For the European readers: in the United States, an entree is the main course—it's not what you are used to.)

There is one very important thing to remember: tips are not included in any of the Disney Dining Plans. In most cases, the wait staffs at Disney restaurants are hard-working individuals who will seem happy and accommodating at all times. But even if they're awesome, they are trying to make a living like the rest of us. They are putting themselves through school, or supporting a family, or trying to make it on their own. Please, please tip them. When you complete a meal, you'll be given a receipt that shows how many dining plan meals you have left. That receipt will also list the price you would have paid for the meal had you not used the Disney Dining Plan. Please tip at least 15 percent of that amount; tip more if you received excellent service. Bring cash so that you are prepared to do that.

Now, here is my frank opinion. If you love the Disney Dining Plan, that's great. Just skip to the next section of this book. (Pausing to wait for them to leave.) OK, now that they're gone, let's have a candid discussion. I always do my homework. I've worked the numbers on many occasions for all sorts of groups. I've considered the math for just one traveler all the way up to a group of ten. In no instance is the Disney Dining Plan saving anyone any money. Just think about it: do you really think Disney is going to lose money on this?

The problem with the dining plan is that I don't eat that much food on vacation. If I buy it, I'll be paying for food that I simply don't need or want. In order to get the full monetary value out of a Disney Dining Plan, you must choose your restaurants carefully. You'll want to eat at the most expensive places and always choose the most expensive meal that you're eligible to order. But you must also avoid choosing restaurants that require more than one meal credit because that's not always in your best financial interest. And you must remember that you're going to have to tip more because you went to an expensive place.

Most people will hate to waste any of their dining plans. But sometimes you may just want a quick-service hamburger. You could just go quick service and pay cash, saving a dinner credit to use later. Or you could go to quick service and use a dinner credit, but then you'll have the crushing guilt of wasting a dinner on a hamburger. Or you could go to a full-service restaurant and order something you don't want because it's the most expensive thing on the menu. (And then have to tip.) It all seems like a lot of stress to me.

A few times each year, Disney will offer a free Disney Dining Plan with booked packages. This usually happens during the slower times of November and January to February. Guests staying at a value resort will get a free cheaper plan, and those lodging at a deluxe resort will get a free upgraded plan. In this instance, it must be a good value, right? I mean it's completely free! Well, sorry to disappoint, but I've done the numbers, and it's still a bad choice. Nothing is free on this planet, especially at Disney. In order to get a free dining plan, you must book your room at the rack-rack. This rate will always be at least 20 percent higher than a rate that doesn't come with a free dining plan. So you are paying for the dining plan after all.

There is only one case where the Disney Dining Plan is absolutely worth it for you. If you are someone who likes to prepay for the entire vacation so as not to think about money while traveling, then the dining plan is for you. And I have no judgment in this regard. For some people, prepayment provides an enormous amount of comfort and relaxation. I get that, and I fully support your decision. Remember, only you can do your homework, and you get to vacation the way you want to vacation. Just don't forget to tip!

### Fastpass+ and MyDisneyExperience

Is that little "+" after Fastpass really necessary? Yep. Fastpass is the system that all other Disney Parks use. Fastpass+ is only at Walt Disney World, and it's quite different. A Fastpass is a little ticket you get at the park while you are actually there. A Fastpass+ is a time you reserve to experience an attraction while you're at home.

In order to utilize this huge perk, you'll need to access MyDisneyExperience. You can do this with either the Walt Disney World app or at disneyworld.disney.go.com. Sixty days before your arrival, you are able to begin booking Fastpass+ experiences using MyDisneyExperience. This is another example of why it's important to have a rough itinerary sketched out. You'll already have made your dining reservations; you won't want to reserve a Fastpass+ for an attraction at Epcot if you're already booked to have lunch at the Magic Kingdom.

When your window of opportunity opens, you'll simply choose the Fastpass+ tab. MyDisneyExperience will already know your hotel reservation arrival date. Then you'll input the date and park you are visiting. You'll be presented with a list of Fastpass+ eligible attractions for that park. You can choose up to three. MyDisneyExperience will then generate a list of those three attractions and the times you can visit them without waiting in line. You can accept this list or change any portion of it. However, some attractions are very popular, and they might already be out of Fastpass+. Frozen Ever After at Epcot is the hottest Fastpass+ right now. If it's not available, you can try for a different day—just remember that you may have to change your itinerary (and any dining reservations) to accommodate Elsa and Anna.

Using MyDisneyExperience, you can change the attraction, the time of Fastpass+, or both. You may choose three Fastpass+ experiences for each day of your vacation. When you complete those three experiences, you can use MyDisneyExperience (on your phone or at an in-park kiosk) to select another. Your Fastpass+ arrangements are stored on your MagicBand. You'll scan your band at the Fastpass+ entrance to the attractions you've selected.

Fastpass+ is not just for rides. It's also available for special seating areas to shows, parades, and fireworks. It's also not available for every attraction in each park. I've noted which attractions use the system in this guide.

In addition to organizing all your Fastpass+ selections, MyDisneyExperience is really the visual representation of what's on your MagicBand. You can view your park tickets, dining reservations, and hotel arrangements. It's also the quickest way to discover which restaurants at any given park have an open table. During your initial use, you'll create a MyDisneyExperience profile for everyone in your party. You can link profiles together—even with guests who are not directly in your party. This is a great way for several families to travel together and have the same times for Fastpass+. It sounds like a lot more work that it is. Trust me, you'll get used to the app and appreciate how easy it is to make, and change, your arrangements.

## Accommodations

Walt Disney World Resort offers the most Disney accommodations close to the theme parks of any other Disney property. There truly is something for everyone and every budget. We'll focus on three main categories of lodging: Disney resorts, non-Disney hotels that are located on Disney property, and non-Disney hotels located elsewhere.

### *Disney Resort Hotels*

Walt Disney World Resort contains no less than twenty-six Disney-owned resort hotels. Each of the hotels has its own theme and amenities. Disney groups their hotels into three categories: deluxe, moderate, and value.

There are some excellent benefits to staying at a Disney hotel. For starters, every Disney hotel has an elaborate, themed pool. Most people have definite opinions about which hotel has the best pool, but even the value properties offer pools that are better than what you'll get most anywhere else. In addition to great pools, Disney hotels also provide:

- free airport transportation via Magical Express
- free transportation around Walt Disney World via Disney transportation
- the ability to charge all purchases to your room account
- free delivery to your hotel of items purchased at theme parks

- Extra Magic Hours in the morning and evening at one theme park
- free parking on the hotel property
- free parking for hotel guests at any of the theme parks
- the ability to make dining reservations 120 days in advance
- the ability to make Fastpass+ selections 60 days in advance

Deluxe hotels are obviously the most deluxe—and the most expensive. Deluxe rooms are large, and most have outdoor balconies. They are in the best locations by being the closest to a specific theme park. All deluxe resorts contain several full-service restaurants and at least one quick-service option. Deluxe rooms usually start at $325 during an off season and can be as much as $800 during a peak season. Expect to pay even more for a better view. These hotels are comparable to Hiltons and Marriotts.

Moderate hotels are perhaps the best value on the property. They offer large rooms but do not come with a balcony. All the moderate hotels contain outside entry rooms; there aren't any interior hallways. They each contain at least one moderately priced restaurant and other quick-service options. Moderate rooms start at $180 during an off season and can be $350 during a peak season. These hotels are comparable to Hampton Inn and Fairfield Inn.

Value hotels still offer all the benefits of staying at a Disney hotel. The rooms are smaller with less-luxurious furnishing. All the value hotels are closer to Disney's Animal Kingdom but farther from the Magic Kingdom. They are all outside-entry rooms without balconies. There are quick-service cafés at each value resort but no full-service restaurants. Expect to pay $100 during an off season and $180 during the peak season. (As an exception, Disney's Art of Animation is a value resort with many family suites that cost a bit more.) These hotels are really not comparable to anything. They are better than your average Motel 6 but not as good as a Hampton Inn.

Next, I'll list all the Disney hotels in alphabetical order. As always, do your homework. Look at your budget and determine what works for you. Also, tripadvisor.com will be an excellent resource while choosing a hotel. (Note: each hotel, officially, begins with the Disney name. I'm omitting this name because they are listed in alphabetical order.)

### *All-Star Movies*

Category: Value

Location: Animal Kingdom

Theme: *Toy Story, The Mighty Ducks, Fantasia, 101 Dalmatians, The Love Bug*

Transportation: Bus to everywhere

Dining: **World Premier in Cinema Hall**—quick-service food court

Oversized icons of Disney movies fill the landscaping. It's a no-frills value hotel with all the benefits of staying on Disney property.

### All-Star Music

Category: Value

Location: Animal Kingdom

Theme: Broadway, country, jazz, rock, calypso

Transportation: Bus to everywhere

Dining: **Intermission in Melody Hall**—quick-service food court

A guitar-shaped pool and a piano-shaped pool provide plenty of fun at this affordable hotel.

### All-Star Sports

Category: Value

Location: Animal Kingdom

Theme: Baseball, football, tennis, surfing, basketball

Transportation: Bus to everywhere

Dining: **End Zone in Stadium Hall**—quick-service food court

Huge footballs, helmets, tennis rackets, and other sporting equipment hold up this hotel's buildings. It's a place for those on a budget, but, remember, it comes with all the benefits of those staying in deluxe Disney hotels.

### Animal Kingdom Lodge

Category: Deluxe

Location: Animal Kingdom

Theme: African safari

Transportation: Buses to everywhere

Dining: **The Mara**—quick-service, **Sanaa**—table-service Indian cuisine, **Boma**—very popular African buffet, **Jiko**—table service with South African wines

Gorgeously themed to fit the Animal Kingdom surroundings, this is the most unique hotel you're likely to experience (unless you go on a real safari in Africa). Wildlife from nearby Disney's Animal Kingdom wanders around the grounds. From the lobby and other public areas, you are likely to see zebras, giraffes, gazelles, some kind of cowlike thing, and others.

### *Art of Animation*

Category: Value

Location: Animal Kingdom

Theme: *The Little Mermaid, Cars, Finding Nemo, The Lion King*

Transportation: Bus to everywhere

Dining: **Landscape of Flavors**—quick-service food court

Art of Animation sits on one side of Hourglass Lake. The rooms in *The Little Mermaid* building are standard value rooms. The rooms in the other three buildings are all family suites. These suites are very popular and can sleep six in 565 square feet.

### *BoardWalk Inn*

Category: Deluxe

Location: Epcot

Theme: Atlantic City (in the early years, before it got crappy)

Transportation: Walk or boat to Epcot and Disney's Hollywood Studios, bus everywhere else

Dining: The BoardWalk Inn is so authentic that it has a boardwalk (it's Disney, after all). The boardwalk has many dining options and it's a destination in itself. Restaurants include **Big River Grille & Brewing Works, BoardWalk Bakery, BoardWalk Pizza, ESPN Club, Flying Fish Café, Seashore Sweets,** and **Trattoria al Forno.** In addition to the restaurants, there are four late-night clubs: **Atlantic Dance Hall, Belle Vue Lounge, Jellyrolls Dueling Pianos,** and **Leaping Horse Libations.**

The BoardWalk Inn is almost a theme park in itself. This property has many devoted fans who are eager to talk about how great it is. Most of the hype is true.

### Caribbean Beach

Category: Moderate

Location: Epcot

Theme: Islands of the Caribbean

Transportation: Bus to everywhere

Dining: **Shutters at Old Port Royale**—table-service affordable; there are five quick-service options.

This sprawling resort contains over twenty-one hundred rooms. There's a lot of water everywhere, and many prefer the pools at this hotel. For an extra charge, you can book a themed *Pirates of the Caribbean* room.

### Contemporary
Category: Deluxe
Location: Magic Kingdom
Theme: Tomorrowland
Transportation: Walk or monorail to Magic Kingdom; monorail to Epcot; bus everywhere else
Dining: **California Grill**—table-service restaurant on the top floor, **Chef Mickey's**—character dining buffet, the **Wave of American Flavors**—table service on the first floor, **Contempo Café**—quick service in the middle of the atrium
One of the original Walt Disney World hotels, this property will always be famous as the building where the monorail passes right through it.

### Coronado Springs
Category: Moderate
Location: Animal Kingdom
Theme: Mayan ruins
Transportation: Buses to everywhere
Dining: **Las Ventanas**—table service for breakfast and lunch, **Maya Grill**—table service for dinner, **Café Rix**—quick service, **Pepper Market**—quick-service food court
One of the larger Disney hotels, this hotel's pool surrounds a Mayan pyramid and has a large waterslide.

### Fort Wilderness Campground
Category: Campground
Location: Magic Kingdom

Theme: Wilderness is great

Transportation: Boat to Magic Kingdom; bus everywhere else

Dining: **Trail's End**—buffet that many locals say is the best value in Orlando; quick-service options are available at the several Trading Posts scattered throughout.

Fort Wilderness offers eight hundred campsites. There are several comfort stations with showers, restrooms, and laundry facilities. There are also a number of cabins that sleep six and have complete kitchens.

### *Grand Floridian*

Category: Deluxe

Location: Magic Kingdom

Theme: Victorian splendor

Transportation: Boat or Monorail to Magic Kingdom; monorail to Epcot; bus everywhere else

Dining: **Gasparilla Island Grill**—quick service, **Cítricos**—table-service European restaurant, **Narcoossee's**—table-service restaurant right on Seven Seas Lagoon, **Grand Floridian Café**—table-service affordable option, **1900 Park Fare**—character buffet, **Victoria and Albert's**—the most exclusive restaurant in all of Walt Disney World with a dress code and high prices

The Grand Floridian is Walt Disney World's flagship hotel. It's elegant with a grand lobby that truly soars above it all.

### Polynesian Village
Category: Deluxe
Location: Magic Kingdom
Theme: Hawaiian/South Seas
Transportation: Boat or monorail to Magic Kingdom; monorail to Epcot; bus everywhere else
Dining: **Kona Café**—table-service restaurant, **'Ohana**—table-service restaurant with family-style dinner and character breakfast, **Captain Cook's**—quick service near lobby, **Pineapple Lanai**—snacks near the pool

The relaxing property hosts a nightly luau (extra charge) and a volcano-themed pool. The whole place is stunning.

### Pop Century
Category: Value
Location: Animal Kingdom
Theme: Iconic moments of the twentieth century
Transportation: Bus to everywhere
Dining: a quick-service food court
This hotel has three pools, one of them in the shape of a computer. It sits on one side of Hourglass Lake and has some nice walking paths.

### Port Orleans French Quarter
Category: Moderate
Location: Disney Springs
Theme: New Orleans

Transportation: Boat to Disney Springs; bus everywhere else

Dining: **Sassagoula Floatworks and Food Factory**—quick service with large Mardi Gras masks

Most often referred to as just "French Quarter," this charming property offers big rooms and quaint walkways. It's along the Sassagoula River, and guests here can also use the facilities at the nearby Riverside.

### *Port Orleans Riverside*

Category: Moderate

Location: Disney Springs

Theme: Old South plantation

Transportation: Boat to Disney Springs; bus everywhere else

Dining: **Riverside Mill**—quick service, **Boatwright's Dining Hall**—affordable table-service restaurant

Most often referred to as just "Riverside," this hotel has two sections: Mansion and Bayou. Bayou rooms have an extra smaller bed and can accommodate five. Mansion rooms are more traditional. For an extra charge, you can book a Royal Room that is themed to the Disney princesses. The enormous pool, Ol' Man Island, is a favorite for many guests. It's also along the Sassagoula River and an easy walk to the French Quarter.

### *Wilderness Lodge*

Category: Deluxe

Location: Magic Kingdom

Theme: National parks of the American West

Transportation: Boat to Magic Kingdom; bus everywhere else

Dining: **Whispering Canyon Café**—fun table-service restaurant in lobby, **Roaring Fork**—quick service, **Artist Point**—table service with a focus on seafood

Usually the cheapest of the Magic Kingdom Resorts, Wilderness Lodge has a lobby that must be seen to be believed—it's amazing. The rustic theme is tastefully executed. Near the pool is a geyser that erupts periodically.

*Yacht and Beach Club*

Category: Deluxe

Location: Epcot

Theme: New England seaside

Transportation: Walk or boat to Epcot and Disney's Hollywood Studios; bus everywhere else

Dining: **Yachtsman Steakhouse**—table-service steak and seafood, **Beach Club Marketplace**, quick service, **Cape May Café**—buffet with character breakfast, **Captain's Grille**—table service, **Hurricane Hanna's**—quick service with bar

These two beautifully designed hotels are operated as one. There are a lot of activities going on and a mini water park called Stormalong Bay.

Dreamlly's Disney Direction

Disney manages its own version of a timeshare called Disney Vacation Club. I'm not going to divulge my opinion of timeshares; I'll just remind you to do your homework. Only you can run your numbers and do what is best for your financial future. However, regardless of whether you buy into Disney Vacation Club or not, you can still stay at their properties.

Rooms that Disney Vacation Club has not sold yet can be booked just like any other hotel room. You still get all the benefits of staying at a Disney hotel, and you'll get daily housekeeping. (Disney Vacation Club owners do not get daily housekeeping when they stay in their units.)

Disney Vacation Club rooms range anywhere from a regular two-bed studio to multi-bedroom villas with full kitchens. All of these rooms, if available, will be displayed when you search for hotels at disneyworld. disney.go.com. Cast members can also assist in booking these rooms if you call the resort. Depending upon season, the prices are comparable to Disney deluxe hotels with multi-bedroom units being considerably more expensive.

All Disney Vacation Club properties either have their own pools, or they have access to the pool at an attached hotel. The same applies to restaurants and food courts. There are two hotels that are exclusive Disney Vacation Club properties. This means that they don't operate as regular hotels and are not attached to anything that does. **Saratoga Springs** and **Old Key West** are the two Disney Vacation Club properties.

Several regular hotels at Walt Disney World have a wing or attached building devoted to Disney Vacation Club. These are Animal Kingdom Lodge, Contemporary (Bay Lake Tower), Beach Club, BoardWalk, Grand Floridian, Polynesian Village, and Wilderness Lodge.

▲ ▲ ▲

### *Non-Disney Hotels on the Property*
There are nine hotels that are physically located on Disney property but are not owned or operated by Disney. These hotels offer a great location, but they vary on the resort benefits they offer. For example, all of these hotels provide some type of theme park transportation, but only the Swan and Dolphin use actual Disney transportation. Package delivery is available at the Four Seasons but not at any of the others. Disney benefits at these hotels can change at any time; make sure you confirm directly with the hotel to ensure they have the benefit you want most. You can book directly with these properties online or by calling them directly.

### Swan (Westin) and Dolphin (Sheraton)

These distinctive hotels, designed by Michael Graves, are unforgettable in appearance. While they are not operated by Disney, they offer most of the benefits of Disney hotels. Guests can use Extra Magic Hours, Magical Express, and Disney Transportation. However, guests may not charge purchases to their hotel account. The Swan and Dolphin are located near Epcot, and guests can walk to the BoardWalk.

### Four Seasons Orlando

This luxury hotel provides the famous Four Seasons customer service with a Disney flare. It opened in 2014, and no expense was spared—it's simply spectacular. The hotel contains a mini water park and several restaurants. Transportation, via a Four Seasons bus, is provided to the Magic Kingdom Ticket and Transportation Center. From there, guests can take a boat, monorail, or bus to wherever they want to be. Consequently, transportation may take a little longer from this hotel. It's not cheap but comparable to a Disney deluxe hotel.

The following seven hotels are located on Hotel Plaza Boulevard. This is Disney property, but these hotels are the most loosely associated. You can walk from any of these hotels to Disney Springs. There is some form of transportation provided to the parks via hotel shuttles and vans. However, Magical Express from the airport is not provided, and guests do not get any priority to make dining reservations and Fastpass+ selections. Guests cannot use Extra Magic Hours. The main reason to stay at one of these properties is if you are loyal to the brand and want to get some frequent customer points.

**B Resort and Spa**
**Best Western Lake Buena Vista Resort**
**Buena Visa Palace Hotel and Spa**
**Doubletree Suites by Hilton**
**Hilton Orlando Resort**
**Holiday Inn**
**Wyndham Lake Buena Vista Resort**

*Non-Disney Hotels off the Property*
There are many hotels in the Orlando area for every budget. However, unlike Disneyland, off-property hotels will require a bit of a drive to get to Walt Disney World. For reference, the following is the rush-hour drive time from each location to the Magic Kingdom parking lot.

Kissimmee area—forty-one minutes
Universal Studios area—twenty-nine minutes
Orlando International area—forty minutes
Downtown Orlando—forty-five minutes
Winter Haven Legoland area—fifty-eight minutes
Seaworld/International Drive—twenty-seven minutes
St. Cloud area—fifty-three minutes
Celebration area—twenty-three minutes
Busch Gardens Tampa—one hour, thirty-one minutes

Cocoa Beach—one hour, sixteen minutes

Lake Buena Vista Hotel area—sixteen minutes

As you research, remember that hotels can call themselves anything they want. Fred's Hotel Maingate doesn't necessarily mean that it's located near Walt Disney World. In fact, there isn't one main gate; there are several entrances from different highways onto the Disney property. Use maps.google.com to calculate the driving time, keeping in mind that Walt Disney World is huge. Calculate the driving time to specific places within Walt Disney World. (It can take thirty minutes to drive from the Magic Kingdom to Disney's Animal Kingdom. Consequently, an off-property hotel may require ten minutes to get to one park and forty minutes to get to another.)

If at all possible, choose a hotel that will allow for flexible theme park days. Theme parks are best enjoyed when guests have a chance to take a break from them. The ability to quickly leave a theme park and return later in the day is worth some of your budget. When I plan a Walt Disney World vacation, my priority is always the ability to take a nap and swim during the afternoon. I will sacrifice expensive dining in order to choose a better-located hotel.

▲ ▲ ▲

## Magic Kingdom

Congratulations! You've made it to the most magical place on earth—and the most-visited theme park on the entire planet. As you approach, you may be able to see the graceful spires of Cinderella Castle. The first view of the castle will always send shivers down your spine. Remember, it's the world's most-photographed building.

If you're staying at a Disney hotel, your Disney transportation will drop you off right at the entrance to the Magic Kingdom. When you're ready to leave, you will return to this transportation hub to catch the bus back to your hotel. Some hotels offer boat and/ or monorail transportation to the park. These options will also deliver you directly to the Magic Kingdom entrance plaza.

If you've driven a car, you'll pay for parking and enter one of the largest parking lots on earth. The parking lot is divided into villains and heroes and then divided again into specific characters. For example, Cruella is a character within the villains lot, and Peter Pan is located in the heroes lot. All the rows within each lot are numbered. Take a picture of your parking spot with your phone. At the end of the day, you'll have seen a lot of characters.

Did you really park in Rapunzel, or was she that one princess who greeted you between entree and dessert?

There are many trams that will take you from your parking lot to the Magic Kingdom Ticket and Transportation Center. Be very clear on this: there is no way to drive to the other side of Seven Seas Lagoon. Even those with a disability must proceed to the Ticket and Transportation Center to access transportation to the Magic Kingdom. First, make sure you have a valid ticket, pass, or MagicBand. If not, buy one. Then you will need to choose how to make your grand entrance.

Your choices to cross the lagoon include express monorail, resort monorail, and ferry. The express monorail travels directly to the Magic Kingdom without stopping. It takes about five minutes. The resort monorail will make two stops on the way to the Magic Kingdom, one at Polynesian Village and one at the Grand Floridian. It can take ten to fifteen minutes, depending upon the length of each stop. A ferry boat takes seven minutes to cross the lagoon, plus time for loading and unloading. If it's not busy when you arrive, the express monorail is your quickest option. If you notice long lines for the monorail, then the ferry will be much faster; the ferry takes more time but holds many more people than the monorail.

However you make your journey, you'll eventually find yourself standing before the Walt Disney World Railroad Station. Pass through security, have your pass or MagicBand scanned, grab a map and Times Guide, and walk underneath the train station. Welcome to the Magic Kingdom!

## Main Street, USA

The first thing you'll notice about Main Street, USA is that it's dominated by a European castle. Cinderella Castle is much bigger than Sleeping Beauty's residence in California. It's graceful, and you won't be able to take your eyes off of it. Even though a castle at the end of an American Main Street doesn't make sense, somehow it just works. Everything looks like it belongs together and was always meant to be that way.

Starting at Town Square and proceeding toward the castle, Main Street, USA is the commercial district of the Magic Kingdom. Here you'll find shop after shop mixed with a bakery or two.

### *Walt Disney World Railroad*

Enter the train station to begin a twenty-minute journey around the Magic Kingdom. There are two other stations: one in Frontierland and one in Fantasyland. You'll ride on one of four vintage locomotives. Trains arrive about every ten minutes.

The journey will take you through Adventureland and around the Rivers of America. You'll pass through Splash Mountain; it's a great way for nonriders to get a look at the climactic animatronic scene. Around the backside of the park, you'll get a glimpse of the Beast's Castle and Dumbo's Big Top over in the new part of

Fantasyland. After a sojourn along Tomorrowland, you'll find yourself back on Main Street, USA.

The Magic Kingdom is considerably larger than Disneyland. The train is a great option to get from the very back of the park to the entrance. Whenever there's a parade, Main Street becomes as packed as the Mall of America during the weekend before Christmas. By taking the train, you can avoid all the Main Street pedestrians and arrive right on top of the park exit.

### Town Square Theater

*Fastpass+* You don't have to walk far to meet the Magic Kingdom's most famous resident. Mickey Mouse is always rehearsing at the Town Square Theater, and he will be happy to take a break and meet you backstage. In addition to taking a great photograph, meeting Mickey at this particular Disney Park is quite special. Often Mickey is quite chatty here—this doesn't occur at any of the other parks. You will be amazed. You will probably cry.

If meeting Mickey is one of the main goals of your visit, get a Fastpass+ before you arrive. The lines here can get a bit long, and they tend to move slowly—Mickey likes to take his time with guests.

### Main Street Vehicles

In addition to the railroad and Mickey, the only other attraction on Main Street is a few vehicles. Look for signs around Town Square and you can wait to ride a trolley, fire engine, or some smaller old-fashioned cars.

You'll slowly ride down the street and be dropped off somewhere along the central hub (in front of Cinderella Castle.) You can also take a vehicle in the opposite direction. The vehicles stop about an hour before any parade.

### Shops of Main Street, USA

You'll find it all here. **The Emporium** is the largest shop in the park. But the best part of this store isn't the merchandise—it's the elaborate window displays. Make sure to check them out. There's also a jewelry store, candy shop, bakery, clothing shop, and just about anything else you could want.

The best place you'll ever get your hair cut is right in Town Square. **Harmony Barber Shop** is open from 9:00 a.m. to 5:00 p.m. daily. Anyone is welcome to stop by for an affordable haircut—no appointment required. In addition to adult cuts and trims, it's a popular place for children to have their first haircut. (They'll get a certificate to prove it.) If you want, the barbers will get some help from Tinkerbell to give your hair that extra sparkle.

### Dining in Main Street, USA

**Tony's Town Square:** This table-service Italian restaurant is inspired by 1955's *Lady and the Tramp*.

**Plaza Restaurant:** An elegant table-service restaurant for lunch and dinner with fantastic ice-cream creations.

**Crystal Palace:** Character dining for breakfast, lunch, and dinner featuring Winnie the Pooh and Friends. In true Pooh fashion, many of the words in this restaurant are spelled creatively—I've learned to just accept that and move on.

**Casey's Corner:** Main Street's baseball-themed quick-service café for hot dogs and such.

## Adventureland

Adventureland at Walt Disney World seems to have a bit more atmosphere than its sister at Disneyland. Perhaps it's because the Florida humidity makes the jungle environment more real.

### Jungle Cruise

*Fastpass+* Quite similar to the Jungle Cruise in California. You'll be entertained by your skipper as you float past animatronic animals from around the world. The corny jokes change from boat to boat, and no two rides are ever quite the same. I find this attraction almost unbearable in the daytime Florida heat, but at night it's a beautiful and entertaining ride. The Jungle Cruise turns into the Jingle Cruise during the holiday season; your boat skipper and all the animals get into the spirit of the season.

### Swiss Family Treehouse

Disneyland's Adventureland is home to Tarzan's Treehouse. Here, we get to visit Swiss Family Robinson from the 1960 Disney film. The artificial tree is officially known as Disneyodendron Eximus, or "an extraordinary Disney tree." The Robinson Family has its entire home on display for you to explore. You'll see their living room, kitchen, and bedrooms on the multiple levels. It's really much nicer than what you'd expect of a family marooned on a deserted island.

The tree is open to explore on your own, and there is seldom a line. Head here if you have anyone in your party who needs to burn off some energy.

### The Magic Carpets of Aladdin

*Fastpass+* Similar to the Dumbo ride, except guests ride around on flying carpets. FYI, there is a camel near this attraction's entrance that is the bane of my existence. It periodically spits water and always seems to hit me.

### Pirates of the Caribbean

*Fastpass+* Like the Jungle Cruise, Pirates of the Caribbean is another nostalgic attraction imported from Disneyland. However, while the two American versions of the Jungle Cruise are similar, the two versions of these pirates are a bit different. Geography altered the Florida experience. Also, the Disneyland version begins in New Orleans and passes through a restaurant; there is no restaurant in Florida, and the attraction begins in the Caribbean itself. Still, it's the famous ride that inspired the multi-billion-dollar movie franchise. Pirates of the Caribbean was updated to include characters from the films.

The queue is well themed and air-conditioned. Just be advised that there is a lot of walking here before you reach the actual ride.

**Dreamlly's Disney Direction**

Are you tired of waiting in line and want to exercise your mind and body? Try one of the Magic Kingdom's two interactive games.

Near Pirates of the Caribbean, look for **A Pirate's Adventure...Treasure of the Seven Seas.** When you check in with a cast member, you'll be given a map and a talisman. You'll follow the map and discover various locations around Adventureland. When you get to a location, your talisman will make all sorts of magical things occur. You're doing all this to help Captain Jack Sparrow locate a treasure and avoid the bad guys.

**Sorcerers of the Magic Kingdom** is a similar experience, but it uses the entire park. Visit the Firehouse on Main Street or look for the sorcerer behind Ye Olde Christmas Shoppe in Liberty Square. A cast member will give you a map and five magic spell cards. You're attempting to stop the Disney villains from stealing Merlin's crystal ball. You'll use the map to find locations where your magic spell cards will produce all sorts of wonderful effects. You can get a new set of cards each day that you visit the Magic Kingdom; collecting the cards has become a popular hobby, and another guest may even offer to trade with you.

▲ ▲ ▲

### Walt Disney's Enchanted Tiki Room

Back to the original version that premiered in 1963, Walt Disney's Enchanted Tiki Room features two hundred audio-animatronic birds, flowers, tikis, and other surprises. For a brief period, the tiki room was under the new management of Iago (*Aladdin*) and Zazu (*The Lion King*), but they have flown the coop, so to speak. This is a fantastic place to sit in air-conditioned darkness and take a break. There is hardly ever a line.

### Shops of Adventureland

The shops of Adventureland fit the theme. Think safari, Aladdin, and pirates. You may also notice several items featuring the Orange Bird. The Orange Bird is...well, he's a bird that's orange. This citrus-inspired bird has a cult following and is almost as much a symbol of Florida as the alligator.

### Dining in Adventureland

**Aloha Isle:** Adventureland's quick-service café is famous for Dole Whip, and there will always be a line.

**Tortuga Tavern:** Another quick-service food option with a bit of spice.

**Sunshine Tree Tavern:** This quick-service establishment offers ice cream, beverages, and fruit; it's where the Orange Bird likes to eat.

**Jungle Navigation Co. Ltd. Skipper Canteen:** a brand-new table-service option inspired by the Jungle Cruise. It opened to mixed reviews; however, a recent overhaul of the menu has made it popular. Like most table-service restaurants, adult entrees run $15 to $35.

### Frontierland
Visit 1770 to 1880 in this land of cowboys, rocky mountains, and bears. The Walt Disney World Railroad makes a stop here along the banks of the Rivers of America.

### *Tom Sawyer Island*
Located in the middle of the Rivers of America, this is an explore-on-your-own attraction. There are lots of trails, suspension bridges, floating barrels, and an entire landscape to explore. This is an actual island, and you must take a raft in order to get here. If you have children with lots of energy and no patience to wait in line, this attraction is a lifesaver. There are several places for adults to sit and wait in the shade. As you can tell, I'm a huge fan of giving yourself permission to relax on your vacation—even if it means skipping another "must-do" attraction.

### *Country Bear Jamboree*
Head to Grizzly Hall for the best air-conditioned sixteen minutes you'll have all day. There are two things that people better not speak ill of in my presence: Dolly Parton and the Country Bear Jamboree. (Now that I think about it, these two things are oddly similar.)

The Country Bears are sort of a combination of the Grand Ole Opry, technology, and *Saturday Night Live*. You might not recognize any of the songs, but you'll be quite entertained anyway by a large cast of audio-animatronic bears. The Country Bears aren't the most politically correct folks around as they perform "Mama Don't 'Cha Whup Lid'l Buford" and "All the Guys That Turn Me On...Turn Me Down." You'll never have to wait long for the show, and every seat is a great one.

This is the only place in the United States to see the Country Bear Jamboree. It's worth the trip to Florida!

### Splash Mountain

*Fastpass+* Themed to the 1946 film *Song of the South*, this is a log flume on steroids. You'll float past hundreds of audio-animatronic characters that tell the story of Brer Rabbit. Just like for the version at Disneyland, you'll want to get that rain poncho out of your theme-park satchel. You will get wet on this ride. It's possible you'll get completely soaked. This ride will feel extra good on a hot summer Florida day; the line will prove that other people thought of that as well.

The ending scene features a spectacular riverboat filled with all sorts of critters singing "Zip-a-Dee-Doo-Dah." You can see this scene from the Walt Disney World Railroad if you're not inclined to get wet.

### Big Thunder Mountain Railroad

*Fastpass+* Sometimes you've had it with life and you just want to scream as you slide down the rock formations of Arizona's Monument Valley. Big Thunder Mountain Railroad lets you do just that. You'll sit in a runaway mine train and careen through valleys, peaks, streams, and dinosaur fossils.

I believe this ride is ten times better at night than during the day. The darkness and unique lightning of the area make the fantasy realness much scarier. Even though it technically is a roller coaster, Big Thunder Mountain's track is fairly tame; it's a great introduction to coasters for younger riders.

### Shops of Frontierland

With no shortage of flannel and Davy Crockett caps, you'll find everything for that Western hero in your life. **Briar Patch** offers Splash Mountain souvenirs, and **Frontier Trading Post** has the largest selection of Western shirts and cowboy/cowgirl hats.

What's with all the pins? No matter which Disney Park you visit, from California to Shanghai, you'll notice large walls in some of the shops that are covered with pins. The Frontier Trading Post has the largest selection in the Magic Kingdom. These pins will be of all different characters doing all sorts of different things. All these pins are part of the popular hobby of Disney pin trading.

Look around at other guests and you'll soon spot someone wearing a lanyard full of pins around his or her neck. If you buy a pin in a shop, you can ask that person to trade a pin with you. That's how your collection will start. Now, there's no guarantee that the other guest will want to trade—you see, some pins are much more valuable than others. There are pins that were only released for a limited time. There are also pins that are only available for certain experiences, like taking a Disney tour or running in a Disney race.

If you can't find another guest to trade with, ask cast members who are wearing pins. They will almost always trade.

▲ ▲ ▲

### Dining in Frontierland
**Pecos Bill Tall Tale Inn & Café:** Quick-service hamburgers and BBQ sandwiches are offered with an enormous toppings bar. This café is near the Country Bear Jamboree.

**Golden Oak Outpost:** This wagon offers quick-service fries and sandwiches.

### Liberty Square
The place: Philadelphia. The time: 1776. Step back in time and meet the people who defied a king and started a new nation. This colonial land has it all: shops, restaurants, and two of the most famous attractions in the

park. By the way, 1776 was a long time ago—Brits are now welcome to visit this land.

### Liberty Belle Riverboat

Take a seventeen-minute journey around Tom Sawyer Island on the Liberty Belle Riverboat. This steam-powered vessel journeys down the Rivers of America. The ride is narrated as you pass Big Thunder Mountain, a wilderness full of animals, and a huge, creepy mansion. There aren't any seats on the boat, but you can lean against one of many railings and enjoy the scenes as they pass before you. It's a nice way to take a relaxing break.

### The Hall of Presidents

Disneyland has Abraham Lincoln. The Magic Kingdom has him, too, plus over forty of his friends.

This twenty-five-minute air-conditioned show begins with a film about the US presidency. The good times and bad times—from inspiring moments to war—are featured. You'll learn about the roots of the presidency after the American Revolution, the challenges of the Civil War, and the constant media spotlight on modern presidents.

After the film, a giant curtain rises, and you'll meet all the presidents of the United States in their animatronic glory—from George Washington to Barack Obama. President Obama provided the voice for his audio-animatronic. There is a roll call of presidents, and every one of them reacts in some way to the sound of their name. Watch for your favorites, but out of respect, the audience is asked to remain silent. I love watching the presidents as they wait for their names. Some of them fidget and look around at their contemporaries.

This is the only Disney attraction that gets an automatic renovation every four to eight years—depending upon the will of the people. As this book was going to press, Mr. Obama's successor had been elected the forty-fifth president of the United States. The Hall of Presidents closed on January 17, 2017, for the necessary renovation. Typically, it will reopen around Independence Day with the new audio-animatronic in place.

### The Muppets Present...Great Moments in American History

If you didn't learn enough about American history inside the Hall of Presidents, you can learn even more right outside. Several times each day, Kermit the Frog, Miss Piggy, Gonzo, Fozzie, and, of course, Sam Eagle share iconic moments in US history. They are dressed in their colonial best. You can stand anywhere that you can see the second-story windows next to the Hall of Presidents.

As you know, the Muppets are quite a serious bunch. The telling of these important stories is done with the greatest respect—there is no tomfoolery or hijinks allowed. (Well, that's the way Sam Eagle wants it. Apparently, not everyone got the memo.)

### The Haunted Mansion

*Fastpass+* Over at Disneyland, the Haunted Mansion is a large New Orleans plantation house. That wouldn't really fit in Liberty Square. Here at the Magic Kingdom, the Haunted Mansion is a large old house styled after the mansions in New York's Hudson River Valley.

Part of the fun, and different than Disneyland, is the interactive queue. While waiting in line, you'll meander through the mansion's cemetery. Take time to read all the humorous tombstones. Go ahead and touch anything you want; many of the memorials will respond with various sounds.

As you enter the mansion, you'll visit the famous stretching room and then be escorted onto your doom buggy. Winding through the mansion's corridors, your doom buggy will narrate what you're seeing in all its eerie glory.

Similar to the version at Disneyland, the Haunted Mansion is more fun than it is scary. Very young children will be intimidated, but most others come away more or less intact. At the end of the ride, keep your eye on any ghost that tries to ride in your doom buggy. These ghosts somehow know your name (a nifty trick courtesy of your MagicBand).

### Shops of Liberty Square

Two fantastic shops in Liberty Square are my favorites at the park. **Ye Olde Christmas Shoppe** is a year-round store for the holiday lover in you. If it's Disney and Christmas, it's for sale in this shop.

**Memento Mori** is your year-round Halloween store. As the Haunted Mansion's official shop, it offers everything from candlesticks to T-shirts to dinnerware. But my favorite item can be purchased in the rear of the store. For $20, you can have your photograph taken by an old-fashioned camera. Then you'll wait in the shop for about five minutes. When you hear a bell ring, you'll be instructed to open a cabinet. You'll find an awesome portrait of yourself inside. When you look at the portrait from one direction, you look like yourself. When you look from another direction, you will see all your facial bones! It's creepy and fantastic.

### Dining in Liberty Square

**Liberty Tree Tavern:** Dine in colonial Philadelphia, and enjoy an all-you-can-eat Thanksgiving dinner. I don't know why, but having Thanksgiving dinner in the summer is a lot more fun than it sounds.

**Columbia Harbour House:** A quick-service seafood café for lunch and dinner.

**Sleepy Hollow:** Another quick-service option, this is your place for funnel cakes.

### Fantasyland

After a recent expansion, Fantasyland has doubled in size since the park opened in 1971. The quintessentially iconic land of the Magic Kingdom, it features the most attractions of any land in the park—many of them as classic and famous as Snow White. It's a gorgeous land with meticulous landscaping and stunning waterfalls. Many think of Fantasyland as a place only for children, but they are quite incorrect. The land is so charming, with many nooks to explore, that people of all ages can easily fill their time here. Fantasyland is also home to the most unique dining in the park; one of them is the only place inside the Magic Kingdom where alcohol is served. Enjoy your time among the royalty, fairies, and all sorts of magical beings. This is what Disney is all about.

### Cinderella Castle

It's more than twice the height of Sleeping Beauty Castle at Disneyland. Inspired by the real castles of Europe and the animated castle of the 1950 film *Cinderella*, this iconic building stands 189 feet tall (57.6 meters). It has more than twenty-five turrets, some of them covered in real gold, and is surrounded by a moat.

Walt Disney was quite surprised that guests at California's Disneyland wanted to see inside the castle. He had envisioned it as a gate to pass through. Imagineers corrected this situation at the Magic Kingdom. Here, guests can enter the castle and dine at Cinderella's Royal Table, the hardest reservation to land in all of Walt Disney World. But even if you don't plan on dining here, make time to pass through the castle on the ground floor. Intricate mosaics tell the story of Cinderella with over a million pieces of glass, silver, and real gold.

Cinderella Castle is a perfect example of forced perspective. To the naked eye, the castle appears much taller than its 189 feet. Each floor of the structure is slightly smaller than the floor below. The railing on the tallest turret is only eighteen inches high. However, when your eyes see that railing, your brain interprets it as being standard in size. Consequently, the castle seems to tower above everything, when it would look quite small compared to any big city skyline.

Cinderella Castle does not have a dungeon. What's underneath? A doorway into the strange world of pipes, conduits, maintenance facilities, and cast members taking breaks.

In the early years of Disneyland, Walt was once looking through a bit of fan mail that his secretary had selected for him. Among the letters was one from a mother telling about the fantastic time her family had in the park. She enclosed a photograph of her kids having fun in Tomorrowland. To Walt's horror, there was a cowboy walking in the background! After immediately investigating, he learned that the cast member had to get to work somehow; in order for a cowboy to get from cast member parking to Frontierland, he had to impede through Tomorrowland. Walt had one of those "if I ever do this again" moments.

Years later, the Magic Kingdom imagineers remembered this story well. They found that a solution to the problem would also solve numerous other operational challenges faced at Disneyland. They simply created a world underneath the Magic Kingdom where all the transportation of people and products could occur.

It's absolutely true. The Magic Kingdom you see is actually the second floor of a gigantic structure. Underneath, long corridors called utilidors are filled with the buzzing presence of cast members bustling from one place to another. Periodically, the utilidors contain an upward staircase. Signs near the stairs indicate where they lead. Need to go to Liberty Square? Just take these steps. Need to get to Tomorrowland? Head down to the end of the hall, take a right, and look for the sign.

The utilidors also contain the trash, climate control, and technology conduits for the entire park. It's a whole city of its own—all with the purpose of hiding that unmagical stuff from park guests.

If you're as enthralled by all this as I am, you may want to see it for yourself. There are a few tours that take guests into the utilidors. Visit disneyworld.disney.go.com and click on "tours." Every tour I've ever taken at a Disney park has been fascinating and well worth my time. However, in order to visit backstage, you must be at least eighteen years old (nobody wants to spoil the magic for the younger folks—and you might see a railroad engineer hanging out with a prince).

▲ ▲ ▲

### Mickey's Philharmagic

*Fastpass+* As a huge Donald Duck fan, I've always loved this attraction. Even though Mickey gets his name in lights, it's Donald F. Duck who is the star of this show. (Donald's middle name is Fauntleroy—he is from Duckburg, which is in the US state of Calisota.)

An enormous movie screen greets guests who are coming to watch a performance of Mickey and his orchestra. But Donald gets into the picture and sort of borrows Mickey's magical hat. Donald tries very hard to return the hat as he gets thrown into one iconic Disney scene after another. He swims with Ariel, eats with Belle, flies with Jasmine, and dances with Simba.

Guests wear 3-D glasses for this attraction. The effects are outstanding. You'll smell Belle's dinner and feel the splash of an ocean wave. At the conclusion of the show, make sure you turn around and see poor Donald's fate in the back of the auditorium.

As you exit this attraction, you'll pass through a gift shop that carries the largest selection of Donald Duck merchandise at Walt Disney World.

### Prince Charming Regal Carrousel

This beatific piece of nostalgia (with an extra "r" in its name) was built in 1917 for an amusement park in New Jersey. There are ninety horses that gracefully glide around to the tunes of recognizable Disney melodies. This carousel is well cared for.

### Peter Pan's Flight

*Fastpass+* Always with one of the longest lines in the park, this iconic attraction tells the story of Peter Pan, the Darling children, and evil Captain Hook. You'll fly inside a sailing ship that soars above London and over Never Land.

A couple of things set the Magic Kingdom's version apart from its sister at Disneyland. The ships in Florida are set onto a constantly moving conveyer system; they stop for loading in California. Also, the queue in Florida is much better. Guests waiting at the Magic Kingdom are escorted through the very detailed rooms of the Darling Home in London.

### "it's a small world"

*Fastpass+* As iconic as it gets. Relax as you float through all the continents of the globe. Try to identify as many of the world's countries as you can. Listen for words being sung in native languages. And attempt to not let the song get to you too much.

Disneyland's version is the original from the New York World's Fair. It was literally plopped down in place. In Florida, this attraction was designed along with the park. The channels that you float in are dug into the foundation here, making it easier to get a good look at all the hundreds of audio-animatronic children.

### Princess Fairytale Hall

*Fastpass+* This is another attraction with rather long lines. Enter the fairytale hall to meet Snow White, Cinderella,

Aurora (Sleeping Beauty), or one of their other royal friends. Signs posted at the entrance will indicate which princess you are waiting for. Normally, you can see two princesses on each visit.

The inside of the hall is beautifully crafted. After all, we are talking about meeting royalty here. And when you do meet them, it is unforgettable. The princesses take time to chat with each guest and pose for photographs. A Disney photographer will take a few shots, and then he or she will offer to take some photos with your camera.

### Mad Tea Party

*Fastpass+* I can't handle this ride, but maybe you can. Whip around in teacups inspired by 1951's *Alice in Wonderland*.

### The Many Adventures of Winnie the Pooh

*Fastpass+* Sit in a hunny pot (yes, that's the correct spelling) and visit with Pooh, Piglet, Rabbit, Tigger, and the whole gang from the Hundred Acre Wood. There are some neat special effects, and it's an enjoyable ride. The queue is also interactive with fun things for children to do while they wait.

### Seven Dwarfs Mine Train

*Fastpass+* Get a Fastpass+ because the popularity of this ride is not waning. The Seven Dwarfs Mine Train is a family roller coaster—it's tame enough for kids but interesting enough for adults. The track is very smooth, and guests ride in mine carts that swing slightly with the motion of the ride. There are some drops. It's just a little more intense than your typical kiddie coaster.

It's the theming that really brings out the magic in this ride. You'll travel through a mine and see all the dwarfs working the day away to the tunes of "Heigh-ho, heigh-ho!" The music is perfectly timed to the animatronics and the story unfolding around you. The giant jewels of the mine glow and shine in the darkness. It's a treat for your eyes and ears.

At the conclusion of the ride, you'll pass the dwarfs' humble home, where Snow White is living with her woodland friends. Don't miss the next chapter of the story; the evil queen, as the old hag, is ready to knock on the door with that infamous apple.

### Enchanted Tales with Belle

*Fastpass+* It's hard to describe this attraction: part ride, part show, part interactive experience—but all Disney. Storytelling is what Disney does best, and, boy, do they do it here.

You'll enter Belle's provincial village house and be transported, via magic mirror, to the Beast's Castle. (The magic mirror effect must be seen to be believed.) Inside the castle, animatronic characters will help you and other guests recreate the story of how Belle fell in love with the Beast. The technology is amazing and the experience is quite interactive. Lumiere moves so smoothly that you'll swear he's made of wax.

Then, just when you think it couldn't get any better, Belle enters the room. Yes, the real Belle—not an animatronic version. She wears her gold ball gown and entertains everyone as she interacts with your small group of guests. There are many hardworking cast members at Walt Disney World, but I can't imagine that anyone works as hard as Belle.

It takes thirty minutes to experience this attraction, but the time will fly by. There really is nothing else like it in the world.

### Under the Sea—Journey of the Little Mermaid
*Fastpass* + Sit in a clamshell and hear the story of *The Little Mermaid*, inspired by the work of Hans Christian Anderson. You'll learn about Ariel, her friends, and the evil sea witch Ursula. You'll even get to meet handsome Prince Eric at the ride's conclusion.

### Dumbo the Flying Elephant
*Fastpass* + The theming of Fantasyland changes slightly when you're near Dumbo. You will have entered Storybook Circus, as evidenced by the large circus tents in the area.

This is the best version of Dumbo on the planet. The queue begins inside a large circus tent, where you don't have to wait in line in order to wait in line. Here, you'll be given a pager that will vibrate when Dumbo is ready for you. In the meantime, you're free to explore all the wonderful things inside the tent; it's an interactive play zone. Even kids who are not interested in riding an elephant will enjoy playing inside this air-conditioned space.

The ride is basically the same as elsewhere except there are two. Cutting the wait time in half, you'll ride one of two sets of flying Dumbos.

### The Barnstormer

*Fastpass+* This is a standard kiddie coaster. It's a one-minute ride that follows a daredevil pilot known as the Great Goofini. Spoiler alert: he's not the best pilot, so the ride has a few curves.

### Casey Jr. Splash 'N' Soak Station

Casey Jr. is the name of the train that transports Dumbo and his mother from town to town. He's parked here in Storybook Circus, filled with all the animals featured in the circus. Everything squirts water here, and adults will want to be careful where they stand. It's a great way for very young kids to cool off. In a brilliant marketing move, a nearby kiosk sells swim diapers and towels.

### Pete's Silly Sideshow

What's a circus without a sideshow? The sideshow here is brought to you by some very popular and famous folks. This is the place to meet Donald Duck, Goofy, Minnie Mouse, and Daisy Duck. You'll choose one of two queues: one line is for Donald and Goofy, the other for Minnie and Daisy.

Disney photographers are present and are happy to snap a few photos with your own camera as well.

### Shops of Fantasyland

**Bibbidi Bobbidi Boutique**, inside Cinderella Castle, offers kids the chance to get dressed up as a princess or knight. Right outside, **Sir Mickey's** has the largest selection of *Frozen* merchandise in the park. In Belle's village, you'll find **Bonjour Village Gifts** and its elegant selection of gifts. The largest shop in the land, **Big Top Souvenirs**, has tons of character merchandise and a large candy counter.

### Dining in Fantasyland

**Prince Eric's Market:** The healthiest food in the park served quick service.

**Storybook Treats:** Quick-service ice cream served near Pooh's attraction.

**Cheshire Café:** A quick-service café for beverages and baked goods.

**Cinderella's Royal Table:** This table-service restaurant is inside the castle, where royalty will visit with you as you dine. Reservations are required 180 days before you arrive; expect to pay $58 per person for breakfast and $73 per person for dinner.

**The Friar's Nook:** Hot dogs and snacks are served quick-service style.

**Gaston's Tavern:** A well-themed tavern with surprisingly healthy options, it's quick service for food and fun drinks (no alcohol—sorry, Gaston).

**Pinocchio Village Haus:** My favorite quick-service option in Florida. Pizza and subs with lots of other items are offered in an ideal Alpine atmosphere.

**Be Our Guest:** Reservations are highly recommended for this table-service restaurant inside the Beast's Castle. It's quick service for breakfast and lunch and table service for dinner with beer and wine—one of just a few places at the Magic Kingdom where alcohol is served. It runs about $15 per entree for breakfast and lunch, up to $60 for dinner.

### Tomorrowland

A 2016 paint job has left Tomorrowland sparkling with space-age colors. Tomorrowland is a vision of the future from the past. It's especially captivating at night, when lighting makes the land look like a thriving metropolis on another planet. From one of Walt's 1964 projects to the cutting-edge technology of Buzz Lightyear, Tomorrowland spans the centuries.

### *Astro Orbiter*

A ramped-up version of Dumbo where guests ride around on rockets. Enough said.

### *Stitch's Great Escape or Some Other Thing That Is Similar*

To begin, I absolutely love the film *Lilo & Stitch*. It has it all: Hawaii, Elvis, and aliens! However, Stitch's Great Escape has received lackluster reviews at best and is not worthy of the film it's based on.

In this twenty-minute show, you'll meet Stitch as you sit under a safety restraint. (It's a little confusing to me too.) Stitch isn't known for his manners, and you'll experience all of his mischievous actions.

There is a persistent rumor that a *Wreck-It Ralph* attraction may replace Stitch for at least part of the year.

### Monsters, Inc. Laugh Floor

*Fastpass+* Fans of the movie know that Monstropolis runs on scream power. Well, Mike Wazowski is attempting to find an alternative fuel source in the form of laughter. A few of his friends will entertain you—sort of—with jokes aimed at the five-year-old set. While waiting in line, you can text a joke to Mike, and it might end up in the show.

### Buzz Lightyear's Space Ranger Spin

*Fastpass+* If you suffer from motion sickness, don't let the word "spin" scare you. You get to control how much your vehicle spins with a joystick, and they never spin very fast. It takes just over four minutes to help Buzz Lightyear defeat the evil Emperor Zurg.

On this interactive journey, you'll use a space-age ray gun to shoot at targets. When you hit the targets, all sorts of effects occur. You're also trying to get as high a score as possible in order to make your brother very jealous.

There's a lot to look at during this ride. You may find yourself so involved in racking up points that you forget to look at everything. If the line is short, ride this twice and don't shoot on the second pass.

### Tomorrowland Transit Authority PeopleMover

Based on one of Walt's ideas, the PeopleMover uses induction motors that do not emit pollution and require very little energy. There are no moving parts necessary to make the PeopleMover move. It's fairly brilliant.

You'll know you've met a true Disney fan if you hear him or her call this attraction the WEDway PeopleMover. WEDway was the original name for Disney Imagineering; W. E. D. are the initials of a certain famous animator.

I often crave this ride, usually when I'm tired and just want to sit and watch people. On the PeopleMover, you'll glide for about twelve minutes over the streets of Tomorrowland. You'll pass through Space Mountain and get a brief respite from the sun. More importantly, you'll get to see Walt's original model for his Experimental Prototype Community of Tomorrow.

### Tomorrowland Speedway

*Fastpass* + Take a lap around part of Tomorrowland in these little vehicles. It's a bit jerky; there are no brakes, and the cars come to a sudden stop when you pull your foot off the gas. You'll hear this ride before you see it.

### Space Mountain

*Fastpass*+ A fairly tame "mad-mouse"-style coaster that seems very untame in the dark. The building that houses Space Mountain is almost as iconic as Cinderella Castle, and it makes a fantastic photo background. Also, take an opportunity to do another study of forced perspective.

Space Mountain does not use the technique and looks much shorter than Cinderella Castle. In reality, it's only eight feet shorter; that's how much taller the castle appears due to forced perspective.

The queue winds its way around a distant space port as you wait for your transportation. When it's your turn, you'll board your vehicle and be rocketed off through stars and planets. There are many twists and turns in the darkness. You'll hear lots of others screaming around you.

Space Mountain was refurbished in 2009; you might not recognize it if you haven't ridden since then. For those who like to know what they're getting into, Space Mountain's maximum speed is twenty-eight miles per hour.

### Walt Disney's Carousel of Progress

This attraction will always be Walt Disney's Carousel of Progress—never just Carousel of Progress. It's his original creation from the 1964–65 New York World's Fair. It's brilliant.

Built for part of the General Electric Pavilion, Walt Disney's Carousel of Progress wowed crowds at the fair. It made an appearance at Disneyland and moved to Florida in 1975. Walt Disney's Carousel of Progress has had more performances than any other show in the history of American theater.

It was Walt's idea that great theatrical efficiency could be attained by having the audience move while the show stayed put. This means that the scene never has to change; it just waits while a new audience arrives and then repeats itself. Every few minutes, one audience rotates to the right while another one arrives from the left.

The show is all about progress. You'll follow a family through different decades, each one featuring the new advancements of the time. Older guests may remember actually using some of these advancements, while younger guests will laugh at the absurdity.

Walt Disney's Carousel of Progress was one of the original audio-animatronic productions. I'm not going to beat around the bush: it's a priceless piece of history that must be preserved, but it's also in need of a refurbishment. (You'll understand what I mean when you see the last scene.)

### Shops of Tomorrowland

Tomorrowland offers the smallest shops in the park. Still, you'll find plenty of merchandise, especially items themed to *Star Wars* and Marvel Comics. Near Space Mountain, you can design your own smartphone case using a kiosk.

### Dining in Tomorrowland

**Cosmic Ray's Starlight Café:** This enormous quick-service option contains different bays that serve hamburgers, sandwiches, chicken, and a galaxy of other items. Cosmic Ray, an animatronic lounge singer, entertains the diners. This is the highest-revenue-producing restaurant in the United States.

**Auntie Gravity's Galactic Goodies:** Quick-service ice cream is offered in the middle of Tomorrowland.

**Lunching Pad:** Hot dogs and snacks served quick service.

**Tomorrowland Terrace:** A quick-service restaurant for lunch and dinner. The Tomorrowland Terrace operates seasonally and is the site of a special fireworks-viewing dessert party.

## Parades, Evening Shows, and Special Events
### Mickey's Royal Friendship Faire

You won't have any trouble finding the stage for this show; it's in the middle of it all, right in front of Cinderella Castle. Check the daily Times Guide as there are usually at least four performances each day. There is plenty of space to watch, but the audience stands for the twenty-minute show.

Any show in front of the castle is worth your time. They are well done with lots of characters, costumes, and, of course, the spectacular backdrop of the castle itself. The moral of the show is that you should give up and spend your life sitting on your couch—just checking that you are still paying attention. It's the Magic Kingdom! Of course the message is about following your dreams and surrounding yourself with good people.

In this show, new in 2016, Mickey, Minnie, Donald, and Goofy bring friends together that they've met on their travels. The friends include some wonderful people (or other animals) from *Tangled, The Princess and the Frog,* and *Frozen*. Expect lots of music and dancing with a surprisingly large cast.

There is no cover for this show. During the summer, see it later in the day when the sun isn't quite so high.

### *Move It, Shake It, Dance & Play It!*

Also right in front of the castle, this parade and party combination occurs once each day, and is a favorite for younger guests. The Disney characters ride on floats that park themselves around the castle hub. Lots of cast members jump from the floats and get the kids all riled up with a little dancing and a lot of jumping around. It's organized chaos that only Disney can do.

### *Festival of Fantasy Parade*

*Fastpass+* The very definition of a Disney parade, Festival of Fantasy has everything you want: incredible floats, characters, choreographed music, and hundreds of cast members. The parade will occur at least once per day. If you're lucky enough that it happens twice on the day you're in the park, the second parade will be much less crowded. Guests start picking their spots early on a busy day—about an hour before parade time.

The parade route is marked on all park maps. The floats are enormous, and you can see the parade from anywhere along the route. However, most people love the atmosphere of Main Street and Town Square. Also, this is a daytime parade, so wear sunscreen if you're not in the shade. If you have a Fastpass+ for the parade, you'll find your special viewing areas around the hub in front of the castle.

If you're not interested in the parade, this will be a great time to ride anything that normally has a line. However, it's not a great time to do any shopping on Main Street, USA.

### Once Upon a Time

This ten-minute show occurs nightly on the castle. Yes, on the castle itself. It's fairly amazing to consider how advanced light-projection technology has become. Using nothing but light, Cinderella Castle is transformed into all sorts of other things. It can become a rocket that blasts off, an icy home, a metropolitan skyline—it's an endless array. During the holidays, the castle appears to be made of gingerbread.

### Fireworks

*Fastpass+* The iconic image of Cinderella Castle under the sparkle of fireworks occurs nightly at the Magic Kingdom. The regular show, called Wishes, will be replaced with a new show in 2017. Wishes is a spectacular presentation that is narrated by Jiminy Cricket. Expect beautiful music and over-the-top pyrotechnics. The new show, Happily Ever After, is sure to be just as spectacular. On some nights, especially during any kind of holiday, the regular fireworks show may change to some other extraordinary display. Guests will see special fireworks for Christmas, New Year's Eve and, of course, Independence

Day. You'll never be disappointed with fireworks at the Magic Kingdom unless the weather doesn't cooperate (which is surprisingly rare).

You can see the fireworks from anywhere in the park, but the best spots are in the central hub, Main Street, and the middle of Town Square. If you can see the front of the castle, then you are in a good spot.

### Night Parade

As this book was going to press, the spectacular Main Street Electrical Parade ended its long run at the Magic Kingdom. No information about its replacement is available. But you should expect something big and sparkly. Night parades are a staple of the Magic Kingdom's entertainment offerings. (They're also a good business move as evening parades ensure that guests stick around.)

Expect amazing effects, characters, and beautiful music. If the night parade is performed more than once, it's worth your time to skip the first one and watch the less-crowded second performance.

### Electrical Water Pageant

I wasn't going to write about this because it's a bit bizarre, but my husband threatened to divorce me if I didn't. He, and dozens of other fans, loves this nightly event. All kidding aside, the Electrical Water Pageant is the oldest continuing entertainment event at any Disney park. It's been occurring nightly since 1971.

The pageant is a series of barges that slowly sail around Seven Seas Lagoon and Bay Lake. Each barge carries an animated light display. The whole show lasts about ten minutes, and it's all choreographed to music. There is a patriot finale that is well done and worth your time. It's all free even if you don't stay on the property or have a park ticket.

The water pageant usually starts near Disney's Polynesian Village around 9:00 p.m. From there, it makes the rounds past the other Magic Kingdom Resorts and the Magic Kingdom front entrance itself. Check with any cast member for that evening's schedule.

### Halloween

Halloween is amazing at the Magic Kingdom. Decorations are everywhere beginning right after Labor Day and lasting through October 31.

The main event is **Mickey's Not So Scary Halloween Party.** This party occurs on select nights during September and October. You need a special ticket to attend; a normal Magic Kingdom pass does not work for Mickey's Not So Scary Halloween Party. The party runs from 7:00 p.m. to midnight, but you can enter the park anytime after 4:00 p.m.

Do they really kick everyone out at seven? Sort of. If you have a ticket for the party, either on paper or on your MagicBand, you'll be given a wristband. They don't kick anyone out, but starting at 7:00 p.m., there is absolutely nothing you can do without a wristband—you'll need one to step inside a shop, to eat, to visit any attraction, and to watch a show or parade. Cast members are constantly checking for the wristband.

It's absolutely worth it to attend the party. Just don't waste your money by buying a park pass for the daytime. Find something else to do, and enter the park at 4:00 p.m. Most everyone, including adults, wear some sort of costume for the event. Expect lots of creative Disney-inspired attire. But don't forget that it's Florida. Even though it's October, it will still be very humid. Go for a T-shirt, shorts, and Jedi robe instead of your whole Darth Vader uniform.

The parade during Mickey's Not So Scary Halloween Party is the best one at Walt Disney World. The headless horseman rides an actual horse through the park. He does this without a head as he holds a glowing pumpkin up in the night. You'll also see all the villains and the folks from the Haunted Mansion. Everything here fits the "not-so-scary" theme; you don't have to worry about your kids.

There are a lot of trick-or-treating opportunities in every land of the park. You could possibly end up with a boatload of candy. Cast members provide bags for you to haul your loot back to your hotel. In addition to all of this, an amazing show occurs several times in front of the castle. The show stars the Sanderson Sisters of *Hocus Pocus* fame. It's fun with lots of music, dancing, and special effects.

The price for the party changes depending upon the date. Parties closer to Halloween are more expense than those in early September. As an average, expect to pay $70 to attend.

### Christmas

Cinderella Castle alone gets 250,000 Christmas lights. That's in addition to the millions of lights put elsewhere on the property. Christmas is stunningly beautiful at the Magic Kingdom. Town Square hosts the most amazing Christmas tree you are likely to see.

Just like Halloween, the main event for Christmas is a special event that occurs on select nights. **Mickey's Very Merry Christmas Party** requires a separate ticket. The party runs from 7:00 p.m. to midnight, but you can enter the park anytime after 4:00 p.m. Again, don't waste a park ticket on this day; find something else to do, and enter the park at four.

During Mickey's Very Merry Christmas Party, you'll get as much complimentary hot chocolate and cookies as you can handle. On average, it will cost $70 to $90 to attend the party, so eat at least that much in cookies.

Mickey's Once Upon a Christmas Parade occurs twice during each party. It's the parade you'll see broadcast in the United States on Christmas Day. There is also a special show in front of the castle.

The main draw for many people is the ability to have your photo taken with Disney characters in their holiday best. It's fun to see Donald all snug in his winter coat, scarf, and hat. You'll also get to meet some characters that normally do not appear in the park, like Scrooge

McDuck and Santa Claus (separately, not together). People will line up quite early (starting at 6:00 p.m.) for the "holy grail" of Disney characters pictures; you can have your photo taken with all seven dwarfs together!

I'm from Minnesota, so I couldn't care less. But for those of you from south of the Mason-Dixon Line, it snows on Main Street, USA. Actually, it is quite fun for me to watch people experience the only snow they'll see during the season.

The holidays are not just relegated to the Magic Kingdom. Every square inch of these forty square miles is decked out in holiday glory.

In addition to the special events and decorations inside the parks, each hotel on the property has over-the-top decor. If you have some extra time during your holiday visit, it's worth it to take a short tour of the Magic Kingdom hotels. Take a bus from your hotel to the Magic Kingdom. From there, walk to the Contemporary to see the lobby. Exit the rear of the hotel and walk toward Bay Lake. There, take a boat to Wilderness Lodge; you will be amazed at all the Christmas glory in the woods. Take the boat back to the Contemporary and hop on the monorail. Get off at Polynesian Village for some Mele Kalikimaka. Then take the monorail to the Grand Floridian to see one of the world's largest and most elaborate gingerbread houses—it's all edible! Buy some of the gingerbread at the Grand Floridian and enjoy it as you ride the monorail back to the Magic Kingdom.

If you're as fanatical about Christmas as I am, you may want to take a Disney Yuletide tour. They are offered during November and early December only and can be booked online at disneyworld.disney.go.com. You'll spend four hours learning how Disney decorates for the holidays, including a stop backstage at Disney's massive holiday warehouse (those hundreds of trees and millions of lights don't just store themselves).

▲ ▲ ▲

## Epcot

Walt's Experimental Prototype Community of Tomorrow is no longer an acronym. Now it's a word all of its own. Epcot is like a never-ending World's Fair. It's where you can experience technological achievements and celebrate the world in one place.

Epcot is large—three times the size of the Magic Kingdom. It's a 1.2-mile (1.9-kilometer) walk around the World Showcase alone. By meandering into each country, you'll easily add many more miles to your day.

It's home to the two most popular Disney festivals on the planet. In addition to Epcot's springtime Flower and

Garden Expo, fall's International Food and Wine Festival has become an international destination. Each day during the festival, thousands of travelers from all over the globe travel to Epcot to eat and drink their way around World Showcase Lagoon.

It's not quite what Walt imagined. Nobody lives at Epcot. But it is a successful Disney park that is consistently one of the most visited destinations in the world.

Whether you arrive via monorail, Disney transportation bus, or car, you'll enter Epcot at the same place. Parking lot trams drop guests underneath the monorail station and near the walkway to the bus loading area. After passing through security and bag check, you'll present your MagicBand and enter the park.

In front of you is the massive Spaceship Earth; we'll explore that in a bit. For now, enjoy the 1980s look and feel of the entrance plaza. Epcot is going through a lot of changes. Hopefully, one of them will be a refurbishment of the entrance plaza. The park opened in 1982, and some of it still looks like that. Wasn't this supposed to be a prototype of tomorrow? Well, just bury that thought for now.

Head toward Spaceship Earth and get ready to explore Future World.

**Future World**
The front of Epcot is Future World. Originally, this was Disney's pride of edutainment: quite academic subjects presented in amazing and fun ways. We'll have to see

where the future of Future World takes Epcot. Right now there's a little bit less of the "edu" and more of the "tainment," but that may change with new leadership.

However, with that said, there are still some great examples of the golden age of Disney's edutainment. One of them is Spaceship Earth.

### Spaceship Earth

*Fastpass+* First, let's get technical. You'll often hear people refer to Spaceship Earth as a geodesic dome—even I do this sometimes. But if any true Epcot fans are within earshot, they'll quickly remind you that a dome is only the top half; Spaceship Earth is a geosphere. Or you can just call it the giant golf ball like most others do. Whatever you call it, it's the 180-foot iconic symbol of Epcot.

Yes, you can go inside, and you should. It's home to a classic Epcot attraction that has stood the test of time. Spaceship Earth is a fourteen-minute ride through the history of human communication. It's incredibly detailed, and you will surely be amazed.

After boarding your time machine, you'll be led by Dame Judi Dench's soothing voice back to Cro-Magnon days. You'll learn about the Egyptians and their papyrus, the Romans and their roads, the Italians and their art, and the Americans and their computers. At the very top (the geodesic dome part of the geosphere), you'll be treated to an unforgettable image of our wonderful home. Then as you travel back to the modern age, you'll get a private interactive experience in your time machine.

After answering a few questions, you'll get to see how you'll live in the future—complete with photographs.

### Innoventions

The two low buildings behind and on either side of Spaceship Earth are called Innoventions. This was a large space where new technologies were featured. Guests could experiment with all sorts of things involving sound, light, motion, and so on.

Right now there isn't a lot going on inside either building of Innoventions. Perhaps something will be happening when you visit the park. Most guidebooks direct you to this website to get the most current information: innoventions.disney.com. But don't waste your time; the website is defunct.

### Universe of Energy

Don't worry; there are some fantastic attractions in the park. But like Innoventions, sadly, Universe of Energy featuring Ellen's Energy Adventure will probably be empty when you visit—it's scheduled to close sometime in 2017. Many Epcot fans required heavy medication when this announcement was made. The rumor is that Ellen is being replaced with an attraction based on Marvel's *Guardians of the Galaxy*.

### Mission: Space

*Fastpass+* You can't miss this building with its massive planets around the entrance. Mission: Space is an interactive attraction where you and three others will take a journey to Mars. You'll be assigned a job: pilot, engineer, navigator, or captain. You'll be asked to perform assigned duties on the journey, but you can also just sit back and enjoy the experience—no one will know, and I won't tell on you.

There are two versions of this attraction: the Orange Team version is for high intensity, and the Green Team is for less intensity. When this ride first opened, there was only the Orange Team and a lot of vomit. Please use caution. If you experience any sort of motion sickness, do not ride with the Orange Team. Seriously. Do not. This attraction is famous for offering a realistic sensation of extreme G-force. The sensation is produced by putting riders inside a centrifuge. In fact, Mission: Space was the first ride in theme park history to provide vomit bags to the riders. (This is no joke; it actually occurred.)

When the custodians just couldn't take it anymore, the less-intense version became a choice. The Green Team offers all the spectacular effects without the spinning. It's still a bit claustrophobic but much more doable for normal people.

### Test Track

*Fastpass+* First, you'll spend some time at a computer designing a car. It's easier than it sounds. You'll choose the shape, engine, and other items. Each choice comes with benefits and disadvantages. Then you'll board a test vehicle to see how your car performs.

The test phase is really the heart of this attraction. You and five others will ride through a track where your vehicle is tested on all types of terrain. You'll see how your car does with some quick stops. And you'll feel the extreme temperature testing area. Then, in order to perform a test for speed, you and your car are hurled around an outdoor track. At the conclusion, you're shown how the car you designed responded to the tests.

The car design portion of the experience is just so-so. Some people really get into designing the best vehicle they can. I enjoy just sitting back and experiencing the various tests on the track.

There are often long lines. If you don't have a Fastpass+, consider using the single-rider line. This line moves much faster, and you can't talk while on the ride anyway.

### *Journey Into Imagination with Figment*
*Fastpass+* Disclaimer: if you find yourself speaking with a diehard Epcot fan, don't mention this ride. It's not worth your time to have to clean up the mess after his or her head explodes. In the days of yore, this was a legendary ride with legions of fan. Now it's a watered-down version.

With that said, I still enjoy this ride. It's basically a dark ride where you learn about the power of imagination with a small purple dragon named Figment. It's not going to change your life at all, but it will provide some nice air-conditioned time in a dark place.

### Disney & Pixar Short Film Experience

Also located with Figment in the Imagination Pavilion, this movie theater shows short clips from the Disney and Pixar archives. You never know what will be showing. If there is any upcoming release imminent for either studio, you can bet it will be featured here.

### Living with the Land

*Fastpass+* Located inside the Land Pavilion, this fourteen-minute boat ride highlights how humans use land to produce food. First, you're shown recreations of various landscapes and natural environments. Next, you're floated through a number of Disney's indoor gardens. This is actually a fascinating look at how fruits and vegetables can be grown in innovative ways. Do not touch any of the plants that are close to the boat; yes, they are real.

There are tomatoes growing in the air using a drip technology that provides only as much water as necessary. There are other types of melons and pumpkins that use some sort of nutrient-rich mixture instead of soil. Then you'll see a fish farm where fish feed the plants and plants feed the fish.

If you find this ride interesting and want to learn more, Epcot offers a Behind the Seeds Tour, where you can spend a morning learning from the researchers who work here. Go to disneyworld.disney.go.com for more information.

### Soarin' Around the World

*Fastpass+* Recently reopened with an all-new experience, Soarin' is now better than ever. A third screen was added, meaning that lines move faster.

On this flight-simulator attraction, you'll hang just a few feet above the floor as a huge screen provides the sensation of flight. You'll feel the wind and smell the smells. Everything is perfectly choreographed to the motion on the screen.

The original version gave guests the ability to fly over California. (It was imported from Disney California Adventure in Anaheim.) Now the new version provides the chance to fly over famous world landmarks. There is an excellent musical score that accompanies the journey.

Soarin' Around the World is located in the Land Pavilion.

### The Circle of Life

Also in the Land Pavilion, this is a twenty-minute film that teaches the importance of respecting the environment. It uses the characters of *The Lion King* to underscore the message that everything on earth is connected in some way.

### The Seas with Nemo and Friends

*Fastpass+* This pavilion is one of the largest aquariums on earth. It holds six million gallons of seawater and contains thousands of sea creatures. When you enter the building, you'll be directed to the signature attraction: The Seas with Nemo and Friends.

You'll board a clam mobile and take a journey to find Nemo—he's lost...again! Some of the technology is pretty cool. However, by far, the best part of the attraction is when you get to look for Nemo among the real fish of the aquarium. Yes, animated fish swim with their real cousins.

When you exit your clam mobile, stick around the building to explore the aquarium from various viewing platforms. If you arrive in the morning, you may be able to see feeding time. At other times, you can watch researchers work with the animals, including the dolphins and sharks.

### Turtle Talk with Crush

*Fastpass+* Spend ten minutes with totally awesome turtle Crush. He'll interact with the crowd in real time. He may ask you a question or even answer one of yours. It's a technological marvel that is very popular. There is often a line.

### Shops of Future World

Each attraction offers a small gift shop, usually at the ride's exit, where you can purchase items specific to that attraction. For example, there is everything for the car lover in your life at Test Track. The largest Disney shop in the park is **Mouse Gear** near Spaceship Earth. This is the main store of Epcot-themed merchandise and other Disney items.

### Dining in Future World

**Garden Grill:** Unique character dining offered inside the Land Pavilion. The Garden Grill is a revolving restaurant that serves family-style dinners for around $45 for adults, $21 for kids.

**Coral Reef:** A table-service steak and seafood restaurant inside the Seas with Nemo and Friends. Reservations are recommended; some adult entrees are up to $60. Try not to freak out that you are eating seafood while their relatives swim past your table.

**Electric Umbrella:** A large quick-service café near Spaceship Earth with refillable fountain soda—a rarity inside a Disney park.

**Sunshine Season:** Inside the Land Pavilion, this massive food court with lots of different options is a very popular air-conditioned place to dine.

### World Showcase

Opening two hours later than Future World, usually around 11:00 a.m., World Showcase is a collection of eleven pavilions. Each pavilion is a tribute to a nation—from its architecture to food to shops. For many guests, this may be the closest they ever get to visiting some of these countries.

Through a special exchange program, most of the cast members in the pavilions are actually from that country—as are that nation's musicians, who perform live each day. When Epcot opened in 1982, the World Showcase pavilions were actually paid for by the represented countries.

The reason these particular ten countries are present is because those are the countries that Disney was able to convince to provide financial support. (There are eleven pavilions but only ten countries; the eleventh pavilion represents the United States and was produced by Disney.)

World Showcase has become a resortwide destination for adults after dark. There's romantic magic in strolling through the various lanes when the sun is down. Each country also provides plenty of their homeland's liquor of choice. And there are the restaurants. Some of the finest international restaurants in the United States are located right here at Epcot. For your information, most World Showcase table-service restaurants offer entrees for around $25 per adult, $15 per child, with a few quite expensive exceptions. Quick-service counters in the pavilions will be much cheaper.

### Mexico

Under a great Aztec pyramid, you'll find the Mexican Pavilion. Most of this pavilion is indoors. You'll enter into a bustling marketplace called the Plaza de los Amigos. Here you can purchase authentic baskets, musical instruments, and other wares made in Mexico.

The Mexican Pavilion is home to a very nice, and relaxing, boat trip through Mexico. **Gran Fiesta Tour Starring the Three Caballeros** is a charming ride. The Three Caballeros, Panchito, José Carioca, and Donald Duck, were made famous in a 1944 Disney film. Here, they have reunited to perform a concert in Mexico. Unfortunately, one of them is missing. It's the one of the three who's most likely to get into some sort of trouble—Donald, of course! You'll spend your slow boat ride attempting to find him. The attraction uses live footage to provide plenty of beautiful scenes of Mexico.

There are two table-service restaurants in Mexico. **San Angel Inn** is the place for romance and atmosphere. It's located well inside the pyramid and next to the stream used for the Gran Fiesta Tour attraction. It's a dark, candlelit establishment with upscale Mexican fare. Outside the pavilion, **La Hacienda de San Angel** is located on the shore of the World Showcase Lagoon. It's a bit louder, but it's also fun to watch other guests as they stroll past. If you get lucky, you might get a water-view table during Epcot's evening show on the lagoon.

In addition to these restaurants, Mexico offers a quick-service option and a very nice lounge. Tequila is the drink of choice at this pavilion.

### Norway

The Norwegian Pavilion is sort of under siege right now. Anna and Elsa, from the fictional Norwegian village of Arendelle, have set up shop here. There are legions of *Frozen* fans everywhere.

**Frozen Ever After** (*Fastpass+*) is the main attraction here. Set on the site of the former Maelstrom ride, Frozen Ever After is a new dark ride that brings guests into the story of the famous sisters. The attraction uses a combination of sets, audio-animatronics, and projections. All the memorable music from the film is featured.

When Frozen Ever After debuted in summer of 2016, it was met with record-breaking lines as long as six hours! While the lines have toned down a bit, expect to wait two hours to ride through Arendelle. Fastpass+ is the best option here, although you must be ready to select this option sixty days before your arrival date. You could also try to get to Norway as soon as the World Showcase opens at 11:00 a.m.

While the ride features animatronics, you can meet the actual sisters next door at the **Royal Sommerhus** (*Fastpass+*). Anna and Elsa meet with guests separately and are quite charming.

One shop, the **Puffin's Roost,** is filled with all sort of Norwegian merchandise. If you want a troll, you can find one, or one thousand, here. This is also the main shop for *Frozen* souvenirs.

Also in Norway is one of the more popular restaurants in the park. **Akershus Royal Banquet Hall** offers character meals in a Norwegian castle setting. The Disney princesses are featured at this establishment, and it's a good alternative to Cinderella's Royal Table at the Magic Kingdom. The other place to get food in Norway is at a quick-service bakery. The pastries are amazing, as are the soups.

### China

A recreation of Beijing's Temple of Heaven signals that you are in China. You'll notice quite a difference in music from the pavilions on either side. The Chinese Pavilion includes lovely authentic landscaping with beautiful gardens.

*Reflections of China* is a film shown continuously in this pavilion. You'll stand in the middle of a round theater as the film is projected all around you. Serene scenes of China are featured.

As this book went to press, most of the remainder of the Chinese Pavilion was dedicated to exhibits about the construction of Shanghai Disneyland. (You can visit these exhibits or just read that chapter in this book.)

**House of Good Fortune** is a shop full of Chinese merchandise. Three things are heavily featured in the shop: silk, Buddha, and pandas.

**Nine Dragons** is the table-service restaurant of the Chinese Pavilion. You can order from a menu or choose the buffet. There is a nice assortment of Chinese tea if you want an afternoon break. **Lotus Blossom Café,** located next to the shop, is a quick-service option.

*Germany*

When you hear a glockenspiel at the top of the hour, you'll know you're at the German Pavilion. This idyllic German village is more Bavarian Munich than it is German Berlin. There isn't a main attraction here, but there are several shops. The German Pavilion also serves lots of something called beer—whatever that is.

**Der Teddybar** is a large toy shop, and **Das Kaufhaus** is a clothing store. **Karamell-Küche** is an extremely popular candy store where chocolate lovers will not survive. **The Stein Haus** sells—well, steins. There's also a beautiful glassware shop and, of course, a shop full of clocks. The last store is dedicated to Germany's love of Christmas. You won't find Santa Claus here, but you'll see plenty of St. Nicholas.

**Biergarten** is the liveliest restaurant at Epcot. It's located in the St. Georgsplatz portion of the pavilion, but you'll hear it before you can see it, especially if you venture here at night. The Biergarten is a Bavarian-style restaurant. This means that you'll sit on long tables next to strangers who won't be strangers for long. There is, of course, a polka band and lots of pretzels, sausages, and spaetzle.

You can also visit the quick-service **Sommerfest** for bratwurst, Black Forest cake, and apple strudel. They have something called Jägermeister here as well.

### Italy

Forget Rome, Florence, and Naples. Italy's pavilion at Epcot is decidedly Venice. Look for the gondolas tied up in the lagoon for ambiance. You'll also see architecture reminiscent of St. Mark's Square. There isn't a main attraction at this pavilion.

The shops of Italy feature items dedicated to two Italian loves: cooking and football (that's soccer, for the Americans). **La Bottega Italiana** is where you want to head if you love to cook with wine and olive oil. **Il Bel Cristallo** is the shop for the sports lovers.

It's no surprise that the rest of the Italian pavilion is dedicated to food. **Via Napoli** is the pavilion's extremely popular pizza joint. It's a table-service restaurant where the pizza is baked in one of three stone ovens; each oven is themed to a different Italian volcano. Disney spares no effort to provide the most authentic experience possible. The flour for the dough is imported from Italy. The water used for the dough is specifically treated to make it taste as close as possible like the tap water of Naples, Italy.

**Tutto Italia** is a very upscale restaurant in Italy. There are indoor and outdoor tables. It's as expensive as it is popular. Nearby, **Tutto Gusto** is a wine bar that supposedly has the largest selection of Italian wine outside of Italy.

### The United States of America

Directly opposite the lagoon from Spaceship Earth sits the US Pavilion, officially called the American Adventure. This pavilion is another great example of forced perspective. However, in this case, the building uses perspective to make it seem smaller. When the park was designed, it was thought inhospitable to the other countries if the American Pavilion was twice the size. So imagineers played a trick to make the building seem the same size as those on either side. The American Adventure is actually a five-story building. But if you look at the outside, the windows only indicate a building of two stories plus an attic. The windows are all false. Your eyes see the three rows of windows, and your brain tells you that the building is just a tiny three-story structure.

**The American Adventure** is also the name of the show inside the pavilion. This is a massive show full of effects. It uses film and audio-animatronics to tell the story of America, from the pilgrims through the modern age. Huge sets lift the animatronic characters into view at the appropriate time in the film. You'll see and hear a parade of famous Americans. Mark Twain and Benjamin Franklin, two people who lived a century apart, act as your narrators as they discuss various aspects of American history.

But this attraction does not provide a rose-colored view of the United States. The more terrible and unfortunate parts of history are included. Frederick Douglass talks about slavery, Chief Joseph rises from the floor to tell of the horrible treatment of Native Americans, and Susan B. Anthony represents the inequality of women. The film portion of the show displays the civil rights movement of the 1960s and the gay rights movement of the modern age.

This is not an attraction that you just watch and forget. It's one that you discuss over dinner later that evening. How did George Washington and his soldiers survive living outside during a cold winter? Why didn't the nation listen to the appeal of Native Americans? Is it OK that Lance Armstrong and Tiger Woods are featured as great American heroes? There are no easy answers.

Outside the theater, there is a shop that sells merchandise that's been made only in the United States. **The**

**Liberty Inn** is quick service with—what else?—hot dogs and hamburgers.

Jutting out into the lagoon, across from the pavilion, is the **America Gardens Theater.** This large amphitheater hosts special concerts and other events. Check the daily Times Guide to see if anything is showing on the day you're there.

## *Japan*

A beautiful and graceful torri gate rises above World Showcase Lagoon. It's a replica of a torri gate in Hiroshima Bay. This is the pavilion of Japan. A horticulturist's dream, the Japanese Pavilion is home to authentic gardens and pools of koi. Everything is in perfect balance at this pavilion.

**Mitsukoshi Merchandise Store** is easily the most unique shopping opportunity in the park. This is as close as you can get to a real Tokyo department store while staying on this side of the Pacific. You'll find kimonos, dishware, and a wall of sake. Japan is a country of contradictions and a constant balance between tradition and progress. When you see chopsticks being sold next to Godzilla T-shirts, you'll know what I mean.

Mitsukoshi is located in a building that is a replica of a palace in Kyoto, Japan. An equally authentic building houses **Bijutsu-Kan,** a small museum of Japanese cultural artifacts. The exhibitions here change. If you see a lot of teenagers hanging around, then you'll know that the current exhibition has something to do with anime.

**Teppan Edo** is the pavilion's version of a Japanese steakhouse. You will sit around a large grill and watch as your food is prepared. It's as much a show as it is a dinner. Next door, **Tokyo Dining** is table service for sushi, sashimi, and tempura. You can also order a bento box as a meal.

Two quick-service options are available in Japan. **Kabuki Café** offers icy drinks, green tea, and miso soup. You can also get quick-service versions of sushi. **Katsura Grill** is the place to go for teriyaki chicken and other dishes with rice.

### *Morocco*

When the Moroccan Pavilion was being constructed, the king of Morocco was so impressed with Epcot that he sent his own architect to oversee the progress. Consequently, this is the most authentic of the World Showcase pavilions. Over nine tons of handmade tiles were shipped from Morocco during construction. If you love mosaics, then you must wander through the streets of this pavilion.

**The Brass Bazaar** sells all sorts of items that, like the tiles, were made in Morocco. **Casablanca Carpets** is a shop for high-end carpets and books. Baskets, sandals, and clothing are offered inside **Marketplace in Medina.** Lamps and coffee are found in **Souk Al Magreb**, and leather products are available at **Tangier Traders.**

One of the newer restaurants in the park, **Spice Road Table** has become a quite popular table-service venue.

It has fantastic views of the lagoon and a large menu. Reservations are highly recommended here.

An older restaurant, **Marrakesh**, is decorated with thousands of tiles. There may be Moroccan musicians and belly dancers to entertain you while you dine.

**The Tangierine Café** is quick service for falafels, hummus, and couscous.

### *France*

There's no doubt that the French Pavilion was inspired by Paris. A replica Eiffel Tower rises above mansard roofs and other Belle Époque buildings.

Wander into the Palais de Cinéma to watch an eighteen-minute film called *Impressions de France.* You'll visit the French Alps and the famous Hall of Mirrors in Versailles. Of Epcot's country-based films, this is the best.

I'm not exactly sure what a Givenchy fragrance is. **Plume eat Palette** is the only shop outside Paris that offers the entire line of Givenchy products. I'm told this is a very big deal. Another shop, **Les Halle's Boutique de Cadeux**, sells anything you can imagine with the French flag on it. Nearby, wine lovers will want to visit **Les Vins de France.** They sell many types of French wine at a range of prices. There are also lots of books about wine for sale.

Of all the countries around the lagoon, France probably has the best reputation when it comes to food. And it should—everything here is amazing.

**Les Halles Boulangerie Patisserie** is a pastry shop and bakery. I can't even type this paragraph without pausing to dream of this food: croissants, éclairs, baguettes, mousse...and that's just the start. This is a quick-service café with sandwiches on fresh bread with French cheese.

**Monsieur Paul** is the most exclusive restaurant at Epcot. You must have a reservation to dine here. Also, dress modestly—no tank tops or anything cut off is allowed. This is one of the most expensive restaurants in all of Walt Disney World. Monsieur Paul is located on the upper floor of the pavilion.

Downstairs from Paul, you'll find **Chefs de France.** This is more affordable but is just as popular. You must have a reservation here. The dining room is well lit, and you will feel like you are in an energetic Parisian brasserie.

### United Kingdom

At Epcot, you can walk from Paris to London in a couple of minutes—no need to deal with that pesky English Channel. Also, these two pavilions coexist well without centuries of war.

If you love *Downton Abbey* and *Dr. Who*, then head to the **Crown & Crest.** In this shop, you'll find all sorts of British merchandise and pop-culture items. Soccer fans should head to **Sportsman's Shoppe** for lots of items with the word "united" on them. The **Toy Soldier** is stocked with merchandise based on famous English works such as *Winnie the Pooh.* And the **Tea Caddy** is a charming cottage catering to the quite civilized act of afternoon tea.

**Rose & Crown Pub** is an authentic British pub right in Epcot. It has a fantastic atmosphere. The main staples of this restaurant are fish and chips and bangers and mash. Get a reservation to eat here without a long wait.

If you want to save a few pounds and some time, look for the **Yorkshire Country Fish Shop.** They offer the exact fish and chips from the Rose & Crown at a quick-service price; they even have the malt vinegar.

### Canada

The United States' beautiful northerly neighbor, Canada is well represented here at Epcot. Look for the Ottawa-style architecture and pine-lined waterfalls. The Canadian Pavilion also features a small bit of Victoria's Butchart Gardens.

*O Canada!* is another country-based film. It's shown on a circular screen, much like that inside China's pavilion. You will have to stand. Martin Short, famous Canadian, leads guests on a tour of Canada. It's quite funny but also extremely beautiful.

Hockey fans should visit the **Northwest Mercantile** and its NHL merchandise. It's the only shop in Canada.

Outside, the quick-service **Refreshment Port** offers croissant doughnuts. These cronuts, just like Canada, are a mix of English and French.

Everyone used to tell me to eat at **Le Cellier Steakhouse.** I ignored them because I love the San Angel Inn over at Mexico. But then I tried it. Yep, it deserves all the hype. You must have a reservation to eat at Le

Cellier Steakhouse. It's quite romantic with low lighting and stone walls. First, you'll be served a bread basket with pretzel rolls. Then, if you're smart, you'll order the cheddar cheese soup with Moosehead beer. That's all I need to say about Canada.

Epcot is the only Disney park in the world that lets you physically see the middle of the park without paying a cent. That's right—you can get inside Epcot without any sort of ticket or pass.

Take the monorail from the Magic Kingdom's Ticket and Transportation Center to Epcot. At the end of the ride, you'll pass over the Epcot gates and be treated to a free tour of the park. You'll curve around Spaceship Earth and get a bird's-eye view of the World Showcase countries.

Want to see some of the topiaries of the Flower and Garden Expo? Just hop on the monorail. Want to see Epcot's amazing Christmas tree? It's just a free monorail ride away. Of course, you're not going to get to stop and ponder over the sights as the monorail keeps moving. But it's a great way to experience Epcot if you don't have much time and/or you're not interested in any of the attractions.

▲ ▲ ▲

**Parades, Evening Shows, and Special Events**
There aren't any parades here, but there is a lot of entertainment available all day and night. Particularly, the countries of the World Showcase constantly offer live performances of authentic musicians. Disney is the largest employer of musicians on earth. Also, Epcot hosts the two most popular festivals in all of the Disney universe.

### *Illuminations—Reflections of Earth*
*Fastpass+* This is Epcot's nighttime show. It's a spectacle that's beyond compare, and many guests say it's the highlight of their trip. You can get a Fastpass+ to enjoy a special viewing place or grab a place anywhere along the lagoon. You may have to get a spot an hour before show time as the lagoon will get crowded.

This show has it all: fireworks, water effects, projections, music, lasers, and lots of other things that I can't even comprehend. It's all done over the water and on the ball of Spaceship Earth. During Christmas, there is an added "Peace on Earth" finale.

At the end of the show, there is a mad dash to exit the park. The monorail and buses will be packed. Instead, take your time and linger around the lagoon. Enjoy all the lights and slowly walk around the whole world. See Paris at night. Hear the raucous music of Germany. Smell that wonderful Mexican cooking.

### International Flower and Garden Festival

Running the entire months of March, April, and May, the International Flower and Garden Festival brings thousands of guests into the park each day. Every inch is decked out with blooms, foliage, and topiaries.

The plaza areas surrounding Spaceship Earth are transformed into large gardens. Because this is a true exhibition, the flowers and plants are labeled, and there is a lot to learn. There are always horticulturists on hand; check the daily Times Guide for presentations and lectures.

Each country of the World Showcase has some type of floral display. The displays are designed to complement the look of that country's pavilion. Indigenous plants from each country are also featured.

The post memorable part of the festival for many people is the Disney topiaries that are spread around the park. They are nothing short of phenomenal. Plants and flowers are sculpted to look like Snow White, Donald Duck, the Beast, and many other iconic characters. The topiaries are always the most popular picture spots in the park.

In addition to the organic displays, there is also a concert series that complements the festival. Held at American Gardens Theatre outside the American

Adventure, the weekend concert series features performers that you may or may not recognize, but you can rest assured that Disney insists on high quality and G-rated lyrics.

The best part: all of this is completely free with Epcot admission.

Where does Disney get all this stuff for the parks? Well, in the case of the horticulture, Disney grows and maintains everything onsite.

All this magic happens backstage—areas of the property that are off limits to guests. In fact, you will never know that tucked away behind the forests are acres of facilities dedicated to making the parks look great. If you are interested, Disney offers tours. I highly recommend the **Backstage Magic Tour**; find out more at disneyworld. disney.go.com.

Several giant greenhouses are hidden on the property. There, Disney grows everything for use in the fours parks and all the resort hotels. All the hanging baskets, and there are hundreds of them in the Magic Kingdom alone, are crafted in this facility. Outside the greenhouses, groves of different types of trees are maintained. In case a palm or pine tree dies, Disney has a ready replace-ment. Some of the special trees in the parks have identi-cal twins. For example, the Liberty Tree—a large tree with lanterns featured in Liberty Square—has an iden-tical twin growing near the greenhouses. The twin was grown from a cutting of the original tree. The original has been growing inside the Magic Kingdom since 1970, but if anything happens to it, it will be replaced, and an-other twin will be planted.

In addition to the greenhouses, Disney also hides other facilities. The largest fiberglass workshop on earth is located at Walt Disney World. This is where many of the ride vehicles for all the Disney Parks are produced. All the façades for Hong Kong's Main Street were made here. Every character costume is designed and made in Florida and shipped throughout the world. The audio-animatronic facility creates and repairs everything from pirates to tiki birds to Howard Taft. If you go on a tour, you can see animatronic limbs lying around here and there.

There are also giant holiday warehouses where enor-mous fiberglass pumpkins, Christmas trees, and brightly painted Easter eggs are stored. The Walt Disney World transportation network is one of the largest in the nation, comparable to the size of those found in many large cities. The buses, monorails, trains, and trams are maintained in special facilities. Disney operates their own trash, com-posting, and recycling programs. Mickey Mouse has his own power plant and water treatment center.

There's a lot more than fairy dust used to create all the magic—most of it is well concealed so that the illusion, and your vacation, is maintained.

▲ ▲ ▲

### International Food and Wine Festival

The International Food and Wine Festival gets bigger every year, and so do the crowds. This is a massive event held from the middle of September through the middle of November.

There are eleven countries represented around World Showcase Lagoon. But during this time of year, many more are included. In 2016, over forty kiosks were assembled throughout the park, all of them offering food and beverages from countries not normally present at Epcot.

There's also the wine. And there's a lot of it. Guests over the age of twenty-one (I apologize to the European visitors) can purchase beautiful wine goblets and carry them around the world. As you journey, you'll be treated to wine from places you never realized could make it.

The **Eat to the Beat Concert Series** is presented in American Gardens Theatre. Hundreds of acts are scheduled each year.

For many people, the main draw is the endless list of seminars and lectures. All sorts of chefs and wine experts take over several event areas in the park. Most of these education opportunities are free for everyone. Check out the daily Times Guide for a schedule. In addition to the free demonstrations, there are many classes that guests can register for. These cost extra, but you'll get personalized attention from an expert in a classroom setting. There are pastry classes, cheese classes, wine classes, and pretty much anything else you can think of.

Usually around August, the Epcot website is updated to include all the classes being offered at that year's festival. Visit disneyworld.disney.go.com to get this information. You can register for classes before the festival in order to ensure your place.

### International Festival of the Arts

Initially, I thought this festival was just a ploy to attract guests during a slower time of the year. Even if the festival was conceived that way, its quality makes it worth your time.

Occurring only on weekends in January and February, the International Festival of the Arts brings visual and performing arts from around the globe to Epcot. Each of the countries around the World Showcase feature displays and interactive demonstrations about various artistic endeavors. There are many lectures, classes and lessons taught in various locatins inside the park. You can find a complete schedule of the events online.

The crown jewel of the festival is the nightly Disney on Broadway Concert Series. Occurring in the United States Pavillion, this series brings the best of New York to Orlando. For no additional fee beside park admission, you can see what people pay hundreds to watch in Manhattan. All the music is live and incredibly high caliber. If you want a seat for one of these concerts, arrive very early.

### Christmas

Christmas is a festive and educational time to visit Epcot. First, there is a gigantic Christmas tree that dominates World Showcase Lagoon. Then there are the pavilions. Each country is decorated authentically. Cast members from the various countries are available to explain the holiday traditions of their country.

However, the highlight of Christmas at Epcot is the **Candlelight Processional.** Held on most nights between Thanksgiving and Christmas, the Candlelight Processional takes place at the America Gardens Theatre. A professional choir and full orchestra present the music of the season. They are joined by a visiting high school or college choir. There are candles everywhere. Then a celebrity narrator will rise and read the Christmas story. Some of the more popular narrators include Whoopi Goldberg, Neil Patrick Harris, and Ashley Judd. It's a moving scene. This event is extremely popular. The best way to get a seat is to book a Dining and Candlelight Processional package at one of the park's restaurants. These packages are available online and will offer a meal combined with a ticket to a reserved seating area. If you don't have a ticket, then get to the theater early and get in line. It's worth it.

## Disney's Hollywood Studios

Opened in 1989 as Disney-MGM Studios, this park used to provide days of attractions. It was part theme park and part movie studio, where Disney's next films and television shows were created before your eyes. It was...

I'm not going to say anything more about what was here; that's going to be annoying for you. I'll focus on what is here now, which is—well, not much. Excuse my brutal honesty, but this is a theme park in transition. Of all the Disney parks on earth, I rate this the lowest. Still, there are a couple of attractions to note. Plan to spend maybe half a day in this park.

Hopefully, my disappointment in this park won't last long. Star Wars Land and Toy Story Land should begin construction soon. There's also a name change in the works. Rumors indicate that the park will become Disney's Hollywood Adventure at some point in the near future.

The new name may also come with a new iconic symbol. The Earfel Tower (studio water tower with Mickey ears) that was the symbol of the early days is gone, as is a giant version of Mickey's magical hat that was the symbol in the later years. Here's to new lands, a new name, and a new symbol. This is one instance where you really will want to stay tuned.

All guests arrive at the same place. Walkers from the Epcot resorts are led to the same entrance plaza as guests from the parking lots and Disney transportation buses. Disney's Hollywood Studios has the closest general parking lot and is probably the easiest park to get in and out of for most people. After a security bag check and scanning your MagicBand, you'll find yourself on Hollywood Boulevard.

## Hollywood Boulevard and Sunset Boulevard

There aren't really any separated lands in this park—instead, there are small areas of grouped attractions. The streets of Hollywood Boulevard and Sunset Boulevard are the closest areas this park has to a themed land.

Hollywood Boulevard runs straight from the entrance plaza to an exact replica of Grauman's Chinese Theatre. (The original Grauman's is in Hollywood; it's where the stars put their handprints.) Sunset Boulevard runs perpendicular from Hollywood Boulevard toward the Tower of Terror.

These streets comprise the shopping area of Disney's Hollywood Studios. It's similar to Main Street, USA over in the Magic Kingdom, except this has a golden age of Hollywood feel. The entire park is dedicated to the Hollywood that everyone thinks existed but never really did. This is the area that represents that sentiment.

The items you find for sale will either be Disney-centric, movie-centric, or both. Just like in real Hollywood, some of the shops offer high-end fashions but with a Disney flair. You'll also find lots of stuff representing classic Hollywood movies and Academy Award statues for various categories that don't really exist, like Best Teacher and Husband of the Year (I won both in 2009).

### Beauty and the Beast—Live on Stage

*Fastpass+* In a large covered theater, you'll be treated to a thirty-minute version of the classic animated film. All the songs are presented, and you should expect elaborate sets and fantastic costumes. Show times will be listed in the daily Times Guide.

This show actually predates the Broadway version of *Beauty and the Beast.*

### The Twilight Zone Tower of Terror

*Fastpass+* This was the first version of the now-iconic ride; it's also the best. You can find this ride in Florida, California, Tokyo, and Paris, but Florida's version is unique.

On this attraction, you'll sit with others in a large elevator car. The car will ascend, and you'll see odd scenes when the doors open on various floors. Then your entire car will leave the elevator shaft, and you'll travel through one of the upper floors. You'll see more eerie things from the classic television show. Walt Disney World contains the only version of this ride where the elevator cars leave the shaft for a tour. The other versions around the world were built later and spared this outstanding feature in the interest of budget.

When you're finished with your tour, giant doors will open, and you'll get a fantastic view of central Florida—for a few seconds. Suddenly, the entire car will drop quickly, and you will lose your stomach. That may be the end of the ride—or it may not. A computer randomly generates each ride's sequence. You may be brought all the way back up to drop again, you may be brought just halfway up, or any combination could occur. This ride will be different each time you try it.

It's amazingly themed and conceived from queue to plummet. The outside of the building reaches 199 feet (60.6 meters) in height—that's sixteen feet taller than Cinderella Castle.

### Rock 'n' Roller Coaster Starring Aerosmith

*Fastpass+* This is the fastest coaster at Walt Disney World. It seems even faster because the whole thing is located in the dark.

In true Disney fashion, there is a bit of a story. The rock band Aerosmith has invited you to party with them. But first you have to get from one side of Los Angeles to the other during rush hour. You'll board a limo and be strapped in. Speakers on either side of your head will continue the story as you ride. You'll be treated to a lot of Aerosmith's music. ("A lot" is a reference to volume; there are actually five speakers per person.)

You won't have any time to get used to the limo because it will blast off on a journey. This is a launching steel coaster themed as a limo. There are several inversions as your limo driver attempts to avoid large fluorescent Hollywood icons. The music is well synchronized, and you'll be immersed in the action.

This is a fairly aggressive ride.

### Disney Junior—Live on Stage!

*Fastpass+* If there are any young fans of the Disney Channel with you, then check the Times Guide to see when this show is being performed. They'll get a chance to see all their friends from *Mickey Mouse Clubhouse, Sofia the First, Doc McStuffins,* and *Jake and the Never Land Pirates.*

Most people sit on a carpeted floor during the show.

### Star Tours—The Adventures Continue

*Fastpass+* This attraction takes place between the first two trilogies. For fans, that's between *Revenge of the Sith* and *A New Hope.*

This is a simulator ride where you'll be strapped onto a StarSpeeder that moves with images on a screen. There are more than fifty different versions of this ride; it will be different each time you try it.

The effects are spectacular. You'll run into many of your favorite characters and be treated to that fantastic score from John Williams.

### Voyage of the Little Mermaid

*Fastpass +* This seventeen-minute live show is presented at scheduled times. Check the daily Times Guide for show times. If you get a Fastpass+ for it, you won't have to arrive as early to find a place to sit as you'll be escorted to a reserved seat.

Puppets and live actors present Ariel's story with all the music you'd expect. Prince Eric and evil sea witch

Ursula make appearances. There are some great special effects, including a thunderstorm at sea.

### Walt Disney—One Man's Dream

Visit this part-show, part-museum to learn more about the life and work of Walt Disney. First, you'll tour a museum of artifacts that includes Walt's second-grade desk, lots of models for Disneyland attractions, and costumes from live-action Disney films.

For the second part of the experience, you'll sit in a theater to view a fifteen-minute film, *In Walt's Words*. There's a lot of history here, and it's all quite inspirational. This is actually a very nice place to recharge your batteries for the day—and for life.

### The Great Movie Ride

*Fastpass+* The park's original marquee attraction is located inside Grauman's Chinese Theatre. But be advised: there are a lot of rumors that the Great Movie Ride could close at any time to make room for a Mickey Mouse-themed attraction.

If it's still there when you visit, it's worth your time to ride; it's a well-done attraction for everyone who loves going to the movies. First, you'll wander around the lobby of the theater as you look at costumes and props from famous films. There is a priceless gown worn by Scarlett O'Hara in *Gone With the Wind* among many other items.

Eventually, you'll board a large vehicle for a trip through the movies. Here's where the audio-animatronic magic begins. Each room you encounter showcases iconic scenes from classic movies. You'll see Gene Kelley with his umbrella, Julie Andrews and Dick Van Dyke as Mary Poppins and Bert, Harrison Ford as Indiana Jones, and many others. For many people, the highlight of the ride is an enormous set from *The Wizard of Oz*, filled with plenty of animatronics.

There are a few scenes that may scare children. You'll visit the spaceship from *Alien* complete with the aliens. Also, a certain ill-mannered green woman from the west makes an appearance during *The Wizard of Oz*.

Everything concludes with a montage of the films that made Hollywood great.

### Toy Story Midway Mania!
*Fastpass+* This interactive attraction is quite popular for all ages; expect long lines if you don't have a Fastpass+.

You'll don 3-D glasses and ride through a crazy midway. During each scene, *Toy Story* characters will help you shoot at various targets. The scenes are all based on historic midway games like shooting at rubber ducks or plates.

At the ride's conclusion, you'll be presented with your score. You can also check a screen to see how your score compares to others. But the main point of this attraction is to notice all the intricate theming and delightful characters. Don't worry too much about your score and just enjoy all the organized chaos.

### Muppet Vision 3-D

*Fastpass+* If you love the Muppets, then you must see this show. If you don't love the Muppets, then—who doesn't love the Muppets?

This show has it all. After a short preshow, you'll be seated in an auditorium. You're there to watch the unveiling of Muppet Lab's newest invention: Waldo, the Spirit of 3-D. In typical Muppet fashion, chaos soon ensues, and the inevitable chickens start flying around.

In all seriousness, this really is quite a show. Every tool in Disney's toolbox is on display: film, live action, animatronics, sets, costumes, and special effects. There is enough detail in the design of the theater alone to occupy your time.

Including the preshow, expect to spend thirty minutes here.

### Indiana Jones Epic Stunt Spectacular

*Fastpass+* This show is the last remaining of the "this is how they do it in Hollywood" experiences that used to occupy most of the park. However, the fate of this show is unknown. It's been taking a break for most of 2016; it may or may not be showing in 2017.

When playing, guests are shown how various stunts are accomplished in adventure films. There are some lavish backdrops and, of course, lots of action from the live-action performers. The extras are chosen from the audience.

There are enough effects to keep you occupied during the thirty-minute duration. Check the daily Times Guide to see when, and if, Indiana Jones is in the park.

### For the First Time in Forever: A Frozen Sing-Along Celebration

*Fastpass+* "Zip-a-Dee-Doo-Dah" from Splash Mountain and "it's a small world" are well known for their ability to stay in your head. I'd like to argue that there's a third song that is equally difficult to forget. It's a song so memorable that you just won't be able to "let it go."

Actually, I really like what Disney has done with this *Frozen* show. It's not a retelling of the story as at Disney California Adventure. Instead, the royal storytellers of Arendelle arrive on the scene. It's their job to get everyone singing in anticipation of the arrival of Queen Elsa. The words for the songs will appear on a huge screen; all you have to do is follow the bouncing snowflake. But most parents can probably sing these in their sleep.

As the various songs are sung, live actors portraying characters from the film make an appearance. You'll meet Anna and Hans, along with animated versions of Sven and Olaf. The grand finale includes an appearance from Queen Elsa and her famous song. Seriously, though, there are some fine singers at Walt Disney World, and Elsa always gives me goosebumps.

Oh, and it snows. A lot!

### Dining in Disney's Hollywood Studios
*Quick Service*

There are a number of quick-service places to grab a bite to eat. However, many of them are in a state of flux. This park is changing a lot, and it's easier to close and/or change quick-service options than it is to tamper with table-service restaurants.

It's a fairly safe bet that the **ABC Commissary** will remain open, although it may change its name. Right now, the commissary is the largest café in the park. This place serves hamburgers, salads, sandwiches, and desserts. While you dine, ads for various ABC shows are displayed on big screens. (Disney owns ABC.)

*Table Service*

**Mama Melrose's Ristorante Italiano:** Homemade pastas and other Italian offerings are available here at a moderate price. Reservations are highly recommended.

**Sci-Fi Dine-In Theater:** Dine in a 1950s car while you watch sci-fi B-movies on a large screen. The choices include hamburgers, shakes, sandwiches, and salads. You'll either love or hate this place. I love it!

**Hollywood Brown Derby:** A recreation of the famous (and former) restaurant in Hollywood; even the caricatures on the walls were painstakingly recreated from the original. The Cobb salad was invented at the Hollywood location in the 1930s by a man named Bob Cobb. It's really very good.

**'50s Prime Time Café:** One of the more famous, and infamous, dining locations in all of Walt Disney World. Here, you'll sit in small 1950s kitchens. Everything looks authentic, and, depending upon your age, you may be transported to another time. Even the small televisions are authentic. The waiters at the '50s Prime Time Café are as much actors as they are food servers. They will play the part of Mom, Dad, Brother, or Sister as they take your order and deliver your food. They will make sure that you behave and eat all your vegetables. There are many staples of American home cooking to choose from. This place is famous for its shakes.

**Hollywood & Vine:** An art-deco restaurant that offers a character breakfast with the Disney Junior characters. Lunch is a character meal that's a buffet; dinner is just a buffet without the characters.

**PizzeRizzo:** Rizzo is the Muppet rat featured in *The Muppet's Christmas Carol.* Apparently, he's also an Italian chef. Rizzo serves pizza and other Italian food in a Muppety atmosphere.

### Parades, Evening Shows, and Special Events

"Stay tuned" has become the motto of Disney's Hollywood Studios. Nowhere is that more apparent than in the entertainment category. Currently, there are no parades and limited holiday events. Hopefully, we'll see some of those things return with the opening of Star Wars Land and Toy Story Land. (*Toy Story* has a natural tie-in to Christmas. *Star Wars*...not so much. Yes, I'm making an inference to the infamous *Star Wars Holiday Television Special*.)

### Fantasmic!

*Fastpass+*  The evening show at Disney's Hollywood Studios is the fantastic Fantasmic! It's similar to the version at Disneyland, but here guests are seated in the Hollywood Hills Amphitheater. Sometimes it's nice to have a seat.

You'll watch all the dazzling effects as Mickey attempts to quell the villains so that his good dreams can return. There is the giant dragon of Maleficent that battles Mickey with lots of fire. The show features heavily in the pyrotechnics and water effects. In the end, Mickey does prevail with the help of a host of Disney friends.

The amphitheater opens ninety minutes before show time, and there will already be people in line. If you have a Fastpass+, you can enter the theater later and sit in a special section. Also, several restaurants in the park offer special Fantasmic! Dinner Packages. For the packages, you'll eat dinner at a preassigned time. When you complete dinner, your server will give you a ticket to a reserved viewing location.

### Star Wars: A Galactic Spectacular

*Fastpass+*  In front of Grauman's Chinese Theatre is the park's version of a fireworks spectacular. Projections, pyrotechnics, and lots of fireworks are used in this *Star Wars*-themed show.

For me, the best part of the experience is the outstanding music. John Williams's score for the entire franchise is so dynamic that it doesn't need fireworks. But they don't hurt it either. It's a spectacular combination of music and visual effects.

Any place where you can see the front of the theater and large screens on either side is a good place to stand. With a Fastpass+, you can get access to a reserved viewing area. Also, there is a fireworks dessert party where guests eat special *Star Wars*-themed desserts before they view the show. You can reserve the dessert party at disneyworld.disney.go.com.

### *Jingle Bell, Jingle BAM! Holiday Party*

During Christmas, the *Star Wars*-themed fireworks show is replaced with Jingle Bell, Jingle BAM! Again, arrive early and choose a place where you can see the front of Grauman's Chinese Theatre and the screens on either side.

Wayne and Lanny, the elves from *Disney's Prep & Landing* holiday special, guide guests through a spectacular montage of famous Disney Christmas scenes. You'll spot iconic moments from *Mickey's Christmas Carol, Beauty and the Beast,* and *The Nightmare Before Christmas.* As the scenes unfold on the screens, fireworks erupt overhead to the choreographed strains of gorgeous melodies. And, of course, it snows a lot.

Similar to the *Star Wars* fireworks show, there is a Jingle Bell, Jingle BAM! Dessert Party prior to each performance. After enjoying a plethora of decadent holiday desserts, you'll get access to a reserved viewing area for the show.

## Disney's Animal Kingdom

Disney's Animal Kingdom is geographically the largest theme park on the planet. It's more than five times the size of the Magic Kingdom and twice as large as Epcot. But don't worry about having enough stamina to visit such a big place. Much of the space is not for you—it's for other types of mammals, reptiles, and amphibians.

This park is gorgeous. You could spend an entire day just roaming through the lush landscaping without even seeing one animal. But you'll never forget about animals entirely because they are the focus of this park. In fact, Disney is adamant that this is an animals-first, people-second environment. Disney's Animal Kingdom is located in the far corner of Walt Disney Resort; it's the farthest from any other theme park. The reason is simple: zookeepers involved with the design process didn't want fireworks from the other parks to spook the animals. In 2017, Disney's Animal Kingdom will, for the first time, offer a nighttime show. However, this show will not feature any pyrotechnics or loud noises.

There are close to two thousand individual animals here—and zero iron bars. Cages were not part of the original design and philosophy. You may even get a bit jealous at how much nicer these animals live than you do at home.

Everyone will arrive by bus or car to this park. Even guests of the nearby lodge are not able to walk. Once again, the surrounding area belongs to the lions and elephants, who don't necessarily want you taking a shortcut through their home. If you arrive by car, trams will whisk you from the parking lot to the entrance plaza.

Right on the entrance plaza you'll find the park's first restaurant, the **Rainforest Café.** You can access this establishment either with or without a pass to Disney's Animal Kingdom. The Rainforest Café is a national chain that you might be familiar with back home. As you dine, you'll be immersed among and entertained by animatronic animals. Periodically, it even storms in the café. There is another location at Disney Springs; both locations are popular, and reservations are highly recommended.

At the entrance plaza, you'll pass through security and bag check. After scanning your MagicBand, you'll find yourself facing something strange: a theme-park entrance with no gift shops in sight.

**The Oasis**

Whoever thought of the idea for the Oasis should be given a medal. There is no better way to acclimate guests to the world of animals then to give them the chance to meander through nature. There are no shops, restaurants, or even restrooms in the Oasis. But there are plenty of flowers, streams, and waterfalls.

There are several paths crossing through the Oasis. If you're heading for an attraction, you can stay straight and keep your eye on that big tree up ahead. But if you have time, take one of the circular routes that wind around a bit more. The entire park is designed to make it seem like guests are walking among the animals. The Oasis is no exception.

The vegetation is thick, but you'll be able to spot deer, anteaters, birds, and many other smaller animals. Remember to look down, up, and all around as the animals will not always be right in front of you.

Eventually, regardless of the path you choose, you'll cross a bridge and step onto an island. You'll know you're in the right place when you see an enormous tree in front of you.

**Discovery Island**
Discovery Island serves as the hub of Disney's Animal Kingdom. It unites all the other lands and offers the most food options. The Tree of Life, the giant symbol of the park, sits in the middle of Discovery Island.

*The Tree of Life*
The symbol of Disney's Animal Kingdom is the massive Tree of Life. At 145 feet (44.2 meters), it can be seen from anywhere within Discovery Island. Although the tree

isn't living, it has more life to it than any other tree in the park.

Intricately carved into the truck and limbs are hundreds of animals. Disney states that around 350 different animals make an appearance somewhere on the tree. It's a dramatic work of art that deserves all the praise it gets.

However, it's at night when the tree really comes alive. **Tree of Life Awakenings** occur several times each night that the park is open. Check the daily Times Guide for the exact times. When the show begins, projection lights illuminate the animals and make them seem to move. It's really quite amazing to see the lion leap and critters crawl all over the tree.

### Discovery Island Trails

To get a close-up look at the tree, and you'll want to, take a hike on the Discovery Island Trails. You can meander on the trails and get close to the Tree of Life. But the carved animals on the tree aren't the only ones you'll see here.

Keep your eyes open to all your surroundings because you never know what the zookeepers have planned. You may get a close view of an exotic bird or a small mammal as a zookeeper provides an informative summary.

### It's Tough to Be a Bug

*Fastpass+* You can actually go inside the Tree of Life! Yes, it's not just a work of art; it's also a building. Inside and underneath is an auditorium that seats over four hundred guests. You can wander around the tree's root system as you make your way to the show.

It's Tough to Be a Bug is a 4-D show. This means that you'll wear 3-D glasses as you learn about all sorts of bugs. The fourth D occurs when you smell and even feel the bugs. Things will touch you during this show; none of them are real, but, nonetheless, be advised that you will feel as if spiders are really crawling on you. This is great fun for some but terrifying for others.

### Winged Encounters—The Kingdom Takes Flight

Near the Tree of Life, Winged Encounters is a bird show unlike all others. Typically, bird shows focus on birds of prey. But here, the show is all about tropical birds and their amazing colors.

One of Disney's pet projects (pun intended) is a program to save macaw habitats in South America. Six types of the beautiful macaw are featured in this show. You'll see some of nature's most vibrant colors as they spread their massive wings. The birds will soar about the Tree of Life, making an unforgettable image.

After the show, its stars will stick around, and you can ask their keepers any questions you may have. You'll also learn about Disney's program to save them.

### Shops of Discovery Island

The shops here focus on safari clothes and official theme-park merchandise. **Island Mercantile** is the largest shop in the park with all the souvenirs and such. **Disney Outfitters** is the place for safari clothing.

### Dining in Discovery Island
**Flame Tree Barbecue:** A quick-service barbecue joint that smells as good as it tastes.

**Pizzafari:** Pizza, pasta, and salads are offered quick service.

**Creature Comforts:** It's actually a Starbuck's.

### Africa
You can't really have a discussion about animals without devoting a lot of attention to one continent: Africa. Disney spared no expense in duplicating the architecture and terrain of this amazing place. This is where you'll see the largest animals in the park.

### Harambe
Harambe, meaning "welcome" in Swahili, is Disney's authentic recreation of an East African village. The theming here is unbelievable. Every detail was thought about from loose tiles on the roofs to the display racks in the shops. For several years, imagineers traveled to and photographed real African villages.

There are a few restaurants and several shops. Much of the food and merchandise is authentic to what you'd find in Africa. This is the village you'll stop at on your way to the animals.

### Kilimanjaro Safaris

*Fastpass+* This one attraction is bigger than the entire Magic Kingdom! Kilimanjaro Safaris is the park's premier experience, and it's extremely popular. Try to grab a Fastpass+ when the opportunity arises.

You'll board a safari vehicle and take a twenty-five-minute journey around the savannah. Your driver and guide will point out the animals that you pass. In the vehicle, there is a sign mounted above you with pictures to help identify what you see.

Expect all the stars of *The Lion King* to make an appearance but in their unanimated realness: warthogs, elephants, lions, hippos, giraffes, zebras, rhinos, crocodiles, and various forms of antelope. The animals wander freely, and some will get quite close to the vehicle. (But don't worry about the carnivores. Disney does a great job of making it appear that they roam free; in actuality, it's impossible for a lion and a zebra to get near each other.)

Remember that all the animals on the safari are real. There are no animatronics here. Consequently, each trip will be different, and there is no guarantee that you'll see your favorites. The animals are out all day, but just like in Africa, they are more active in the early morning and evening. For the first time, night safaris became an option in 2016. Google the sunset time for when you'll be in the park, and grab a Fastpass+ near that time.

The safari vehicles are actually being driven; there is no smooth track. Expect to be jostled around a bit as you cross over bridges and pot holes.

### Festival of the Lion King

*Fastpass+* This is the first of two unbelievable shows at Disney's Animal Kingdom (the other is Finding Nemo: the Musical). In fact, these two shows alone are worth the price of admission. They are as good as many of the things I've seen in New York.

Festival of the Lion King is part live performance and part giant puppetry. The audience sits around the stage, which makes you feel like you are involved in all the action happening around you. And by "around you," I mean all around you. The enormous cast fills every space of the theater, including the air.

Festival of the Lion King is not a retelling of the story. Instead, it uses the film's famous songs to celebrate Simba and his bravery. The live singing is extraordinary. You won't likely see such dancing and acrobatics anywhere else.

The theater is quite large; it seats almost fifteen hundred guests. But everyone in the park will want to see this show. You must arrive forty-five minutes before show time to get a place. Or, if you have a Fastpass+, you'll be escorted to a reserved section.

### Rafiki's Planet Watch

You can't walk to Rafiki's Planet Watch; it's a bit of a journey. You'll catch your ride at the **Harambe Train Station.**

The expertly themed **Wildlife Express** will transport you via train from Harambe to Rafiki's.

On the way, you'll see some of the behind-the-scenes action. A narrator will point out the various facilities where the animals rest when they're not in the park. After you arrive at Rafiki's Planet Watch Station, it's a brief walk to the exhibits.

This is truly the educational center of Disney's Animal Kingdom. Here is where veterinarians and zoo-keepers conduct research and care for the animals. Part of the park's mission is to improve the lives of animals in their natural habitats. This is where some of the work to meet that goal is performed.

There is a discovery trail, a sort of petting zoo, and a couple of multimedia presentations. All of this has the aim of education and conservation.

When you are finished, you'll have to take the train back to Harambe as you really don't want to walk through the lion habitat.

### *Pangani Forest Exploration Trail*
I can't get enough of this park's exploration trails; there's another one coming up in Asia. I love that you can walk at your own pace and take as much time as you want observing the animals.

The Pangani Forest Exploration Trail focuses on African animals. There is an aviary where the birds are permitted to fly all over. You'll also see many types of African fish and the extremely large hippo tank. (You can watch the hippos through underwater glass—perhaps the most graceful animal you'll see all day.)

Keep walking, because after you cross a suspension bridge, you'll see a truly amazing sight: gorillas in a seemingly natural environment. There can be a crowd watching the gorillas. Just take your time and you'll get a good vantage point.

### Shops of Africa

**Mombasa Marketplace** and **Ziwani Traders** offer African-themed merchandise. Many of the items are imported. **Zuri's Sweet Shop** sells animal-themed candy and spice rubs from Africa. There is a small shop near Rafiki's Planet Watch offering souvenirs and toys.

### Dining in Africa

**Tusker House:** A large buffet with table-service character meals. Reservations are highly suggested for any of the Rivers of Light packages (explained at the end of this section).

**Harambe Fruit Market:** Quick-service fruits and snacks are offered.

**Harambe Market:** Here you'll find African-style street food offered quick service.

**Kusafiri Coffee Shop and Bakery:** There's always a line for this quick-service bakery.

**Tamu Tamu Refreshments:** A quick-service café with lots of curry.

## Asia

The lush jungles of southeast Asia and India are represented here. Throw in a salute to the Himalayas, and you'll have this well-rounded Asian experience. As with Africa, the architecture and landscaping are authentic and inviting.

### Maharajah Jungle Trek

The second of the exploration trails, Maharajah Jungle Trek is another chance to explore on your own. No Fastpass+ is required to meander the trails and search for animals.

After viewing the colorful birds and reptiles, most guests are on a mission to find the tigers. One of the most gorgeous animals in the entire park, the Asian tigers are regal and a lot larger than you'd expect. The tigers are free to explore their lush habitat that even includes the ruins of an ancient Thai temple.

However, even though the tigers are what people come to see, they're not what people end up talking about on the way out. That honor belongs to the giant fruit bats. The bats are giant. They fly around. There is no glass. To summarize: giant bats fly around without a glass barrier! Apparently, this type of bat is not at all interested in humans—at least that's what the nearby zookeeper says.

### Kali River Rapids

*Fastpass+* This is the typical river raft ride but themed as only Disney can. Twelve guests sit together in giant rafts that are sent hurtling down the Kali River.

Also in true Disney style, there is a story that aims to teach a lesson. On this ride, you're exploring the rainforest while on the lookout for unscrupulous loggers. Eventually, the logs do cause some problems for your raft.

You'll get soaked on this ride. Use the poncho from your theme-park satchel. Very few people leave this ride without dripping water everywhere.

### Expedition Everest

*Fastpass+* The only attraction you can see from the parking lot is Expedition Everest. This recreation of the tallest mountain on earth is 199 feet (60.6 meters). It's tied with the Tower of Terror as the tallest point in Walt Disney World. The mountain is beautifully portrayed with just the right proportions. It makes an excellent photograph.

Guests begin as they walk through the Himalayan village of Serka Zong. After a themed queuing area, you'll board an old train that was meant to deliver tea. Of course, something goes wrong, and part of the track is missing. You'll go forward, backward, up, down, and through. You'll meet the famous yeti.

This ride is not for the faint of heart. It's a major roller coaster with all of the associated thrills and screams.

### Flights of Wonder

The bird show in Discovery Island focuses on tropical macaws. This bird show showcases predatory raptors (except there are some chickens, which seem more like Muppets than birds).

You'll sit in a large outdoor amphitheater as the birds fly about. The show lasts about twenty minutes and is quite educational. Check the daily Times Guide for show times.

### Finding Nemo—The Musical

*Fastpass+* Situated between Asia and Dinoland USA is Theater in the Wild, the indoor home to Finding Nemo—The Musical. This is the second of the park's unforgettable live theatrical events.

The forty-minute show retells the story of Disney-Pixar's *Finding Nemo*. You may remember that the original film is not a musical. Songs were composed for this version by Robert Lopez (who eventually went on to write songs for another Disney project, a little-known film called *Frozen*).

You'll see all the characters from the film as they "swim" in the air around you. Many innovative puppets are used to accomplish all this action. There are some beautiful moments when you'll feel that you are in the ocean.

The theater is air-conditioned, and you should plan to arrive at least thirty minutes before show time.

### Shops in Asia

**Mandala Gifts** is the place to go for the tea lover in your life. Authentic Asian merchandise can be found at

**Bhaktapur Market**, and **Serka Zong Bazaar** is the souvenir shop.

### Dining in Asia

**Yak & Yeti:** A popular table-service restaurants with Asian food. Reservations are recommended.

**Royal Anandapur Tea Company:** Quick-service cold and hot teas might be the best drink you have all week.

**Yak & Yeti Food Cafés :** A quick-service version of the table-service restaurant.

## DinoLand USA

Don't expect to wander into a paleontological dig. The theme of DinoLand USA is that the dinosaurs never went extinct; they just opened a roadside carnival. Another part of the early mission of Disney's Animal Kingdom was to salute animals past, present, and mythological. This is the salute to animals past. (The mythological presence in the park has never come to fruition; I'll write more about this in a bit.)

### Chester & Hester's Dino-Rama

This is a land within a land that best represents the roadside carnival atmosphere. There are two rides here and a number of midway games.

### Primeval Whirl

*Fastpass+* This is a kiddie coaster with spinning cars. With that said, it's more intense than you think. Once again, I can go on Expedition Everest without a problem, but one ride on this whirl will make me hurl. There's a lot of spinning going on.

### Triceratops Spin

This is Dumbo but with dinosaurs. Enough said.

### Fossil Fun Games

These are all the midway games you've seen before but with a Jurassic twist. You can Whac-a-Packycephalosaur or try your luck at the Bronto-score (basketball game). There are several others. It's $3 to play each game, and, yes, there are prizes.

### The Boneyard

You don't have to wait in a line to explore this area. It's actually a nicely themed dinosaur-bone playground. There are slides, giant footprints, and lots of other things to explore. The bridge that connects the two portions of the Boneyard is labeled the Olden Gate Bridge!

### Dinosaur

*Fastpass+* The only dark ride at Disney's Animal Kingdom, Dinosaur is an immersive attraction. After hearing from Bill Nye the Science Guy, you'll board a vehicle to rescue an iguanodon. On the way, you'll run into lots of other dinosaurs in all their audio-animatronic realness. Some are quite scary.

There's also a meteor storm and other special effects. You will eventually find the iguanodon—it's not as cute as you were thinking.

Please note, even though the whole area seems tailor made for kids, this attraction can be frightening. Also, the ride vehicle moves around a lot.

### Shops in DinoLand USA
Two shops offer all the dinosaur stuff you'll ever need: **Chester & Hester's Dinosaur Treasures** and the **Dino Institute Shop.**

### Dining in DinoLand USA
**Dino-Bite Snacks:** Ice cream and cookies are offered quick service.

**Restaurantosaurus:** Quick-service burgers and such are served in a themed atmosphere.

**Trilo-Bites:** Turkey legs, beans, and cornbread are offered quick service.

## Parades, Evening Shows, and Special Events
### Rivers of Light
*Fastpass+* Another of Disney's unbelievable nighttime shows, Rivers of Light takes place on the Discovery River Lagoon. You must secure a place at least an hour before show time. Or get a Fastpass+ for a special viewing location. There are also some dining packages with priority viewing at disneyworld.disney.go.com. Guests sit in an amphitheater along the lagoon for the presentation. Just note that in order to get a seat without a Fastpass+ or dining package, you must arrive early. The amphitheater has a separate entrance for guests that do not have priority

access. The lines for these standard seats are long—this show is very popular.

There aren't any fireworks during this show since they frighten the animals. But that's the only thing missing, and the rest is so good you won't miss the pyrotechnics. Water is used artfully and functionally to create beautiful shapes. There are projections courtesy of the Disneynature films.

From the depths of the lagoon, huge lotus flowers emerge with live performers concealed within. There are floating vessels, hundreds of lanterns, and a temple. Everything is choreographed. You will probably cry.

After the show and between Tree of Life Awakenings, you can partake in the **Discovery Island Carnivale.** You'll be invited to party with lots of performers in a street dance atmosphere.

### *Pandora—the World of Avatar*

Opening on May 27, 2017, Pandora—the World of Avatar brings the film to Disney's Animal Kingdom. There's been a lot of Disney fan reaction to this—most of it not good. People are concerned that:

1. Few people care about the film.
2. It doesn't belong in Disney's Animal Kingdom but rather at Hollywood Studios.

Perhaps this is a way of incorporating some mythological, or fictional, animals into the park. (Remember the park's early mission?) There may be another connection as *Avatar* contained a heavy theme of protecting natural resources.

Disney has announced some type of river-based attraction, flying-based attraction, and superb theming. It's been under construction for a long time—the film came out in 2009. I guess this is another place where we'll all have to stay tuned.

## Typhoon Lagoon/Blizzard Beach

Florida is the only Disney Resort on the planet that has a Disney water park—and they have two! Walt Disney World is host to two world-class water parks. Both are highly themed with all the attractions you'd expect, and both are open for most of the year.

Periodically, one of the two parks will close for maintenance (during a slow time), but there is always at least one water park open. Another great feature is that when a hotel pool is closed for maintenance, guests of that hotel get to visit a water park for free.

You must have a water-park pass in order to enter. Normally, these passes will be stored on your waterproof MagicBand. For more information, please see the section about tickets earlier in this chapter.

## Typhoon Lagoon

Disney's Typhoon Lagoon opened in 1989 and has expanded many times. The imagineers' back story of the park is that a small resort village in the Pacific was hit by a typhoon. At the same time, there was an earthquake and a volcano. (Why would anyone go to this resort?) Consequently, with their village in ruins, the people decided to just embrace the disaster and open a water park. The theme of Typhoon Lagoon is natural disaster ruins a resort paradise. The theme is better than it sounds and works well.

**Mount Mayday** is the volcano that hovers above the water park. Somehow, the waves perched a fishing boat on the volcano. The Miss Tilly is sort of stuck up there, and she blows her steam every thirty minutes. The rest of the water park involves attractions cleverly disguised as ruined pieces of the resort village.

The centerpiece of Typhoon Lagoon is a large (three-million-gallon) swimming lagoon and wave pool called **Surf Pool.** There is a water coaster, **Crush 'n' Gusher**, and three speed slides named **Humunga Kowabunga.** A twenty-one-hundred-foot (640-meter) lazy river called **Castaway Creek** offers guests a relaxing journey.

There is a series of other waterslides (some require tubes) and three body slides. **Ketchakiddee Creek** is a children's splash pad and play area. **Shark Reef,** a feature you rarely see at other water parks, is an area where guests can snorkel over a coral reef. Children must be accompanied by an adult. And, yes, there are sharks in the reef, but they are extremely tame.

Buses from all Disney hotels make a stop at Typhoon Lagoon, usually on the same route as Disney Springs.

There are plenty of food options, all quick service, and a couple of shops. If you're worried that you've forgotten something at your hotel, the shops will usually carry it and are stocked with swimsuits, towels, and sunscreen.

A note about sunscreen: People close to me know that I can never write anything about water parks without including at least one paragraph about sunscreen. I am a sunscreen fanatic. Please, please, please wear sunscreen. The sun in Florida is intense, even during the winter months. Don't risk ruining your vacation with a painful sunburn. But more than that, skin cancer is disfiguring and deadly.

Restrooms and locker rooms with showers are available inside the water park. There are also lockers for rent. You can rent a towel for two dollars. Tubes for the various slides are complimentary, as are life jackets.

## Blizzard Beach

Disney's Blizzard Beach is surely the most uniquely themed water park you'll ever see. As a Minnesotan, I feel quite at home. The Disney story of the park is that a freak blizzard hit central Florida. The storm was so bad that it dropped a ton of snow on Walt Disney World. So Disney imagineers, not wanting to sit around during all the cold weather, decided to build a ski resort on the property. However, they didn't move fast enough, and all that snow started to melt. Now, what does an imagineer do when the ski runs and bobsled tracks start to run with water? Well, you open a water park.

The symbol of the park is **Mount Gushmore.** The mountain even has a chairlift! It's all expertly themed, and those of you from warmer climates will enjoy being able to frolic in a winter wonderland without freezing.

Above Mount Gushmore, **Summit Plummet** is one of the fastest speed slides in the world. It rises to a height of 120 feet (36.5 meters). Also located on the mountain are several other slides, some of which require tubes.

**Melt-away Bay,** a large wave pool at the base of Mount Gushmore, occupies more than an acre. There is an area for teenagers called the **Ski Patrol Training Camp** that contains its own attractions. **Tike's Peak** is the place for smaller kids to splash around a snow castle. **Toboggan Racers,** one the park's most popular attractions, is an eight-lane waterslide with a few hills.

All Disney transportation buses make a stop at Blizzard Beach, usually on their Disney's Animal Kingdom route. As with Typhoon Lagoon, you must have valid park admission to enter. Parking at both water parks is free. There are plenty of quick-service food options, all of them with a winter theme. If it's an usually cold Florida day, **Frosty the Joe Man** sells coffee and hot chocolate.

Restrooms with showers are located near the entrance. The other restrooms in the park include dressing rooms. Lockers are available for rent, as are towels. Life jackets and inner tubes are free.

A repetitious note about sunscreen: People close to me know that I can never write anything about water parks without including at least one paragraph about sunscreen. I am a sunscreen fanatic. Please, please, please wear sunscreen. The sun in Florida is intense, even during the winter months. Don't risk ruining your vacation with a painful sunburn. But more than that, skin cancer is disfiguring and deadly.

# Disney Springs

The area formerly known as Downtown Disney has a new name and plenty of new appeal. Disney Springs, Walt Disney World's massive entertainment district, occupies no less than 120 acres of property. It's as big as a theme park and contains nearly as many attractions. The entire Disney Springs is free to explore—no pass, ticket, or MagicBand required.

Parking is free, and all Disney transportation buses stop here. There is also boat transportation from nearby Disney hotels (Saratoga Springs, Old Key West, Port Orleans Riverside, and Port Orleans French Quarter). Those staying in a Buena Vista Boulevard hotel can walk here. Disney Springs is normally open daily from 10:00 a.m. to midnight.

Disney Springs is divided into four districts: **Marketplace**, **Town Center**, the **Landing**, and **West Side**. Each district carries a slightly different theme and design, but the tenants aren't grouped in any special way. The use of districts is more an easy way to locate places than it is a division of offerings.

The busiest movie theater in Florida is located here. **AMC Disney Springs** has twenty-four screens—some of them with food and beverage service. There is a luxury bowling alley called **Splitsville**, a **House of Blues**, and a **Cirque du Soleil** show called *La Nouba*. On top of all this, Disney Springs is host to **Orlando Harley-Davidson**, the **Lego Imagination Center**, and the enormous **NBA Experience**.

Shopping is one of the main draws here (the other is eating). Disney Springs is literally full of shops. Some of them you can find back at your local mall, like **Basin** and **Sunglass Hut.** Other stores are much rarer: **Arribas Bros., Eric McKenna's Bakery, Sound Lion,** and **Curl by Sammy Duvall.**

Of course, many people go to Disney Springs to fulfill their Disney shopping fantasy. **The World of Disney** is a ginormous store with everything Disney you could ever imagine. Much of the merchandise from the parks is available here. But if you can't find it at World of Disney, it may be at one of the other Disney-centric shops. **Disney's Days of Christmas** is the largest Disney Christmas store on earth. **Tren-D** is a modern boutique with the latest Disney apparel. **D Street** is the Disney pop-culture store, and **The Art of Disney** is a higher-end collectible shop. If you need a Disney-themed phone case, head to **D-Tech on Demand.**

And lastly, there is the food. There is no shortage of dining options in Disney Springs. And just because it's not technically a theme park doesn't mean you don't need reservations. Many of Disney Springs's table-service restaurants are extremely popular and need to be booked well in advance. You can use the same system to make reservations here as you do for the other resort locations.

Everything for every budget is available to eat and drink. Affordable quick-service options include **Earl of Sandwich**, **Wetzel's Pretzels**, **Wolfgang Puck Express**, and a **Starbucks**. Then there are much more expensive establishments such as **Morimoto Asia**, the **Boathouse**, **Fulton's Crab House**, and **Wolfgang Puck Grand Café Dining Room**.

Families especially enjoy the themed **Rainforest Café** and its cousin, **T-Rex Café: A Prehistoric Family Adventure.** Both of these require reservations.

There are many, many more attractions, shops, and restaurants at Disney Springs. Fortunately, it's easy to discover what's available today inside the entertainment district. Visit disneysprings.com for the most complete list of tenants.

## Area Sights outside Disney

Central Florida is a vacationer's dream. Orlando sits almost in the middle of the Florida peninsula. It's about eighty miles from Walt Disney World to the Gulf of Mexico and about sixty miles to the Atlantic coast. You could easily occupy weeks at just Walt Disney World alone, but in case you want to burst that Disney bubble for a bit, here are the distances to other area attractions. Because the Disney property is so large, these distances are calculated from the Magic Kingdom parking lot.

| | |
|---|---|
| Universal Studios Florida | 16 miles |
| SeaWorld Orlando | 12 miles |
| Busch Gardens Tampa | 73 miles |
| Legoland Florida Resort | 37 miles |
| Kennedy Space Center | 65 miles |
| Port Canaveral | 67 miles |
| Daytona Beach | 78 miles |
| Ringling Museum | 120 miles |
| St. Augustine, Florida | 130 miles |
| Lake Okeechobee | 106 miles |

# 4

## Tokyo Disney Resort

**A**MONG OTHER THINGS, Disney parks are known for cleanliness and excellent service. What happens when you combine Disney with the world's cleanest and most hospitable people? You get Tokyo Disney Resort, the magical place where everything always works. This is the most difficult park to write about because I love it so much and there are just not enough superlatives in the English language. Amazing, fantastic, unbelievable, extraordinary—all these apply and many more.

Even without Tokyo Disney Resort, Japan is a magical place. As an American, I find it refreshing to see every single person take such pride in what he or she does. The people who clean your hotel room know what a vital and important job they are performing for the economy of Japan, and they clean the room in a way that reflects that knowledge. The person driving the train feels the same way about her job, as does the guy who works behind the counter at one of the many 7-Elevens.

I'd have to pee pretty badly before I'd use a public restroom inside a New York City subway station. But a train station restroom in Japan will be much cleaner than yours at home. The only time a public restroom on the Minneapolis rail network was that clean was the day it opened. Recently, I was on the train with my husband in Japan. A woman accidentally dropped a piece of paper as she was exiting the train. I told my husband that the paper would never make it to the next station. And it didn't. Less a minute after the doors closed, another passenger got up and picked up the paper. The whole country is about pride, honor, and thinking of the greater good.

All of the Disney parks have a reputation for perfection. With that said, you will still see things that don't work in California, Florida, Paris, Hong Kong, and Shanghai. One of the pirates might not be moving, maybe the Haunted Mansion's soundtrack stops unexpectedly, or a cash register on Main Street may be down for the day. None of these things happen at Tokyo Disney Resort. There is some Japanese imagineer who is not going to be able to sleep if the third French doll from the left isn't kicking her leg quite as high as the others.

If you're lost in Tokyo, someone will offer to help. But they won't just get you on the right track; they will physically bring you to where you want to be. I've had this happen to me many times. I asked a Japanese friend about it once, and she explained that it's such an honor to be able to help someone. She said that to be late to a meeting because you were helping a foreign traveler is a thing of pride.

If you lose your wallet on the train, just go to the nearest station. You'll get your wallet back—with all its original contents, including bills of Japanese yen. If you forget something in your hotel room after you check out, don't be surprised if there's a message on your phone about it. Return the message before you leave Japan, and the item will be sent, free of charge, to your next hotel. If you forget something in a restaurant, someone will soon come running after you.

In many ways, Walt's philosophy of theme-park operation was quite Japanese from the beginning. He wanted his first Disneyland to be a spotless park where the cast members went above and beyond to deliver pride-filled hospitality. Perhaps that's why Tokyo Disney Resort just works so well—it's the perfect combination of a philosophy and a people.

*Dreamlly's Disney Direction*

Tokyo Disney Resort Pros:

- It's very easy and quick to get between Tokyo and Tokyo Disney Resort.

- It's an amazingly clean resort with unbeatable hospitality.
- Everything that's supposed to function functions well.
- Tokyo DisneySea is the most unique of all the Disney Parks.
- The kitschy, over-the-top cuteness of Japanese culture fills the resort.

Tokyo Disney Resort Cons:

- The sprawling city of Tokyo is well visible from within the resort, which may ruin the illusion (Disney bubble) just a bit.
- Summer weather is unexpectedly humid, and the winter can be cold.
- Japan, in general, is not the most affordable country to visit.
- English is rarely used.

▲ ▲ ▲

# History

Walt's love of the railroad partly inspired him to build Disneyland. It's fitting that the history of Tokyo Disney Resort begins with trains.

Post–World War II Japan was a place of rebirth and rebuilding. At the time, the country was occupied by the United States, and much of it needed to be rebuilt.

It wasn't just the buildings and infrastructure that had been destroyed, but their government and basic way of life had also perished. Railroads were one way to get the people moving again.

Japan is a country with a high population, but it's also an island nation with limited space. Mass transit has always been important in Japan because there simply isn't enough room for highways and cars. To begin the postwar rebuilding process, the United States offered subsidies to Japanese companies that were interested in building rail lines. Many companies stepped forward.

Soon, Tokyo became a grid of rail lines owned and operated by private companies. Toei, JR, and Keisei were three of the many corporations that built commuter railroads. Even though they all had the goal of moving Japan forward, they were still companies in competition with each other for passengers.

The average Japanese worker took the train line that was most convenient, regardless of which train company owned it. But the leisure travelers had a choice. In the 1950s, it became quite a fad for railroad companies to build small amusement parks at the end of their lines. The thought was that people would use the trains to get to these parks at night and on the weekends. The railroad companies were getting the fares of the travelers, and they were getting whatever profits they could get from these small amusement parks. It was actually a fairly brilliant idea.

As the years went by, these large railroad companies started offering various perks to attract riders. Some of them even began to create special train lines for certain passengers. The people, and their government, became concerned that private rail might disrupt their business. A law was passed: every multistop railroad in Japan must be open to anyone in the public who wanted to buy a ticket to ride. This law still applies today. In fact, this is why Tokyo Disneyland does not have a train running around its perimeter. A multistop Disneyland Railroad would have to be made available to the public, even those who didn't want to buy admission to the park. Today, Tokyo Disneyland has a train that operates in Adventureland, but it only has one stop and is considered more of a ride than a train. (However, the Disney Resort monorail does make several stops, and it is open to the non-Disney public.)

In 1960, Chiharu Kawasaki, president of Keisei Electric Rail, gathered a few other executives and formed a new corporation called the Oriental Land Company, or OLC. The sole purpose of OLC was to reclaim and renovate land in Urayasu with the purpose of building a world-class theme park. Even though the project was barely an infant and most of the land was still beneath the sea, the Disney name had already been mentioned.

Urayasu was a small village located right on Tokyo Bay, about ten miles (sixteen kilometers) from Tokyo proper. It was built on flat, low-lying land that was often at the mercy of the tides. The village had been almost entirely destroyed by bombing in World War II. In 1960, it was primarily home to people in the fishing industry. OLC's idea was to reclaim a piece of land near Urayasu that was jutting out into the Pacific Ocean. They believed in this land because it offered beautiful ocean views and was close enough to a massive population that would take the train to get there.

After a few years of dealing with all the politics of obtaining the land, OLC began working on the reclamation in 1964. It took more than five years to complete. OLC soon began construction on some of the land for commercial purposes, but they left space for their dream theme park. OLC executives started to make frequent trips to Disneyland. In 1971, they also journeyed frequently to the brand-new Walt Disney World. Over the years, they met with several of Disney's top people, but Mickey Mouse was too busy with the Florida Project to become too involved in Tokyo.

By 1973, Walt Disney World's Magic Kingdom had been operating for two years. Disney was able to devote their attention to other projects. One of them was EPCOT Center. The other was the possibility of a Disneyland in Europe or Japan. Frank Stanek, the imagineer in charge of research and planning, was asked to consider the possibilities. After extensive research, he concluded that a park in Japan had a higher chance of being profitable than a park in Europe.

In December of 1974, Disney executives made their first official trip to Tokyo. The executives took a helicopter tour of Urayasu and immediately saw the potential of the site. But a project like this had never been done before. Neither side knew where to start. It took months of negotiations alone just to agree on how to agree.

Over the next six years, negotiations between Disney and OLC were sporadic. Sometimes it seemed like the park was imminent, and other times it was deemed impossible. There were lots of questions about designing, building, and managing a park. But the big question was: who should pay for it?

Disney was in over their heads with EPCOT Center, which was costing much more to build than anticipated. They were reluctant to spend even a dime in Japan. OLC had a difficult time securing bank financing when their main partner, Disney, didn't believe enough to take a risk.

Finally, an agreement was reached. It was agreed that OLC would finance, construct, and manage the park. Disney would design the park, provide intellectual property, and train cast members. In exchange for their expertise, Disney would be given 10 percent of admission revenue and 5 percent of merchandise and food sales. To this day, Disney does not own even one doorknob of Tokyo Disney Resort. (But don't cry too hard for Disney; they've made enough from Tokyo Disneyland's candy store alone to buy Daisy Duck several billion pairs of shoes.)

The agreement was signed in California on April 30, 1979. Tokyo Disneyland was going to become a reality.

As you can imagine, a lot of work progressed during the next four years. Constant travel occurred between

Anaheim and Tokyo as the two companies each took necessary steps to build the park. Some of the imagineers focused on park design. Others focused on which attractions would work and how to tweak them for Japanese guests. Still others were involved in the recruiting and training of thousands of Japanese cast members. Over seven thousand people were hired during these years.

One thing was clear: the Japanese wanted Cinderella's larger castle from Florida instead of Sleeping Beauty's more humble abode in California. The shape of Cinderella Castle began to rise on the land that once belonged to the sea. On a clear day in Urayasu, Mount Fuji is visible in the distance. As the spires of the castle were set, construction workers could see the amazing views that would soon be open to guests.

Tokyo Disneyland opened on April 15, 1983. Mickey Mouse, Minnie Mouse, Donald Duck, and all their friends were there to welcome guests to the first Disney park on international soil. And, yes, the characters spoke Japanese—and continue to do so at this park.

Attendance was well above predictions, and OLC began to make plans for the future. In fact, they were encouraging Disney to design new attractions as early as three months after the park's opening.

Over the next fifteen years, Tokyo Disneyland steadily added new lands and attractions. It soon became the third-most-visited theme park in the world, right after Disneyland and Walt Disney World's Magic Kingdom. Five official hotels were built to the rear of Tokyo

Disneyland, right on Tokyo Bay itself. These hotels are owned by OLC, but they were not built with any Disney association.

In 2000, the first Disney-branded hotel, Disney Ambassador Hotel, opened near the park's front entrance. The hotel opened in conjunction with a large shopping, dining, and entertainment district called Ikspiari. Somewhat similar to Downtown Disney in California, Ikspiari is free to visit. Ikspiari is adjacent to Tokyo Disneyland and connects to the main train station with service to central Tokyo.

One year later, the most exciting event in the history of Tokyo Disneyland occurred. A second theme park was added along with another Disney hotel and a monorail system. This was the largest expansion in the park's history. Now, Tokyo Disneyland was just one part of the officially named Tokyo Disney Resort.

Remember the amazing park that Disney designed for Long Beach, California? Well, here it is in Tokyo. On September 4, 2001, Tokyo DisneySea opened to the public. Tokyo DisneySea, with its attached Mira Costa Hotel, quickly became the fourth-most-visited theme park in the world. It is also the fastest theme park in the world to host ten million guests, which it did during just its three hundred and seventh day of operation.

A third Disney hotel, Tokyo Disneyland Hotel, opened on July 8, 2008. Its graceful design and warm colors can easily be seen from the passing Disney Resort Line monorail. A fourth hotel, Tokyo Disney Celebration

Hotel, opened on June 1, 2016. It's the most economical of the Disney properties, but it's not directly located at the resort and requires a shuttle ride.

OLC has a long history of reinvesting in Tokyo Disney Resort. A new port, Arendelle, is currently under construction at DisneySea and will be the home of Anna, Elsa, and all their *Frozen* friends. Tokyo DisneySea is also getting a Leonardo da Vinci-themed version of Soarin'. Over at Tokyo Disneyland, Fantasyland is in the midst of the largest expansion in the park's history with attractions inspired by *Beauty and the Beast.* Tomorrowland will be home to a new *Big Hero 6* attraction.

Japan hasn't just survived its post–WWII trauma—it has thrived. Tokyo Disney Resort is just one part of this amazing country and its incredible people. The future of Tokyo Disney Resort is only limited by the imagination and the ingenuity of the Japanese people. Expect great things.

# Travel Knowledge

*Arrival*

If you're already in Tokyo, it's quite simple to get to Tokyo Disney Resort. But all travelers should first take a moment to thank the Shinto gods for the **Suica Card**. Remember all those rail lines running through Tokyo, each privately owned? It's still like that today. Fortunately, since 2001, all rail lines accept the Suica Card. The Suica Card is a reloadable card used to gain access to the various trains.

You can purchase the card and load money onto it using machines at all train stations.

To ride a train, scan your Suica Card at an entrance. After you conclude your journey, you'll scan your card at an exit, and the correct fare will be deducted from your balance. You don't need to know, or even care, which company operates which track of your trip. But if you don't have a Suica Card and you want to transfer from the Tokyo Metro to a JR Rail, you'll need to buy a separate ticket for each leg of the journey. The Suica Card also works for the Disney Resort Line (monorail). When you leave Japan, stop at any train station to be refunded the balance of your Suica Card (minus a small service fee).

To get to Tokyo Disney Resort from anywhere within Tokyo, make your way to Tokyo Station using the Marunouchi Line of the Tokyo Metro. Once there, look for signs, and transfer to the JR Keiyo Line. (This line only goes in one direction from Tokyo Station, so you don't need to worry about which side of the tracks you're on.) Tokyo Disney Resort is at the Maihama Station on the JR Keiyo Line. From Tokyo Station, there are both express and local trains on the JR Keiyo Line, but all lines stop at Maihama.

As you approach the Maihama Station, there will be no doubt that you've arrived at Tokyo Disney Resort. The station is very Disneyfied, and you can see Cinderella Castle from the Train. At Maihama, exit the station. Then you can walk to Ikspiari, the entertainment complex, or take the Disney Resort Line to your final destination.

The Disney Resort Line is a monorail; however, unlike Florida's monorail, you must pay to ride this one. You can use a Suica Card, and the fare will be deducted. You can also purchase single-trip and multiday passes at station kiosks. For reference, a single trip is ¥260.00 ($2.50) and a three-day pass is ¥1,100.00 ($10.57). Guests of the Mira Costa Hotel and Disneyland Hotel get an unlimited ride pass for the duration of their stay.

You can't mistake the Disney Resort Line for any other rail line. The windows are all shaped like Mickey Mouse, as are the handles you hold if you stand on the monorail. The trains are usually decorated to match whatever is going on in the parks.

There are four stations. Resort Gateway Station serves Ikspiari and Disney's Ambassador Hotel. This is also the station you'll use to access the JR Maihama Station with service to Tokyo. The next monorail stop is Disneyland Station. This station serves Tokyo Disneyland and the Disneyland Hotel. Next is Bayside Station, which serves the official partner hotels located on Tokyo Bay. The final station is Tokyo DisneySea Station with access to Tokyo DisneySea and the Mira Costa Hotel.

If you're not already in Japan, then most likely you'll be flying into one of Tokyo's two international airports. Tokyo Narita Airport is sixty kilometers (thirty-seven miles) northeast of Tokyo Disney Resort. It's the busiest international airport in Japan, although Tokyo Haneda Airport is busier overall. From Narita, you can take a train to Tokyo Station and then transfer to the JR Keiyo

Line to head to Tokyo Disney Resort. This whole journey will take about one hour and forty minutes. But there is a much more convenient way. The Airport Limousine Bus is affordable and quick (limousinebus.co.jp). This orange-colored bus runs often and takes about fifty-five minutes to reach Tokyo Disney Resort. You will easily find their orange-colored desk after you clear customs. You can buy your ticket there, and they will deliver you directly to your hotel's front door. It costs ¥2,450.00 ($23.55) for a one-way transfer.

Tokyo Haneda Airport is twenty-three kilometers (fourteen miles) directly across Tokyo Bay from Tokyo Disney Resort. You can actually see planes landing at Haneda from several places inside Tokyo Disney Resort. Once again, you can take a train to get from Haneda to Tokyo Disney Resort, or you can take the Airport Limousine Bus (limousinebus.co.jp). The buses are still orange, and they will bring you to your hotel's front door in about forty minutes, but allow plenty of extra time if there is traffic. The cost to ride from Haneda is ¥830.00 ($7.97).

I don't recommend using taxis in Tokyo. They will cost a significant amount of money and will certainly take a lot longer. A taxi from Narita to Tokyo Disney Resort will run you about ¥22,894.00 ($220.04). If you do take a taxi, don't ever touch the door—seriously, don't. The door will open and close by itself, and the driver will not like you to tamper with that. The driver will also wear white gloves and will probably not speak English, but all drivers in Tokyo recognize the word "Disneyland."

I also do not recommend Uber in Tokyo. Due to regulations, it's actually much more expensive in Japan to take an Uber than it is to use a taxi. Just do yourself a favor: if you're at an airport and are going to a hotel, use the Airport Limousine Bus. If you're in Tokyo and want to go anywhere else, use a train.

### Entry Requirements

All travelers must have a valid passport to visit Japan. A tourist can stay in Japan for ninety days, and your passport must be valid the entire time. Citizens of the United States, the European Union, the United Kingdom, Australia, Canada, and some Eastern European countries may visit Japan without a visa. Before you depart, check with your country's travel department to learn if you need a visa to enter Japan.

All visitors to Japan are photographed and finger-printed at the passport control point. Lines at both Haneda and Narita can be quite long for this process. Allow plenty of time to pass from your aircraft to ground transportation. After passport control, you will proceed through customs. This can also take a while as Japanese officials are extremely vigilant when it comes to firearms. Firearms are illegal to possess in Japan, and they do whatever they can to keep their island nation free of guns.

### Parking

Nobody drives here, so don't worry about it. But if you are worried, it costs ¥2,500.00 ($24.02) to park for a day at either park. It costs ¥2,000.00 ($19.21) to park for a night at a Disney hotel.

## Time

Tokyo is sixteen hours ahead of California, thirteen hours ahead of New York, and seven hours ahead of Europe in the summer. Japan does not observe daylight saving time. In the winter, add one hour difference between these times.

## Language

It shouldn't surprise you that the language of Japan is Japanese. (If it does surprise you, then you need to spend a lot more time riding "it's a small world.") You will see and hear very little, if any, English anywhere in Tokyo. The same pride that makes the Japanese such excellent hosts is also the pride that makes them reluctant to speak English. Most Japanese people study English in school, but they are afraid of offending English speakers. Consequently, they will almost never attempt to speak it in front of you even if they can.

Most hotels, and everywhere at Tokyo Disney Resort, have employees who went to college in the United States. These people are much more confident and will be able to assist you in English. At Tokyo Disney Resort, the cast members who can speak other languages will have a tiny flag representing that language on the bottom of their name tags. Just remember that the flag representing English is not the stars and stripes—it's the Union Jack, the flag of Great Britain. (We'll let them have this one being that they invented the language and all.)

But don't let a fear of language keep you from having an adventure in Japan. The international travel language of gestures can get you quite far. Most restaurants in Japan, and all restaurants in Tokyo, will have an English menu. You can also rest easy knowing about the Japanese obsession with plastic food. All restaurants, even those inside Tokyo Disney Resort, have a display of plastic versions of their food near the door. You can always point to the dish you'd like to try.

If you are venturing into Tokyo, which you absolutely should, take a rail map along that is in English. You can easily find these online. The rail stations along a given route will be numbered. You can use your map to find the number of the station you want. Don't worry about recognizing the Japanese characters; just look for that number.

Most of the shows and attractions at Tokyo Disney Resort will be entirely in Japanese. Often, cast members will recognize non-Japanese speakers and hand them a small card that contains a translation. But even if you don't know what's being said, you'll enjoy the experience of trying to figure it out. And it's a lot of fun listening to Mickey and Donald having a conversation in Japanese!

### Weather
Tokyo enjoys long periods of pleasant weather in the fall and spring. Tokyo Disney Resort is located on land that

juts out into the ocean. There are nice ocean breezes that make for long, enjoyable evenings. Winter can get cold in the middle of January. The daytime highs can drop to the midforties (4°C). It can snow in the winter, which turns Tokyo Disneyland into a gorgeous winter wonderland. But crowds are considerably lower in winter; just dress in layers and enjoy the season.

Summer, on the other hand, is horrendous. The temperature isn't all that bad, with summer highs reaching eighty-five (29°C), but the humidity is almost unbearable. People don't normally think about Japan as being humid, but, trust me, Tokyo is worse than Florida from July through September. I spent a week in mid-September at Tokyo Disney Resort and was constantly wet. When I wasn't soaked in sweat, I was drenched from sporadic rainstorms. I could never quite decide which was more uncomfortable. Fortunately, there are a lot of air-conditioned places inside both parks.

The rainy season in Japan begins in early June and lasts through the month of July. This season can actually be quite nice in June. Crowds in the parks are always less when rain is present. However, as June turns into July, the humidity will return, and the rains will do nothing to break it.

### Money

Japan's currency is the yen (¥). The exchange rate is usually around one hundred yen to one US dollar. It's easy to do rough conversions in your head by moving the decimal over two places. Of course, the exchange fluctuates, and you can always find the most current rates online.

It's no surprise that Japan is a hotbed of technology. But it might surprise you to learn that this advanced technological society still prefers cash. Most restaurants and shops in Tokyo take credit cards, but you will rarely see anyone use them. It seems that Japanese people reserve credit cards for larger purchases like hotel rooms and expensive merchandise. The rest of the time, they'll use cash.

There's pride in the notion that a guest has cash and is willing to give it to Disney in exchange for a Donald Duck keychain. I believe cash is preferred because it's more ritualistic. The cast members at the register will accept your cash with as much pride as you present it with. They will take great care in returning any change. Also, all your purchases will be well wrapped.

On April 1, 2017, the sales tax in Japan will raise to 10 percent. This amount is usually already included in any printed prices you'll see. At some stores, both the pre- and post-tax amounts for an item will be printed on the price tag. A lodging tax of 5 percent is imposed when your hotel rate is less than ¥15,000.00 ($131.33). If your nightly rate is above ¥15,000.00, the lodging tax rises to 8 percent.

In Japan, tipping for service is not customary—it will also be quite insulting. Good service is something that everyone should always provide without any need for monetary incentives.

## Tickets

Tickets for Tokyo Disneyland and Tokyo DisneySea are available online, at the entrance gates, and at any Disney Store in Japan. The official website is tokyodisneyresort. jp. Look for the small globe in the upper right corner to change the language to English.

There is one huge difference between a ticket to Tokyo Disney Resort and a ticket to one of the American Disney parks. At Tokyo Disney Resort, you must choose the date, or dates, you are visiting before you purchase a ticket (called a "passport" in Tokyo). There are no peak or value seasons here; all days cost the same. The resort makes you buy a specific date in order to control crowding in the park.

For the purpose of this discussion, a child is anyone age four to eleven, and a junior is anyone twelve to seventeen. Those younger than four are free, and those older than seventeen are all adults.

A one-day passport is ¥7,400.00 ($71.32) per adult, ¥6,400.00 ($61.68) per junior, and ¥4,800.00 ($46.26) per child. You must declare which park you are visiting, Tokyo Disneyland or Tokyo DisneySea, and you must state the date you will arrive. You can only visit one park using this passport.

A two-day passport is ¥13,200.00 ($127.22) per adult, ¥11,600.00 ($111.80) per junior, and ¥8,600.00 ($82.89) per child. For a two-day passport, you must declare which park you will visit on the first day and which you will visit on the second day. You must visit each park, and you cannot hop between parks. To visit the same park on two consecutive days, you will need to purchase two one-day passes to that park.

A three-day passport is ¥17,800.00 ($171.56) per adult, ¥15,500.00 ($149.39) per junior, and ¥11,500.00 ($110.84) per child. To get a three-day passport, you will declare which park you are visiting on day one. The other park will be assigned to you on day two. On day three, you are free to hop between the two parks.

A four-day passport is ¥22,400.00 ($215.87) per adult, ¥19,400.00 ($186.96) per junior, and ¥14,400.00 ($138.78) per child. You must declare a park for the first day, visit the other park on the second day, and hop on days three and four.

Tokyo Disney Resort offers a Starlight Passport for admission after 3:00 p.m. This passport is only good on Saturdays, Sundays, and Japanese national holidays. Starlight Passports cost ¥5,400.00 ($47.30) per adult, ¥4,700.00 ($41.17) per junior, and ¥3,500.00 ($30.66) per child. On weekdays, including Fridays but excluding holidays, guests can enter either park with an After 6 Passport. An After 6 Passport is ¥4,200.00 ($40.48) for all ages and means you can enter...well, after 6:00 p.m. However, there are some days when these nighttime passports aren't valid—mostly when the parks close before 10:00 p.m., these types of tickets are not available and wouldn't be a good investment anyway. Check the resort's calendar at info.tokyodisneyresort.jp (change the language by clicking on the globe at the top and then choose "resort schedule").

### Park Hours

While the hours at both Disneyland and Walt Disney World fluctuate wildly, hours at Tokyo Disney Resort are fairly standard all year around. Most days, the parks are open from 8:00 a.m. to 10:00 p.m. During the slower season, from December through February, the parks might delay opening until 9:00 or 10:00 a.m. on Tuesdays, Wednesdays, and Thursdays.

One other huge difference between the American and Japanese Disney parks has to do with closing time. When it's closing time at an American Disney park, this means that the attractions stop and guests slowly meander out. The shops on Main Street are open until everyone has left the park. It's not uncommon at all for there to be guests in the US shops well over an hour after closing. This does not happen at Tokyo Disney Resort. Here, closing time is closing time. Everything will stop, and shops will close—even if you're waiting in line to pay. You'll be asked to put your merchandise back and to promptly leave the park.

Another item of note: opening time is a spectacle at Tokyo Disney Resort. Long lines will begin to form at the gates up to an hour before opening time. There are many more guests here at opening than at any other Disney park. When the gates open, the Japanese guests will run to get a Fastpass or reserve a spot for the day's first parade. Think of Black Friday at a US big-box store, and you'll get the picture. (You'll be reprimanded if you run at any of the other Disney parks, but in Tokyo, it's part of the culture.)

## Accommodations

There is no shortage of hotel rooms in Tokyo. There are four Disney hotels, six non-Disney hotels on the Disney property, and countless hotels in Tokyo itself. Because the rail system is so efficient, it's easy to stay in Tokyo and take the train to Tokyo Disney Resort for the day.

If you're staying in Tokyo, a hotel around Tokyo Station is the most convenient because it requires only one train to get to Tokyo Disney Resort. But there are many other parts of the city to consider. Shinjuku is where you should stay if you want endless nightlife. Ginza is for shopping; Asukusa is for visiting a shrine and Tokyo's SkyTree Tower. Ueno is the neighborhood for the zoo and museums.

### *Disney Hotels*

Disney hotels at Tokyo Disney Resort are fabulous with elaborate theming and legendary service. But compared to the Disney hotels in the United States, there are fewer special benefits. Really, the only benefit is the ability to enter either park fifteen minutes before they open to other guests. Fifteen minutes is not a lot of time, but it does give you a head start to the more popular attractions.

Now for the bad news: it's slightly easier to get a reservation at a Tokyo Disney hotel than it is to actually build your own Tokyo Disney Hotel. In order to grab a reservation, you must be prepared, diligent, and rehearsed. Reservations for the four Disney hotels open exactly six months in advance at tokyodisneyresort.jp. They open at 6:00 a.m., Japan time, on that day. By 6:15 a.m., most of the rooms will have been reserved by people in Japan.

You need to rehearse in advance. Practice getting used to the website. Use the reservation system to discover exactly what time you'll need to be online. Decide in advance what type of room you want at which hotel. Practice booking a room—just don't enter your credit card information, and the room will be canceled. When it's your actual day to book, you'll be glad that you rehearsed. This time, you can enter your credit card and finalize the booking. You will be charged for the first night when you make a reservation.

### Disneyland Hotel

Across the entrance plaza from Tokyo Disneyland is the graceful Disneyland Hotel. It's a large hotel with 701 rooms, restaurants, and a pool complex. The Tokyo Disneyland Station of the Disney Resort Line is directly in front of the hotel's entrance. Guests staying at this hotel get a pass for unlimited rides on the monorail during the duration of their stay.

The hotel offers several different types of rooms and views. Standard rooms without a park view are the most affordable. Themed suites with a view of Cinderella Castle are the most expensive. Overall, Tokyo's Disney hotels are not cheap. Expect to pay ¥52,000.00 ($501.06) for a standard nonview room. Suites with a view can run upward of ¥100,000.00 ($963.57).

Regardless of room, you will find that it's large, immaculately clean, and full of small Disney touches. A themed suite will be even larger with multiple rooms, and it will be full of items dedicated to a Disney film. A *Beauty and the Beast* suite, for example, comes with everything you'd expect Belle to find inside the Beast's Castle. The other themed rooms include Tinker Belle, *Alice in Wonderland*, and *Cinderella*.

There will be a lot of convenience items in the room. The Japanese people don't like to travel with necessities. You'll not only find shampoo, conditioner, and soap but also toothbrushes, toothpaste, ear cleaners, sewing kits, slippers...and pajamas! Yep, they don't travel with pajamas and expect all higher-end hotels to provide them. You can take any of the toiletries, but leave the pajamas to be laundered for the next guest.

The largest restaurant is the **Sherwood Gardens Restaurant.** It's a buffet for breakfast, lunch, and dinner. Expect to pay around ¥5,000.00 ($48.18). There is also a table-service, upscale restaurant called **Canna** and a café called **Dreamers Lounge.**

### Hotel Mira Costa

One of my favorite hotels in the entire world, Hotel Mira Costa is a marvel of architecture and convenience. This is the only Disney hotel in the world that is inside a Disney park. (Yes, the Grand Californian lies alongside Disney California Adventure. But Hotel Mira Costa juts out into Tokyo DisneySea and forms a large portion of the park's Mediterranean Harbor.)

Hotel Mira Costa has 502 rooms. The theme of the hotel is Venetian Renaissance. The theme is everywhere—beautiful paintings on the ceilings, sculptures in lush gardens, and gondolas floating right next to the hotel.

The Tokyo DisneySea Station is attached to the hotel via a covered walkway. Complimentary monorail rides are included with each stay. Guests staying here can access either park fifteen minutes before the general public. However, guests of the Hotel Mira Costa can enter Tokyo DisneySea via a special entrance that only they can use. The entrance is right inside the park. I can't tell you how amazing it is to be walking through a theme park and in less than three minutes be inside your hotel room.

This is the most expensive hotel on the property. Most of the rooms are standard, and there aren't any themed suites, but rooms with Tokyo DisneySea views are highly sought after. If you want a room with a view into the park, you must be ready to book exactly when the window of opportunity opens. Expect to pay ¥60,000.00 ($577.98) for a standard room with no view. A room with a view will cost around ¥80,000.00 ($770.68). A view room with a small balcony can be as much as ¥150,000.00 ($1,444.92).

All the rooms are exquisite inside this hotel. They are very large by Japanese standards and tastefully decorated.

The amenities included with the rooms are luxurious, as is the bedding. The corridors and lobby are as amazing as the rooms; even the elevator uses Mickey's voice to announce each floor.

The indoor and outdoor pools are themed like an ancient Roman bath. Sculptures of the Disney characters in togas line the outdoor pool. There is also a beautiful wedding chapel and a charming shop, **MickeyAngelo Gifts.**

The large buffet restaurant of the hotel is called **Oceano.** This establishment also has an a la carte menu for lunch and dinner. **Silk Road Garden** is a table-service restaurant that serves Chinese food. This beautiful restaurant tells the story of Marco Polo with large murals on the ceilings and walls. The lounge at Hotel Mira Costa, **BellaVista Lounge,** has stunning views of Tokyo DisneySea. Full meals are served in the lounge.

### Disney Ambassador Hotel

Think art deco when you walk into this hotel. Disney Ambassador Hotel is connected to the Ikspiari entertainment district. Guests staying here do not get a complimentary pass to the monorail system. Instead, Disney Ambassador Hotel offers a shuttle van that brings guests to each park. The shuttle service is quick and efficient.

There are 504 rooms at this hotel. One of the great features of Disney Ambassador Hotel is the many character rooms. You can choose a room themed to one of these characters: Mickey Mouse, Minnie Mouse, Donald Duck, Chip 'n Dale, and Stitch. In each one of these rooms, expect over-the-top theming. For example, Donald's rooms come with beds that look like his iconic blue sailor suit.

The standard rooms are a bit more affordable, around ¥40,000.00 ($395.33). However, the character rooms can be as much as ¥70,000.00 ($674.34) even during a slower season. There is a hotel shop and a nice pool that will remind you of classic Hollywood.

**Chef Mickey** is the hotel's largest restaurant. It's a character buffet for breakfast, lunch, and dinner. Because guests tend to linger and play with the characters, there is a ninety-minute limit on the amount of time you can spend eating here. **The Empire Grill** is an American restaurant in the art-deco style. **Hana** is a table-service Japanese restaurant, and **Tick Tock Diner** is a traditional American diner from the 1950s. There is a lounge, **Hyperion Lounge,** with food and drinks.

### Disney Celebration Hotel

Disney Celebration Hotel was an existing hotel located near, but not on, the Tokyo Disney Resort Property. OLC purchased the hotel and gutted it. After an extensive renovation, it reopened during the summer of 2016. Guests get to the parks by riding complimentary buses. The efficient buses are themed and take around fifteen minutes to get to either park.

The hotel is themed after classic Disney parks attractions. Large teacup chairs welcome you in the lobby. Canoes from Tokyo Disneyland's Westernland are featured, as are murals of other Disney attractions.

The rooms are located in one of two buildings: Wish and Discover. Each room features a large mural of Disney characters enjoying attractions at one of the Disney parks. This is the most family-friendly hotel with each room having four twin beds. Some of the rooms contain a set of bunk beds and can sleep up to five.

The prices of the rooms vary by view and size. There are garden views and ocean views, with ocean views being a bit pricier. Large corner rooms are more expensive than standard rooms. Overall, expect to pay ¥25,000.00 ($240.80) for a standard garden view and ¥40,000.00 ($395.33) for a large corner ocean view.

There is a café in each building: **Wish Café** in the Wish building and **Discover Café** in the Discover building. However, these cafés are only open for breakfast. There are no options for eating lunch and dinner in this hotel.

### *Non-Disney Hotels on Tokyo Disney Resort Property*
Do not overlook these six hotels. They are all beautiful properties located on the backside of Tokyo Disneyland. All of these hotels are perched directly on Tokyo Bay and offer stunning ocean views. For many of the rooms, the choice is either a view of the Pacific or of Cinderella Castle—what a choice to make!

The prices at these six non-Disney hotels are considerably cheaper. You can find the exact price online, but you'll pay less than half the cost of even the most affordable Disney option.

Besides theming, the only real advantage to staying in a Disney hotel is the fifteen-minute early park access. You can almost negate that benefit by arriving at the park early to be one of the first in line. So when you consider price and the lack of Disney benefits, it may be in your best interest to stay at a non-Disney hotel.

The Bayside Station of the Disney Resort Line is located near the middle of the six properties. Guests staying here do not get a pass to ride the monorail, but you can purchase one at any of the hotels. Guests of these six hotels do get complimentary rides on a shuttle van. The van will bring you to the Bayside Station or the JR Maihama Station with service to Tokyo.

I've stayed at the **Hilton Tokyo Bay** many times. The service is excellent, and the rooms are clean. This Hilton is the closest hotel to the Bayside Station; you can just walk. Rooms here have fantastic views of either Tokyo Disneyland or the Pacific Ocean. Those on the Pacific side look out over the city of Tokyo and a distant Haneda Airport. On a clear day, Mount Fuji is visible from this hotel.

Just do your homework. Look at the rates and see what fits into your budget. The Disney hotels are fabulous, but the difference in price could more than pay for your next airfare to return to Tokyo.

Sunroute Plaza Tokyo—sunroute-plaza-tokyo.com

Sheraton Grande Tokyo Bay Hotel—sheratongrande tokyobay.com

Tokyo Bay Maihama Hotel—maihamahotel.jp

Tokyo Bay Marihama Hotel Club Resort—tbm-clubresort.jp

Hilton Tokyo Bay—hilton.com/Tokyo

Hotel Okura Tokyo Bay—okuratokyobay.net

# Tokyo Disneyland

Congratulations! You've not only made it to the incredible country of Japan, but you've come to the extraordinary Tokyo Disneyland. Just think of it like Walt's original dream with a small twist. The dream is the world of imagination, where yesterday, tomorrow, and today are perfectly rendered; the twist is that you're 5,139 miles (8,271 kilometers) from American soil or 3,852 miles if you count Hawaii, which you absolutely should. (More on Disney's presence in Hawaii can be found in chapter 8.)

This is the first Disney park outside of the United States. It's the culmination of three decades of negotiation, planning, and execution. But as much as it's based on Walt's dream, this is not your Walt's Disneyland. It's every bit as much Japanese as it is American. And that's why you should be proud to be here. Tokyo Disneyland is the ultimate symbol of two countries who were once bitter enemies, now choosing to work together for the purpose of creating happiness.

Regardless of how you got here or where you stayed, everyone enters Tokyo Disneyland through the same entrance plaza. You'll immediately notice the beautiful landscaping and floral arrangements. Have your passport (ticket) scanned, and enter the plaza.

Before you head into the actual park, take a moment to look for any characters in the area. There are usually a couple of them greeting guests and posing for photographs in the entrance plaza. However, you'll probably notice one big different between the American parks and Tokyo Disneyland: here, secondary characters are as popular as the stars. You might not see Mickey and Donald in the plaza, but you very well may see Gus Gus and Pearla, two of Cinderella's mice. Or you might get a glimpse of Miss Bianca and Bernard from *The Rescuers*. You may even see Pinocchio's Blue Fairy or Clarabelle, a cow from the early years of Disney animation. These are characters you will never see anywhere else.

Now, after you've had a chance to get those rare photos, keep walking. There's no railroad here, so you don't need to enter under the train station. You'll hear the music change as you enter—hey! What's going on here? Is this Main Street or not?

## World Bazaar

It looks like Main Street, USA—sort of. The first major difference you'll notice is an enormous glass roof hovering above the entire land. Yes, every square inch of World Bazaar is covered by an architectural wonder: a metal and glass structure that gives the land a half-indoor, half-outdoor feel. Since it does rain often in Tokyo, especially during the summer, this structure was considered a necessity during the park's initial design. It functions well, and World Bazaar can keep thousands of guests completely dry.

Under the glass, the familiar streets of Main Street exist. Like its American cousins, the theme of this area is turn-of-the-century American small town. However, unlike all the other Main Streets around the world, World Bazaar does not use forced perspective. All the buildings are full scale with the second floors the same size as the first floors. The glass cover makes the land feel much bigger than it is; forced perspective was not required.

In early research, it was discovered that the name "Main Street" meant nothing to the Japanese. While Americans think of Main Street as more of a concept rather than an actual street, the Japanese took the words literally. Park designers were concerned that the name Main Street would make guests believe this was the most important place in the park; consequently, they might neglect to even explore other areas. The name World Bazaar has been in place since the park opened. To the Japanese, the name works well. To me, I picture a world bazaar as being much more international than what this area really represents.

If you look down World Bazaar, you'll see the familiar spires of Cinderella Castle in the distance. If you're visiting anytime in November or December, you won't see Cinderella Castle as it's obscured by an enormous Christmas tree in the very middle of the bazaar.

Similar to Main Street, USA, there are no major attractions here. There is an omnibus that makes trips from the entrance plaza to the castle, but this is the only ride in World Bazaar. The rest of the land is dedicated to shopping, dining, and more shopping.

**The Grand Emporium** is the largest shop in the park with all the appropriate park souvenirs. (Note: Only Tokyo Disneyland merchandise is sold at Tokyo Disneyland. Tokyo DisneySea sells only Tokyo DisneySea items. To buy both in one location, you'll need to visit the large **Bon Voyage** shop that sits between Tokyo Disneyland and Ikspiari. You do not need a ticket to shop at Bon Voyage.)

Also in World Bazaar, you'll find **Town Center Fashions**, **Disney & Co.**, **Toy Station, Pastry Palace**, the **Home Store,** and many others. These shops sell the type of items that their names suggest. The busiest shop, and the most lucrative in all of Japan, is **World Bazaar Confectionery**. Here, you can purchase hundreds of prepacked snacks in delightful Tokyo Disneyland tins. There is an entire row of cash registers. This shop will be extremely busy close to closing time.

There are several places to eat under the protective glass of World Bazaar. As a general rule throughout all of Tokyo Disney Resort, expect to pay ¥1,000.00 ($9.70) for a quick-service meal and ¥2,000.00 ($19.40) for a table-service meal. Character meals will run around ¥5,000.00 ($48.46).

*Dining in World Bazaar*

**Eastside Café:** A table-service restaurant with pasta and other Western cuisine.

**Great American Waffle Company:** A wonderful quick-service option with waffles in the shape of Disney characters. The waffles are highly recommended by the author of this book.

**Sweetheart Café:** Quick-service hamburgers, sandwiches, and snacks are offered.

**Refreshment Corner:** The most American option in World Bazaar; hot dogs and other quick-service items are offered.

**Restaurant Hokusai:** A popular table-service Japanese restaurant.

I love buying anything at Tokyo Disney Resort. Making a purchase is a ritual anywhere in Japan but especially at Tokyo Disney Resort. After exchanging money in a proud and deliberate manner, your purchase will be well wrapped in paper and/or bubble wrap. Then it will be placed in a plastic Disney bag. But that's not all. Before it's handed to you, the cast member will put another unused bag inside with the purchase. One last step: the cast member will always secure the top of the outer bag with a piece of Tokyo Disney Resort tape.

This is all part of the tradition of omiyage. When Japanese people visit a destination, it's practically required that they bring back a gift for absolutely everyone they know. The World Bazaar Confectionery is so popular because the tins of treats are a perfect omiyage.

The reason you're getting an extra bag for each item you buy is because you're supposed to put each gift in a new bag before you give it to the recipient. In Japan, the presentation of a gift is much more important than the gift itself. It's almost like saying, "I thought of you so much on my journey that I carried this item back for you. I took such great care of it that the bag it came in does not have even one wrinkle."

This ritual is so rewarding to watch that I always buy something, even if it's just a ¥100 pen. But be advised: omiyage is such a proud tradition that everyone will take part. The lines to get into some shops at Tokyo Disney Resort can get extremely long when the parks are crowded. Yes, I do mean the lines to get *into* the stores; I've seen them become a two-hour wait! Cast members will stand at the end of the line with a sign indicating the approximate wait time until you can enter the store. When you do finally gain entrance, the lines for checkout will not be as long because they will only admit a set number of shoppers at a time. If you're in the parks on a holiday or weekend, shop as early in the day as possible.

▲ ▲ ▲

### Adventureland

On a cold winter day, Adventureland can feel somewhat out of place. But you'll feel quite in the jungle on a humid summer day. As you leave World Bazaar, Adventureland has a New Orleans look and feel. The farther you explore the land, the more tropical it will become.

#### *Pirates of the Caribbean*

The beginning of this version of Pirates is similar to Disneyland. You'll gracefully float past the diners at the Blue Bayou Restaurant. Then the ride becomes more similar to the Florida version.

Expect all the zany pirate antics and the appearance of Captain Jack Sparrow. You'll sit in boats. Please note: The Japanese find it horribly rude to step on anyplace where someone will sit. Consequently, step all the way into the boat; do not use the bench as a step. This is quite different from what occurs in the United States.

#### *Western River Railroad*

The only train at Tokyo Disneyland is this narrow-gauge rail that acts more like a ride. You'll get off the train at the same station where you initially boarded; there is only one station on this railroad. But that doesn't mean you shouldn't ride.

It's a scenic and relaxing journey around Adventureland and Westernland. During the fifteen-minute expedition, you'll pass through a frontier town and spot plenty of animals. As a special treat, Western River Railroad passes through a prehistoric world of dinosaurs, similar to the railroad at Disneyland. Every time I ride, I'm astounded at how rural the train feels. I almost forget that I'm in the middle of the largest metropolitan area on earth.

### Jungle Cruise: Wildlife Expeditions

If you want to know exactly how it feels to be "lost in translation," then you must ride this version of the jungle cruise. It's probably the most fun you'll have all day.

The cruise is basically the same as the American versions. You'll sit in a boat and be guided through some of the world's most famous rivers. Along the way, you'll pass lions, hippos, elephants, and all sorts of jungle creatures. There is an upgraded ending in Tokyo with a cool temple effect.

The best part, however, is watching the Japanese guests; they are much more interesting than the animatronic zebra. The boat's skipper serves as a guide and constantly talks during the ride. They are telling Japanese versions of the same corny humor you hear at the American parks. If you don't speak the language, you won't be able to understand a single word. But the Japanese guests will—and they will laugh hysterically. Then you'll laugh with them. The experience of laughing just because someone else is laughing—well, it's priceless. Every English speaker should experience this attraction.

### Swiss Family Treehouse

A replica of the Swiss Family Treehouse at Walt Disney World. You'll see all the modern amenities that the Robinsons created in their primitive jungle surroundings.

### The Enchanted Tiki Room: Stitch Presents "Aloha E Komi Mai!"

This version of the Enchanted Tiki Room is quite a bit different than the versions in California and Florida. Stitch, from Disney's *Lilo and Stitch,* is adored by the Japanese people. They've embraced him in a way that hasn't occurred in the United States. Japan has a love affair with Hawaii; perhaps that's why they love Disney's most Hawaiian film (at least it was until *Moana* premiered in November of 2016).

The tiki birds and all of their Hawaiian friends are still present in this show. But Stitch, that mischievous alien, corrupts the show with music from the film. "Aloha E Komi Mai" basically means "a very special Hawaiian welcome." Once it begins, the show lasts ten minutes. Rarely with a line, this attraction is perfect for cooling down on a summer day.

### Minnie Oh! Minnie

This small stage show takes place near Pirates of the Caribbean. Minnie, Mickey, Donald, Goofy, and Chip 'n Dale entertain guests for thirty minutes. The music is very Caribbean in style. Check the daily Times Guide for show times.

### Mickey's Rainbow Luau and Lilo's Luau & Fun

These two luaus take place inside the Polynesian Terrace Restaurant. You'll enjoy a Hawaiian dinner while several characters put on a show. Each luau lasts around eighty minutes. You must have a separate ticket to attend; however, the reservation system is online and only in Japanese. Tickets open thirty days before the date you want to attend; they are often sold out within a day or so. Once again, English speakers will not be able to navigate the website enough to purchase tickets to these luaus. If you know someone who reads Japanese, he or she can help. Otherwise, go to guest services when you enter the park and inquire about any last-minute tickets.

### Shops of Adventureland

Think pirates and jungle while visiting the shops in this land. **Pirate Treasure** and **Adventureland Bazaar** feature all those items. There are a few more upscale shops in the New Orleans portion of this land, such as **La Petite Perfumerie** (it sells perfume).

### Dining in Adventureland

**Café Orleans:** Quick-service snacks are offered in a themed environment.

**Crystal Palace Restaurant:** Table-service character meals are served with Western and Japanese food.

**The Skipper's Galley:** A quick-service jungle café with snacks.

**Squeezer's Tropical Juice Bar:** Ice cream is offered quick service here.

**China Voyager:** Chinese food shaped liked Mickey Mouse is cute to look at while ordering at this quick-service establishment.

**Blue Bayou Restaurant:** This restaurant is table service and upscale. Located inside the Pirates of the Caribbean, it's one of the park's signature dining experiences.

**Boiler Room Bites:** There's always a line here for quick-service steamed buns.

**Polynesian Terrace Restaurant:** Requiring a separate ticket, this table-service character luau has Western food and a Hawaiian theme.

## Westernland

Apparently, the word "Frontierland" doesn't translate to anything that makes sense for the Japanese guests. Westernland is the official name for this land, and it's the only Westernland in the world.

### Country Bear Theater

You might remember how much I love the Country Bears. What could be better? Well, the Country Bears in Japanese! It's the same fifteen-minute show, but the down-home bears perform all their country hits in mostly Japanese. Often, there are English—I mean American—words that really don't translate like "y'all" and "whoop." It's fun to hear these words mixed in with the Japanese language.

Unlike Florida, the Country Bears in Tokyo present two other shows. During the summer, they perform a vacation version with all sorts of summery songs. You will recognize the melodies but not the words. During November and December, the Country Bears perform a Christmas-themed show. Once again, you'll recognize all the tunes, but you'll have to sing along to your own words inside your head.

### Mark Twain Riverboat

Westernland comes complete with a Rivers of America. This may seem a bit strange because you're not in America. But remember, Japan is an island nation without the enormous and broad rivers you'll find on a continent; they are simply enthralled by all the romantic space that the American frontier provides. You can board this authentic riverboat for a twelve-minute journey around Tom Sawyer Island.

### Tom Sawyer Island Rafts

The only way to get to Tom Sawyer Island is by riding one of these rafts. Once on the island, you can explore Tom's territory. It's a bit less politically correct than the American versions. There's a lot to explore here, and you'll be given a map to use as a guide. You can visit Tom Sawyer's Treehouse, Injun Joe's Cave, and Huckleberry Swamp.

Again, no matter which park you're in, Tom Sawyer Island is a great place to go if you are sick of lines and just want to get some exercise.

### Big Thunder Mountain

*Fastpass* The wildest ride on the fron—I mean in Westernland. You'll board an old mine train and race around canyons and mines. Again, it's better at night.

The Tokyo Disney Resort version of Fastpass is similar to the system at Disneyland. Unlike with Walt Disney World, you won't reserve your passes until you get to the park. At Tokyo Disneyland, you just insert your park ticket in a Fastpass machine near the attraction's entrance. You'll be given a coupon that will state the time you should return. When you return, use the special Fastpass entrance to access the ride without a line.

### Super-Duper Jumpin' Time
This outdoor show is geared toward the smallest guests. During this thirty-minute show, you'll watch as the Disney characters sing, dance, and basically run around to everyone's delight. Check the daily Times Guide for show times.

### Horseshoe Roundup and Mickey & Company
Both of these dinner shows take place in the Diamond Horseshoe. Similar to the luaus, you must have a separate ticket to attend either of these special shows. Again, the ticketing system is only in Japanese. Get a Japanese friend or ask at guest services when you visit the park.

### Camp Woodchuck
Fans of Donald Duck will recognize the Junior Woodchucks, the scouting organization that nephews Huey, Dewey, and Louie belong to. This mini land within Westernland is incredibly well themed and absolutely

adorable. You can eat like a Junior Woodchuck, play like a Junior Woodchuck, shop like a Junior Woodchuck, and meet Donald in his complete Junior Woodchuck attire. There is a lot of detail here, and you can spend hours learning how to become a full-fledged Junior Woodchuck.

### Shops of Westernland

**Western Wear, Country Bear Bandwagon, General Store, Trading Post**—you get the picture. The shops here range from Western-style apparel to lots of pins for trading. **Happy Camper Supply** is the shop at Camp Woodchuck. Stop here for all your scouting and Donald Duck supplies.

### Dining in Westernland

**The Canteen:** Quick-service snacks are offered with a Western flair.

**Camp Woodchuck Grill:** Adorable quick-service waffle sandwiches and s'mores.

**The Diamond Horseshoe:** You must have a special ticket to enjoy the dinner shows inside this restaurant.

**Check Wagon:** Desserts are served quick service here.

**Hungry Bear Restaurant:** Asian food is offered quick service and themed to the Western surroundings.

**Plaza Pavilion Restaurant:** Get your quick-service burgers in the shape of Mickey Mouse here.

**Pecos Bill Café:** The line will be long here as everyone in Japan wants to purchase a Mickey-shaped churro.

## Critter Country

The smallest land in the park, Critter Country is home to one of the most popular attractions.

### Splash Mountain

*Fastpass* Nearly identical to the Walt Disney World version, you'll sit with seven others and enter the world of *Song of the South*. (Don't worry if you haven't seen this movie because nobody in Japan has either.) During the ten-minute ride, you'll slosh around in a log as the story unfolds around you. Then you'll take a huge splash down the mountain.

You will get wet on this ride. You will probably get soaked. Use the poncho in your theme-park satchel for protection. Or if it's summer and you're soaked from sweat anyway, just go ahead and ride in order to cool down.

### Beaver Brothers Explorer Canoes

There are no motors on this ride. You and fifteen others will have to paddle your large canoe around the Rivers of America. The canoes are a fun activity on a winter day. In the summer, they're just about as close to hell as you'll experience.

Also, this attraction makes a great picture. Just have one person in your party stand on the shore, and they will get a fantastic photograph of you with your paddle. You can burn off the calories from the Mickey churro while on this ride.

### Shops of Critter Country
Only one shop, **Hoot & Holler Hideout,** offers souvenirs with a focus on Splash Mountain.

### Dining in Critter Country
**Grandma Sara's Kitchen:** Grandma Sara offer quick-service hamburgers and beverages.

**Rackety's Raccoon Saloon:** Rackety sells snacks in a quick-service style. Once again, everyone seems to buy a churro.

### Fantasyland
To the Japanese people, Fantasyland is the epitome of the Disney experience. This land of fairy tales, walking brooms, and talking animals is the main draw of Tokyo Disneyland. Fantasyland has the most attractions in the park, including a dark ride with a legendary reputation that is only found here.

A massive addition is making this large land even larger. *Beauty and the Beast* and *Alice in Wonderland* are each getting their own mini lands within Fantasyland. But don't worry about construction having an impact on your experience; Tokyo Disney Resort is great at hiding work behind themed walls.

### Cinderella Castle
The symbol of Fantasyland, and an icon of the entire resort, is Cinderella Castle. It looks exactly like the Cinderella

Castle at the Magic Kingdom in Florida. However, it's not a carbon copy.

This castle at Tokyo Disneyland is 168 feet (fifty-one meters) tall; it's exactly fifteen feet shorter than its twin in Florida. The color schemes of the two castles also differ. The blues are not quite the same shade, and the gold accents are in different places.

The interiors are also different. When Cinderella is at her Florida home, she welcomes guests to visit her second-floor restaurant. When she travels to Tokyo, Cinderella welcomes guests to Cinderella's Fairy Tale Hall, an indoor attraction.

### Cinderella's Fairy Tale Hall
In this beautifully executed attraction, you'll enter the castle to begin a journey through the interior. As you progress, the story of Cinderella is gorgeously told through paintings, stained glass, dioramas, and various artifacts. You'll see the actual glass slipper that Prince Charming put on her foot to prove that she was his love. The highlight of the experience is a look at the throne room where Cinderella and her prince hold court.

### Alice's Tea Party
The teacup ride—it's still nauseating in Japan.

### "it's a small world"
This version of the iconic ride is similar to the version at Walt Disney World except the main chorus of the song is in Japanese. Again, it's more fun to watch the

Japanese guests on the ride than it is to watch the singing dolls.

### Castle Carousel

This beautiful carousel is meticulously maintained and spelled correctly! Every horse is white, but they wear all sorts of colorful harnesses. The ride lasts two minutes.

### Snow White's Adventure

The name just says Snow White's Adventure, but, trust me, it's the same as Disneyland's Snow White's Scary Adventure. The evil queen turns into the old hag right before your eyes. She will continue to jump out and scare you for the duration of the ride. It's great fun for most people but terrifying for kids.

### Dumbo the Flying Elephant

The nostalgic among us will appreciate that Tokyo Disneyland's version of this famous ride has not been redesigned. Here, Dumbo still retains the 1950s colors of the original version at Disneyland—even though that original is more modern now.

You have probably heard that Japan is a society obsessed with photography. Well, for many of them, taking a picture of their children on this ride is an absolute necessity. Consequently, the line can be quite long.

### Pinocchio's Daring Journey

Similar to Disneyland's version, during this two-minute ride you'll learn the story of Pinocchio and all the poor choices he makes. I love *Pinocchio* because there is no absolute villain in the film; Pinocchio is his own worst enemy—just as it happens for most of us.

### Peter Pan's Flight

The ride itself is almost identical to the version at Walt Disney World. However, the queue is not as nice here in Tokyo. Don't let that stop you—the gorgeous journey over London and to Never Land is captivating no matter where you take it.

### Pooh's Hunny Hunt

*Fastpass* All right, here is the legendary ride that I wrote about earlier. As soon as you enter the park, you must immediately go to this ride to get a Fastpass. They will run out of Fastpasses for this ride just an hour or so after opening. In fact, when the gates open, you'll see throngs of Japanese people running into the park. Most of them are heading to this attraction. If you don't have a Fastpass, expect a long line.

When it debuted, Pooh's Hunny Hunt was the first dark ride in the world to use trackless technology. After passing through many large pages of a storybook, you'll be immersed into the world of Pooh and his friends. However, as soon as you board your hunny pot, you'll notice that it isn't attached to anything—it just sort of goes on its own.

A complex computer system controls each self-motivated hunny pot throughout the ride. As you progress, you'll proceed into a number of rooms that contain images of the iconic story. When you enter a room, you'll explore the area, barely missing any other hunny pots that are already in the room. The computer works all this out so that every hunny pot gets a close-up view of the scene.

Each time you ride Pooh's Hunny Hunt, you'll have a different experience. The computer randomly generates a path for your hunny pot and makes sure that your path doesn't cross too closely with any other pot. You'll jump with Tigger and get blown away during Rabbit's windy day.

The whole ride is fantastically immersive. Pooh's Hunny Hunt is amazing and deserves all the hype it gets.

### Haunted Mansion

*Fastpass* This is the only haunted mansion in the world that's located in a Fantasyland. That was done purposely. The Japanese people are very superstitious. It's almost their national pastime. The early designers of Tokyo Disneyland were told that guests would never enter a house if there was even a remote possibility that it contained ghosts. The imagineers put the Haunted Mansion in Fantasyland so that there would be no confusion: these ghosts are in a fantasy; they are not real.

To fit the Fantasyland theme, the mansion is a large, gothic-style house that looks like something out of *The Wind in the Willows*. The inside of the attraction is similar to the version at Walt Disney World. After the stretching room, guests are put into doom buggies to tour the rest of the mansion. But like the Disneyland version, this

Haunted Mansion does get the *Nightmare Before Christmas* overlay during the holiday season.

**Dreamlly's Disney Direction**

You've probably heard about the hidden Mickeys. These are subtle shapes of Mickey Mouse that are cleverly hidden on most attractions and architecture. There are some famous ones imbedded in the ceiling mural at the Hotel Mira Costa. There are lots of books and blogs out there to help you seek hidden Mickeys during your visit to any Disney park or resort.

But did you know there are hidden Donalds? Yep, it's true. Subtle shapes of Donald Duck appear from time to time. They are rare but exciting to find. The best example occurs inside the Haunted Mansions at Anaheim, Orlando, and Tokyo. Just after you pass the corridor with "hot and cold running chills," look at an upholstered chair to the left. The pattern on the upholstery is a hidden Donald.

▲ ▲ ▲

### Mickey's PhilharMagic

Mickey's PhilharMagic is the same high-tech immersive attraction from Walt Disney World, but it's in Japanese.

After the short preshow, guests use 3-D glasses to watch the show. Donald Duck soon gets into trouble and finds himself searching for Mickey's hat through iconic Disney scenes.

All the special effects from Orlando are here, including the sights, sounds, and smells. But all the famous music is sung in Japanese. It's incredibly fun to hear something familiar sung with a different voice and in another language.

There is rarely a wait or line for Mickey's PhilharMagic. This immersive show makes a nice, relaxing place to sit in air-conditioning during the summer. It also makes a great place to warm up during the winter. Allow fifteen minutes once the preshow begins.

### Shops of Fantasyland

Gifts based on the classic Disney films and their royal characters are the focus of shops in Fantasyland. **Kingdom Treasures, Harmony Faire,** and **Fantasy Gifts** are three of these shops. **Pooh Corner,** near Pooh's Hunny Hunt, offers merchandise based on A. A. Milne's famous stories. One of my favorite Disney songs is "Baby Mine" from *Dumbo.* Here, **Baby Mine** is the cutest baby store you'll ever see. Lastly, **Pleasure Island Candy,** based on *Pinocchio,* is another candy store inside the park.

### Dining in Fantasyland

**Captain Hook's Galley:** Although a nasty man, Hook makes fairly good quick-service pizza in his galley.

**Queen of Hearts Banquet Hall:** This quite large cafeteria-style restaurant has Western food and a lot of theming. If you love *Alice in Wonderland*, you must eat here.

**Cleo's:** Pinocchio's adorable fish offers quick-service snacks in this kiosk.

**Village Pasty:** Quick-service snacks are made fresh here—and, yes, more churros.

The sun can be intense in Tokyo, especially during the summer. Surprisingly, it's difficult to find sunscreen in Japan. Bring your own! It's not that the Japanese are pro-melanoma. It's actually quite the contrary; the Japanese are so careful to avoid the sun that sunscreen isn't really necessary. Staying out of the sun has been part of the Japanese culture for centuries. You'll see many people walking around Tokyo on a sunny day with umbrellas. You'll never see Japanese people lying out in the sun by the pool.

Here's another odd juxtaposition of Japanese culture: you would think that people who like to avoid the sun would also love sunglasses. Nope. Nobody wears sunglasses in Japan, and they are impossible to buy. You can find a few pairs at the resort, but they are always themed with Mickey ears and fairies attached to them. As someone who's constantly breaking his sunglasses and doesn't like his vision obscured by Tinker Bell, I've learned to bring along an extra pair to Tokyo Disneyland.

▲ ▲ ▲

## Toontown

Step into the neighborhood where Mickey, Minnie, Donald, and all their friends live. It's an animated city within a real theme park. Everything is as full of color as you might imagine. The version of Toontown at Tokyo Disneyland is far more immersive than the version in California. You can really step into Mickey's world and explore the interactive streets toward the back of Toontown.

### Gadget's Go Coaster

This simple kids' coaster is well themed and includes a small splash at the conclusion of the ride. Nobody gets wet, but it adds a level of fun to an otherwise tame ride.

### Goofy's Paint 'n' Play House

Goofy's house is an attraction unique to Tokyo Disneyland. Here, kids and adults can splash all kinds of "paint" onto Goofy's walls. (The painting is actually accomplished with some pretty cool lighting effects.) After a usually short line, you'll get a few minutes to paint before you're escorted back outside to Toontown.

### Chip 'n Dale Treehouse

Children can climb around and explore the home of Disney's two rascally chipmunks. This is a nice place to try if you have a kid who's done waiting in lines.

### Donald's Boat

This is another chance to climb and play without waiting in a line. Donald has parked his boat, the Miss Daisy, here in Toontown for you to explore. All the items inside are things you'd expect Donald to have. From the upper level of the boat, you can get great photographs of Toontown.

### Minnie's House

The third play experience in Toontown. Here, kids can explore Minnie's very interactive abode. Go ahead and open the oven, answer the phone, and look at her pictures. Her bedroom is just as cute as it should be.

### Mickey's House and Movie Barn

Here is your chance to meet the famous mouse in his first international home. After touring the home and noticing all the special things that Mickey has acquired, you'll journey into the backyard. Here, Mickey has converted his old barn into a movie studio.

You'll watch trailers of Mickey's many movies as you wait in line. The line can get long, but it seems to move surprisingly fast. Soon you'll be escorted backstage, where Mickey has taken a break from filming in order to meet you.

### Roger Rabbit's Car Toon Spin

Similar to the ride at Disneyland, you'll spin your way through the back alleys of Toontown. The ride lasts almost four minutes; that's four minutes too long for me. However, many enjoy this spinning experience.

### Shops of Toontown

**Toontown Five & Dime** and **Toontown Delivery Company** are the only stores in this land. The merchandise is centered around Mickey and his friends.

### Dining in Toontown

**Dinghy Drinks:** Quick-service beverages are offered in this kiosk near Donald's boat.

**Toontown Treats:** Desserts and snacks are sold in a weird-looking truck that only makes sense in Toontown.

**Toon Pop:** This popcorn cart is themed as well as the land it's in. (More about Tokyo Disney Resort's obsession with popcorn is coming in a bit.)

**Huey, Dewey, and Louie's Good Time Café:** Donald's nephews operate this quick-service restaurant that serves burgers, pizza, and other snacks.

**Mickey's Trailer:** Mickey sells quick-service snacks and spring rolls here. The pizza spring rolls are amazing.

### Tomorrowland

Pretty much all of the city of Tokyo seems like Tomorrowland to me. But if you're not going into the city, then step inside Tomorrowland for a look at the future.

Tokyo Disneyland's Tomorrowland is in the midst of a renovation and an addition. A large attraction themed to *Big Hero 6* is in construction. You'll also notice many successful attempts to update this entire land.

### StarJets
Just like the Dumbo ride but with small rockets. That's it.

### Star Tours: The Adventures Continue
*Fastpass* This is the same simulator ride from Disney's Hollywood Studios in Florida. The five-minute ride uses technology and 3-D glasses to make guests believe they are battling Storm Troopers and Darth Vader. The simulation is computer driven, and there are endless versions. Each time you ride will be different.

Also, any dialogue on the ride will be in Japanese. It's fun to hear how Darth Vader speaks in another country.

### Stitch Encounter
Another attraction unique to Tokyo Disneyland. After waiting in an interactive queue, guests are ushered into an air-conditioned theater. Here, you'll meet Stitch, presented as an animated technological marvel.

Stitch will interact with the audience. He'll ask and answer questions in his Stitchy voice. The entire experience will be in Japanese, but if you follow what the Japanese guests are doing, you'll be OK. Japan has a love affair with the film *Lilo & Stitch*; consequently, this attraction is always popular.

### Space Mountain
*Fastpass* You'll notice the iconic building that houses Space Mountain when you approach the resort on the train from Tokyo. The indoor roller coaster is similar to the version at the Magic Kingdom. It's a three-minute ride through the stars and planets.

### Buzz Lightyear's Astro Blasters
*Fastpass* The same attraction from the Magic Kingdom. You'll help Buzz Lightyear defeat the evil emperor Zurg by blasting at targets. You can control when to turn your vehicle for better aim. You'll be given a score at the ride's conclusion. The attraction lasts around four minutes.

### Monsters, Inc. Ride & Go Seek!
*Fastpass* If guests aren't running toward Pooh's Hunny Hunt when the gates open, they're running here. Monster, Inc. Ride & Go Seek! will also run out of Fastpasses about an hour after the park opens.

You'll sit in a vehicle and travel through the incredibly themed city of Monstropolis. As you ride, you'll use a flashlight to find any monsters you see hiding. When you hit a monster with your beam of light, all sorts of things will happen.

This attraction will be different each time you ride as you find new monsters to spotlight. The ride lasts four minutes and is very immersive. Like Pooh's Hunny Hunt, it's worth your run to the Fastpass line.

### One Man's Dream II—The Magic Lives On

This is one incredible show. Full sets, costumes, and special effects tell about the impact that Walt Disney's imagination had on the world. The show opens in black and white and will colorize as the action unfolds.

You'll see all your favorite characters, especially those from the early years of Disney animation. It's a thirty-minute show. In case you're wondering, the original *One Man's Dream* had a good run in this same theater. The show was updated and given a new name to entice guests to return.

Not everyone who visits the park will be able to see the show; there isn't enough space in the theater. Consequently, this show requires a free ticket that is distributed via lottery. Early in the day, go to the One Man's Dream lottery center that's near the theater. You'll scan your park admission ticket and use a screen to select which performance you'd like to attend. You'll also scan the tickets of anyone else you may want to sit with during the show. The machine will decide if you've won the lottery. If you have, then you will get a free ticket from the machine. The ticket will have a seat number on it. If you have not won the lottery, you will not be able to try again that day.

However, you still may get to see the show even if you didn't win the ticket lottery. You can wait in a line before the show, and any unclaimed seats will be released. You might not be able to sit with everyone you came with, but it's worth it to see this show. Also, on days of lower attendance, the lottery may not be required for certain performances.

### Shops of Tomorrowland

*Star Wars,* Stitch, and Pixar dominate most of the merchandise in Tomorrowland. **Cosmic Encounter** is the shop for Stitch, **Treasure Comet** for *Star Wars,* and **Monsters, Inc. Company Store** for Pixar merchandise.

### Dining in Tomorrowland

**Space Place FoodPort:** Ice cream is offered quick service with a futuristic flair.

**Tomorrowland Terrace:** This large quick-service restaurant is for burgers and sandwiches. It can be quite crowded and has excellent views of Cinderella Castle.

**Pan Galactic Pizza Port:** Get the best pizza in the galaxy at this quick-service café.

**Plaza Restaurant:** Here, the Plaza Restaurant is not table service. This is a quick-service café for Japanese food.

**The Popping Pod:** Another popcorn cart—many more to come!

**Lite Bite Satellite:** Head here in case you need another Mickey-shaped churro. Apparently, many of the Japanese guests do.

## Parades, Evening Shows, and Special Events
### Happiness Is Here Daytime Parade

Parades at Tokyo Disneyland are amazing. You'll see incredible floats, great performers, and all the characters you can imagine. Check the daily Times Guide for the parade times on the day you're at the park. You may also notice that many Japanese guests start getting a place to sit way in advance—think hours. They often bring small plastic mats with them to sit on.

The parade route is marked on all park maps. One big difference to parades in the United States: parades at Tokyo Disneyland never go down their version of Main Street. Because of the park's design, parades have no place to go inside World Bazaar.

As a tip, when the parade passes through Toontown, there is only one side of the street open for viewing. (The other side of the street is a wall.) So the performers will give all their attention to the crowd on your side of the street. It's a little more interactive to watch the parade from here.

### Tokyo Disneyland Electrical Parade Dreamlights

Disney has some amazing parades around the world, but this one is the best. There aren't enough superlatives in the English language to describe it. It's something you just have to see. Everything works. Everything glows and goes together. The whole thing is so perfectly beautiful that you will cry. Seeing something like this reaches that inner humanity we all have, and you can't help but feel proud to be a person.

Park guests will claim a seat two hours before the parade...sometimes more! Just get a cheap plastic mat at the grocery store in Ikspiari and join in the fun!

### Once Upon a Time

This projection show occurs on the front of the castle a few times each night. Check the daily Times Guide for the exact show time. It's a short but fairly amazing use of projections and music to stir the nostalgic Disney emotion inside us all.

### Sky High Wishes

You'd think that the amazing Tokyo Disney Resort would have equally amazing fireworks each night. You'd be wrong. Yes, there are fireworks every night, but they aren't that amazing. This is one department where Tokyo Disneyland is a bit lacking. If you're around to see them, great. Just don't make it a special point to attend.

### Halloween

It may seem odd, but Tokyo Disneyland entirely embraces three holidays that aren't prominent in Asia. Halloween is well celebrated here. You'll find all sorts of amazing decorations, special foods, and merchandise. In fact, you'll often see Japanese guests walking around with a catalog of all the special Halloween items.

There are Halloween-themed parades each day. On certain days, adults are allowed to wear Disney costumes. Americans have absolutely nothing on the Japanese when it comes to costumes; these people go all out. It's worth the price of admission just to see how good the costumes are.

### Christmas

Christmas is the second holiday that Tokyo Disneyland adores. You'll see the same catalog, but this time it will show all the Christmas food and merchandise.

There are Christmas-themed parades and shows each day. The decorations are incredible.

### Easter

Easter isn't really celebrated all that much at the Disney parks in the United States and Paris. It's surprising how much Tokyo has embraced the nonreligious side of this holiday. Like Christmas, decoration will be everywhere, and, yes, there is an amazing Easter-themed parade. (New in 2017, Judy Hopps from *Zootopia* will lead the parade. I wonder why…)

One of the centerpieces of Easter at Tokyo Disneyland are things called the Usatama. These are Easter egg-like characters that are scattered around the park. They also show up in the parade and require the Disney friends to keep them well-behaved. Like a lot of the added Japanese touches at the resort, I'm not exactly sure what the Usatama are all about, but I sure do like seeing them.

All the Easter hoopla at Tokyo Disneyland reminds me of what it must have been like in the United States when my grandma was a kid. You can even buy an elaborate Easter bonnet with mouse ears.

### Golden Week

Japan celebrates Golden Week from around April 28 to May 5 each year. Tokyo Disney Resort goes all out for Golden Week with merchandise, food, parades, and shows.

For foreign visitors, Golden Week is actually a collection of Japanese holidays that happen to lie within the same week. It's the longest holiday vacation time in Japan, similar to Christmas in the United States. Many companies close altogether for this week.

Tokyo Disney Resort will be packed. This is their highest season, and prices will reflect that. The hotels will be full. Unless you have a specific reason for visiting during Golden Week, don't.

### Winter: Anna and Elsa's Frozen Fantasy

During the months of January and February, *Frozen* takes over most of the area in front of the castle. In addition to a nightly spectacular projection show on the castle, large sculptures of the *Frozen* characters surround the park's central hub. A special *Frozen* parade occurs each morning during this festival. The parade contains fantastic floats and is synced with the film's catchy music. In true Tokyo Disneyland style, unique *Frozen* merchandise and food fill the shops and restaurants.

What's will all the popcorn? All over Tokyo Disneyland and Tokyo DisneySea, you'll see carts selling popcorn. But it's never the plain salted kind. Over the years, I've seen these flavors: soy sauce, honey, coconut, curry, chocolate, milk tea, cappuccino, jalapeño, and strawberry.

No visit to Tokyo Disney Resort is complete without popcorn. You can purchase it in a single cardboard cup, but who would do that? You can also purchase it in an adorable plastic container that will be themed to a Disney character. I have a Mickey-as-a-snowman popcorn container that I will never part with. All the special containers come with a strap so you can wear it. Seriously. There is nothing better than walking around a theme park with a plastic Donald-Duck-as-an-Easter-egg bucket strapped around your body. When you want some popcorn, you just have to open it and enjoy.

However, here is another strange thing about Japanese culture: the Japanese people find it rude to walk and eat. Yes, in the land of crazy vending machines, you won't see people walking and eating or drinking. Beside every group of vending machines, you'll notice a collection of trash receptacles. This is because the people will buy their products and consume them right there next to the vending machine and then dispose of the trash. You will never see hordes of people walking while sipping Starbuck's like you do practically anywhere else.

You won't see many guests walking around with food at Tokyo Disney Resort. This is why the plastic popcorn containers are so popular; you can close them while you walk. Also, notice that you never see even one kernel of popcorn on the ground. Diligent cast members make sure that every kernel ends up in someone's mouth or in the compost.

▲ ▲ ▲

## Tokyo DisneySea

*It must have been a dream*, I thought as I went to sleep my first night after visiting Tokyo DisneySea. *No place could be that good.* But in the morning, I woke up and visited the park again. It wasn't a dream. It was all real.

Tokyo DisneySea is the best theme park on the planet. It's probably the best theme park in the universe. Normally, I would never say such a superlative statement without having hard facts to back it up. But somehow I feel like I have the hard facts. Tokyo DisneySea is really that good. Throughout my life, I've never met anyone who has been to Tokyo DisneySea who didn't also think it was the best theme park on earth.

Everything came together during the formation of this park: the location, the theme, the ingenuity—and the money. Tokyo DisneySea's final price tag was ¥335 billion yen ($3.2 billion). You can see every yen. There's not an inch of this park that wasn't thought about, themed, constructed, and then thought about again.

You're going to get sick of me going on and on about this park. Everyone else in my life has. So let's just get started.

However you get here, everyone arrives at the same entrance plaza. You'll pass through security and have your ticket scanned. As you enter the plaza, take some time to consider the amazing sculpture/fountain in front of you.

The large earth-shaped fountain is the **DisneySea Aquasphere.** It's a wonder of design and technology. The large planet seems to float effortlessly on the water. Cascading streams highlight the surface of the planet. Take some time and locate your home on this big blue ball.

When you've completed your earth ogling, turn toward the park. To enter, you'll pass underneath the spectacular Hotel Mira Costa. And now, finally, you can see the enduring symbol of Tokyo DisneySea: Mount Prometheus. We'll get to the mountain later; for now just enter Venice and its Mediterranean Harbor.

**Mediterranean Harbor**

Mediterranean Harbor encompasses all the land, and the water, that you see in front of you. Rest assured, there are more amazing lands in this park—you just can't see them from here. Each land of Tokyo DisneySea is themed to a different type of harbor. This is Italy, and it's right in the middle of a Renaissance.

Hotel Mira Costa serves as the backdrop for this entire area. The hotel's façade is painted using a technique called trompe d'oeil. Using this technique, a flat surface is painted to seem three dimensional. Have a closer look at the hotel. What you thought were several separate buildings at various distances is actually just one really big flat wall. It looks like huge shutters frame some of the windows, but there are no shutters here. It's all smoke and trompe d'oeil.

The water in front of you, also called the Mediterranean Harbor, is the prime location of all the park's shows. You'll see guests getting an early seat for whatever show is next.

Like most Disney parks, with the exception of Disney's Animal Kingdom, this entrance land has few attractions and many shops. Still, there is plenty to see and do here.

### Venetian Gondolas

Located in a small channel that juts into the Hotel Mira Costa, you'll find the Palazzo Canals. On these small waterways the lovely Venetian gondolas float to the strains of Italian music. Two guides accompany each gondola on an eleven-minute trip. Sixteen people can fit into each boat.

### DisneySea Transit Steamer Line

Further back on the main water of Mediterranean Harbor, you'll see the dock for the DisneySea Transit Steamer Line. These steamer ships offer the very best way to see the park. From this dock, you can take a steamer all the way to the farthest land in the park: Lost River Delta.

While on the steamer, you'll begin to appreciate the park's extensive theming and beautiful views. You'll steam through small channels into wonderful harbors. One harbor is more intricate than the last.

### Fortress Explorations

Located on the far side of the water, underneath Mount Prometheus, is the Fortress Explorations. If DisneySea was just this attraction, it would be worth it. You can explore for hours and never see the same thing twice. I've been to this park many times, and I always discover new areas. (Sometimes I think there is a computer that keeps track of my movements and changes the rooms to surprise me.)

This area is similar to Tom Sawyer Island at Disneyland (in the way that you can explore on your own), but it's much more intricate. As you explore the fortress, you'll discover turrets, rooms, and entire ships that you can board. You'll see odd rooms where Renaissance scientists are using models of planets to explain the universe. You can make them move. In fact, you can make anything happen here just by rotating a wheel or pulling a level. Whenever you encounter an object on the fortress, just try it—you'll never know what will happen.

You may try the **Leonardo Challenge** by obtaining a map from a cast member. Follow the clues as you try to become a member of the Society of Explorers and Adventurers.

The Fortress Explorations is where you want to come to get some exercise and to avoid waiting in line. I really can't get enough of this area.

### Shops of Mediterranean Harbor

There are a lot of shops here. **The Emporio** is the largest of DisneySea's gift stores. Here is where you'll find all of the park's souvenir-type items. **Figaro's Clothiers** (themed after Pinocchio's cat) is for clothes, and **Il Postino Stationery** sells all sorts of pens and fine paper. The busiest shop in the park is **Merchant of Venice Confections.** Here is where you can get any size of DisneySea tin filled with any variety of candy. At **Villa Donaldo Home Shop** you can purchase lots of household items. There is an entire wall of Donald Duck-themed dishware!

### *Dining in Mediterranean Harbor*

**Café Portofino:** A Mediterranean table-service restaurant with pasta and other Italian cuisine.

**Gondolier Snacks:** Quick-service ice cream is served near the Palazzo Canals.

**Zambini Brothers' Ristorante:** Large quick-service café that offers pasta and pizza. There is an upper outdoor seating area with great views of Mediterranean Harbor. The spaghetti bolognese is cheap and awesome (though a small portion, so get two).

**Magellan's:** This table-service restaurant has Western food. It's one of the park's signature dining experiences with a nice lounge. Some people claim it's the best Disney restaurant in the world. I can't confirm because it's a little too fancy for me.

**Mamma Biscotti's Bakery:** Italian snacks and hamburgers are quick service here.

**Ristorante di Canaletto:** Another fine table-service restaurant with Western cuisine.

**Refrescos:** Fantastic soups are served quick service here.

## American Waterfront

It's a bit of the United States right here in Japan. As soon as you set foot in American Waterfront, you'll know you're in 1920s New York City. The streets are filled with shoppers, and an ocean liner has pulled into the port. Up ahead and over a bridge, you can just barely see a quaint Cape Cod village across the water.

### *Tower of Terror*

*Fastpass* You can't miss the Tower of Terror as it looms high over New York City. The outside of the building is expertly themed, and you'll feel as if you're about to enter a large hotel near Central Park.

The ride is similar to the version that was at Disneyland in California. But the story is quite different. *The Twilight Zone* was never televised in Japan. So gone is any reference to that classic show. Instead, there is a new story here about the owner of a New York hotel who mysteriously disappeared in 1899. You're entering the hotel as part of the New York City Preservation Society's tour. You'll be given the tour, but, of course, something goes wrong in the elevator shaft.

Like the other Towers of Terror around the world, each ride is different. A computer randomly generates each ride's sequence.

### Turtle Talk

The same attraction from California and Florida—except it's in Japanese. You'll meet Crush, the turtle from *Finding Nemo,* and he'll answer all your questions about turtle life. It's not as much fun as other attractions if you don't speak Japanese.

### DisneySea Electric Railway

This elevated train takes guests from American Waterfront to Port Discovery. There are some excellent views of Mount Prometheus from the railway.

### DisneySea Transit Steamer Line

One of the things I love about Tokyo DisneySea is all of the transportation options. Here is another dock for the DisneySea Transit Steamer Line. From here, you can make an entire loop through all the park's harbors. It's a fantastic way to see the whole thing.

### S.S. Columbia

A large ocean liner has pulled into American Harbor, and you can explore the whole thing. This is another of my favorite places at Tokyo DisneySea. There is an expensive restaurant inside and a bar, but it's open to everyone to explore the decks.

Yes, this is an actual ship. It might not be ocean ready, but you can tour all the decks for great views of the American Waterfront. You should make sure to venture all the way to the front of the ship. This is one place where you can see outside the Disney bubble. Here, you'll get a great view of Tokyo and airplanes landing at Haneda Airport. If it's a clear day and you look in the distance, you will get an amazing view of Mount Fuji.

Back in the park, directly on the starboard side of the ship, you'll discover a stage with a seating area. Prior to 2017, the amazing *A Table Is Waiting* was performed several times each day on this stage. I was inconsolable for weeks after this show closed—it was so good! However, a brand-new show will debut here sometime in 2017. All we know is that the new show will feature the Disney friends. (I'm sure Duffy will be in it. I have such a love/hate relationship with him that I might have to take an upper—and a downer—in order to survive the show. Keep reading for more information about Duffy.) But if the new show is even half as good as *A Table Is Waiting*, we will be well entertained.

### Toy Story Mania!

*Fastpass* Until the new Nemo attraction debuts, this is where everyone is running when the park opens.

All of the Fastpasses for Toy Story Mania! will be gone within thirty minutes of the park opening. If you must ride this attraction, then you must get to the park early and be one of the first through the gate. Without a Fastpass, the line will be extremely long.

The ride is similar to the versions in the United States. You'll ride through the colorful midway and shoot at targets while the *Toy Story* gangs help you. You will get your score at the conclusion of the ride.

Even if you're not riding, you should still visit this area. It's themed like an Atlantic boardwalk that's attached to New York. At night, the whole place glows with thousands of lights.

### Big City Vehicles

Nobody else is ever in line for these vehicles. I always ride them. While in American Waterfront, look for signs advertising Big City Vehicles. Wait by the sign, and a themed vehicle will show up. You never know what kind of ride you might get. You may get a nice tour of American Waterfront in a luxury car, or you may get put in the back of a paddy wagon. Regardless, it will be a relaxing journey and a nice way to see the whole land.

### Big Band Beat

This fantastic show, located in the Broadway Music Theatre, is a thirty-minute review of jazz hits. There is a huge cast, and all the music you hear is live. The singing is extraordinary.

All your favorite Disney characters make an appearance at some point; however, the focus is on the music and the talented dancers.

You will need a free ticket to see this show. Just like with *One Man's Dream* at Tokyo Disneyland, go to the ticket lottery center sometime during the day. Insert all your group's park tickets into the lottery machine, and choose the time you want to attend. If you win the ticket lottery, you'll be presented with tickets. The lottery center is located back in Mediterranean Harbor by the gondolas.

Any talking in the show will be in Japanese, but this incredible music is so enjoyable that it doesn't matter what language it's in.

### Cape Cod

Across a bridge from New York Harbor you'll see a charming Cape Cod fishing village right out of Massachusetts. There are no attractions here, just a themed shop and restaurant. The Cape Cod mini land is the home of Duffy. Read on!

### My Friend Duffy

In the Cape Cod section of American Waterfront, you'll find a restaurant called **Cape Cod Cook-Off.** If you purchase a meal here, you will be treated to a ten-minute show as you dine. My Friend Duffy tells the story of how Duffy met his friend ShellieMay.

You must purchase a meal in order to see the show. The ten-minute show repeats every fifteen minutes, but there is a time limit for how long you can eat. In order to keep families from seeing the show all day (which, oddly, many will want to), the cast members usher tables of diners out once their limit has been reached.

It's not a great show, and the food is just OK. But if you are a fan of Duffy, then you must attend. If you don't know who Duffy is...well, you will.

## Shops of American Waterfront

The largest store in American Waterfront is **McDuck's Department Store.** Yep, Scrooge McDuck runs a retail empire in Tokyo. The store is themed as you'd expect Scrooge to have decorated it. In the Cape Cod area, **Aunt Peg's Village Store** sells the most Duffy merchandise on the plant. Who's Duffy? You'll be afraid you asked.

## Dining in American Waterfront

**S.S. Columbia Dining Room:** An expensive table-service restaurant on the S.S. Columbia with Western food.

**Cape Cod Cook-Off:** This quick-service café offers hamburgers with a show and a time limit.

**Sailing Day Buffet:** A buffet restaurant with Western and Japanese dishes.

**Teddy Roosevelt Lounge:** A unique lounge with food located on the S.S. Columbia. It's cozy and makes a wonderful place to relax in the evening.

**Delancey Catering:** Quick-service hot dogs served as you'd find them in New York.

**New York Deli:** What's New York without a deli? Quick-service hamburgers and sandwiches are available here. The famous Mile High Sandwich may be the best Western-style entrée you'll have all day.

**High Tide Treats:** Here, churros have invaded DisneySea as well.

**Hudson River Harvest:** The place for quick-service snacks in American Waterfront.

**Barnacle Bill's:** Another of the land's quick-service snack locations.

**Liberty Landing Diner:** The last of America's quick-service snack options.

**Restaurant Sakura:** A fine table-service restaurant with Japanese cuisine.

What's a Duffy? Well, that's a very good question. You'll see Duffy all over Tokyo Disney Resort, especially at American Waterfront.

Duffy is the Disney Bear. Several years ago, someone at Disney merchandising was trying to find a way to tap into the Japanese *kawaii* culture. Kawaii culture is a multi-billion-yen industry in Japan. Kawaii means "cuteness," and the entire culture celebrates things that are over-the-top cute. Think about Hello Kitty and all of her friends—you'll get the point. Some folks at Disney started selling cute American teddy bears with the hope of attracting kawaii fans. But they didn't buy it or any of the teddy bears. You see, for something to be kawaii, it has to have a story and lots of accessories.

And so Duffy was born. (Yes, Duffy is a complete fabrication for marketing purposes, but we'll just ignore that.) Here's the story: Mickey had to go on a very long voyage by ship, and he was worried that he'd get lonely. Minnie, being the wonderful girlfriend that she is, sewed a teddy bear for Mickey and gave it to him in a duffel bag. She thought the bear would be a great companion on Mickey's journey. Of course, Mickey loved the gift and named him Duffy because he came in a duffel bag. Duffy became his travel buddy, and soon all the Disney friends wanted their own. Somehow, Duffy came to life. (I'm not sure how Minnie accomplished this—no doubt she made a deal with Ursula.) Duffy, as living teddy bears are apt to do, got a girlfriend named ShellieMay and a cat friend named Gelatoni.

The whole marketing idea worked, and Duffy took over the entire country of Japan. There are no less than 24,601 outfits for Duffy. And in true Japanese style, you should also make clothes for Duffy using your own skills. It's not just good enough to have a well-dressed Duffy. You must have several. Also, in an act that seems strange to everyone else, true Duffy fans bring all their Duffys with them when they visit the parks. I guarantee that you will see Japanese guests carrying several Duffys, all dressed in different ways. These fans treat Duffy like a person (many times, better than a person). You will see Duffy get the best spots to watch a show. Duffy will get his own seat at a restaurant, and I have seen people buy food for Duffy. (I'm not kidding about any of this.) When a fan takes Duffy on a ride, he'll get a seat. These fans believe so strongly in Duffy that they will not move him to accommodate anyone who might actually be alive. Several Duffys can take up an entire row on the monorail. No matter how packed the train gets, Duffy will keep these priority seats. You could be a ninety-five-year-old survivor of Hiroshima, Nagasaki, and the 2011 tsunami. It won't matter. You can stand because Duffy needs a seat!

Disney attempted to make Duffy popular in the United States and Paris. The Europeans didn't want anything to do with him. Duffy made appearances at Epcot and Disney California Adventure. He did OK but not well enough to keep him around. Disney has recently started promoting Duffy at Hong Kong Disneyland and the new Shanghai Disneyland. We'll have to wait and see how that goes.

I really wasn't a fan of Duffy. Then I got one for a birthday present. He's just so cuddly and cute. My Duffy has three outfits, and I'm not buying anymore—except that I really want this Santa Claus suit that I saw at McDuck's Department Store. But I will never, ever give him my seat on the monorail...I think.

▲ ▲ ▲

**Port Discovery**

This is Disney TokyoSea's answer to Tomorrowland. It's not a port that exists in reality—at least not yet. Port Discovery is a futuristic vision of what a high-tech harbor may look like someday. This is the closest land to the real

Pacific Ocean. The line between fantasy and reality is quite blurry here. I love it!

### Aquatopia

There are so many attractions at Tokyo DisneySea that are unique to this park. Here is another one. On Aquatopia, you'll sit in a little boat that is self-propelled. A computer will guide you around a very shallow pond. As you ride, you'll narrowly miss other boats and lots of shooting water jets. You won't get wet on this ride.

Aquatopia at night is fantastic. Lots of unique lighting features make the ride an unforgettable experience. There is never much of a line.

### DisneySea Electric Railway

From here, guests can take the electric railway back to American Harbor. There are excellent views of the real Pacific and fantasy Mount Prometheus.

### Nemo and Friends SeaRider

This attraction, which replaced the popular StormRider, is scheduled to open on May 12, 2017. It's an indoor experience in which guests will be shrunk down to size in order to explore the ocean from the vantage point of Nemo and Dory. It's sure to be amazing as everything else seems to be inside this park.

It hasn't been announced yet whether Nemo and Friends SeaRider will be included in the Fastpass system. I'm willing to bet that it will. When a new attraction opens at Tokyo Disney Resort, hordes of people will line up every morning for months outside the park's gates. At opening, these people will run at top speed, and a multihour line forms easily. All Fastpasses are usually gone within a few minutes. If you want to ride this attraction and you are going to DisneySea anytime in 2017 or 2018, you must arrive at the park at least two hours before opening and secure a place right near the entrance gates.

### Shops of Port Discovery
**Discovery Gifts** and **Skywatcher Souvenirs** offer merchandise with a futuristic theme.

### Dining in Port Discovery
**Seaside Snacks:** Chinese pork buns are served quick service.

**Breezeway Bites:** A quick-service kiosk with snacks.

**Horizon Bay Restaurant:** This cafeteria-style restaurant is open for most meals. However, on certain days, it offers character dining. Check at the restaurant for the day's schedule.

## Lost River Delta
Part of the amazing charm of this park occurs when you pass between lands. Often, you'll walk through highly themed passages that serve as a transition between worlds. You'll know you're near Lost River Delta when you see the lush foliage of a South American river delta.

Some of the fun back here is the chance to meet more rare characters. The Three Caballeros—Panchito, José Carioca, and Donald Duck—often greet guests in this land. This is Tokyo DisneySea's answer to Adventureland with a large Latin flare.

### Indiana Jones Adventure: Temple of the Crystal Skull

*Fastpass* Similar to the version at Disneyland but with a different story, you'll join Dr. Jones on a tour of an ancient temple. You'll sit with eleven others during this three-minute adventure in a Jeep-type vehicle.

There are a lot of special effects used, and you will feel immersed in the action. It's not as intense as most roller coasters, but the ride vehicle does move a lot. I'm prone to motion sickness (hence my fear of the tea cups), and I don't have a problem on this ride.

Grab a Fastpass if you can. Japanese teenagers love this ride, and the line will reflect that.

### Raging Spirit

*Fastpass* Tokyo DisneySea has a number of rides that are more intense than anything they have over at Tokyo Disneyland. This is another one of those.

Raging Spirit is a highly themed steel inversion coaster. After boarding the train, you'll spend two minutes careening around the ruins of an ancient ceremonial site. You will twist and turn a lot. You will go upside down.

Again, teenagers keep this line long most of the day.

## DisneySea Transit Steamer Line

From this dock, you can take the steamer back to Mediterranean Harbor. This leg of the steamer network is my favorite because it passes through Mysterious Island.

## Out of Shadowland

This brand-new show takes place in a theater that's themed like an old airplane hangar. Out of Shadowland is the story of a young girl named Mei and the interesting things she sees while lost in the forest—at least that's what I think it's about; the show is in Japanese. Here is my synopsis that may be completely incorrect: Mei, a very shy girl, gets lost and befriends a deer. She does some good things to help the forest but then gets set on fire. When her dear deer friend is killed, Mei stabs a large bird. That's it. But it doesn't really matter if you can't understand any of the lyrics to the beautiful music.

Out of Shadowland is full of visual sensory. The forest sets are amazing with lots of special lighting effects. Most of the action is told through dance and movement, similar to a Cirque du Soleil show.

In order to see this show, you must have a free ticket that is given through a lottery. Just like Big Band Beat, you'll scan all the park passes for those in your group. If you win the lottery, your free tickets will be printed. If you don't win the lottery, you can still try to get a last-minute seat by showing up at the theater and waiting in line. Also, for this show, the first performance of the day does not require a free ticket; you can just go to the theater and watch the show.

Out of Shadowland is twenty-five minutes in length.

### Shops of Lost River Delta

Exploration and safari are the major themes for the retail in this section of the park. **Lost River Outfitters** is the largest store with most of the souvenir-type items. Some of the smaller shops will have a focus on Indiana Jones and the Raging Spirit coaster.

### Dining in Lost River Delta

**Expedition Eats:** Quick-service hot dogs are served here in a lush setting.

**Tropic Al's:** Snacks and desserts are served quick service at this café.

**Miguel's El Dorado Cantina:** This quick-service shop offers soup and other Mexican food.

**Yucatán Base Camp Grill:** This Mexican-themed restaurant is the only table-service location near the rear of Tokyo DisneySea.

**Lost River Cookhouse:** Another quick-service snack option.

### Arabian Coast

When the music changes as you leave Lost River Delta, there will be no doubt that you've entered Arabian Coast. This incredible land has layer after layer of theming. Go ahead and explore the streets. Let them lead you well into the land. Look in the windows and at all the things attached to the buildings. You'll run into lots of carpets, camels, and even a few magic lamps.

### The Magic Lamp Theater

*Fastpass* Part live action and part 3-D experience, this show is continuously performed throughout the day. After a preshow, you'll be escorted into the theater for a ten-minute show. A magician named Shaban is the head-liner for this performance, and his partner is none other than Genie from *Aladdin*.

The show is in Japanese, but you'll enjoy the special effects even if you don't speak the language. There are two continuous live shows at DisneySea; the other is in Mermaid Lagoon. Both of these shows are quite popular, and you may need to wait for more than one show cycle before you get in. To avoid this, you can get a Fastpass.

### Jasmine's Flying Carpets

Just like Dumbo except it's carpets.

### Sindbad's Storybook Voyage

It's not a typo. The Japanese call him Sindbad with an extra D. But I don't care what they call him because this is the best ride in the entire Tokyo Disney Resort. In fact, this is my absolute favorite Disney attraction on the planet. If I was told I was dying and could only experience one more Disney attraction, I would choose Sindbad's Storybook Voyage.

After the queue, you'll sit in a boat and sail through the story of Sindbad and his tiger, the unbelievably cute Chandu. During your journey, you'll see hundreds of audio-animatronic performers—the most of any Disney attraction anywhere. Some of the performers are as small as mice, and one in particular is a giant-sized giant who sings and plays an instrument. For the full fifteen minutes of the ride, you'll be completely overwhelmed by the spectacle of it all.

The music for the entire attraction was written by Alan Menken, the composer of *The Little Mermaid, Beauty and the Beast, Aladdin, Newsies,* and about one thousand other award-winning titles. Sindbad's main song, "Compass of Your Heart," is gorgeous and will stick with you even though the dialogue and lyrics are in Japanese. When you enter the ride, ask for an English translation. You'll be handed a colorful small brochure that will tell you the story. You can shellac the brochure when you get home and make a nice Christmas ornament!

Here is a fact that baffles my mind: the Japanese guests do not think this ride is anything special. There is never, ever a line. I just can't get my head around this. Every non-Japanese person I know thinks this ride is amazing. I don't get it. Anyway, I'm often the only person in my boat, and you probably will be too. If you see a very handsome man shellacking an English brochure alone in a boat, that's me! If they ever close this ride, I'll probably jump off Mount Prometheus because life will have no meaning anymore.

### Caravan Carousel

This double-decker carousel is themed to the film *Aladdin*. You can ride on Genie, or you can ride on a horse, elephant, griffin, and other types of wonderful animals. It's a bit more fun to ride on the top layer because you'll get great views of Arabian Coast. The carousel is especially beautiful at night. The entire Arabian Coast glows with soft street lights, and you'll appreciate the three-minute break to enjoy them.

### Games of Arabian Coast

Whenever you go to Arabian Coast, there will undoubtedly be a long line to play one of two carnival games. The reason these games are so popular is that the chance of winning is high, and the prizes are really good. The games can change, but think along the lines of trying to get a ball into a hole or something like that.

They normally cost ¥500.00 ($4.86) per play. You can win a large prize fairly easily. There is always a cast member at the end of the line explaining what to do. These cast members have instructions in English. As an added bonus, the cast members are really supportive and will scream with joy if you win a prize.

### Shops of Arabian Coast

**Agrabah Marketplace** and **Abu's Bazaar** are the two shops here. The items are very *Aladdin*-centric, but you can also buy a stuffed Chandu from the Sindbad ride.

### Dining in Arabian Coast

**Open Sesame:** Here is another spot for churros, just in case you haven't had one yet.

**Casbah Food Court:** Japanese food is served at this quick-service establishment. Even if you don't eat here, go inside this gorgeous establishment and look around.

**Sultan's Oasis:** The Oasis offers quick-service snacks, including a steamed bun in the shape of Chandu's tail. It's filled with creamed chicken and is delicious.

## Mermaid Lagoon

The colorful spires of shells will signal that you've entered Ariel's kingdom under the sea. This land is brilliantly executed. The entire thing is indoors with air-conditioned, shaded comfort. Most of the rides here are geared toward children. It's fantastic that parents can sit in this one land and keep an eye on them. There is also a large restaurant and an amazing show.

Mermaid Lagoon is especially beautiful at night. The outside of the structure contains millions of fiber-optic lights that sparkle in the darkness. There is nothing like this anywhere else in the world.

### Ariel's Playground

Children can explore, and fall, as much as they want in this interactive playground. Everything is soft and well protected.

### Jumpin' Jellyfish
Float up and down on a shell that's being carried around by a giant jellyfish. This ride will make for the best photograph you'll take inside Ariel's world.

### Blowfish Balloon Race
Just like Dumbo, but you're in a shell that's being carried by a giant blowfish. There's a bit of a theme going on, I guess.

### The Whirlpool
Just like the teacups, but you'll sit inside kelp that's taken for a spin in the ocean. You couldn't pay me enough to ride.

### Scuttle's Scooters
One of two outdoor rides in Mermaid Lagoon. You'll sit in a hermit crab and rotate around Scuttle, Ariel's bird friend. There is a slight dip that occurs; it's a tame version of the traditional caterpillar-type ride.

### Flounder's Flying Fish Coaster
A traditional kiddie coaster themed like a fish. There is often a long line here.

### Mermaid Lagoon Theater—King Triton's Concert
*Fastpass* This is the other continuously performed show in the park. Remember that scene in *The Little Mermaid* where King Triton is holding a concert and Ariel doesn't show up? Well, here you get to go to that concert. You also get to see what Ariel was up to that whole time.

This fifteen-minute show is full of fantastic effects. King Triton, Ariel, Flounder, and Sebastian are present, as are lots of other performers. Some of them, especially Ariel, swim all around the water...er, air around you. It's a spectacle that should not be missed.

This show is quite popular, and you may need to wait for more than one cycle to get in. You can get a Fastpass.

### Shops of Mermaid Lagoon

There are surprisingly a lot of shopping opportunities inside Ariel's undersea kingdom. Most of the merchandise is themed to the ocean, but there is a large store that offers all the park souvenirs you'll need. **Mermaid Treasures** and **Sea Turtle Souvenirs** offer gift-type merchandise. **Kiss de Girl Fashions** is where you should head if you have a true Ariel lover in your family. **The Sleepy Whale Shoppe** is the place for general DisneySea merchandise. It's actually inside a giant whale that slowly closes his eyes, attempting to stay awake.

### Dining in Mermaid Lagoon

**Sebastian's Calypso Kitchen:** This large quick-service restaurant serves hamburgers, sandwiches, and pizza. It's well themed, just like everything else inside Mermaid Lagoon.

### Mysterious Island

Welcome to Mysterious Island—the most unique theme-park land you'll ever see in your life. The entire land is located around the bottom of Mount Prometheus. In fact, the mountain is so large that you can't see any other land from Mysterious Island. It's a wonder of design and construction.

Jules Verne was the inspiration for Mysterious Island. Every inch reflects his writing: futuristic fiction rooted in industrial-age style. This land was steampunk before steampunk became a thing. Mysterious Island's two main attractions are both themed to famous works of Jules Verne.

There isn't so much background music here as there are sounds. There is water pouring everywhere and anywhere. Mount Prometheus erupts sporadically and calls your attention. Again, there is nothing else like it in the world.

### Mount Prometheus

Standing above all of Tokyo DisneySea is Mount Prometheus. At 189 feet (fifty-eight meters), it's the iconic symbol of the park. Mount Prometheus is made out of 750,000 square feet (69,600 square meters) of poured concrete rocks. It is one of the largest poured concrete buildings in the world. Yes, it is a building, and you can go inside.

And it should be known that Mount Prometheus is an active volcano. Inside are water cannons and actual rocket burners that create the sporadic eruptions. You can hear the eruptions from all over the park, especially when the rocket burners fire up.

To get a great picture in front of Mount Prometheus, you'll have to be in Mediterranean Harbor. Stand in front of the water with the mountain a little off center, and you'll get a great photo.

### 20,000 Leagues Under the Sea

*Fastpass* You'll board one of Captain Nemo's submarines and search for the lost city of Atlantis. Along the way, you'll encounter lots of fish and many strange creatures. Some of the creatures are quite large and may even attack your vessel.

This attraction is a marvel of engineering. Spoiler alert: You are never submerged in water during this attraction. The windows of your submarine are actually two panes of glass with a small amount of water between them. As the submarine dives, air is injected into the water, creating bubbles. By controlling the amount and direction of the bubbles, it seems that you are gliding around under the water. You may not believe it, but everything you see from fish to shells is actually completely dry.

There is always a line for this ride. My suggestion is to skip Toy Story Mania; you can ride that elsewhere. Let the Japanese guests run to Toy Story while you run here and grab a Fastpass. Then ride Journey to the Center of Earth and come back to use your 20,000 Leagues Fastpass later.

### Journey to the Center of the Earth

*Fastpass* This is a second unbelievable ride themed to a Jules Verne novel. Journey to the Center of the Earth is much like the Indiana Jones ride but with a lot more theming. You'll board a subterranean vehicle and explore the wonders underneath Mount Prometheus. There are amazing things to see down here, and some of them are quite dangerous.

Your vehicle will move a lot, but it's never been a problem for me. There is a brief roller-coaster section where your vehicle will careen around the mountain; you can even see this section from the outside.

This ride will also build a very long line as the day progresses. Again, skip Toy Story Mania and head here in the morning. Get a Fastpass for one of the Jules Verne rides and then ride the other and return later with your Fastpass.

### Shops of Mysterious Island
**Nautilus Gifts** is the only store here. It's small but full of steampunk Disney items.

### Dining in Mysterious Island
**Nautilus Galley:** This kiosk sells quick-service snacks and always has a very long line for Chinese hot dogs.

**Refreshment Station:** Even Jules Verne may want a quick-service churro.

**Vulcania Restaurant:** This amazingly themed cafeteria features Chinese food. Vulcania is my favorite place to eat at Tokyo DisneySea. You should get the spicy tofu and rice.

## Parades, Evening Shows, and Special Events
Instead of traditional parades, all of Tokyo DisneySea's events take place on Mediterranean Harbor. You'll see people, and their Duffys, stake a place to sit well in advance of any performance. Think in terms of hours, not minutes.

### *Crystal Wishes Journey or Something Else Like It*

A few times each day (check the daily Times Guide), Tokyo DisneySea presents a character party on the water. The current version, Crystal Wishes, is scheduled to run until the middle of March 2017. But don't worry—anything that replaces it will be quite similar.

As the music starts, huge floats (this is one parade where the floats actually do float) sail into Mediterranean Harbor. The floats are filled with characters and lots of dancers. The whole harbor will come alive with other speedy watercraft zipping colorfully around.

The floats will dock close to the shore, and the characters will depart the vessels. They'll dance around and perform choreographed movements. After a bunch of fireworks and an eruption from Mount Prometheus, everyone will get back on their floats and depart.

It's fun to see these shows because there's nothing else like them. But don't sit around for hours. Just walk around close to show time and you'll be sure to find someplace to stand, even if your view isn't perfect.

### *Fantasmic!*

The evening show at Tokyo DisneySea is Fantasmic! It's the same show from Disneyland and Walt Disney World, and it's spectacular no matter where you see it.

Mickey will again attempt to defeat the evil villains using pyrotechnics and lots of music. Maleficent will make an appearance and turn into a fire-breathing dragon. And all of Mickey's friends will come to his aid.

The effects are outstanding. Here at Tokyo DisneySea, the water is used a bit better than at the other parks. There are lots of water effects, including large fountains and water cannons. Also, the backdrop of Mount Prometheus is unforgettable, especially when it erupts.

You'll see people finding a space quite early. But, again, don't worry about sitting. The show lasts twenty minutes, and you can find a spot to stand shortly before show time.

### Halloween, Christmas, and Easter

All three of these Western holidays are celebrated well at Tokyo DisneySea. You'll see amazing decorations throughout the park, but most of the festivities occur on Mediterranean Harbor.

During Halloween, the Crystal Wishes show will be replaced with...well, basically the same show. But the characters will ride on floating pumpkins.

During Christmas, the Crystal Wishes show will be replaced with...well, basically the same show. But the characters will ride on floating Christmas stuff.

During Easter, the Crystal Wishes show will be replaced with...you get the picture, right?

### Fireworks

Tokyo DisneySea has the same lackluster fireworks show as Tokyo Disneyland. When I say same, I mean same. The fireworks are aimed so that they appear over Westernland in one park and off the side of the harbor in the other.

I hate ending this whole section about the amazing Tokyo DisneySea on such a lackluster note, but that's the way it is. Just spend your day doing all the other incredible things. Then enjoy the fact that you don't have to rush to get to the fireworks.

*Dreamlly's Disney Direction*

Japan has extremely strict employment restrictions. It's virtually impossible for a non-Japanese citizen to gain employment inside the country of Japan. You will encounter very few, if any, non-Japanese cast members at Tokyo Disney Resort.

One exception is the face characters. A face character is any character that doesn't wear a mask over his or her head. Cinderella, Belle, and Prince Charming are all face characters. Disney insists that all their characters look as close to the films as possible. Consequently, Disney has made a good case to the Japanese government that Caucasian people need to be hired for most face characters except for Mulan, Tiana, Pocahontas, and Moana.

Many Disney-loving Americans would love to work at the fantastic Tokyo Disney Resort. But unless you look like Ariel or Prince Eric, you will not get a job here. (Also of note, Cinderella's fairy godmother is a face character all around the world, always portrayed by a lovely older woman. For some reason, here in Tokyo, the fairy godmother wears a very creepy old-woman mask. It's really not as creepy as it is terrifying. You will see her as she's never not near the Tokyo Disneyland entrance or in Fantastyland.)

▲ ▲ ▲

## Ikspiari

Ikspiari is Tokyo Disney Resort's sprawling entertainment and shopping district. To pronounce it, my Japanese friend told me to think about the word "experience" but don't say the "ence."

Ikspiari is like Downtown Disney and Disney Springs in the way that it has shops and restaurants, but it looks completely different. Ikspiari is an indoor mall. It's free to visit Ikspiari, and it's an easy walk from both the Resort Gateway Station and Maihama Station.

There are hundreds of shops and restaurants here. There's even a grocery store. (Wouldn't it be nice if the American properties had one of those?) Ikspiari has a movie theater with all films in Japanese.

The largest shop inside Ikspiari is the **Disney Store.** But this shop should not be confused with another that sits outside the complex. I'll explain. Between Ikspiari and Tokyo Disneyland is a large store that's shaped like a bunch of suitcases. This store is called **Bon Voyage.** Here, you can buy all the souvenir merchandise that's sold inside the parks. The Disney Store inside Ikspiari sells the merchandise that you can find at all other Disney Stores in Japan. These stores do not sell the same items. Nor do they sell items that you find at the American Disney Stores. A true Disney fan will want to visit both shops at Tokyo Disney Resort.

## Area Sights outside Disney

There is a lot to see outside Tokyo Disney Resort—a lot. Tokyo is not just the largest, but it's also one of the world's greatest cities. The fantastic rail system makes it easy to be as active as you want.

It's also fairly quick and convenient to visit places outside of Tokyo. The bullet trains, called Shinkansen in Japanese, are quick, to say the least. The maglev lines of the Shinkansen run up to 375 miles per hour (603 kilometers per hour). Tokyo Station, easily accessible from Tokyo Disney Resort in around fifteen minutes, is the station where you can find the Shinkansen to all points around Honshu (the island that includes Tokyo).

Here are some of my favorite places to visit in Tokyo proper and the accompanying train station.

**Meiji Shrine**—Beautiful forested shrine of the Emperor Meiji. The parklike grounds are expansive and well manicured. Station: Harajuku.

**Harajuku**—This is a street where people dress in cosplay; you'll see everything here, especially on a Sunday night. When I say everything, I mean literally everything. Harajuku offers the strangest sights you're likely to behold in Japan. Station: Harajuku.

**Shinjuku**—A haven of nightlife where all the lights and people will blow your mind. Shinjuku is a combination of Times Square, Las Vegas, your local arcade, and an episode of *Hoarders*. Shinjuku also contains the seat of Tokyo's government and the world's busiest train station. Here is where you'll find white-gloved "pushers" cramming people onto subway cars during rush hour. This ward of Tokyo is the unofficial home of Godzilla; you can see the giant lizard towering over Shinjuku. Station: Shinjuku.

**Shibuya**—There's shopping all around, but the main draw is Shibuya Crossing. This is the world's busiest pedestrian crossing. When the lights change, thousands of people come from seemingly out of nowhere to cross the street. It's truly a sight to behold. Station: Shibuya.

**Asakusa**—This area includes my favorite shrine, Sensoji Temple (it's Buddhist, not Shinto). There is an amazing souvenir shopping street leading to the temple called Nakamise Dori. If you can't find it here, then it doesn't exist. Station: Asakusa.

**Akihabara**—The technology center of Tokyo. The newest gadgets you didn't even know existed are for sale here. This is also the animé center of Tokyo. Station: Akihabara.

# 5

---

## Disneyland Paris

BIENVENUE A PARIS! What many consider the most beautiful city in the world, and it very well may be, Paris has been thriving with art and culture for centuries. It's a city with a gorgeous river, famous art museums, unbelievable architecture, romantic avenues, and pastry shop after pastry shop.

Disneyland Paris Resort is equally beautiful. No expense was spared while creating the original park, and it shows. This is the best constructed of the "Magic Kingdom"-style parks in the world. It's simply gorgeous.

Currently, Disneyland Paris Resort is the most-visited attraction on the entire continent of Europe. You may have heard that there are other things to do and see in Europe, but none of them attract as many visitors as La Château de la Belle au Bois Dormant.

However, no other theme park on this planet has the turbulent history of Euro Disneyland/Disneyland Paris. It's a story of complex cultures coming together. It's a story of some failure and much success. It's a story where the loudest people in the room are not necessarily correct.

Disneyland Paris Resort includes two theme parks: Disneyland Parc and Walt Disney Studios. There is an entertainment district called Disney Village. Seven Disney resort hotels are located on the property, as is a large train station with direct service to Paris.

In a city of beauty, Disneyland Paris Resort is Disney's beautiful jewel.

Disneyland Paris Resort Pros:

- The incredible city of Paris is a direct train ride away.
- The most beautiful of all the Disney castles is here.
- It's easy to walk between the parks and most Disney hotels.
- Disneyland Parc was built with amazing attention to design.

- Walt Disney Studios is expanding but retains its educational attractions.

Disneyland Paris Resort Cons:

- There aren't enough cast members.
- The resort's restaurants tend to close early, making dinner sometimes difficult.
- Not everything works all the time.
- There aren't enough cast members.

▲ ▲ ▲

## History

If you ask most Americans about Disneyland Paris, you'll likely receive some comment referring to it as the failing Euro Disneyland. For many, the only headlines they remember are the early ones. Stories about failure sell more papers than stories about success; consequently, the media doesn't really report on the park's successes—and there have been many.

The idea of a Disneyland in Europe is nothing new. In fact, even Walt mentioned this idea during the early years of Disneyland. It just made sense. Many of Disney's early successes were built on European tales. In addition, the Mickey Mouse films were extremely popular in Europe because their stories were told through action with little English dialogue. However, Walt was preoccupied with

Disneyland and then the Florida Project during the end of his life.

It was after the tremendous success of Tokyo Disneyland in 1983 that Disney executives started taking a second look at Europe. These were the Michael Eisner years as the head of Disney. Mr. Eisner was many things but lazy was not one of them. He was ambitious to a fault.

In 1984, two imagineers were tasked with scouting locations in Europe. By this time, European governments had heard rumors of Disney's quest for land, and they were hungry to have the massive, job-creating park in their countries. At one time, over one thousand possible locations had been identified by the scouts.

After much research, only four locations remained in 1985. Two of them were along the Mediterranean coast of Spain. The third location was also near the Mediterranean in the French town of Toulon. The fourth location was a plot of farmland about twenty-five miles (forty kilometers) east of Paris in Marne-la-Vallée.

As time progressed, the French were able to put together a financing package that was far superior to Spain's. The location near Toulon was preferred because it had a warmer climate. However, early land exploration revealed a type of bedrock that made it unsuitable for theme-park development. On December 18, 1985, Michael Eisner signed the first letter of intent with the French government to build a theme park in Marne-la-Vallée, France.

The final preconstruction deal was made in March of 1987. Disney wasn't interested in the same deal they received in Tokyo. Here, they wanted more of the pie and were willing to pay for it upfront. The French agreement created a company called Euro Disney SCA. One-third of this company was owned by Disney. The second third was owned by Saudi Arabian Prince Al-Waleed Bin Abdulaziz. The last third was publicly owned by French shareholders. The three partners would split the construction cost. They would also equally split all profits after Disney received a percentage for use of their intellectual property.

Construction on the park began in August of 1988. At the same time, Euro Disney SCA decided to build seven hotels on the property. A council of architects, including Frank Gehry and Michael Graves, was hired to design the hotels and an entertainment complex.

As soon as the first shovel hit the dirt, the controversies started to fly. Ariana Mnouchkine, a theatrical director from Paris, called the park a "cultural Chernobyl." The phrase stuck. Soon, much of the Parisian media was calling for an end to the project, stating that it was the death of French culture by the Americans. Article after article appeared condemning Euro Disneyland and directing Mickey Mouse to stay in America and Japan.

However, history has shown us that the loudest people in the room are not always the most representative. These early negative opinions were from a few in the Parisian media; the general population of France was supportive of the resort. In fact, by November 1991, twenty-four thousand people had applied to work at the park.

Mr. Eisner was well aware of the critiques, and his response was to meet them head on—he had a bit of an ego. He began to pour money into the project; he was going to show the French how to build something beautiful. Initially, this decision led to a decade of financial stress for Euro Disney SCA. Now that we look back, we can appreciate his decision as it created one gorgeous park.

The second round of controversy was even more intense. As soon as cast members started training at the newly constructed Disney University, Disney stared having run-ins with organized labor in France. The French have the most organized and powerful labor unions on the planet. This was but the first time Disney and French Labor collided—there would be many more. In fact, these disputes have been the top problem of Euro Disneyland/Disneyland Paris Resort since its opening.

The unions did not like Disney's rules about appearance and hygiene. They believed that Disney was infringing on the rights of workers. Disney argued that their entire theme-park empire was built on an image. They insisted that the park would only succeed if the guests encountered the experience they were expecting, and that experience counted on a clean-cut image.

Organized protests and demonstrations plagued the construction site. Interestingly, very few of the actual cast members had an issue with Disney; it was the organized labor activists who were instigating the demonstrations.

Construction proceeded despite the criticism. On April 12, 1992, Euro Disneyland opened to the general public. But only twenty-four thousand of that general public showed up on opening day. The French media had scared people away by warning of massive traffic jams that never occurred. Meanwhile, in the United States, the American media was having a field day with one negative story after another.

To make matters worse, Europe began to experience a recession soon after the park opened. Park attendance held steady at twenty-five thousand per day (the park was designed for an average of sixty thousand per day). Hotel occupancy fell, and the largest of the seven hotels was closed. Euro Disney SCA announced a sizable loss for the first year of operation. Things were not looking good, and the enormous debt encumbered during construction was starting to show its ugly face.

On the brink of financial disaster, Euro Disney SCA was reorganized in March of 1994. Disney agreed to use money from its other divisions to pay off half of Euro Disneyland's debt. Disney also agreed to waive their right for compensation to use their intellectual property. Finally, Disney agreed to purchase half of $1.1 billion in new shares. The other half of the shares was split between French shareholders and Prince Adbulaziz. Again, the American media published their stories.

With less debt and a new source of income, Euro Disneyland forged ahead. A new investment in advertising resulted in a spike in attendance and hotel occupancy. The park's attendance increased by 21 percent between 1994 and 1995. At the end of 1995, Euro Disney SCA returned a profit for the first time. A turnaround had begun. (No stories were written about this in the United States.)

By 1998, things were looking up around the entire resort. In fact, things were so good that consideration could now be given to building a second park. Disney-MGM Studios in Orlando was enjoying tremendous success at this time. It was decided that a Hollywood-themed park would do well in France. Construction began adjacent to Euro Disneyland.

The year 2002 was a pivotal one for the park. Walt Disney Studios Park opened on March 16, 2002. Euro Disneyland also opened that day but under a new name. The Americans conceded that they'd made a mistake. For Americans, the word "Euro" has a connotation of travel and adventure. But for Europeans, the word "Euro" sounds like a no-fun business term. The name of the park was officially changed to Disneyland Parc. The entire property was now Disneyland Paris Resort.

The new additions and changes paid off, and attendance once again grew. Occupancy at all seven hotels was now over 90 percent, and profits were being made. But, again, the economy came back to bite Disneyland Paris. The world recession of the late 2000s hit the park hard.

Now, enter Mickey Mouse with his recession-proof pockets. Disney does well in America and Japan during recessions. People tend to flock to movie theaters when they can't afford anything else. Disney's acquisitions of Marvel Comics and Lucasfilm started to turn huge profits. Not only did Mickey have the money, but he also had a desire to bring Disneyland Paris more fully into the Disney family.

In September of 2012, the Walt Disney Company bought most of Disneyland Paris Resort from Prince Adbulaziz and French shareholders. Disney paid $1.5 billion and now owned 82 percent of Disneyland Paris Resort. Then, in February of 2017, Disney purchased 90 percent of Kingdom Holding Company and its remaining shares of Disneyland Paris Resort. Currently, the Walt Disney Company owns all but 14.3 percent of the resort. However, that won't last long as Bob Iger has announced an aggressive $1 billion compaign to aquire the remaining shares.

Today, Disneyland Paris Resort is experiencing renovations as a result of Disney's cash flow. Disney is banking that future profits of the resort will be high, and they'll get to keep 95 to 100 percent of all that cash. A new land based on the film *Ratatouille* just opened at Walt Disney Studios. There are many rumors about other new lands themed with *Star Wars* and Marvel Comics.

Despite what many in America believe, Disneyland Paris Resort is not going anywhere. Attendance figures are good, and there is excitement for future attractions.

And perhaps all the controversy and financial distress make this park the realest of them all.

## Travel Knowledge

### Arrival

If you're already in Paris, Disneyland Paris Resort is just one train ride away. There are two train systems that run underneath Paris. The Paris Metro is the subway system that serves the city itself. The Paris RER is a regional train system that serves the outlying areas. RER trains go below the ground in Paris and above the ground when they reach the suburbs.

To get to Disneyland Paris Resort, make your way, either by Metro or foot, to Châtelet Les Halles. Here you'll catch the RER A4. It will take forty-five minutes and cost €7.60 ($8.52). You will ride all the way to the end of the line and depart at Marne-la-Vallée–Chessy. Most RER maps also call this station Parcs Disneyland. When you exit the station, you'll be right in the middle of Disneyland Paris Resort. It's an easy walk to either park, Disney Village, Disneyland Hotel, and Hotel New York. If your destination is another Disney hotel, you'll find shuttle buses that will take you there right outside the station.

The largest airport in the area is Charles de Gaulle International Airport. By far, this airport has the most international flights in France. France is in the Schengen Zone, a collection of European nations that act with a single border. When you clear customs and passport control at Charles de Gaulle, you are entering the Schengen Zone and can travel anywhere within it without having to pass through border control again.

The quickest way to get from Charles de Gaulle to Disneyland Paris Resort is to take a TGV train. TGV is a rail network that operates even farther from the city than RER. The TGV will take just twelve minutes and will cost €17.50 ($19.61). However, the TGV train only runs during the middle of the day. During other times, your best option is to take RER B3 from the airport to Châtelet Les Halles. There, transfer to the RER A4 and depart at Marne-la-Vallée–Chessy.

A taxi from Charles de Gaulle to Disneyland Paris Resort will cost around €49.00 ($54.91). Unfortunately, an Uber in France is about the same price as a cab. However, Uber is constantly in French courts, and this may change.

Many people, especially Europeans, drive to Disneyland Paris Resort. The property is located off the A4 motorway, just east of Paris. Exit 12.1 serves Val d'Europe and the non-Disney hotels, Exit 13 is for Disney's Davy Crockett Ranch, and Exit 14 serves everything else. Once you take your exit, follow signs to your destination. The entire area is a well-marked tourist destination.

### Entry Requirements

People entering France (and all the Schengen Zone) need to have a valid passport and proof of return flight. Citizens of the United States, Australia, Japan, New

Zealand, and Canada do not need a visa to enter Europe. Citizens of other countries should check with their government's department of travel to discover if they need a visa to visit the Schengen Zone.

Of course, anyone already living in the Schengen Zone doesn't need to even go through border control. Citizens of the United Kingdom may visit the Schengen Zone with a passport and no visa.

### Parking

It costs €20.00 ($22.41) to park for a day at Disneyland Paris Resort. It's free to park if you're staying at a Disney hotel. Some of the non-Disney partner hotels also include a free parking pass; you'll know if they do at the time of reservation.

### Time

Disneyland Paris Resort is in the central European time zone. It's the same time as Madrid, Berlin, Rome, and most of western Europe. Paris is one hour ahead of London and Lisbon. It's six hours ahead of New York City, nine hours ahead of California, and seven hours behind Tokyo in the summer, eight hours behind in the winter.

Europe observes daylight saving time, but it doesn't change its clocks during the same weekends as the United States. Europe begins DST on the last Sunday in March and ends DST on the last Sunday of October.

### Language

Paris is decidedly French—that should be no surprise. But you'll find that Disneyland Paris Resort is decidedly multilingual. You'll see that every sign is in French, German, English, Italian, Dutch, and Spanish. However, most of the main dialogue during shows will be in French and English.

Cast members will have one or more little flags on the bottom of their nametags. Those flags will let you know which language(s) that person speaks. If you're looking for the US flag to find someone who speaks English, you'll be looking for a long time. The British flag is the official flag of the English language here.

### Weather

Paris has fairly good weather most of the year. It's colder than California during the winter and has more humidity than California during the summer. But the summer is not nearly as oppressive as Florida, Tokyo, Shanghai, and Hong Kong.

Fall and spring are gorgeous in Paris. The beautiful landscaping around the resort is lovely during these times. It's rare, but it can snow at Disneyland Paris Resort. If it does, you'll find that a magical layer of sparkling white makes the whole place even better. Snow does not generally last for very long.

Weather in Europe is extremely relative. The British will think that any day with sun is perfect, even if it's cold.

The Italians will be freezing, even in the summer. The French are only happy when it's cold enough to wear a fashionable jacket but warm enough to take the jacket off to reveal a fashionable outfit underneath.

## *Money*

The euro (€) is the official currency of France and most of the European Union. Credit cards are accepted everywhere at Disneyland Paris Resort. Just make sure that your credit card has a chip and that you know your international PIN. Your international PIN may be different than your PIN back home; check with your bank to make sure.

You can exchange British pounds and US dollars at most hotels in the area. Or for a better exchange rate, you can get euros from an ATM. Recently, the European markets have taken a tumble due to the British vote to leave the European Union. I remember when €1.00 was worth $1.30. As this book was going to press, €1.00 was worth $1.12.

France employs a VAT (value added tax) system. All food prices contain a 5.5 percent VAT. Other goods will require a VAT of 19.6 percent. Almost all the time, the VAT is included in any printed price. If you spend more than a threshold amount at certain shops, as a tourist you are qualified to receive a VAT refund. If you qualify, you'll be given information at the time of purchase. It's easy to get a VAT refund at the airport or electronically on your credit card.

Lodging tax in France is a bit complicated. Normally, there is a flat tax of 10 percent plus a per-person fee included in your hotel rate. The per-person fee changes as to the type of accommodation; higher-end hotels have a higher fee. Hotels are categorized according to level and not price. A more expensive three-star hotel will have a cheaper fee than a lesser expensive four-star hotel. Anyway, you don't really need to understand this lodging tax because it's usually included with the rate at time of booking.

Service tipping in France is a gesture; it's not a necessary act. Nobody will think poorly if you don't leave a tip. Normally, it's customary to round your bill to an amount that makes sense. If your bill is €9.23, just hand the server €10, smile, and walk away. For a bill of €72.34, give the server €80. In any case, hand the money to the server and do not just leave it on the table as in the United States. Leaving money in the open is quite rude and will make the server feel less like a server and more like a servant.

### Tickets

Now that Disney controls the majority of this resort, it's easy to purchase tickets online. Tickets can be purchased separately or as part of a hotel reservation. For the purposes of this discussion, everyone twelve and older is an adult, those three to eleven are children, and humans younger than three are free. The prices listed are the prices you'll pay on the day of your visit. If you prepurchase tickets online at least one day in advance, you'll save €4.00 ($4.48) per ticket.

A one-day, one-park ticket is €75.00 ($84.04) per adult and €67.00 ($75.08) per child. Once you use this ticket to enter one of the parks, you cannot enter the other park. A one-day, two-park ticket is €90.00 ($100.85) per adult and €82.00 ($91.89) per child. On this ticket, you can hop between the two parks as much as you want during a single day.

Once you purchase a multiday ticket, you will always get the option to hop between parks. A two-day, two-park ticket is €140.00 ($156.88) per adult and €126 ($141.19) per child. A three-day, two-park ticket is €174.00 ($194.98) per adult and €159.00 ($178.17) per child. And a four-day, two-park ticket is €212.00 ($237.56) per adult and €192.00 ($215.15) per child.

### Park Hours

Disneyland Parc is normally open from 10:00 a.m. to 10:00 p.m. on weekends and 10:00 a.m. to 7:00 p.m. on weekdays. During higher seasons, the park may stay open until 10:00 p.m. even on weekdays.

Walt Disney Studios normally opens at 10:00 a.m. and closes about two hours before Disneyland Parc.

Please note that restaurants are apt to close much earlier than the parks. If Disneyland Parc is closing at 7:00 p.m. or earlier, you will not be able to find a place to eat dinner inside the park. In that case, your best options include the hotels and Disney Village.

I'd also like to officially apologize to my international friends for using the a.m./p.m. system in this book.

## Accommodations

Yes, it's possible to get a hotel in the city of Paris and take the train to Disneyland Paris Resort. This is fine if you plan to visit the resort for one day and spend the rest of your time in Paris. The train ride is about forty-five minutes each way.

If you want to spend more time than that in the parks, it's best to stay closer. There are seven Disney hotels located on resort property.

At Val d'Europe, the train stop right before Disneyland Paris Resort, you'll find a huge mall and many nice non-Disney hotels. These hotels are closely associated with the resort and will offer ticket and parking packages. Most of these hotels also run some sort of scheduled shuttle to the parks. You can book with these hotels directly via their websites. Just do a search for "Val d-Europe hotels," and you can easily find a list.

### Disney Hotels

All Disney hotels at the resort are wonderfully themed. They are also very American. Earlier research into the typical guests revealed that Europeans wanted an American experience when they stayed at the resort. The seven Disney Hotels are themed to reflect seven different areas of the United States.

Each of these hotels comes with a continental breakfast for a fee (you're on the continent, remember?). They also include free parking. Some of the more expensive properties have character greetings during the breakfast time. Also, guests of Disney hotels can enter one of the two parks early on certain days. You can check online if Extra Magic Hours are occurring during your stay. If they are, you may enter the designated park two hours before the general public.

When you book an online reservation for a Disneyland Paris hotel, your booking will automatically include park tickets. These tickets are for hopper admission to both parks for every day of your stay. For example, a two-night reservation will include tickets for three days at both parks. Even if you book using a non-Disney site like hotels.com, the reservation will include tickets. The only way to reserve a Disneyland Paris hotel without tickets is to call the hotel directly. Hotel rates without tickets are not much cheaper; only do this if you absolutely do not want to enter either park.

Each of the hotels has restaurants and lounges. As a general rule, the more expensive properties have more expensive dining options.

### Disneyland Hotel

The elegant Disneyland Hotel is themed to match Main Street, USA. It's Victorian splendor that's beautifully done. The 496-room hotel opened with the rest of the park in April 1992. You can enter Disneyland Parc by just going downstairs. It's a very short walk to Walt Disney Studios.

This hotel has a fantastic location right above the entrance gate to Disneyland Parc. Rooms on one side of the hotel have amazing views of the Disneyland Paris

Railroad Station and Main Street, USA. Some of the more spectacular rooms have balconies and/or windows that look directly at Main Street and the castle. From these rooms, you will have a bird's-eye view of all parades and fireworks. Rooms on the other side of the hotel are a bit cheaper but also have great views of the Fantasia Gardens. You really can't go wrong with a view at this hotel.

Most of the rooms are standard with two double beds. There are also larger rooms with multiple beds that sleep more people.

This is the most expensive hotel in the area; it's also one of the most expensive in Paris. A standard room with no view starts at €610 ($683.55).

### Disney's Hotel New York

This property was designed by famed architect Michael Graves. The outside gives the impression of the New York City skyline without being too literal. The front of the hotel faces Disney Village, and the back faces Lac Buena Vista, a small body of water that was Disney-made.

You can walk to either park easily from Hotel New York. It's also a very short walk to Disney Village and the train station to Paris.

The interior is themed like art-deco Rockefeller Center. You'll also see some nods to taxi cabs, apples, and Central Park. The hotel has 565 rooms.

Rooms of this hotel are full of little touches of New York City. The furniture and fixtures will remind you, in a clever way, of the Big Apple. Most of the rooms have two beds, but some offer multiple beds for families. This has become my hotel of choice while visiting the resort.

Hotel New York is much cheaper than the Disneyland Hotel. It still offers great amenities and has an excellent location. A standard room with no view starts at €300.00 ($336.17).

### Disney's Newport Bay Club

The theme of this hotel is Cape Cod and New England. With 1,098 rooms, it's the largest hotel on the property. When it opened, it was the largest hotel in all of Europe.

Newport Bay Club is located directly on Lac Buena Vista. All the water fits well with the theme of this hotel. Even if you're not staying here, the hotel makes a nice background for a photograph. You can walk to the parks, or there is a free shuttle bus.

Most of the rooms are standard with two beds. There are some nice views of Lac Buena Vista on one side and parking lot views on the other. Prices at this hotel are comparable to those at Hotel New York, just a bit cheaper. A standard room with no view starts at €290.00 ($324.97).

### Disney's Sequoia Lodge

Disney's Sequoia Lodge is just slightly smaller than Newport Bay Club. It contains 1,011 rooms. This beautiful property sits directly across Disney Village on Lac Buena Vista.

The theme of this hotel is American national park lodge. Thousands of trees were planted near the hotel to give the illusion that it's in the woods. The trees have grown nicely, and the atmosphere feels great.

You can walk to the parks in about twenty minutes, or there is a free shuttle bus.

Disney's Sequoia Lodge contains mostly standard rooms. On one side, rooms face the lac (lake) and Disney Village. Rooms on the other side face the wooded property. This is another hotel with all-around good views.

This property is slightly cheaper than Newport Bay Club, mostly because the location is just a little farther from the parks. Expect to pay €250.00 ($280.14) for a standard room with wooded view.

### Disney's Hotel Cheyenne and Disney's Hotel Santa Fe

These are two separate hotels, but they're fairly similar. Each hotel contains one thousand rooms. They sit across from each other on the Rio Grande, a Disney-made river. Neither hotel is on Lac Buena Vista. You can walk to the parks in about fifteen minutes or take a free shuttle bus.

Hotel Cheyenne is an American western-themed hotel. Woody and Jessie from *Toy Story* are heavily featured here. Hotel Santa Fe is themed to the American southwest. It has more of a desert feel and features the *Cars* characters. There are lots of pine trees around Hotel Cheyenne and many cacti around Hotel Santa Fe.

Most of the rooms are standard. These are the most affordable properties at Disneyland Paris Resort. The furniture and fixtures aren't as nice as the hotels around Lac Buena Vista. But guests still get Extra Magic Hours and the ability to walk to the parks. Some of the rooms have views of the Rio Grande and other themed areas of the hotels.

A standard room without a view starts at €170.00 ($190.50).

### Disney's Davy Crockett Ranch

This is the farthest property from the parks. It's a fifteen-minute drive via your own vehicle as there isn't a shuttle. It's really not possible to walk from Davy Crockett Ranch. However, guests still get the use of Extra Magic Hours and free parking at the theme parks.

Davy Crockett Ranch is comprised of 595 cabins. They are surrounded by a wooded environment. All cabins come with a small kitchen and full bathrooms. Some have one bedroom, and others have two bedrooms. They are not air-conditioned. Also, housekeeping is not available during your stay.

The entire property is surprisingly large with several trails, pools, a tennis court, Crockett's Tavern restaurant, a video arcade, and a small store.

The privacy that the ranch offers makes it appealing; however, the distance makes it less convenient. Consequently, the rate per night is similar to the Hotel Cheyenne and Hotel Santa Fe. A one-bedroom cabin starts at €170.00 ($190.50). Two-bedroom units are €40.00 ($44.82) more.

## Disneyland Parc

Les félicitations! Congratulations! You've made it to Disneyland Parc at Disneyland Paris Resort. You've come many miles, but no matter if you came by boat, plane, train, or automobile, you're standing in front of the Fantasia Gardens.

Normally, bag check and security occur when you enter the plaza that connects the two parks, train station, and Disney Village. Since the entrance to the Disneyland Hotel is within this plaza, guests will have their bags (and luggage) checked when they enter the hotel.

Fantasia Gardens is a lovely area that looks great no matter the season. There are several paths that meander through the flowers. In order to enter the park, you must cross the garden and proceed underneath the Disneyland Hotel. That's where you'll have your park ticket scanned. When you exit through the other side of the Disneyland Hotel, you'll notice another plaza. This plaza sits between the hotel and the park.

Up ahead is the Disneyland Paris Railroad Station. Just like in the United States, you'll pass underneath the railroad station and enter Town Square. Here you'll get your first view of the very best Disney castle in the world: Le Château de la Belle au Bois Dormant (Sleeping Beauty Castle). There will be more about the fabulous castle later. Right now, enter Town Square. Even though you're in France, welcome to Main Street, USA.

## Main Street, USA

Guests who have been to Disneyland or the Magic Kingdom at Walt Disney World should feel right at home here—except there are a lot of French words on the buildings. This isn't, exactly, what Main Street looks like in the United States. It's more like what an ideal Main Street would look like if the British had lost the colonies to France. It's always a bit odd, and often it feels more like Main Street, Canada. But I've learned that the more I embrace these differences, the more I learn from them. It's kind of cool being on Main Street, USA and hearing so many different languages being spoken.

Aside from the language, the design of the street and the forced perspective are similar to the American parks. However, the large Disneyland Hotel as an anchor behind the train station adds a layer of Victorian theming that I really like.

There is another hidden feature to Main Street that is absolutely brilliant. In the very corners of Town Square, the corners farthest from the train station, you will notice two covered walkways, one in each corner. These walkways are called arcades. They are themed to the Victoria era and stretch all the way from Town Square to the central hub in front of the castle. This means that when an evening parade or fireworks show is over, the crowds have three ways to exit: down Main Street or through one of the two arcades. I sure miss this feature when I'm back in the United States and the entire nation has to exit down Main Street.

### Liberty Arcade

Facing the castle, the arcade on your left is Liberty Arcade. This covered walkway is designed as a salute to one of the best gifts ever given: the Statue of Liberty. As you walk down the arcade, the story of Lady Liberty is told from conception to placement in New York's harbor. You'll learn about Gustav Eiffel; the same man who built the tower designed the inner framework for the statue. Frédéric Bartholdi, the statue's sculptor, also makes an appearance. In the middle of the arcade, you'll see a reproduction of the statue's dedication ceremony. The reproduction is complete with life-size figures and a recording of US President Grover Cleveland's original speech.

### Discovery Arcade

Back in Town Square and facing the castle, the arcade on your right is Discovery Arcade. This arcade is dedicated to great American inventions of the nineteenth century. The walls are lined with reproductions of diagrams from the US Patent Office. You will be able to recognize many of the inventions here; some are even still in use today.

Also in this arcade are posters of large American cities. The posters are reproductions of actual art that was created in the nineteenth century but depicts the cities as people thought they'd look in the twentieth century. It's fun to look at the posters and see how close people's imaginations came to what was actually realized.

### Disneyland Paris Railroad Main Street Station
Up in the train station, you can board the Disneyland Paris Railroad for a round trip around the park. There are three other stations along the route where you can depart: Frontierland, Fantasyland, and Discoveryland.

The train ride is narrated mostly in French, but you'll hear lots of English words that really don't translate.

### Main Street Vehicles
Similar to the parks in the United States, you can also ride different types of vehicles up and down Main Street. Wait by one of the signs in Town Square, and some type of vehicle will deliver you to the central hub. There is a trolley, a fire engine, and also some horse-drawn streetcars.

### Shops of Main Street, USA
Just like its American cousins, Main Street is dedicated to shopping. You'll find the largest stores in the park and the most merchandise. This is where you can get Disneyland Paris Resort souvenirs.

**The Emporium** is the largest shop. But there are also **Disney Clothiers, Disneyana Collectibles,** and **Disney & Co. Boardwalk Candy Palace,** where you'll want to go if you're Japanese and need to purchase tins of candy for all your friends.

### Dining in Main Street, USA

**Walt's: An American Restaurant**: This table-service restaurant on Main Street offers American food.

**Plaza Gardens Restaurant:** This table-service buffet is located near the central hub.

**Casey's Corner:** The same quick-service hot dog café from the United States.

**Market House Deli:** Stop here for quick-service sandwiches.

**Victoria's Home Style Restaurant:** More American food is offered quick service here, including hamburgers.

### Frontierland

Europeans love Frontierland—mostly because it's something they never had. I once drove on a two-lane highway across Arizona with my friend from London. He constantly made me stop so that he could get out and take a picture of absolutely nothing. The nothingness fascinated him.

At Disneyland Parc, Frontierland is more cowboyish than the Frontierlands in the States. There is no Midwestern Tom Sawyer Island here.

Frontierland at Disneyland Parc is currently under extensive renovation. All the work is scheduled to be completed in the summer of 2017.

### Thunder Mesa Riverboats

Located along the Rivers of the Far West, Thunder Mesa is where you can board one of two riverboats.

The Mark Twain is recognizable because it has a paddle wheel in the back. While on this ship, you'll cruise the river and listen to narrations by Mark Twain. The narration is in English.

The Molly Brown is the only Disney riverboat that has paddle wheels on its side. Named after the famous *Titanic* survivor, while riding this ship you'll hear Molly Brown tell about her life in Colorado. Molly's speech is also in English. (Prior to 2011, both boats featured narration in French.)

The real Molly Brown was extremely famous in Europe. Her rags-to-riches appeal made her quite popular. The fact that she survived one of history's most famous disasters just added to her appeal.

Regardless of vessel, a riverboat journey takes about fifteen minutes.

### Big Thunder Mountain

*Fastpass* This is the fourth version of the ride on the planet, and it's also the best. Big Thunder Mountain occupies the island in the middle of the Rivers of the Far West (right where Tom Sawyer Island normally is located). You'll recognize the rock features of Monument Valley while you look across the river.

The fact that this coaster is on an island adds immensely to its appeal. After boarding the old mine train, you're immediately plunged into a tunnel that takes riders underneath the Rivers of the Far West. You'll pop out on the island and begin to climb the coaster's first hill.

From that point, you'll careen up, down, and around the rock formations. The theming on this ride is excellent with lots of special effects. You'll enter the mine, narrowly miss lots of obstacles, and get into an explosion. Eventually, you'll be plunged back underneath the river in order to return to the station.

Some rides that have world duplicates are so similar that it's not worth your time to ride if you're already used to the attraction. Big Thunder Mountain is not one of those. If you love the other versions of this ride, then it's well worth your effort to experience the Disneyland Parc version.

### Phantom Manor

Disneyland Parc's version of the Haunted Mansion is located in Frontierland. Like Big Thunder Mountain, this is the best version of this attraction on the planet.

Phantom Manor looks like an old Victorian mansion that you see on the outskirts of some prairie towns. It fits well into the Frontierland surroundings. You'll already notice a difference from the other parks on the outside. The versions in Disneyland, Magic Kingdom, and Tokyo Disneyland look fairly normal from a distance. It's when you get up close that you realize something weird is going on. Here at Disneyland Parc, the Phantom Manor looks creepy from any distance and angle. There's no way this house could not be haunted. A professional exorcist could live in this house, and it would still be haunted.

The queue and preshow are fairly similar to the other versions around the world. Then things start to go differently. As you climb aboard your doom buggy, you'll notice a beautiful, elegant staircase on your right. There is a more substantial back story inside this attraction than there is at the other Disney parks. The story is told through narration in both English and French. It's a bit difficult to piece together and was inspired partly by *The Phantom of the Opera.*

So it turns out that Thunder Mesa was founded in 1795 by a man named Henry Ravenswood. He built his manor on Boot Hill; from there he could see the whole town. Henry was responsible for the gold mine inside Big Thunder Mountain. As the miners dug deeper, they awoke the evil spirit of the Thunder Bird. It was told that this bird would appear in the form of an earthquake.

Henry and his wife, Martha, had a daughter named Melanie. She was quite beautiful and became engaged to a train engineer. The engineer had plans to move away from Thunder Mesa. Henry just couldn't stand the idea of his daughter leaving. He tried hard to stop the wedding, but, instead, he was killed in a massive earthquake.

On her wedding day, a mysterious phantom appeared and lured Melanie's groom into the attic. There, the phantom hung the groom from the rafters. The townspeople claimed that the phantom was actually Henry, having come back from the dead with the help of the Thunder Bird during the earthquake. Melanie went into a deep depression and refused to take off her wedding dress. She still sits inside the manor, wearing the dress, waiting for her groom to return.

Is everyone OK? There is actually a lot more to the story. You can read about it online. Imagineers often write a story to frame the attraction they are working on; in this case, they spared no detail.

Phantom Manor is the most macabre of all the Disney haunted attractions. At one point, your doom buggy will dip below the ground so that you can see the decaying corpses and bones in the cemetery. At the conclusion of the ride, you'll pass through a creepy frontier town. Apparently, these are the spirits of those who woke the Thunder Bird in the mine.

### Pocahontas Indian Village
In this interactive play area, young kids can climb and slide down several structures. Pocahontas makes appearances in this area.

### Disneyland Railroad Frontierland Depot
From here, you can catch the train to Fantasyland, Discoveryland, and Main Street, USA.

### Shops of Frontierland
**Thunder Mesa Mercantile** is the largest shop in this land. This store was probably built by Henry Ravenswood; it may be haunted. It's also the place to go for souvenirs and western-inspired items.

### Dining in Frontierland

**Silver Spur Steakhouse:** A table-service restaurant with grilled steaks.

**The Lucky Nugget Saloon:** Tex-Mex is served quick service here.

**Fuente del Oro Restaurant:** Quick-service American Southwest food can be found inside this spicy café.

**Cowboy Cookout Barbecue:** There's a lot of American food in Frontierland. Here is another quick-service place for hamburgers and chicken.

## Adventureland

You'll know you're in Adventureland when the desert turns into the jungle. Disney landscape designers worked hard to choose foliage that would thrive in this cooler environment. Those who miss Tom Sawyer Island and its opportunities to explore will find a great replacement here. You won't find a Jungle Cruise in this Adventureland, but you'll see the familiar sights of Aladdin and pirates.

### Le Passage Enchanté d'Aladdin (Aladdin's Enchanted Hallway)

At this walk-through attraction, you'll explore the story of Aladdin, Jasmine, and Genie. Beautiful vignettes recreate the story in great detail. You can journey through this attraction at your own pace, and there is never a line.

### Indiana Jones and the Temple of Peril

*Fastpass* At Disneyland Parc, this Indiana Jones attraction is a steel coaster. It's not the vehicle-adventure ride you find in California and Tokyo, but the theming is still great.

You'll ride in a runaway wagon through the jungle and around ruins of an ancient temple. There are no inversions, but the ride is fast and thrilling. Use a Fastpass to avoid a line on days of high park attendance.

### Adventure Isle

In the middle of Adventureland, you'll find an island surrounded by water. This is Adventure Isle. It's similar to Tom Sawyer Island in the fact that you can explore on your own. It's different because you don't have to wait for a raft to bring you there. There are several bridges that connect the island to the mainland. (This can be accomplished because there is no riverboat that needs to be accommodated.) I quite like this feature because as much as I love Tom Sawyer Island, I hate waiting for a raft to bring me back.

A large portion of Adventure Isle is full of caverns that wind and twist. You can spend a good deal of time exploring all the themed nooks and crannies.

Moored next to the island is a pirate galleon. You are welcome to board the galleon and discover how the pirates lived on this ship.

Also on the island is **Le Cabane des Robinson** (Robinson's Hut Shanty). This is a replica of the Swiss Family Robinson Treehouse from the Magic Kingdom. You can also journey through the tree house on your own.

Spend some time exploring Adventure Isle, especially if you're with kids who want to run and are tired of lines.

### Pirates of the Caribbean

Similar to the Disneyland version, you'll board a boat that floats through a restaurant on its way to see the pirates. All the familiar audio-animatronics and scenes are here. If you've never been on this attraction and don't have plans to visit a Disney park again, then you should ride it. Otherwise, this one is so similar to the others that you can skip it.

### Shops of Adventureland

**Les Trésors de Schéhérazade** (Scheherizade's Treasures) offers *Aladdin*-themed merchandise. **La Girafe Curieuse** (The Curious Giraffe) is for all your safari needs. **Temple Traders Boutique** and **Indiana Jones Adventure Outpost** are where you'll head for souvenirs and Indiana Jones items. **Le Coffre Du Capitaine** (The Captain's Chest) has all your pirate gifts and gifts for pirates.

### Dining in Adventureland

**Blue Lagoon:** This table-service restaurant is inside Pirates of the Caribbean. Some of the sunken tables have extremely poor views. I once ate here, and all I saw were others guests' feet. For a better table, get a reservation as close to opening time as possible.

**Colonel Hathi's Pizza Outpost:** Apparently, the elephant from *The Jungle Book* also makes quick-service pizza.

**Restaurant Hakuna Matata:** *Lion King*-themed café with quick service and no worries.

**Restaurant Agrabah Café:** A Mediterranean buffet with an *Aladdin* theme.

## Fantasyland

Of all the Disney Parks around the world, Fantasyland looks more at home here. Most of the iconic attractions of this land were inspired by tales that originated in Europe. That bit of belonging, plus the detailed design of the land, makes Fantasyland the sparking gem of Disneyland Parc.

Everything is romantic and charming here. From the gilded spires of the castle to Toad's rustic English pub, Fantasyland is very much like a dream.

### Le Château de la Belle au Bois Dormant (Sleeping Beauty Castle)

With my apologies to the people of Shanghai and their brand-spanking-new Enchanted Storybook Castle, I proclaim that Le Château de la Belle au Bois Dormant is still the best Disney castle on earth.

Imagineers had a huge problem: how do you make a spectacular castle in a country of spectacular castles? This had been easy in the United States. The only former royal residence on American soil is Iolani Palace in Hawaii, and that's not an iconic building most people recognize. The castle in Disneyland Parc (then Euro Disneyland) had to be something special.

One of the early ideas was to forget about a fairy tale castle entirely. Early sketches show Discoveryland, instead of Fantasyland, in the middle of the park. Replacing a fairy tale castle was to be a futuristic tower of iron and other metals. Then Michael Eisner entered the discussions. He was not going to be intimidated by European castles. He directed the imagineers to work on a spectacular fairy tale castle. (And he encumbered the debt necessary for construction.)

The result was Le Château de la Belle au Bois Dormant, Sleeping Beauty Castle, as only Paris could host. (Many people ask me why Paris's castle isn't named for Belle. After all, Belle seems to be the most French princess. However, *Beauty and the Beast* premiered just a few months before the park opened—well after the design phase. Had *Beauty and the Beast* premiered a couple of years earlier, the castle would most likely be called Le Château de la Belle et la Bête.)

Le Château de la Belle au Bois Dormant stands fifty meters (160 feet) tall. Unlike the other fiberglass castles, this one was constructed the old-fashioned way: using stone, masonry, glass, and gold. To give you an idea of how obsessed Disney was with this castle, each of its stained glass windows was created by Peter Chapman, the world's foremost expert in the art. In order to make time for Disneyland Parc, he had to take a break from his current project at the time: the restoration of all the stained glass of Notre Dame Cathedral in Paris.

Everything associated with this castle is gorgeous and graceful. The tapestries are real. The curtains are made out of the finest fabrics. All the woodwork was hand-shaped by Bavarian craftspeople. From the outside, it looks as if the castle is simply rising out of solid rock. The best masons in the world were brought to the park to complete this effect.

Does this castle compare to the real castles just down the road? Well, it doesn't have to. Le Château de la Belle au Bois Dormant is the embodiment of a fantasy. Unlike real castles, there isn't anything utilitarian about it. That's why I can't keep my eyes away from it.

### La Taniere du Dragon (The Dragon's Lair)

As if the castle weren't spectacular enough, it comes complete with its own dragon. Hidden deep underneath the structure is a network of winding tunnels. You'll explore on your own until you come face to face with a giant dragon. The dragon is twenty-seven meters (eighty-nine feet) long. When the park opened, this dragon was the largest audio-animatronic figure ever created.

The dragon is often sleeping. You'll see its massive body breathing slowly. But every once in a while, the dragon wakes up. You'll hear a sort of growl and see smoke bellow from its nose. The dragon's movements are controlled by a randomized program; you never know how long you can linger before the dragon springs awake.

### La Galerie de la Belle au Bois Dormant (Sleeping Beauty's Gallery)

This is where you want to head to get a closer look at Peter Chapman's extraordinary stained glass. On this walk-through attraction, you'll enter the castle and view various dioramas that tell the story of *Sleeping Beauty*. Some of the story is told in tapestry, other parts are told with figures, and still other parts are told via the amazing stained glass.

You can explore this attraction on your own. Seriously, even those not interested in *Sleeping Beauty* should experience the gallery. Everyone needs to see the stained glass and all the intricate details that can be accomplished with creativity and hard work.

### Le Carrousel de Lancelot (Lancelot's Carousel)

Lancelot, the French knight from Camelot, has a carousel here at Disneyland Parc. It's a stunning ride with gilded horses and painted scenes. You can get an amazing photograph by standing on the far side of the carousel. You won't forget the image of the castle rising above these beautiful horses.

### Blanche-Neige et les Sept Nains (Snow White and the Seven Dwarfs)

The same attraction as Snow White's Scary Adventure in Disneyland. It's not for the young and faint of heart, but others enjoy this dark ride.

### Les Voyages de Pinocchio (Pinocchio's Travels)

Similar to the versions in California and Tokyo. You'll travel through the world of Pinocchio and visit Pleasure Island before coming face to face with Monstro the whale.

### Peter Pan's Flight

*Fastpass* Similar to the version at the Magic Kingdom but without the interactive queue. You'll board a sailing galleon and fly with Peter over London. Eventually, you'll end up in Never Land with the evil Captain Hook.

The real London is only 343 kilometers (213 miles) from this attraction. Every Brit loves the story of *Peter Pan*, and they all will be in line for this attraction. Get a Fastpass to avoid a long line.

### Dumbo the Flying Elephant

As a general rule, when a story originates from continental Europe, its accompanying attraction is titled in French. When a story originates from England or the United States, the attraction is titled in English. Consequently, since Dumbo is an American story, the attraction is not L'éléphant Volant Dumbo. But the ride still includes sitting in a fiberglass Dumbo and rotating around a mouse.

### Mad Hatter's Tea Cups

The place to le puke and la barf if you are prone to motion sickness.

### Disneyland Railroad Fantasyland Station and Meet Mickey Mouse

From the station, you can take the train all the way to the front of the park. This can be a nice way to exit at the end of the day, especially if there is a parade or fireworks scheduled.

In front of the railroad station is where you can meet Mickey Mouse. The line often moves faster than it will appear.

### Alice's Curious Labyrinth
Explore this topiary maze on your own. There are many sculptures of characters from the film hidden inside the maze. It's fun to come around a corner and accidentally run into one of them—except when it's the Queen of Hearts.

### Princess Pavilion
Here is where you can meet one or more of the famous Disney princesses. Yes, not too far from Disneyland Parc lives actual royalty, but none of them are nearly as approachable as these. You never know which princesses will be featured, but it's often Cinderella, Belle, and Sleeping Beauty.

### "it's a small world"
The same attraction from the Magic Kingdom except that most of the song is in French.

### Casey Jr. Circus Train
Casey Jr. is the train that brings Dumbo and his mother around to different circus locations. Similar to the version at Disneyland, the small train circles around the vignettes of Storybook Land, although many of the vignettes are different here.

### Le Pays des Contes de Fées (Literally "Fairytale Country." It's also "Storybook Land.")

I love this version of Disneyland's Storybook Land Canal Boats. Here at Disneyland Parc, the boats are continuously loading, which saves a ton of time waiting in line.

You'll sit in a small boat and float around the various vignettes of Storybook Land. The vignettes are meticulously made miniatures (say that three times fast) of Disney scenes. Here in Paris, they have included a scene from *Peter and the Wolf,* an often-overlooked Disney short film that I love.

### Shops of Fantasyland

Stores here focus on gifts, princesses, and classic Disney characters. There are two shops inside the castle that you should check out, even if you don't buy anything, because they are quite beautiful. **Merlin l'Enchanteur** offers glass and other works of art. **La Boutique du Château** is a gorgeous Christmas shop inside the castle.

**La Chaumiere des Sept Nains** is the seven dwarfs shop, and **La Confiserie des Trois Fées** is a candy store owned by the three fairies from *Sleeping Beauty.* Near the Pinocchio ride, **La Bottega di Geppetto** offers hand-crafted items from Germany and Italy. Lastly, **Sir Mickey's Boutique** is where you'll go for Fantasyland souvenirs.

### Dining in Fantasyland

**Toad Hall Restaurant:** This themed quick-service English pub offers fish 'n' chips. It's the best restaurant in the whole resort.

**Au Chalet de la Marionnette:** Here, you can order quick-service hamburgers and sandwiches at Paris's version of Pinocchio Village Haus.

**Auberge de Cendrillion:** Literally Cinderella's Inn, this elegant restaurant features character dining with Disney princesses.

**Pizzeria Bella Notte:** Enjoy quick-service pizza at this café themed to *Lady and the Tramp.*

**Fantasia Gelati:** Continuing the Italian theme, you can order quick-service gelato here.

## Discoveryland

Disney made a small departure from their normal Tomorrowland here. Since French author Jules Verne practically invented the future for many Europeans, it was decided that a land inspired by him would be appropriate.

The colors are warmer here and the machinery more visible. There are plenty of gears and pistons in the architecture. It's not quite as steampunk as Tokyo DisneySea, but it's more so than the American versions of Tomorrowland.

### *Buzz Lightyear Laser Blast*

*Fastpass* The same ride as in the United States and Tokyo. Help Buzz Lightyear defeat the evil Emperor Zurg by shooting at targets.

### *Orbitron*

Just like Dumbo, only rockets.

### Autopia

You'll drive around in a little car with lots of colorful scenery passing by. If you've ever wanted to brag to your friends that you drove on the Autobahn, here is your chance. You don't even need an international driver's license.

### Les Mysteres du Nautilus (Mystery of the Nautilus)

Dive under the sea in Jules Verne's submarine. Unlike the claustrophobic Nemo submarines in California, this is a walkthrough attraction based on the Disney film *20,000 Leagues Under the Sea.* You'll see the engine room, Captain Nemo's room, and a variety of other spaces essential for life on a fictional submarine. The whole experience is well done, especially an encounter with a giant squid.

I'm about to share a secret. If you don't want to spoil your theme-park magic, skip this paragraph. As you approach this attraction you'll see the submarine Nautilus in a lagoon near Space Mountain. Most guests believe that this is the submarine you're touring during the attraction. However, in reality guests are never even close to this prop. During the queue, a winding staircase helps to disorient guests. While crossing through the underwater tunnel, you're actually walking away from the lagoon and into a building outside Discoveryland. Not only is this attraction not in a submarine—it's not even physically inside the park!

### Space Mountain: Mission 2

*Fastpass* There is no comparison between this Space Mountain and all the others. It's a completely different ride. This version at Disneyland Parc is much more intense than any of its siblings. Be advised: this is a major coaster. You may fare well on the tame Space Mountains in the States, but this is a totally different experience.

First, Space Mountain: Mission 2 is a launching steel coaster. You'll launch quickly from the ground station to the top of the structure. Then you'll ride in the darkness as you twist and turn through space. There are inversions on this coaster.

It's hard to say which version is better. Thrill-seekers love the launching and twisting that this ride in Paris provides. Others like to be thrilled by the theming instead of the ride. It's up to you.

Note: It's been announced that Space Mountain: Mission 2 will receive a *Star Wars* makeover in 2017. Normally when this occurs, the track of the ride remains the same but new effects and music are added. Stay tuned.

### Disneyland Railroad Discoveryland Station
Hop on the train here to quickly get to Main Street, Frontierland, and Fantasyland.

### Star Tours
*Fastpass* Watch out for Darth Vader on this simulation ride. Similar to the other versions, you'll sit in a simulator and journey through space as you use the force to defeat the Empire.

The ride system will be completely new in 2017. Each time you ride will be different as a computer randomly generates a sequence. There are audio-animatronics as part of the queue and preshow.

### Disney and Pixar Short Film Festival

In this indoor theater, you'll see short films made by Disney and Pixar. The films are shown in a variety of languages, which can be a lot of fun to view. This theater is a nice place to relax. If there are any upcoming releases from either studio, they will be heavily featured here.

### Jedi Training Academy

Several times each day, young padawans (gifted kids) are shown the ways of the force. This is an interactive show. Check the daily Times Guide for show times.

### Shops of Discoveryland

**Constellations** and **Star Traders** offer futuristic merchandise and lots of *Star Wars* items.

### Dining in Discoveryland

**Buzz Lightyear's Pizza Planet Restaurant:** Pizza is served buffet style in this *Toy Story*-themed restaurant.

**Café Hyperion:** Great quick-service burgers are served in this unique place themed as a futuristic zeppelin hangar.

You've probably heard that Parisians are rude and unfriendly. Forget all that—nothing could be further from the truth.

The people of Paris are not rude. However, they don't want to be your best friend either. Waiters have a job to do, and they will do it. When they go home, they have fulfilling lives with lots of friends and family. They don't need to have small talk with you. This may make some Americans uncomfortable.

I'm not saying that one way is better than the other. It's just different. French workers are well organized and paid. They don't rely on tips. Again, they're not being rude; they are doing their jobs.

You'll notice quite a difference in cast members at Disneyland Paris Resort. First, there are far fewer of them. Employment laws in France are strict, and Disney has had their share of run-ins with them. Consequently, employers want to be absolutely sure about hiring anybody before they do. It's nearly impossible to terminate employment in France.

Many of the cast members you'll interact with are rotating European workers. In France, people can work for twenty-one days before they are considered permanent employees. Many companies use rotating workforces to avoid French law. People will actually work for four weeks in one location and then change to a completely different job the next month. It's not an ideal situation and doesn't provide the employee with expertise. But it gets the job done.

Again, I'm not stating that one system is better than the other. It's just different.

▲ ▲ ▲

## Parades, Evening Shows, and Special Events
### Disney Magic on Parade!

There are always fantastic parades at this park, and this is no exception. Expect lavish floats with all your favorite characters. Everything is choreographed to iconic Disney music. This parade features hundreds of performers.

Main Street is often the place of choice for viewing the parade. The ambiance of the street and views of the castle add to the spectacle of it all. Check the daily Times Guide for parade times.

### Disney Dreams

Disney Dreams is the nighttime show at Disneyland Parc. This is one fantastic show and has about everything you'd want it to. Consequently, I highly recommend Disney Dreams; it's amazing.

If you have time and like to relax, grab a place early in the central hub. If you don't have time, then wait a bit. Right before show time, they will let people stand in the middle of Main Street. You can get some great views from here. Basically, in order to enjoy this show, you must be able to see most of the castle and the area around it.

Other Disney Parks have parts of this show in different places, but only Paris has it all together. Projections light up the castle in different shapes. Huge water screens are used to project iconic Disney scenes. Large fountains blast high in the air. Memorable Disney melodies come from all over. Fireworks explode over the caste. It's a combination of World of Color, Fantasmic!, Once Upon a Time Castle Show, and Wishes Fireworks. Disney Dreams is everything choreographed perfectly together to create a spectacle you will not forget.

In 2017, Disneyland Paris will celebrate its twenty-fifth anniversary. A special anniversary edition of Disney Dreams will run through the entire year.

### Halloween and Christmas

Halloween and Christmas are well celebrated at Disneyland Parc. Expect incredible decorations and seasonal music. The decorations will spill into the Disney hotels as well.

In addition to the atmosphere, both Halloween and Christmas offer special parades, shows, and character greetings. At Halloween, the Disney villains make frequent appearances near the castle for photographs. At Christmas, it's Mickey and friends in their winter wardrobes.

One nice touch that often occurs here: during these holidays, the special parades are offered in addition to the normal parade, not instead of. (The other Disney parks often replace their normal parades during holiday time.)

Adding to the seasonal fun is the beauty of the city of Paris itself. Halloween is nothing at all, but during

Christmas, Paris adds even more lights to a city already full of them. Also, to make things even more magical, there is the possibility of real snow. It's fairly remote, but it's still a beautiful possibility.

## Walt Disney Studios

When this park opened in 2002, it was rather small and a bit disappointing. However, recent additions have made this a park worthy of the Disney name. In its current form, Walt Disney Studios is far better than its sister park, Disney's Hollywood Studios in Orlando.

Walt Disney Studios and Disneyland Parc are located adjacent to each other. It is a very quick walk between the two. Even though it's been expanded, I still don't think of Walt Disney Studios as being a full-day park. You'll want to be able to visit Disneyland Parc when you're finished here. I'm not a big fan of park hopping in California and Florida. In Tokyo, hopping is not an imperative. But here, you must be able to hop. I would never buy a one-day, one-park pass and use it to visit Walt Disney Studios.

With all that said, there are some incredible things to see here. The biggest thrill rides at Disneyland Paris Resort are in this park, as are its most incredible live shows. There remains a studio tram tour where you can see behind the scenes, and there is an animation studio. Unlike Disney's Hollywood Studios in Florida, in Paris you can still learn about the movie-making process. This park is coming along and growing up.

You'll know you're in the right place when you see a water tower with Mickey Mouse ears. That's the Earffel Tower, the symbol of Walt Disney Studios. As you have your ticket scanned, you'll enter the park through an entrance plaza called **La Place des Freres Lumiere** (the Lumiere brothers were French men who have been attributed with inventing moving cinema). In the middle of the plaza, you'll see a fountain based on a scene from *Fantasia*. You're now ready to enter the studios through the Front Lot.

### Front Lot

The Front Lot serves as an entrance point to the park. Much like Main Street, its function is mainly to provide shopping and food. Most of the Front Lot is occupied by the huge Disney Studio 1.

### *Disney Studio 1*

This structure is a covered pavilion with food and shops. It's a nice place to escape the sun in the summer and the cold in the winter. You must enter and exit the park through Disney Studio 1.

### *Shops of Front Lot and Disney Studio 1*

The largest shop, **Walt Disney Studios Store,** is for all the park souvenirs. This store is located off La Place des Freres Lumiere, outside Disney Studio 1.

Inside Disney Studio 1, **Les Légendes d'Hollywood** is the most unique store in the park. It's themed like the inside of a movie studio.

### Dining in Front Lot and Disney Studio 1

**Restaurant en Coulisse:** One large café fills an entire side of Disney Studio 1. This restaurant provides quick-service burgers and Californian food.

## Toon Studio

This land pays homage to both classic Disney animation and the newer Pixar films. There are two mini lands within Toon Studio: Toy Story Playland and Ratatouille.

### Art of Disney Animation

In this large building next to Mickey's magical hat, you can watch, learn, and experiment with animation. There are always animators present who demonstrate how to draw and animate the famous Disney characters. After they finish, you can try your hand at sketching.

You can also learn how music is put into a film, how voices are recorded, and how special effects are added.

### Les Tapis Volants (The Flying Carpets)

Just like Dumbo except it's magic carpets around the story of Aladdin and Jasmine.

### Crush's Coaster

This attraction is unique to Walt Disney Studios and themed to the totally cool turtle from *Finding Nemo*. Guests will encounter lots of characters from the film.

Crush's Coaster is a relatively minor coaster, but the cars you sit in can spin completely around. This ride may be too intense for some younger fans of *Finding Nemo* and adults, like me, who are prone to motion sickness.

### Cars Quatre Roues Rallye (Cars Four-Wheeled Rally)

Another attraction unique to Walt Disney Studios and themed to the *Cars* franchise. Guests ride in little vehicles that whip around each other.

### Toy Story Playland

This playland is expertly themed, and you'll feel as though you've shrunk to the size of Woody, Buzz, Mr. Pricklepants, and the whole *Toy Story* gang. This mini land within a land will entertain all ages.

### Toy Soldier Parachute Drop

You'll sit on swings that are attached to green parachutes. Your feet will dangle as you're pulled up and then let go in a controlled fall.

### Slinky Dog Zigzag Spin

The cutest ride in the park. You'll sit inside the slinky part of Slinky Dog as he runs in a circle trying to catch his tail. It's basically for kids, but I always ride it.

### RC Racer

I never had one of those Hot Wheels tracks when I was growing up. One of the class bullies had one, and I was always jealous. The fact that I can go to Paris and ride this gives me some vindication. (Am I a bad person for hoping that the bully of my childhood doesn't have enough money to travel?)

You'll sit in a very large model car and race up and down the half-pipe portion of a Hot Wheels track. The track is very orange—as it should be.

### Ratatouille: The Adventure

*Fastpass* An amazing ride in an amazingly themed mini land. I know you're already in Paris, but here you'll really feel like you are in the middle of this beautiful city. Every detail was thought of in this new addition to Walt Disney Studios. Spend some time wandering around the cobblestones and streetlights.

The indoor attraction is a trackless dark ride. After passing through a themed queue, you'll sit inside an enormous rat for a tour of Rémy's famous kitchen. The rats drive themselves. You'll narrowly escape lots of kitchen items and will barely miss collisions with other rats. A computer system keeps all the rats on their course. You will never experience the same ride twice if the line is short enough that you can ride again.

This attraction is Disney at its best. It's great to see this park get a unique experience of this quality. There is no other *Ratatouille* ride in the world.

### Mickey and the Magician

This new show replaced the popular Anamagique in 2016. While I loved the old show, Mickey and the Magician is a fantastic and worthy replacement.

Mickey has been asked by a great magician to help him clean his studio. When Mickey is left alone, he succumbs to temptation and attempts some of the magician's tricks. This gets him into a bit of trouble. But there are plenty of magical friends around to help, including Cinderella's fairy godmother and Aladdin's Genie.

There's a lot going on here: large sets, fantastic costumes, and amazing effects. While the limited dialogue is in French, there is plenty of action to let everyone know what's going on with the story. Also, expect lots of familiar melodies.

Mickey and the Magician is performed several times each day. Check the daily Times Guide for show times.

### Shops of Toon Studio

**The Disney Animation Gallery,** located in the Art of Disney Animation building, sells higher-end collectibles. **Toy Story Playland Boutique** offers Toy Story merchandise, and **Chez Marianne** sells all sorts of Paris (non-Disneyland) souvenirs. Chez Marianne is located in the Ratatouille mini land.

### Dining in Toon Studio

**Bistrot Chez Rémy:** This is the best restaurant in the park. It's a table-service, amazingly themed establishment where Rémy offers all his wonderful food. Of course, you must try the famous ratatouille.

Dreamlly's Disney Direction

There are lots of character meet-and-greet opportunities at both Disneyland Paris Resort parks. Disneyland Parc tends to offer classic characters and villains. Walt Disney Studios provides characters from Pixar, Marvel, and *Star Wars*.

Meeting characters is a staple of all Disney parks. On the various park apps, you can find out exactly who is appearing and when.

In California, Florida, Paris, Hong Kong, and Shanghai, you'll form a nice line as a cast member organizes the meeting. When it's your turn, you'll spend a few moments interacting with the character and then have your photograph taken. Disney photographers will use their cameras and are also happy to take one with yours.

In Tokyo, the procedure is different—and not nearly as good. I'm baffled at how such an organized country can let their character meet-and-greets get so out of hand. There has to be something cultural going on that I don't understand. At Tokyo Disney Resort, characters mingle with guests in the open. There are no lines, and often mobs of people are trying to get close. The character will point to someone in the crowd, and that person gets to approach and have his or her picture taken. It's often frustrating for me because, like most Americans, I crave fairness in everything.

▲ ▲ ▲

## Production Courtyard

This land puts the studio in Walt Disney Studios. Production Courtyard is for movie lovers and all who yearn to escape inside a story.

### Studio Tram Tour: Behind the Magic

This is the last of the Disney parks to offer a studio tram tour—and that's too bad. Sure, there may not be any actual films being made here, but it's fascinating to drive through movie sets that instantly take you to another place and time.

You'll sit in a tram and tour the backlots of the studio. You'll see London, among other environments, and witness a catastrophic explosion. It's the perfect way to get off your feet for a while.

### The Twilight Zone Tower of Terror

*Fastpass* This famous drop attraction has made it to France. Almost identical to Disneyland's former version, guests ride up the elevator shaft of the Hollywood Tower Hotel. There's a lot of inspiration from *The Twilight Zone*, and everything is well themed. Of course, the finale of the ride is a sequence of drops from the thirteenth floor.

As with the others, a computer randomly controls the number, and height, of the drops. No two rides will ever be the same.

### Stitch Live!
Similar to the attraction at Tokyo Disneyland, fans of Stitch can sit and have a chat with the experimental alien. Stitch will sing, dance, and talk with the audience. It's highly interactive and can get a bit loud—as Stitch is apt to do.

### Disney Junior Live on Stage!
This short show occurs several times each day. Disney Junior Live on Stage! brings all your Disney Channel favorites to Walt Disney Studios. *Mickey's Clubhouse* is represented, as well as *Sofia the First, Doc McStuffins,* and *Jake and the Never Land Pirates.*

There's a lot of singing and even more dancing in this show. It's mostly geared toward the younger fans of these television shows. Check the daily Times Guide for show times.

### CinéMagique
I really can't get enough of this show. I hope it never closes, and I often wonder why it has never been brought to Florida.

A history of the first one hundred years of cinema, this show is half live action and half film. It's brilliantly done.

I hesitate to write too much about CinéMagique because I don't want to spoil anything. Just know that the live actors interact with the screen actors in a way that blows my mind. This show is for movie lovers. That's all I can say without ruining what will be a wonderful forty minutes of your day.

CinéMagique is performed several times each day. Check the daily Times Guide for show times.

### Shops of Production Courtyard

**Tower Hotel Gifts** is the only shop here. It offers Tower of Terror souvenirs.

### Dining in Production Courtyard

**Restaurant des Stars:** This buffet restaurant offers international cuisine.

### The Backlot

The Backlot is exactly what it sounds like. It's a collection of stuff that's been assembled toward the back of the studio because there really wasn't any other place for it. That's what real studios in Hollywood do with their back lots. So perhaps, even though this is the least themed land in the park, it may be the most authentic.

### Armageddon: Les Effets Spéciaux (Armageddon: Special Effects)

You may not remember the 1998 film *Armageddon*. History hasn't been kind to this picture, but it was the highest-grossing movie of 1998. Critics hated it, although *Armageddon* was a success at the box office.

This attraction is a look at how special effects are created for motion pictures. Many of the techniques demonstrated are a bit outdated in our current CGI world, but it's still interesting to see how things were done. In many ways, this attraction makes me appreciate pre-CGI Hollywood. Things looked more real back then.

### Rock 'n' Roller Coaster avec Aerosmith (Rock 'n' Roller Coaster with Aerosmith)

*Fastpass* This launching steel inversion coaster provides the highest thrill rating of any attraction at Disneyland Paris Resort. Similar to the ride at Walt Disney World, guests are strapped into long limousines as they race through Los Angeles to join Aerosmith. The coaster is completely enclosed.

This version features the same high-tech sound system as the original in Florida. Aerosmith's music is synced through multiple personal speakers on each seat. You'll twist and turn around a dark Hollywood on your journey.

As one of the few high-intensity rides at the resort, lines can be long. Get a Fastpass if you're at the park when school is not in session.

### Moteurs…Action! Stunt Show Spectacular

This is the original show that was so successful it was cloned in Orlando. (The version in Florida recently closed to make room for the expansion of Disney's Hollywood Studios.) Guests sit in an amphitheater and watch stunt drivers perform amazing feats of daring and skill.

The set looks like a conglomeration of various European cities. Performers in the show use the buildings, bridges, water, and streets to demonstrate their stunts. There are cars, motorcycles, and watercraft involved in the demonstrations.

Everything is coordinated and executed with precision. You'll learn how filmmakers use perfectly timed pyrotechnics to make benign car crashes look like the crash from hell.

### Shops of the Backlot

The only store here is **Rock Around the Shop,** located in the Rock 'n' Roller Coaster building. It sells music-themed merchandise and Aerosmith stuff.

### Dining in the Backlot

**Disney Blockbuster Café:** This quick-service restaurant offers sandwiches and salads. It's located in a warehouse full of props from Disney films.

**Café des Cascadeurs (Stuntman's Café ):** A quick-service burger joint in a 1950s-themed diner.

## Disney Village

Originally, this entertainment district was called Festival Disney when Euro Disneyland opened in 1992. Architect

Frank Gehry designed the original appearance of the district, but it has changed several times since then. Its name was changed to Disney Village when the whole property became Disneyland Paris Resort.

Disney Village sits across the resort entrance plaza from the train station to Paris. It's the smallest of the Disney entertainment districts (although Hong Kong doesn't have one at all), and it's free to explore.

There are several restaurants, including a **Rainforest Café, McDonald's, Planet Hollywood,** and many others. There is a definite American theme going on here, and **Billy Bob's Country Western Saloon** is always packed.

Shopping is not as plentiful here as it is at Downtown Disney, Disney Springs, and Ikspiari. **World of Disney** is the largest shop with merchandise from both parks.

The biggest draw here for Europeans is **Buffalo Bill's Wild West Show…With Mickey & Friends.** This extravaganza is often sold out. Get your tickets online if you are interested in attending. You'll sit around an arena and eat a huge American meal. The meal comes complete with cornbread and apple pie. As you dine, lots of action takes place in the arena. You'll see Buffalo Bill and all his fantastic performers. You'll meet Annie Oakley and a cast of horse-riding cowboys and cowgirls. Mickey and his pals make an appearance dressed in their appropriate western-themed attire.

Disney Village offers concerts throughout the year on an open-air stage. Billy Bob's often has live music inside its saloon. There is also a cinema complex, IMAX, and a large arcade.

## Area Sights outside Disney

Disneyland Paris Resort is near this town called Paris. You may have heard of it; I guess it's kind of a big deal. All kidding aside, Paris is an extremely beautiful city full of history and culture. There's a lot to see here.

All of the Disney hotels offer organized tours into the city. If Disney is your focus and you're staying at the resort the entire time, an organized day tour can be an excellent way to affordably see the main attractions. If you're spending part of your trip actually staying in the city, then skip these organized tours. For reference, Paris is an easy forty-five-minute train ride away.

Below, I've listed some of my favorite things to see in the city. But if you really want to experience Paris, you just need to sit. Find a café with outdoor seating; there are literally thousands of them. Look for one with small tables on the sidewalk and with all their chairs facing the street. It sounds odd to international visitors, but you don't want to face your travel companions here. You want to face the world. Before you sit at one of these tables, just motion to the server (as if to ask if it's OK) and have a seat. If there aren't any servers outside, peek your head in the door and make eye contact with one. Eventually, a server will come over and take your order. Just get "un café, s'il vous plait." Don't worry about ordering anything fancy; whatever they bring will be good enough. Then spend the next few hours sipping and look at all those who pass before you. They won't care how long you sit there. This is Paris.

**Louvre Museum:** Of course, you have to go to the Louvre. It's the most famous art museum in the world. Buy your ticket online to save a very long wait in line. Inside, spend your time meandering. You'll want to see Ms. Mona Lisa and Miss Venus de Milo for sure. But my advice for the Louvre is simple: keep it simple. Just wander around and keep your eyes open. A little-known painting may touch your soul in a way that a celebrated masterpiece never could.

**Orsay Museum:** Initially, the Louvre rejected modern art. Impressionism was considered modern, and all that stuff ended up here. It's a gorgeous museum inside a renovated train station.

**Norte Dame Cathedral:** Make a quick stop to see the interior of this massive building. It's amazing and historical. And, of course, Disney created an animated version of Victor Hugo's *The Hunchback of Norte Dame.* Climb the stairs and get a close-up look at the actual gargoyles.

**Eiffel Tower:** Get your picture taken, but don't go to the top. The lines are too long, and it's too high to have good views. In any city, you never want to go to the top of the tallest point. Always go the top of the second-tallest point so that you can see the tallest point in your photos (see the next attraction).

**Arc de Triumphe:** The best views of Paris are from the top of this monument.

**Palace of Versailles:** A thirty-minute train ride from Paris (in the opposite direction of Disneyland Paris Resort), this is the largest palace in Europe. It's as expansive and ornate as you imagine. Expect to spend a whole day wandering the grounds and buildings.

**River Seine:** Probably the best experience you can have in this city is a nighttime cruise on the river. They're cheap and absolutely spectacular.

# 6

---

## Hong Kong Disney Resort

I s THERE ANY place else even remotely like Hong Kong? Nope. It's a cosmopolitan city mixed up with ancient Chinese villages mixed up with tropical jungles. It's the best skyline in the world (sorry, New York) mixed up with massive tenements mixed up with lush islands.

It's sort of like the Chinese mainland except that it's not. It's sort of like New York City except that it's not. It's got British infrastructure. An incredibly beautiful harbor sits in the middle of it with tropical mountains in the background.

Hong Kong is an island, though what we typically call Hong Kong encompasses a larger area. The large skyscrapers are on the actual Hong Kong Island. Across the harbor from the island and attached to the Chinese mainland is the Kowloon Peninsula. Kowloon is part of Hong Kong. Sitting near all this is the island of Lantau. Lantau, also part of Hong Kong, hosts the city's sprawling airport and Hong Kong Disneyland Resort. Hong Kong is comprised of no less than 263 islands scattered along the Chinese coast.

In order to continue any discussion of Hong Kong, we have to talk about its political construction. In 1860, the Second Opium War ended between England and China. As part of the treaty that ended the war, Hong Kong became an English colony. The Chinese weren't happy with that arrangement, and the two parties went back to the table in 1898. That's when England agreed to a ninety-nine-year lease of Hong Kong.

Hong Kong remained a democratic colony of England, while China continued on its path to become the People's Republic of China. In 1997, Great Britain made good on its word, and Hong Kong was ceded back to the Chinese.

There was, understandably, a lot of consternation over the cessation of Hong Kong. The city had been accustomed to democratic rule and was now to be controlled by a Communist regime from Beijing. Many were afraid of the economic impact of Chinese rule, especially when it came to tourism. The best way for China to deal with all this was to create the Hong Kong Special Administrative Region (SAR). The strategy is basically one country, two systems.

As part of the SAR, Hong Kong retained its own currency. The SAR controls its own borders with policies different than those of mainland China. Yes, Chinese citizens from the mainland must pass through border control to visit Hong Kong, a city in their own country. Likewise, even though most tourists enter Hong Kong without a visa, one will be needed to cross the border between the SAR and mainland China.

The SAR and mainland China continue to have a contentious relationship. Beijing has attempted to tighten its grasp on the SAR for a number of years. Recently, there have been civil demonstrations in Hong Kong to protest Beijing's interference with SAR elections. Some of these demonstrations have become violent. On top of this, the people of Hong Kong have become a bit unwelcoming to "mainlanders," people who live on the mainland of China. There have been some unpleasant demonstrations in this regard as well. (Since all news in mainland China is highly censored, most mainlanders are unaware of any problem that Hong Kong has with Beijing.)

For the tourist, Hong Kong is extremely safe to visit. You can spend weeks in the SAR and never know of the struggle between Hong Kong and Beijing. The main point of this discussion is to understand that Hong Kong and China are one country with two different systems of operating.

▲ ▲ ▲

# History

Like most American companies, Disney was reluctant to develop a relationship with the tightly controlled China of the pre-1990s. But since the regime in Beijing changed its attitude toward foreign investment, Disney became interested in the country. It began with the film studio seeing enormous potential for a Chinese movie audience. It was only natural that the Disney theme park division would be next.

During the mid-1990s, Disney had several discussions with Chinese officials about the possibility of building a theme park in either Hong Kong or Shanghai. But Disney, being understandably prudent, wanted to see how the cessation of Hong Kong from the British to the Chinese would progress. Noting that the SAR system granted continued autonomy for Hong Kong, Disney moved ahead with negotiations.

The SAR was promoting a new piece of reclaimed land called Penny's Bay. It was located on Lantau Island, not far from the brand-new Hong Kong International Airport. The land was fairly protected from other development, and Disney was quite interested in it.

Of course, as with all the international parks, the largest matter was who would pay for it and who would get the profits. Because a single regime in Beijing controls the country's finances, it was simpler to reach an agreement here than it had been in Paris. It was decided that Beijing would own 53 percent of Hong Kong Disneyland Resort. The Walt Disney Company would own 47 percent. Costs and profits would be split accordingly. The agreement was signed on August 8, 1999.

Disney was still feeling some post-traumatic stress about the construction of Euro Disneyland. Consequently, they wanted to be as friendly toward Chinese culture as possible. An early edict was made that the entire project would adhere to the principles of feng shui. Several masters of feng shui were hired to ensure that the park's design would bring good fortune.

Two massive hills sit behind the park. The feng shui masters believed that one hill represented a green dragon and the other a white tiger. They made certain that the park faced east to west. Hong Kong Disneyland Resort is located right on the ocean. All walkways near the ocean were careful to gracefully curve inland so that qi, good energy, did not flow into the sea. Two hotels were planned. But at the last minute, one of the hotels had to be moved to bring more chi, positive energy, to the resort. Crickets bring good fortune according to feng shui. Jiminy Cricket suddenly found himself in the role of ambassador.

The feng shui ideas were positive and led to good results in design and function. However, a second remaining fear of Euro Disneyland would have a negative impact on the new park. Disney was fearful of building too much too fast. The gilded over-the-top Euro Disneyland with seven hotels led to financial disaster. Disney did not want to make the same mistake here. Unfortunately, they overcorrected. The post-Europe stress caused imagineers to think small.

Groundbreaking for the resort occurred on January 12, 2003. Hong Kong Disneyland Resort had a fast construction period, especially by Disney standards. The park, along with two hotels, opened to the public on September 12, 2005.

Attendance was good but not good enough. The concerns that the park was too small were being realized. There just wasn't enough to do. In the first three years after opening, research showed that the typical guest was spending around five hours inside Hong Kong Disneyland. In order for the park to succeed, guests needed to stay there all day. Guests can't spend money on food and merchandise when they're not inside the park.

Both Disney and Beijing agreed that further expansion was not just necessary; it was imperative. Aggressive plans to add mini lands around the perimeter of the park moved ahead. While the new lands were developed, the park moved quickly to add parades and attractions to its existing size. Good marketing promoted these additions, and attendance started to rise.

The first new land, Toy Story Land, opened in November of 2011. The second additional land, Grizzly Gulch, opened in 2012. Mystic Point, the third new land, premiered in 2013.

In 2014, Hong Kong Disneyland turned a profit, and hotel occupancy was 94 percent. Another new nighttime parade and a small *Frozen* area brought more visitors. But 2015 did not fare as well. Chinese people living in the mainland began a boycott of Hong Kong. This was due to the ongoing tensions between Beijing and the SAR. Not only did these tensions stop mainlanders from visiting, but the mainlanders now had an alternative: the upcoming Shanghai Disneyland Resort. Then 2016 saw a further drop in attendance. To complicate matters, the yuan, the currency of China, became quite unstable and fell.

However, both parties are quite committed to the resort. Disney and Beijing are not backing down on their plans. A third hotel will open in 2017, and an entertainment district is currently in the design phase.

In addition to these already scheduled improvements, a major announcement in December 2016 revealed further aggressive plans. The largest expansion in the park's history was unveiled. This $1.5-billion project will completely change the look of both Tomorrowland and Fantasyland. Tomorrowland will get an entire mini land themed to Marvel Comics. (The Iron Man Experience has already opened, but this new Marvel land will be five times the size of that one attraction.)

Fantasyland will be expanded with the Kingdom of Arendelle. Guests will be able to step into the world of *Frozen* for new rides, restaurants, and shops. But above all of this, Disney is reimagining Hong Kong Disneyland's Sleeping Beauty Castle. For the first time in history, an iconic Disney castle is getting a makeover. It will be much larger and will probably come with a new name. Stay tuned.

Overall, it seems that Hong Kong Disneyland has survived the opening of Shanghai Disneyland and is charging ahead with new plans. Just like the city where it's located, Hong Kong Disneyland will continue to grow and change as East and West continue to mix together in a delicious cultural stew.

Hong Kong Disneyland Resort Pros:

- It's very easy and quick to get between the airport, the city, and the resort.
- Hong Kong Disneyland is compact and easy to walk around.
- Hong Kong's mini lands are unique with attractions not found elsewhere.
- It's the most naturally beautiful of Disney's locations.
- Hong Kong Disneyland goes all out for Halloween.
- Its fairly low attendance means shorter lines.

Hong Kong Disneyland Resort Cons:

- The summer weather is unbearable.
- The park is small.
- It's an expensive and long flight from Europe and America.

- There isn't an entertainment district near Hong Kong Disneyland Resort.

▲ ▲ ▲

# Travel Knowledge

*Arrival/Transport*

Hong Kong Disneyland Resort's location between the airport and central Hong Kong makes it an easily accessible destination.

If you are already in Hong Kong, it's easy to get to the resort on the Hong Kong metro. From either the Hong Kong or Kowloon Stations, take the Tung Chung Line in the direction of Tung Chung. Get off at the Sunny Bay Station. From there, you'll take the short Disneyland Resort Line one station to Disneyland Resort.

The Disneyland Resort Line of the Hong Kong Metro connects two stations: Sunny Bay and Disneyland Resort. Because this line only serves Hong Kong Disneyland Resort, its trains are Disney themed.

**Hong Kong International Airport** is located on Lantau Island, the same island as Hong Kong Disneyland Resort. Well, technically, the bulk of the airport is located on a tiny island called Chek Lap Kok, which is indistinguishable from the larger Lantau Island. It opened in 1998 and is a modern, thriving airport. Counting by the number of passengers annually, it's the eighth-busiest airport in the world. In 2011, Hong Kong International

Airport passed Memphis International in becoming the world's busiest cargo airport.

It's simple to secure ground transportation at Hong Kong International. To take the metro to Hong Kong Disneyland Resort, you'll take the Airport Express Line to Tsing Yi Station. There, transfer to the Tung Chung Line in the direction of Tung Chung. Depart at Sunny Bay Station and take the Disneyland Resort Line one stop to the resort.

The Hong Kong metro system is good, but you have a more efficient option. Hong Kong contains one of the most extensive and affordable taxi fleets in the world. A ride from Hong Kong International to Hong Kong Disneyland Resort costs HK$137.00 ($17.66). A cab from central Kowloon to the resort costs HK$165.00 ($21.27). Uber is only slightly cheaper in Hong Kong, and since cabs are absolutely everywhere, I recommend them.

However, the most scenic and best way to arrive at Hong Kong Disneyland is via boat. The Star Ferry makes two round trips daily between Hong Kong Disneyland and the Tsim Sha Tsui ferry terminal on Kowloon. Since the resort's property is right on the water, it just makes sense that Hong Kong Disney Resort has its own pier. The adult fare for a round-trip voyage is HK$180.00 ($23.18). You can also purchase packages from Star Ferry that include park admission and meal vouchers. The ferry leaves right from the heart of Victoria Harbor; you'll sail past the incredible skyline of Hong Kong and then enter the sea for your short trip to Lantau Island. It takes forty-five minutes each way for the voyage.

Your cab driver will probably have at least three phones mounted on the dash. Maybe even more. The driver will continue to monitor these phones during the trip.

First, I'm amazed that anyone can be so important as to use multiple phones. Second, I'm amazed at how much one person can do at a time. This is all complicated by a third feeling, which is general anxiety for my safety.

I've learned to buckle up and not worry about it. These drivers are extremely used to driving this way. I have a feeling that the driver would be even more distracted without any of the devices.

▲ ▲ ▲

### Visa/Passport

Hong Kong is a special administrative region within China. While most tourists need a visa to enter mainland China, one is probably not required to visit Hong Kong. Citizens of the United States, Canada, Australia, the United Kingdom, the European Union, and New Zealand may enter Hong Kong without a visa for ninety days. (Brits may stay up to 180 days since they used to run the place and all.)

Citizens of other countries should contact their department of travel to discover if they need a visa. All travelers must have a valid passport to enter the SAR of Hong Kong. But remember, you cannot cross the border between the SAR and mainland China without a visa.

### Ground Transportation

A car is not required to enjoy the area, and you should not rent one. Other drivers tend to drive quite fast here, and roadways are complicated with lots of bridges and tunnels.

As I stated earlier, taxis are an affordable option here. The Hong Kong metro system is cheap, clean, and easy to use. Hong Kong Disneyland Resort has its own metro station. Also, don't forget that Hong Kong Disney Resort has its own pier with direct access to the city via the Star Ferry.

### Time

Hong Kong, in fact all of China, is in the same time zone. (The United States could take a lesson from them in this regard.) So Hong Kong is in the same time zone as Shanghai and Beijing. Hong Kong is one hour behind Tokyo and twelve hours ahead of New York City. They are six hours ahead of Europe and fifteen hours ahead of California.

The Hong Kong SAR does not observe daylight saving time. In the winter, the time difference between China and Europe/America is one hour greater.

## Language

There are two official languages of Hong Kong: Chinese (Mandarin) and English. A third language, Cantonese, is a recognized regional language and is used often.

Due to Hong Kong's long history with Great Britain, it's easy for English speakers to navigate the city. You will find that most of the city's signs are in Chinese and English. Your hotel's employees will be able to speak English, as will most other workers in the travel industry. Your taxi drivers may not be able to have a conversation in English, but they will be able to understand the English word for any destination in the city.

## Weather

OK, I'm going to be extremely frank here. Please listen to me. Do not go to Hong Kong anytime between April and October. Just don't. It's miserable. You think Florida is humid? You haven't seen humidity. The summer season in Hong Kong is extreme. It's very hot and very humid—all the time.

I was in Hong Kong during the middle of September 2014. I was visiting Ocean Park, a fantastic theme park on the island of Hong Kong. (Ssh...don't tell Mickey!) It was so hot and humid that I started to get disoriented. This feeling was horrible, and I got scared. My husband ushered us into the nearest restaurant. Ironically, it was a penguin-themed restaurant where you eat while penguins frolic behind glass.

At the door, an employee said, "Welcome. Please understand that it's very cold in here because of the penguins." Also, there was a HK$200.00 ($25.78) minimum charge to eat here. We ate there, and it was the best money we ever spent.

I don't want you to think I'm hyperbolizing. I also don't want to scare you away from your travel plans. Just know that you will be quite uncomfortable during the summer periods. If you must travel then, make sure to drink lots and lots of water. The water in Hong Kong is safe to drink right out of the tap.

The rest of the year offers pleasant weather. The winters are like Florida's but with less humidity. (I guess that's Mother Nature's way of rewarding them for surviving the summer.)

### Money

Hong Kong does not use Chinese currency. The Hong Kong dollar (HK$) is the official currency of the Hong Kong SAR. When Britain turned Hong Kong back to China, there was great fear of a massive economic crisis. To prevent such crises, the Hong Kong dollar was pegged to the US dollar. However, now that the SAR has made a complete transition from England, the Hong Kong dollar is a completely separate form of currency.

You may notice that not all the money looks the same. There isn't a central government bank that issues the bills. In Hong Kong, a few banks have the ability to issue currency. A HK$100 issued by one bank will be slightly different in appearance to a HK$100 issued by another. You can find the name of the issuing bank on the bill.

Credit cards are widely accepted. The people of Hong Kong, and indeed all of China, are the largest users of the ApplePay system. In contrast to Japan, the Chinese are much less willing to carry cash.

You will find ATMs everywhere, and money exchange is available in all hotels. At the time of publication, HK$1.00 was equal to US$0.13.

There is no sales tax in Hong Kong. The Hong Kong SAR assesses 6 percent on all lodging rates in the city. Hotels also have the right to assess an additional 10 percent service charge, and most of them do. This extra 16 percent is usually included in your nightly rate. Unlike mainland China, Hong Kong seems to have interpreted their confusing tax law in your favor (see the next chapter for the other interpretation).

Tipping is not customary in Hong Kong. You will probably notice a required 10 percent service charge on your restaurant bill. That is your tip.

### Tickets

It's easy to purchase a ticket to Hong Kong Disneyland online and in person. Online, go to hongkongdisneyland.

com. In person, you can purchase tickets at the park, inside the Disney Store at the airport, and at Disneyland kiosks around the city.

The Avenue of the Stars is one of the busiest tourist sections of Kowloon; it's right on Victoria Harbor. If you buy your tickets at the Disneyland kiosk here, you'll get a free gift. Sometimes I get nice luggage tags and other times reusable grocery bags.

Hong Kong Disneyland offers the simplest ticketing options. There is no hopping here (because there is nothing to hop to). Adults are all those age twelve to sixty-four. Seniors are those sixty-five and older. Children are aged three to eleven. Those younger than three are free.

A one-day ticket to Hong Kong Disneyland is HK$539.00 ($69.47) per adult, HK$385.00 ($49.62) per child, and HK$100.00 ($12.89) per senior. (Can you believe that senior price? I know two grandparents who would kill to be able to walk into Walt Disney World for twelve bucks!)

A two-day ticket to the park is HK$739.00 ($95.25) per adult, HK$525.00 ($67.66) per child, and HK$170.00 ($21.91) per senior. (That's less than eleven bucks per day! I'm moving to Hong Kong as soon as I turn sixty-five.)

*Dreamlly's Disney Direction*

Generally, theme parks are quite good at accommodating people with disabilities. Disney sets the gold standard in this regard. Every attraction, restaurant, and shop is designed to welcome guests of all abilities. However, even at a Disney park, information about how to access these accommodations can be confusing.

It's a good idea for people with disabilities to stop at guest services whenever they enter a park. Each location offers a printed guide for those with disabilities. These policies and procedures can change, and it's a good idea to get the most current version each time.

Booking a hotel is a bit more complicated. Each Disney resort and cruise ship offers rooms for those with a disability. Calling is the best way to get the specific room you may need. Making a phone call to California and Florida is easy. It's also quite easy to get connected with an English-speaking cast member in Paris, Hong Kong, and Shanghai. Unfortunately, the resort with the best service, Tokyo, is the one that's impossible to call. Remember, Disney doesn't own any portion of Tokyo Disney Resort, and I'm afraid this amazing resort's call center is not up to par. It's hard enough to secure any room at a Disney hotel in Tokyo, let alone a specific room. In Tokyo, my suggestion for those with disabilities is to stay at one of the two American hotels that are on the property. You'll have a choice between a Hilton and a Sheraton. Both offer accommodating rooms via their websites. The Tokyo Disney Resort Monorail is accessible, and both hotels offer direct bus service to the Bayside Station.

Lastly, those with disabilities need to consider the complexities of travel to the non-Disney portions of their vacations. Even though it's not perfect, the United States is the most accommodating country among the Disney locations. In Paris, Hong Kong, Shanghai, and Tokyo, guided tours are the best way to see the sights of the city if they provide door-to-door transportation. Portions of all these places are old with streets that are less than friendly. Guidebooks specifically for people with disabilities are available for all these cities.

▲ ▲ ▲

## Accommodations

Tripadvisor.com lists exactly seven hundred different hotels in the Hong Kong SAR. There is truly something for every budget here. You can spend a lot at a luxury high rise on the harbor or very little in a nearby hostel.

Staying off the Disney property makes sense here for two reasons: First, Hong Kong Disneyland is a small park that can easily be explored in one day. Second, the transportation options make it extremely easy to get to the park from an off-site hotel.

I stated before that I'm not in the business of rating off-site hotels. However, I've received such great service at one location that I really feel I should mention it. **Hotel Panorama by Rhombus** is in the Tsim Sha Tsui area of Kowloon. Its location is perfect with easy access to the metro. Many of the rooms have fantastic views of Victoria Harbor. Best of all, I've always been able to get a reasonable rate here. The hotel is very clean, and the staff is friendly.

### Disney Hotels

There are two, soon to be three, Disney hotels at Hong Kong Disneyland Resort. They offer the best location if you want to relax and have multiple days inside the park. It's also quite quick to get into the city using the metro or cabs. As usual, these hotels are immaculately clean and themed.

Unfortunately, there are no other special benefits for staying on the property. There are no Extra Magic Hours here or room-charging ability.

Another item to note: since Hong Kong Disneyland is so close to the airport, the hotels here are some of the closest to the terminal. It's not difficult to transfer from a central Hong Kong hotel to a Disney hotel before the last night of your journey. Then when you wake up the next morning, it's an easy cab or metro ride to the airport.

### Disneyland Hotel

This hotel is gorgeous. In my book, it's second only to the Mira Costa at DisneySea as my favorite international Disney hotel. In appearance, it looks similar to the Grand Floridian at Walt Disney World.

The Disneyland Hotel has a Victorian theme. The amazing grounds include beautiful landscaping and lush gardens. There is even a hedge maze to explore in the shape of Mickey Mouse. The hotel has a large playground and possibly the best indoor/outdoor pool complex in the city, complete with waterfall and slide.

**The Bibbidi Bobbidi Boutique** is located within the hotel. This is where kids can be transformed into princesses, knights, and pirates. Disney characters also make appearances in the lobby. To really get to know some of the characters, have a meal at the **Enchanted Garden Restaurant.** This is a character buffet within the hotel. Other dining venues are the **Crystal Lotus,** a Chinese restaurant, and **Walt's Café.**

But here is the best part: the Disneyland Hotel is located on the shores of the South China Sea. It's spectacular! It's a beautiful body of water to go to sleep next to at night. Also, rooms that are closest to the sea have views of the Hong Kong skyline in the distance. Sitting on a balcony as you listen to the ocean and see all the lights of the city makes a memorable evening.

There are standard rooms and seaside rooms. Most rooms here are large and have two double beds. You can upgrade from these to a room that has a balcony. Standard rooms start at HK$2,600.00 ($335.11) without a balcony or view. Rooms with balconies and a view of the sea start at HK$3,150.00 ($405.99).

It's an easy, and scenic, walk to Hong Kong Disneyland from this hotel. You'll walk down a brick promenade that's full of plants and flowers. There is also a free shuttle that will stop at the metro station.

### Disney's Hollywood Hotel

Art deco of the Hollywood that never was is the theme of this hotel. It's a little scaled back from the Disneyland Hotel, but it's still a well-themed place to stay. Again, Disney did a great job with the landscaping. You can stroll through courtyards that contain vintage cars and famous Hollywood landmarks.

A pool, outdoor only, is shaped like a grand piano. There is a waterslide and lots of lounge chairs to relax on. The hotel contains a large playground, children's activity center, and arcade.

Disney's Hollywood Hotel also has a character restaurant. At **Chef Mickey,** you can dine buffet style while Disney characters come to your table. The hotel has a quick-service café called **Hollywood & Dine.** There is a nice, relaxing lounge.

The rooms here are a bit smaller, but they are still as immaculately clean. There are no balconies here, but rooms on one side of the hotel do face the sea. Most rooms are standard with two double beds.

A standard room with a garden view starts at HK$1,850.00 ($238.44). The same room with a sea view starts at HK$2,150.00 ($277.11).

It's about a twenty-minute walk to the park from this hotel. But guests here can ride the resort shuttle for free. The resort shuttle also stops at the metro station.

### The Explorer's Lodge

Sometime in 2017, a third Disney hotel will join Hong Kong Disneyland Resort. This hotel is located between the two existing properties and is well under construction. Guests here will be able to walk to Hong Kong Disneyland or take the free resort shuttle.

Drawings of the Explorer's Lodge make it look similar to Animal Kingdom Lodge at Walt Disney World. The imagineers have already released a story that goes along with the property. The story is that four explorers built the hotel, but they disagreed on its theme. In true Disney style, they collaborated on the lobby, and then each built his or her own separate wing for the rooms.

The four wings of the hotel will each have a different theme: African savannah, South American rain forest, Pacific Islands, and Asian jungle. The renderings of these areas look spectacular. Themed pools will accompany each wing. The hotel is planned to have more than seven hundred rooms.

The Explorer's Lodge is also located right on the South China Sea. I expect that many rooms will have excellent views of the water.

No prices have been released for the hotel. However, just by looking at the room drawings, I think it will be comparable to Hong Kong's Disneyland Hotel. Just keep in mind that if hotel occupancy for the resort continues to drop, prices will likely be cheaper.

*Dreamlly's Disney Direction*

For those living in the United States, Hong Kong is the farthest of the Disney locations. It's just over fourteen hours to fly from Los Angeles to Hong Kong, just under sixteen hours from New York. But even a short eight-hour flight to Paris will induce jetlag. Jetlag feels like having a cold on the day of your best friend's birthday party. It's unpleasant. I'm often asked how I deal with it. Unfortunately, my answer is a bit complicated.

Anyone who says they have a good fix for jetlag is lying. Most tips and tricks you read online are also useless. The thing is that no two jetlags are the same. Your approach to dealing with it will, and should, change.

First, don't worry about sleeping during the flight; worrying about sleep will just cause unneeded anxiety. And, for Mickey's sake, don't make yourself really tired before the flight in hopes that it will make sleep easier. It won't. Board the plane well rested and ready for your adventure. If you sleep on the flight, great. If not, that's great too.

If you land in the morning and you haven't crossed the International Date Line, it means that you've probably missed one night of sleep. Your body can deal with this. Try hard to maintain a normal eating schedule for your first day and get active. Go to bed that evening. You'll wake up at an odd hour during the middle of the night. Stay in bed and read a book. You'll fall asleep again after about an hour. Repeat this pattern, and you'll acclimate quickly.

Crossing the date line while traveling west means that you'll miss more than one night of sleep. In this case, you must listen to your body. Forcing yourself to stay awake in this circumstance will catch up with you. As annoying as it may be, sleep when you're tired. In a few days, you'll be fine.

Crossing the date line while traveling east means that you've entered hell. Seriously. There is nothing you can do to fix the fact that you've landed before you've taken off. You'll live a day twice, and your body will know it. In this case, it's best to get several rounds of short sleep. Rest for three hours and try to stay awake for the next five, eating a large meal each time you wake. Repeating this cycle, even though you'll often be awake during the night, allows your body time to heal and adjust.

The jetlag situation gets more complex when you want to go to an international Disney park on your first day of vacation. If we all had unlimited time and money, we'd sit around for a week eating bon-bons while our bodies adjusted. But since that's not the reality for most of us, we have to force ourselves out of bed in a very un-Disneylike manner. Fortunately, adrenaline will be your best friend.

Yes, it's possible to run on pure fairy dust and Diet Coke. Let the excitement of the day carry you through until you can crash when you've had enough. Just give yourself permission to enjoy the day, even if that means your day ends in the early afternoon.

▲ ▲ ▲

## Hong Kong Disneyland

Congratulations! You've made it to the most exotic of Disney's properties. A large fountain of Monstro the whale beckons you to walk down the promenade and toward Hong Kong Disneyland. When you look farther down the promenade, you'll see the South China Sea. As you turn to look toward the park, you'll see lush green mountains creating the perfect backdrop. Of all of Disney's geographic sites, this is the most naturally beautiful.

The amount of green everywhere will surprise even those from Florida. Lantau Island is a tropical paradise of rolling mountains that dip into the sea. Standing here, you will hardly believe that one of the world's largest cities is just a five-minute drive away.

As you turn toward the park, you'll see the Hong Kong Disneyland Train Station. It should look familiar because it's based on the original Disneyland design. Have your ticket scanned, and walk underneath the railroad station. It all looks oddly familiar. Welcome to Main Street, USA, the last of Disney's Main Streets.

## Main Street, USA

There a difference to this Main Street, but it's not one you can notice immediately. This was the first Main Street where the façades of most buildings were cast out of fiberglass. They were produced at Disney's fiberglass workshop (the world's largest) in Orlando and shipped to Hong Kong. This means that Main Street will retain its bright colors with a lot less maintenance.

The rest of the land is similar. Main Street connects Town Square and the railroad station to a central hub. As you proceed through Town Square, you'll see another familiar sight: Sleeping Beauty Castle. The structure looks similar to the one at the original Disneyland. However, look at those mountains! Again, the lush green mountains frame the entire park, especially the castle.

Like the other parks, Main Street, USA is primarily for shopping and dining.

### Hong Kong Disneyland Railroad

Hop aboard for a grand-circle tour of Hong Kong Disneyland. There are only two stations inside the park: Main Street and Fantasyland. Basically, there's a station here at the front of the park and another one in the very back.

### Main Street Vehicles

Similar to other Disney parks, wait by the appropriate sign to catch a ride to the castle.

### Art of Animation

In Town Square, you can learn all about how animated movies are produced. Art of Animation is part experience and part museum. After you partake in the learning experience, you're welcome to wander around and see artifacts from Disney's animated films.

### Animation Academy

Next door to Art of Animation, guests can attend a workshop and learn how to draw a Disney character. The workshops last twenty minutes and are offered on a continuing basis. So you'll never have to wait longer than twenty minutes for the next one to begin.

Often, the instruction is in Chinese or Cantonese, but don't let that stop you. It's easy to follow along with the animators' movements. Everything is conducted in a slow, step-by-step process. You'll be amazed at how easily you can draw Donald Duck in Chinese!

### Town Square Characters

Hong Kong Disneyland often presents characters in the middle of Town Square. Many times, you will see several characters scattered about. Just get in line to have your photograph taken. Check the Hong Kong Disneyland app to see exactly who is appearing when.

FYI, Hong Kong Disneyland has daily scheduled appearances by *Zootopia*'s Judy Hopps and Nick Wilde. It takes a while for new characters to make it into the theme-park greeting rotation. Consequently, lines for newer characters are always long. Currently, only Hong Kong and Shanghai have scheduled daily appearances by Judy and Nick.

### Shops of Main Street, USA

Oddly, there are no shops in Town Square. **City Hall** serves as guest services, and the other buildings in the square are occupied by the Art of Animation. However, many fine stores are just up the street.

**The Emporium** is the largest store with all the Hong Kong souvenirs you may need. Remember, for now, there isn't an entertainment district outside the park. If you need to purchase anything, purchase it here.

Other shops offer jewelry, apparel, and Disney toys. Duffy has crossed the sea from Japan and has a new store on Main Street.

### Dining in Main Street, USA

**Market House Bakery:** A quick-service bakery with all the wonderful smells you'd expect.

**Main Street Market:** The best quick-service waffles in the world are served here.

**Main Street Corner Café:** This table-service café offers American and Chinese comfort foods.

**Plaza Inn:** Here is a lovely table-service Cantonese restaurant at the end of Main Street.

Dreamlly's Disney Direction

There are a lot of Mickey-shaped foods available in the Disney parks. Here's what you need to know:

Mickey Ice Cream Bars are awesome. The ice cream to chocolate ratio makes these bars superior to the ones you can get at home—I think it's the ears. These bars are mass produced and are great anywhere.

Mickey Rice Cereal Treats are also awesome. Plain is good, but those dipped in chocolate are infinitely better. But you must be careful. Some parks offer these bars as a mass-produced item. They are not as good. Get them where you can see them being made in front of you. The best Mickey Rice Cereal Treats are at the Magic Kingdom in Florida. There's really no competition here.

Mickey Pretzels are really awesome. These are mass produced but are warmed on the spot and are good anywhere.

Mickey Waffles are the awesomest. Nothing beats a Mickey Waffle with strawberries and whipped cream. But again, you must be careful. Many places serve these well after they've been made. If you see them sitting in a warming pan, move on. You want them when they're right off the iron. The very best place in the world for Mickey Waffles is Main Street Market at Hong Kong Disneyland. These are always fresh and made to your order. You can get just plain, but then you'd have to go to the doctor because something must be wrong with you.

▲ ▲ ▲

**Adventureland**

There is no Frontierland here—only Adventureland. But what an Adventureland it is! Almost one half of the park is Adventureland, and most of that is a single attraction. But it works so well here. As Fantasyland fits right at home in Paris, so does Adventureland fit right at home among these lush mountains.

The water and foliage come together beautifully, as do the meandering paths and thatched architecture. The best version of an iconic Disney attraction is here, and so is the best show in the park.

*Jungle River Cruise*

This is the best Jungle Cruise attraction in the world. It's significantly larger than the others, and the natural environment makes it extremely immersive. Remember, there is no Frontierland at Hong Kong Disneyland—no Rivers of America with Mark Twain riding past. Instead, it's the Jungle Cruise attraction that uses the most water in the park. Here, the Jungle Cruise sails on the Rivers of Adventure. In the middle is an island, but instead of Tom Sawyer, it contains Tarzan's Treehouse.

The Jungle Cruise is narrated. Since this is a multilingual park, you'll have to choose your language before you get in line. Yes, there are three queues for this attraction: Mandarin Chinese, Cantonese, and English. You'll want to ride using your preferred language first in order to understand the narration. After that, you can just choose whatever line is shorter. (Most often, I've discovered that the English line is the shortest.)

You'll board a small steamship and begin your journey. Because this version of the Jungle Cruise is so large, the ships have a lot more space between them. This adds to the immersive success of it all. The first thing you'll see is Tarzan's Treehouse. It's fun to see guests exploring the tree house while you're riding beneath them on a different attraction.

Next, you'll encounter similar animals to the ones you'll see in California, Florida, and Tokyo. But generally the effects are much better here. You'll encounter a hungry school of piranha that is usually successful in scaring a few passengers.

Then the cruise gets significantly different. You'll sail past giant stones that resemble faces. Your skipper narrator will explain that these are the gods of fire and water. As you enter a canyon, you're accidentally in the midst of a battle between these two gods. There's a lot of fire, caused by the god of fire, that gets mixed up with a lot of water from the god of water. Consequently, there's a lot of steam. But your skipper will make sure that you safely navigate the feud and return to the dock.

I'll write more about Halloween later, but this holiday is featured heavily in Hong Kong. During the Halloween season, this attraction changes to **Jungle River Cruise—Curse of the Emerald Trinity.** The ride path is identical to the non-Halloween time, but artifacts placed throughout the attraction change the story.

### Rafts to Tarzan's Treehouse

Tarzan's Treehouse is in the middle of the Rivers of Adventure. There are no bridges, and the only way to get there is by log raft. But first, as you're crossing the water, your driver will have to steer the raft out of the way of passing Jungle Cruise steamers. Then you'll dock next to the tree-house island.

The tree house itself is similar to the one at Disneyland in California. It's located in, around, and on top of a giant tree. You can explore the tree house at your own pace. There's a lot to discover here and no lines on the island. When you're ready, just take a raft back to Adventureland.

### Liki Tikis

This group of Polynesian-inspired tikis spouts water at those who come close. There's often a group of young kids here, cooling off and getting soaked. If you go to Hong Kong Disneyland during the middle of the summer and you see a white guy just sitting in the water... well, that's probably me. Stop and say hi before a cast member evicts me from the park.

### Festival of the Lion King

Performed at least four times each day, this is the best show in the park. It's also far superior to the already fantastic

Festival of the Lion King in Orlando. Check the daily Times Guide for show times. The show lasts thirty minutes.

Similar to the version in Florida, you'll sit in the round and watch as the spectacle unfolds in front of you. There's just more spectacle to watch here. The live music is superb with singing that will provide goose bumps for days. The dancing and acrobatics are choreographed. By the end of it all, there's so much going on that you'll be inspired to just breathe and soak it all in. This is one of those Disney shows that leave you happy to be alive.

### Shops of Adventureland

**Professor Porter's Trading Post** is the only shop here. It's large and packed with merchandise. There's also a large selection of prepackaged candy and cookies.

### Dining in Adventureland

**Tahitian Terrace:** Quick-service Indian food is offered here.

**Chocolate Banana Dippers:** Healthy eaters should head here for fruit served quick service in bowls.

**River View Café:** This is a table-service Southeast Asian restaurant.

**Safari Snacks:** Snacks and beverages are offered quick service at this location.

### Grizzly Gulch

This mini land is the closest thing Hong Kong Disneyland has to Frontierland. It's themed to an old mining town that's been abandoned and taken over by bears. The bear motif is quite noticeable throughout the whole area. To make it even more interesting, it was discovered that the entire town was built on top of a geyser field.

Everything in Grizzly Gulch, even the "wooden" logs, was created out of poured concrete. More than thirty-eight hundred tons of concrete were used during construction. The centerpiece of the land is a bear-shaped mountain that is a miniature replica of Grizzly Peak from Disney California Adventure.

### *Big Grizzly Mountain Runaway Mine Cars*

Most of Grizzly Gulch is taken up by the one ride. It's sort of like Big Thunder Mountain in that it's a runaway mine train, but that's where the similarities end. There are many more animatronics at Big Grizzly Mountain and overall better theming.

After boarding, your train will leave the station. A large Grizzly bear isn't paying attention and accidentally sends your train down track four. (Four is an extremely unlucky number for the Chinese people. Many hotels in China do not have a fourth floor.) Your train will get a bit out of control as it careens around the mountain and through the mine.

At one point, guests come face to face with a broken piece of track. The train will lose momentum, and you'll go backward down a hill before switching to another piece of track. Then there's an explosion courtesy of a bear cub who is also not paying attention. Who's in charge of these bears anyway?

### Grizzly Gulch Geysers
Throughout the land, you'll find geysers that sporadically explode in the air. If you're standing near them, you will get a little wet. Younger guests love to lean against the railing and wait for a cool-down.

### Grizzly Gulch Welcome Wagon Show
This quaint show is performed several times each day. A small cast of performers sings and dances to the music of the Old West. Check the daily Times Guide for show times.

### Shops of Grizzly Gulch
**Bear Necessities** is the only shop here. It's also just a wagon of stuff. This is where you'll find Grizzly Gulch merchandise and other bear-type things.

### Dining in Grizzly Gulch
**Lucky Nugget Saloon:** Grab your spurs and stop here for quick-service chicken, fish, and salads.

### Mystic Point
When you can't hear the hoe-down music and you feel the architecture oddly change, you'll know that you're in Mystic Point. This is the eeriest place at Hong Kong Disneyland.

The story is that Mystic Point was built in 1896 by an explorer named Lord Henry Mystic. He cleared the rain forest and built a large British-style manor. There's a lot of strange stuff around Mystic Point. Most of it was discovered by Lord Mystic on one of his many journeys.

### Mystic Manor

Mystic Manor is Hong Kong Disneyland's version of the Haunted Mansion. Any new entertainment venture must be approved by the Chinese government. The government has a restriction on the depiction of an afterlife. This restriction explains why some movies are not allowed to run in China. (Interestingly, they have a similar restriction on the depiction of time travel.) Knowing that the traditional Haunted Mansion would never fly in Hong Kong, imagineers came up with the concept of Mystic Manor.

This large Victorian mansion is where Lord Mystic lives with Albert, a monkey he befriended. Albert is Lord Mystic's traveling companion and is also the mascot of Mystic Point. In the queue, you'll begin to see some the lord's strange collections. You'll even be treated to a slideshow that he made. Albert peeks out here and there during the preshow.

Soon you'll board one of the lord's Mystic Magneto-Electric Carriages to tour the mansion. In the first room, Acquisitions and Cataloguing, Albert unlocks a box that nobody is supposed to touch. Of course, all sorts of mayhem ensue.

From that point, many of the lord's artifacts are able to move on their own. There are references to the

Haunted Mansions around the world in some of the moving artwork. You'll proceed through several rooms, each containing artifacts that are acting strangely. The Egyptian Antiquities room is especially well done. At the conclusion, Albert finds a way to lock the box that started all the confusion.

Mystic Manor uses the same trackless ride system as Pooh's Hunny Hunt in Tokyo. Your carriage will guide itself through the room. You'll narrowly miss other carriages as you get a chance to see all the artifacts up close. No two rides will ever be the same here.

And one more amazing fact: the music for Mystic Manor was composed by the brilliant Danny Elfman. Mr. Elfman wrote the music for *The Nightmare Before Christmas* and *Edward Scissorhands,* among many other notable compositions.

### Mystic Point Freight Depot
This is really just a photo spot where you can have your picture taken with some of Lord Mystic's stuff.

### Garden of Wonder
Guests stroll through this small garden on their own. There are several artifacts on the paths that create special effects.

### Shops of Mystic Point
**The Archives Shop** sells lots of souvenirs, jewelry, and Mystic Manor merchandise.

*Dining in Mystic Point*
**Explorer's Club Restaurant:** This quick-service restaurant serves Asian food in a fantastically themed atmosphere.

Disney's Fastpass system is barely used at Hong Kong Disneyland. This is the only Disney Park where just two attractions use the line-skipping mechanism. However, there isn't much need for one.

There is a fair amount of major attractions in the park, and attendance is never terribly high. I haven't ever encountered more than a twenty-minute wait for anything, even the very popular Mystic Manor.

As the new hotel opens in 2017 and the entertainment district progresses, perhaps park attendance will climb. There is no doubt that Disney will add a Fastpass system when lines get too long. (Remember, Disney doesn't want you standing in line; you can't eat or buy anything when you're just standing there.)

▲ ▲ ▲

**Toy Story Land**
This is the last of the mini lands, for now anyway. Toy Story Land is nearly identical to Toy Story Playland at

Walt Disney Studios in Paris. Other Toy Story Lands will open in Orlando and Shanghai in the near future.

As in Paris, Toy Story Land is as cute as can be. Guests feel that they've shrunk to the size of Andy's toys when they enter this land. Most of the attractions here are geared for younger visitors.

### Toy Soldier Parachute Drop
Rise up in the air on one of the green army men's parachutes. Then you'll gently float back down to the ground.

### Slinky Dog Spin
Sit on the back of Slinky Dog as he tries to catch his tail. You'll ride around in a circle that has a few dips.

### RC Racer
You'll speed back and forth on a half-pipe track while sitting in an oversized toy car.

### Toy Soldier Boot Camp
Learn to be a soldier by interacting with the green army men. This is a short show/demonstration that occurs in the middle of the land. Check the daily Times Guide for show times.

### Cubut in Toy Story Land
If you see some large blocks sitting around, that's Cubut. A cast member helps guests build the blocks into a person. Cubut then acts like that person. Depending upon how you stack the blocks, Cubut will act accordingly.

### Shops of Toy Story Land

**Andy's Toy Box** is the only store here. All the *Toy Story* merchandise you'll ever need is found within.

### Dining in Toy Story Land

**Jessie's Snack Roundup:** Cowgirl Jessie offers quick-service snacks here.

### Fantasyland

Fantasyland is the closest land to the mountains that line Penny's Bay. Imagineers took great care to preserve the natural views in this land. The attractions are spaced perfectly to allow guests the chance to soak in all the beauty. Again, Hong Kong Disneyland is Disney's best topographical location for a park.

### Sleeping Beauty Castle

The mountains dictated what type of castle the park should have. It was thought that the large Cinderella Castle of Florida and Tokyo would be out of perspective with the lower mountains in the background. Consequently, a replica of Sleeping Beauty Castle from Anaheim was constructed in Hong Kong.

This castle is a near-identical twin of the version in California. It rises to the same height of seventy-seven feet (twenty-three meters). It's extremely difficult to find a difference between these two castles.

The main difference is age. Hong Kong's Sleeping Beauty Castle is much newer. It uses more fiberglass.

Details like faux masonry are easier to spot in Hong Kong. Another difference, and one that's much more apparent, is that there isn't an attraction inside the Hong Kong castle. You can walk through the bottom portion, but there is nothing on the second floor.

However, all of this is changing very soon. Sleeping Beauty will need to find another place to sing to her woodland animals as the castle is getting a major renovation. Sometime in 2017, expect Sleeping Beauty Castle to be covered with large painted canvasses. Behind these covers, the castle is being expanded. It will have a completely different look. No details have been announced yet, but I suspect it will contain some sort of restaurant and walk-through attraction. The castle will also probably get a new name. All this work is expected to be completed in 2019.

### Snow White Grotto
Similar to the structure at Disneyland. Snow White often hangs about here for photos.

### Cinderella Carousel
Another beautiful Disney carousel and perfect picture spot.

### Mickey's PhilharMagic
The same fantastic attraction from Florida and Tokyo except this one is in Mandarin Chinese. It doesn't matter if you can't understand a word. The melodies are all familiar enough that you'll know what's going on.

Again, but here in Hong Kong this time, Donald Duck chases Mickey's magical hat through various Disney scenes. It's a 4-D experiment where you'll smell the apple pie and feel the ocean as it splashes you in the face.

The very best part of experiencing Mickey's PhilharMagic in Hong Kong is that it's a wonderful place to observe culture. You'll see two distinct groups of Chinese guests here. The first group is those who are from Hong Kong itself. These guests grew up with all this technology; they also know all the characters on the screen. The second group, those from mainland China, has never seen anything like this before. They will gasp audibly when a figure from the screen appears to reach out and touch them. Anytime any sort of special effect occurs, guests from the mainland will scream with surprise and joy while those from Hong Kong will shake their heads at them. The whole thing is a lot of fun to watch.

### Dumbo the Flying Elephant

Ride around on Dumbo in the special administrative region of China. What's more to be said?

### Fairy Tale Forest

This newer area is gorgeous. Guests wander through landscaped paths as they encounter miniature versions of famous Disney scenes. You'll see Rapunzel's tower, the Beast's castle, Eric and Ariel's royal abode, and others. In addition, Tinkerbell is often waiting to say hello toward the back of the forest.

This is a great opportunity to explore on your own without waiting in a line. It's very much like Disneyland's Storybook Canal Boats without the boats and canals. OK, it's nothing like Disneyland's Storybook Canal Boats.

### Hong Kong Disneyland Railroad Fantasyland Station

The only other station on the Hong Kong Disneyland Railroad. From here, you can ride all the way to the park's entrance/exit at Main Street. Use this station if you're tired of walking or if you want a quick exit during a parade.

### Fantasy Gardens

Fantasy Gardens is Hong Kong Disneyland's character greeting area. Here, five beautiful pergolas each host a different character. Normally, you'll find Mickey Mouse and his friends waiting to greet you.

Photos are easy to get with a park photographer or with your own camera. Again, all Disney photographers are happy to take a photo with your own camera or phone. Note: if you want to see Anna and Elsa, they're near the castle in a special venue next to Royal Banquet Hall.

During Halloween, Fantasy Gardens turns into **Villains Gardens.** Mickey and Donald don't hang around for this because Maleficent will set up shop with four of her companions. Note: the Big Bad Wolf appears here, the only place on the planet where you can get a photo with him.

### Mad Hatter Tea Cups
Your chance to throw up in Mandarin Chinese or Cantonese.

### The Many Adventures of Winnie the Pooh
*Fastpass* Identical to the version at the Magic Kingdom with a less-interactive queue. You'll sit in the familiar hunny pots and explore the Hundred Acre Woods.

### "it's a small world"
I'd like to apologize to all Disney purists for what I'm about to say: this is the best version of "it's a small world." Yes, I know that the version in Anaheim is the original one that Walt worked on. It's the one that came all the way from the New York World's Fair. I understand the historical significance of the attraction in Disneyland.

But I like this one better. It's the newest of all the attractions of the same name. The water canals were dug to optimize viewing. You can see things better here. This was the first version of the ride to feature Disney characters intermingling with the singing dolls in their specific countries. For example, you can spot Pinocchio in Italy.

Another fantastic difference about Hong Kong's small world is the addition of an expanded North America. You'll see scenes from the United States and Canada. (Mexico was always part of the Latin section.)

Please don't hate me for loving this ride in this place.

### Mickey and the Wondrous Book

Inside Disney's Storybook Theater, this thirty-minute show is amazing. Mickey and Goofy have discovered a book that can bring stories to life. They open the book (why do they always open the book?), and Olaf, the snowman from *Frozen*, falls out. Mickey tries to get Olaf back into his story, when all three of them are sucked into the book. Now, Mickey and Goofy travel through stories, each time hoping to find the story where Olaf belongs.

There are six stories featured: *The Jungle Book, The Little Mermaid, Tangled, Brave, Aladdin*, and *The Princess and the Frog*. They learn a bunch of lessons along the way. Finally, they venture into Arendelle, where Olaf can rejoin his *Frozen* life.

Expect amazing stagecraft here. The sets and costumes are spectacular. I was in love with the previous show at Disney's Storybook Theater, The Golden Mickeys. It was heartbreaking to hear about the end of that show, but Mickey and the Wondrous Book took away all that pain.

### Shops of Fantasyland

**Storybook Shoppe**, located next to the castle, is the largest store in the land with all the souvenirs, merchandise, and cookies. **Pooh Corner** sells housewares (go figure), and **Merlin's Treasures** is a smaller shop for souvenirs.

### Dining in Fantasyland

**Royal Banquet Hall:** Not as regal as the name implies. It's a quick-service restaurant for international cuisine.

**Small World Ice Cream:** Ice cream and snacks are offered quick service here.

**Clopin's Festival of Foods:** Clopin, a little-known character from *The Hunchback of Norte Dame,* sells quick-service Chinese food. I'm not sure why.

Each Disney park is equipped with first-aid stations and medical-response teams. First-aid stations are located on all park maps. They can handle any type of minor problem, with foot blisters being the most common.

In the event of a serious medical emergency, shout for help. Cast members are well trained to call medical personnel. In the United States, simply dialing 911 from any phone will immediately connect you with an operator. In Anaheim and Orlando, 911 operators are able to connect quickly with medical staff already located inside the theme parks.

In the unfortunate event that something serious occurs in your Disney hotel room, call the front desk immediately. Hotel staff will be able to quickly call medical support and get them to your room.

Just remember that there are great people all over the world who want to help. Don't be afraid to ask for help before small problems become medical emergencies.

▲ ▲ ▲

## Tomorrowland

Hong Kong Disneyland's Tomorrowland is a bit on the small side, but it's designed beautifully with lots of metallic elements throughout. And it just got bigger. The newly opened Iron Man Experience has pushed Tomorrowland outside the boundary of the Hong Kong Disneyland Railroad track.

Due to the positions of the mini lands and nearby highways, only Tomorrowland and Fantasyland have room to expand. Interestingly, the only lands that are shared between Hong Kong and Shanghai are also Tomorrowland and Fantasyland. Since new rides can't be duplicated between the parks, it's fun to see the many unique attractions coming to China.

### Orbitron

Just like Dumbo except it's flying saucers.

### Star Wars: Command Post

This is a highly themed character interaction area. Guests journey to a rebel base, where they can have their picture taken with heroes from a galaxy far, far away.

The characters can change but normally include R2-D2 and Chewbacca.

### Hyperspace Mountain

*Fastpass* Someone got Space Mountain on my *Star Wars*. Someone else got *Star Wars* on my Space Mountain! In the summer of 2016, Hong Kong's Space Mountain was given an overlay and turned into Hyperspace Mountain. Disneyland in California previously had this overlay.

The basic structure of the ride is the same, but new effects and sounds provide constant reminders that you are traveling through the *Star Wars* galaxy. To hear John Williams's amazing score while riding a coaster is worth the price of admission to Hong Kong Disneyland!

### Autopia

Autopia is another attraction that pushes the boundary of Tomorrowland over the train tracks. Similar to other versions around the world, you can drive your own car around a curvy track. Just remember, Hong Kong was a former British colony, and they drive on the left!

Note: Autopia closed during the summer of 2016 for refurbishment, and no date has been announced as to when it will reopen.

### Buzz Lightyear Astro Blasters

Another Tomorrowland attraction that's similar to those in other Disney parks. You'll control the angle of your vehicle as you help Buzz Lightyear battle the evil Emperor

Zurg. You'll use a laser gun to shoot at targets and will be given a score at the end.

### Iron Man Experience

Disclaimer: This is a brand-new ride that I have not experienced yet. Here is what I know from research: It's the first Disney attraction based on a Marvel Comics character. Iron Man Experience is a 3-D motion simulator that cost as much money as Tony Stark is worth. And it uses the same simulator mechanisms as the Star Tours rides.

In true Disney style, there is a story. Tony Stark has invited you on a tour of Hong Kong, the city hosting the current Stark Expo. While on the tour, Hydra attacks the city. Tony then becomes Iron Man to help you fight Hydra.

I'm expecting a few things. First, I hope to see a lot of Hong Kong during this ride. Second, I'm expecting that, like Star Tours, no two rides will be quite the same. And third, I hope that Iron Man Experience will accept a Fastpass.

### Jedi Training: Trials of the Temple

During this interactive show, younger guests are shown the ways of the force. Even though the show is mostly in Mandarin, English-speaking children will do fine if they watch the performers' body language. This show occurs several times each day. Check the daily Times Guide for show times.

Jedi Training takes place in an area of Tomorrowland that's partly under the Autopia track. Close by, there are often many *Star Wars* characters that you can meet and photograph.

### Shops of Tomorrowland

There are two stores in Tomorrowland, and both of them offer *Star Wars* merchandise. **Space Traders** is located near Hyperspace Mountain, and **Star Command Suppliers** is over near the Buzz Lightyear attraction.

### Dining in Tomorrowland

**BB-8 Snack Cart:** Tasty quick-service desserts are served here in a giant version of BB-8 (if you don't know what a BB-8 is, then you should probably skip Tomorrowland altogether).

**Comet Café:** Hong Kong's famous street food is served quick service at this fragrant location.

**Starlight Diner:** Head here for quick-service American food.

## Parades, Evening Shows, and Special Events

### Disney Paint the Night Nighttime Spectacular

Hong Kong Disneyland's outstanding night parade is Disney Paint the Night. It's almost the same as the parade that just closed at Disneyland in California but with fewer crowds.

As one approach to attract guests to the park, Hong Kong Disneyland has greatly increased its repertoire of parades. This is one of them.

All the spectacular floats that you'd expect are here, as are all the characters and lots of cast members. This is a high-energy parade with pumped-up music, dancing, and flashing lights galore. Main Street is the most popular place to watch the parade.

### Flights of Fantasy Parade

Another amazing parade, this one usually occurs in the afternoon. The theme of this parade is flying. Disney characters that can fly, like Dumbo, are featured above floats. The characters that can't or won't fly (I'm looking at you, Donald) are carried by floats shaped like hot-air balloons. Again, expect a lot of music and choreographed dancing.

### "Disney in the Stars" Fireworks

Fireworks occur nightly at Hong Kong Disneyland. These are much better than Tokyo's and are worth your time to stay in the park.

Lots of fireworks, other pyrotechnics, and projections are used for this show. It's important that you can see the front of Sleeping Beauty Castle for the full effect. The castle serves as a screen for the projections to appear.

### Christmas

Christmas is celebrated well at Hong Kong Disneyland Resort. Amazing decorations fill the park and the resort hotels. The characters make appearances in their

Christmas finest, especially at the Fantasy Gardens greeting area.

A special parade occurs during the holiday season. Depending upon the expected park attendance, the Christmas parade may be performed in addition to, or instead of, Flights of Fantasy.

### Halloween

Halloween is huge at Hong Kong Disneyland. Disneyland and the Magic Kingdom have their special Halloween parties, but no other park does more to celebrate Halloween than Hong Kong Disneyland. For some reason unknown to me, the people of Hong Kong love Halloween, even though depictions of an afterlife are banned. In fact, if you like Hong Kong Disneyland on Facebook, you'll see that they run Halloween ads constantly during the fall.

The Jungle Cruise gets a Halloween overlay during this time of the year. Mickey and his entourage are replaced with villains at Fantasy Garden. But don't worry that you will miss Mickey and Donald. Every afternoon during this season, the **Mickey & Friends Costume Party** occurs in front of the castle. Guests can interact and have a photo taken with the characters in their Halloween attire.

The Disney villains also get their own show in front of the castle. Nightly, **Villains' Night Out** gives those horrible beings that chance to cause mayhem on the central hub.

**Mickey's Halloweentime Cavalcade** is a parade that occurs daily, usually during the late afternoon. The Disney characters put on their Halloween costumes and ride on giant pumpkins down Main Street, USA. There is a lot of music and tons of creativity.

Hong Kong Disneyland is the only Disney park to have an attraction that is just open for Halloween. Located in a facility off the beaten path, between Adventureland and Grizzly Gulch, is the **Nightmare Experiment.** This is an actual walk-through haunted house attraction. No other Disney park has dared to offer this kind of activity. When you enter, you'll meet your guide, a professor who is to guide you through a land of nightmares in order to return to the real world. You'll journey through a jail from *Pirates of the Caribbean,* a hall of voodoo inspired by *The Princess and the Frog,* an asylum that features the Mad Hatter, and—a thing so scary I can hardly write it—an interaction with giant mutant toys from *Toy Story.* (Mutant toys are scary anyway, but here they're absolutely terrifying.) All right, some teenagers may think the Nightmare Experiment is too Disneyfied, but there are plenty of scares for the likes of me. Needless to say, this is not an attraction for young kids.

Throughout the park, there are a lot of special Halloween foods and merchandise. Just be advised: October is still a very warm month for Hong Kong. Pretend you're a vampire: drink plenty of fluids and stay out of the sun.

## Area Sights outside Disney

With its odd combination of Asian and Western history, Hong Kong is one of the most unique travel destinations in the world. There is a lot to do here. Fortunately, it's quite easy to get around, and most of the city is affordable.

### Ngong Ping 360

Located right on the same island as Hong Kong Disneyland is an aerial tramway called Ngong Ping 360. It's a very short, and cheap, cab ride away. You can take a twenty-five-minute gondola ride over the mountains of Lantau Island. When you begin the journey, you'll get amazing views of Hong Kong International Airport.

At the top of your mountain destination, you'll find Ngong Ping Village, a small collection of shops and restaurants. But the real draw up here is the Tian Tan Buddha. The monks of the nearby Po Lin Monastery built the Buddha in 1993. It's relatively new, especially by Chinese standards. The Tian Tan Buddha is enormous. It's made of bronze and is 112 feet (thirty-four meters) tall. But he appears much taller since you have to climb 268 steps to reach him.

### Victoria Harbor Star Ferry

Usually considered the number-one tourist attraction in Hong Kong, a ride on the Star Ferry is an absolute must-do. The Star Ferry has been bringing passengers between Hong Kong Island and Kowloon since 1888. In fact, twenty-six million people ride on the Star Ferry every year.

The experience is amazing. While crossing the gorgeous harbor, you'll see all the skyscrapers of Hong Kong and Kowloon. You can stand by a railing and watch the other watercraft in the area. The whole organization is a well-run machine.

The best part—it only costs HK$2.00 to ride. That's right: for US$0.23, less than a quarter, you can have one of the most priceless experiences in the word.

### Temple Street Night Market
The Temple Street Night Market occurs nightly in Kowloon. It's a sprawling market with lots of stalls. Nearby, you'll find endless amounts of Chinese food.

### Victoria Peak
Ride a tram up to the top of Victoria Peak for a bird's-eye view of the most amazing skyline in the world. The experience is great if you can time it right to be up there at sunset.

### Hong Kong Tramways
If I had only an hour in Hong Kong, I'd take a cab to the Kowloon Ferry Terminal. There, I'd get on the Star Ferry and travel to central Hong Kong. Then I'd walk to the nearest street and get on a Hong Kong double-decker tram. This is another experience you will never forget. Sit on the top deck and watch the amazing world pass before you. The locals use it for transportation, but you'll use it to experience the dichotomy of cosmopolitan central Hong Kong and the traditional look of residential Hong Kong.

It costs HK$2.30 to ride the tram. Yep, that's US$0.27. For US$0.50, you can experience the very best of Hong Kong.

## Macau

Hong Kong isn't the only special administrative region of China. In fact, there is another quite close by. Macau is a province connected directly to mainland China. You can actually see the enormous casinos of Macau from Hong Kong International Airport.

Macau is a former Portuguese colony that was ceded to China about the same time that the British left Hong Kong. It's also a SAR within China with its own currency, the Macanese pataca. You can travel directly between Hong Kong and Macau via a short ferry. Even though you will need to pass through border control between the two SARs, no visa is required for most tourists to enter Macau.

You may have noticed that I mentioned casinos in the first paragraph about Macau. This is the only reason to visit. I went because I was interested to see any similarity to Las Vegas. Macau was interesting, but I probably won't return.

Enormous casinos line the main streets, and, from the outside, it looks very much like Las Vegas. The Venetian Hotel and Casino is almost identical to its sister in Nevada. You'll also find Wynn, MGM Grand, Sands, Hard Rock, and many others. However, the casino interiors are noticeably different from what is found in the United States. Everything here centers around gambling. I found no shows. The few shops and restaurants were entirely vacant. But every single seat in the casino was occupied. Feel free to form your own opinion about what this means. I'll keep mine to myself.

Aside from the casinos, there is a very small historic district and one interesting church façade. If you want to experience a bizarro Las Vegas, then by all means take the ferry to Macau. Otherwise, spend your time in Hong Kong.

# 7

---

## Shanghai Disney Resort

CHINA IS AN ancient country full of diverse landscapes and people. It's also the most populous nation on earth. There are 161 cities in China with more than one million people. Just to compare, the United States has nine cities with a population greater than one million. Yet, for a country that immense, we know so little about it. Most of us could probably only name two or three of those 161 major cities.

For a large part of the twentieth century, China was isolated from much of the Western world. Slowly, that has changed, and different cultures can now come together and discover what can be done to improve the lives of their people. Providing well-paying jobs and increased tourism revenue is one thing that can have a positive impact.

The brand-spanking-new Shanghai Disney Resort includes one theme park, two resort hotels, a large public park, and an entertainment district. The paint still smells new, and the typical guest is quite curious. The people of Hong Kong had been exposed to Disney over the years. Those in mainland China had not. The whole concept is a gamble. But regardless of whether or not it can succeed, this is certain: Shanghai has one absolutely gorgeous Disney park.

Shanghai Disney Resort Pros:

- Everything is new.
- Shanghai Disneyland is the most different of the Magic Kingdom-style parks.
- Cast members are newly trained and highly efficient.
- It's a big park that provides plenty of exercise.
- The currency exchange rate makes Shanghai Disneyland quite affordable for travelers from North America and Europe.

Shanghai Disney Resort Cons:

- With so much room to expand, the park can feel empty.

- The park is missing some of the more iconic Disney attractions.
- Smog can be a real problem on some days.
- The changing political relationship between the United States and China might impact the future of this beautiful park.

▲ ▲ ▲

## History

Shanghai was on Disney's radar ever since it had been considered as a potential site prior the construction of Hong Kong Disneyland Resort. The massive population of the area was one appealing aspect of Shanghai, as was the rapidly growing middle class. But both parties, Disney and Beijing, wanted to wait and watch Hong Kong Disneyland unfold.

However, in 2002, a rumor started that Disney had already signed an agreement to build a park in Shanghai. This made the leadership of the Hong Kong SAR (special administrative region) quite nervous. Their park hadn't even broken ground yet. Disney assured them that Hong Kong Disneyland was their first priority in the area. Still, Hong Kong SAR had a difficult time with the rumor. In fact, Hong Kong SAR forced Disney to sign an agreement limiting the number of attractions that could be duplicated between Hong Kong Disneyland and whatever was being considered in Shanghai.

Not much else was heard from Shanghai until 2007. At that time, a representative of the Chinese central government confirmed that the local government of Shanghai had asked Beijing for permission to create a partnership with the Walt Disney Company. Permission was granted, but the local government of Shanghai wanted to wait until after the 2010 Shanghai World's Fair before proceeding. This was good news for the folks down in Hong Kong.

The decision to wait until after the fair led to speculation that the fair's location was being considered as the future home for a Shanghai Disneyland. But eventually Disney talked Shanghai out of that site because it limited future development. As Euro Disneyland's large size impacted the design of Hong Kong, so would Hong Kong's small size impact the design of Shanghai. Disney was committed to building a larger park with more attractions in Shanghai than it had in Hong Kong.

Officials began to look at land in the Pudong District of Shanghai. This is the city's most populous district and is also the location of Shanghai's large international airport. The land under consideration was close to major highways. It was also located about halfway between the airport and Shanghai's central business district. Eventually this would become the home of Shanghai Disney Resort.

But again, negotiations turned to the finances. Who would pay for the project, and who would get the profits? Disney was interested in the same deal they got in Hong Kong. In the end, the Chinese created a company,

Shanghai Shendi Group, to co-own the park with Disney. The final agreement stated that Disney would own 43 percent of Shanghai Disney Resort, with Shanghai Shendi Group owning 57 percent. The costs and profits would be split accordingly.

The groundbreaking ceremony occurred on April 8, 2011. Mickey Mouse attended, wearing a traditional Chinese outfit. It was announced that Shanghai Disney Resort would include Shanghai Disneyland and two resort hotels. Future plans included two more parks and several more hotels. Since that day, rumors have persisted about the possibility of an Epcot and Animal Kingdom joining Shanghai Disneyland.

Construction began, and Disney started hiring cast members. The Chinese are well known for their speedy construction ability. However, when Disney imagineers arrived on the scene about one year later, they discovered that some of the early construction work was not suitable for the designs being prepared. Much of the early work had to be redone. A 2014 opening date was pushed to 2015.

But when 2015 arrived, things were not going well. Construction had slowed, and a curious public became restless. Bob Iger, the person in charge at the Walt Disney Company, turned most of his focus toward Shanghai. Budgets were tightened in Anaheim and Orlando to finance the reorganization of Paris and the building of Shanghai. The funds did help, and construction proceeded in China.

A spring 2016 opening was planned as Disney began a massive publicity campaign aimed to educate the Chinese about what a Disney park was. The campaign must have done a good job. On May 20, 2015, the first Disney Store in China opened to the public. It was located in central Shanghai. An hour after opening, the store was completely filled to capacity, and the line to enter the store stretched for more than a mile.

By mid-2015, construction on both resort hotels had neared completion. Disneytown, the resort's entertainment district, was also almost complete. However, the park itself was again behind schedule. The spring 2016 opening date was removed, and no new timeline was revealed.

Finally, as the new year began, information started to flow out of Shanghai. The resort would open during the summer of 2016. Soon, a website went live with the ability to make hotel reservations and purchase tickets.

On June 16, 2016, Shanghai Disney Resort opened to the public. In addition to Shanghai Disneyland, the resort featured two hotels and the Disneytown entertainment district. A large public park, Wishing Star Park, had opened about a month earlier. Wishing Star Park does not require admission. Also opening was a large theater and permanent home of a Mandarin version of Disney's hit Broadway show *The Lion King*.

Shanghai Disneyland Resort is too new to foresee accurately. Articles written in November of 2016 tend to report a lower-than-expected park attendance. Both Disney and Shanghai Shendi Group deny these reports.

The fluctuating Chinese yuan has been seen as the main problem with park attendance at this time.

Only time will tell the future of this infant park. If attendance truly is low, then we'll see additional attractions added to the existing Shanghai Disneyland. However, if attendance is high, we'll probably hear an announcement concerning the development of a second park and additional hotels.

## Travel Knowledge
### Arrival/Transport

Most international visitors will arrive at Shanghai Pudong International Airport. This modern and sprawling airport has five runways that serve over sixty million passengers each year. You will find all the services you'd expect from a major international airport.

After clearing customs, there are a few options for transportation to Shanghai Disney Resort. It is possible to take a train; however, to use the Shanghai Metro, you will need to take three different lines with two transfers. I don't recommend this option as it's confusing, especially when you've just walked off a very long flight.

Taxis are by far your best option at Pudong International Airport. A cab from the airport to the resort is ¥70.00 ($10.19). This makes it the cheapest Disney taxi in the world. Be advised: Only take a cab from the official airport taxi line. Do not go with any driver who approaches you in the terminal. Shanghai continues to be plagued with unregistered cab drivers who will take advantage of you and your tourist ignorance.

If you really want to make things easy for yourself, you can prehire a car to provide transportation from the airport to your hotel. I've found that www.shanghai-carservice.com is a reliable company with great customer service. Their rates vary depending upon your destination and specific needs. Just fill out the form on their website, and they will reply via e-mail within a few minutes. For an extra fee, this car service will meet you right outside the airplane door and guide you through customs.

### Visa/Passport

Most travelers need a visa to enter the People's Republic of China. Remember, this is not true for the Hong Kong SAR. Those who wish to visit Shanghai Disney Resort and stay in China longer than 144 hours will need to obtain a visa. I'll highlight the basic process, but you should visit www.china-embassy.org for the most current information. (Travelers planning to spend less than 144 hours in Shanghai can skip this information and proceed to the paragraph about the Shanghai Visa Waiver Program.)

There are two ways to obtain a Chinese visa: in person or through an agent. To use the in-person process, you'll download and complete the visa application. Then you'll physically go to a Chinese embassy or consulate in your home country. Bring the application, your current passport, a recent passport photograph, and $140. You'll wait in a line until an official can receive all your items. Yes, you'll be required to leave your passport at the embassy or consulate. Around four days later, you'll get a call to return to the embassy or consulate and retrieve your passport. The Chinese visa will be glued to one of your passport's pages.

If you don't live near an embassy or consulate or if you don't want the hassle of an in-person application, you can use an agent. There are many agents available online, and you can find them by doing a simple Google search. However, make sure you are using a reputable agent as there is a lot of fraud in this area. My advice: Call your nearest college or university and ask to speak with their study abroad department. Ask someone there who they use to obtain Chinese visas. Most universities use a local agent that you will be able to trust.

To use an agency, you'll either mail or physically deliver to them the completed application form, your current passport, a recent passport photograph, $140 payable to China, and whatever fees the agent charges. The agents will then do the work of getting your stuff to the Chinese embassy. They will retrieve your completed passport with visa and mail it to you. You'll need to allow a few weeks for the agent to accomplish all this.

However, if you're only visiting Shanghai and you intend to spend less than 144 hours, you can use the **Chinese Visa Waiver Program.** This is a bit complicated. Keep reading carefully. First, those on a visa waiver must stay within the Shanghai metropolitan area. If you are caught breaking this rule, the punishment can include a large fine and time in jail. Just don't leave the city of Shanghai.

The clock of the visa waiver starts at the immediate midnight after your arrival. If you land at 11:00 p.m., you'll have one hour of free time in China; if you land at 1:00 a.m., you'll have twenty-three hours of free time in China—before the 144 hour clock starts ticking. When you enter China, you must prove that you have an airline ticket to leave the country within the waiver period. Here's the catch: when you leave China, you cannot return to your home country. All participants in the Chinese Visa Waiver Program must visit a third country after their departure. However, the Hong Kong SAR does count as a third country. So you can arrive in Shanghai without a visa and spend up to six days at Shanghai Disney Resort. Then fly to either Hong Kong or Tokyo and visit the Disney resort there before returning home. There are a few more complications to note if you want to use the waiver program:

- You may not use any connecting flights inside China.
- Guam, Saipan, and all other US territories are considered the United States and do not qualify as a third-country stopover.
- The entire European Union is considered one country under this policy. Europeans must visit a third country—one that is not China or inside the European Union.

- If, for any reason, you must stay in China beyond the 144-hour limit, then you will need to get a visa. This includes unexpected airplane delays. Getting a visa while inside China will be an enormous hassle; give yourself plenty of wiggle room. I always book a departure flight within 120 hours of my arrival. This gives me twenty-four hours to find a way out of China if my flight is canceled.

### Ground Transportation

Taxis in China are extremely affordable. Just be advised that there is a fair amount of fraudulent drivers in Shanghai. Always use the official taxi line at the airport or Shanghai Disney Resort. Do not accept rides from drivers who approach you outside the taxi line, even if the line is long. It's much better to wait in line for an official cab than to be ripped off by a fraudulent driver. If you're walking around the city, always go to a major hotel to obtain a taxi.

Most taxi drivers in Shanghai will not speak English. Ask someone at your hotel to write your destination in Mandarin for the driver. Most hotels will also give you a card with their address in Mandarin to make it easy for you to return. Reputable drivers will likely know all about Shanghai Disney Resort. Showing them a photo of the castle on your smartphone will get you to the resort entrance.

Shanghai Disney Resort operates a free shuttle between the park, both hotels, and the Disney Resort Shanghai Metro Station. Using the Shanghai Metro, travelers can access most points within the city affordably. Just note that the trains will be extremely busy during rush hours, and the system is not as user friendly as the metros of Hong Kong and Tokyo. Also, Shanghai Disney Resort is at the end of a short metro line, and a transfer or two will almost always be required. Ask at your hotel for exact directions on which train(s) to take.

### Time

Shanghai is in the same time zone as Hong Kong and the rest of China. It's one hour behind Tokyo and twelve hours ahead of New York City. They are six hours ahead of Europe and fifteen hours ahead of California.

The People's Republic of China does not observe daylight saving time. In the winter, the time difference between China and Europe/America is one hour greater.

### Language

Mandarin Chinese is the official language of China, but there are a lot of other languages used. China is an extremely diverse nation with hundreds of different ethnic groups and thousands of dialects.

In Shanghai, you'll find that most people in the hospitality industry will speak English. You can easily find English speakers all over Shanghai Disneyland Resort. If you need to call the resort to make a reservation, by pressing 2, you can be connected to an English-speaking cast member. I've never had any issues understanding a cast member over the phone; they are well trained.

However, you will find that few in the service industry will speak English. If you take a cab, chances are the driver will not speak English. Always ask someone at your current location to write your destination in Chinese on a piece of paper. Show that paper to the driver. The bell staff at any hotel will be used to this and may even have some preprinted cards for you to use with popular destinations already on them.

### Weather

Shanghai has a fairly temperate climate with four distinct seasons. The summer is normally hot and humid, not as bad as Hong Kong but more humid than New York. The average temperature in July is 29°C (84°F). The rainy season of September brings about a nice fall. Winters can be surprisingly cold with an average January temperature of 4°C (39°F). However, it rarely snows. A moderate spring brings back the humidity of summer.

Like many large Chinese cities with the exception of Hong Kong, Shanghai suffers from a fair amount of air pollution. Don't expect to see a lot of blue sky when you're in town. Visitors with allergies and/or asthma should take precautions and carry necessary medication with them. On the positive side, hazy air makes for some spectacular sunsets behind Enchanted Storybook Castle.

### Water

Tap water is not always safe to drink in mainland China. Any major hotel will most likely treat its own water. Ask at the front desk to find out if it's safe to drink and brush your teeth from the bathroom facet. Bottled water is available for purchase in all of the tourist areas of Shanghai.

It's more difficult to discern if water and ice are safe in a restaurant. Modern establishments and fast-food chains should be fine, but be careful in smaller, more traditional venues. If in doubt, order something from a bottle. (Once, in a moment of desperation, I brushed my teeth using some vodka. It was a pleasant experience, and my teeth felt quite clean, although my breath probably betrayed my action.)

### Toilets

Most public restrooms in Shanghai will contain a mix of Western-style toilets with Chinese-style squatting receptacles. (A few stalls will be one way, and the rest will be the other.) You'll find this combination inside Shanghai Disney Resort as well. Don't worry if you've never used a Chinese squatty potty before—it's fairly easy to figure out what to do! All hotels rooms in Shanghai will contain only Western toilets.

The restrooms inside Shanghai Disney Resort are immaculate. You could easily eat off the floor—except the floor around the squatty potties, which you should avoid. All kidding aside, there's no need to be concerned about finding a clean restroom at any Disney property. However, if you venture to other places in China, make sure to carry a travel roll of toilet tissue with you.

## Internet

While in Hong Kong, you won't notice any Internet censorship. The same is not true for mainland China. At Shanghai Disney Resort, you won't be able to access Google or any of its products, including Gmail. Facebook is also off limits. An extremely large team of government workers constantly monitor the Internet and block any site that Chinese leadership finds offensive, including many news sites. The rest of the world has dubbed this team "the Great Firewall of China." I'm not sure why, but some of my favorite theme-park blogs are blocked.

## Money

The official currency of China is the renminbi (it means "people's money"). The basic unit of the renminbi is the yuan (¥). Many people use the term "yuan" to generally describe all Chinese currency. As of publication, ¥1 is equal to fifteen cents American. (Please note: ¥ is the Western symbol for both the Chinese yuan and the Japanese yen. Basically, when talking about China, ¥ = yuan. When talking about Japan, ¥ = yen.)

Much like in Hong Kong, credit cards are accepted all over. However, due to a concern about fraud, some credit card companies get suspicious when a charge occurs from mainland China. It's a very good idea to contact your credit card company and let them know that you'll be traveling in mainland China.

A value added tax (VAT) of 17 percent is added to most goods purchased in China. The VAT rate is 13 percent for food and medical essentials. You can receive a refund of the VAT on goods at the airport. Lodging tax in mainland China is currently a little fishy. In the past, a 15 percent tax and service fee was added to all hotel rates. However, starting in May 2016, this lodging tax changed into a VAT of 6 percent. Consequently, most hotels are still charging the 15 percent and calling it a service while also adding the 6 percent VAT on top of that. It's all in how the hotel is interpreting a poorly written law.

Technically, tipping is illegal in China. But most people seem to want and expect one. Be discreet and give people in the service industry around ¥10. However, don't be surprised if your tip is refused. Some citizens are proud to strongly support the party line, and they will not partake in this illegal activity.

### Tickets

Tickets are available online via the park's app or in person at Shanghai Disney Resort. Note: If you purchase tickets online, you'll be asked to provide your passport number. When you get to the park, you will show your passport and a ticket confirmation number in order to retrieve your tickets. It's important that you enter the passport number of someone who is physically going to be with you when you enter the park for the first time. The resort uses your passport to verify that it is, indeed, the correct person who ordered the tickets. At this time, there is no way for an international visitor to purchase a ticket and give it to someone else.

Shanghai Disneyland is the first Disney park to offer tickets by height. This makes a lot of sense to me. Regardless of age, people over 1.4 meters (four-foot-seven) can ride more attractions than those who are shorter. In Shanghai, people over 1.4 meters buy the standard ticket. Those shorter buy a child ticket. (I understand how demeaning this may be to a shorter adult. Perhaps Shanghai Disneyland could use some enlightenment on this matter.) People over the age of sixty-five can buy a senior ticket.

In addition to height, tickets are also sold based on date. There are standard days and select days. Standard days are normally weekdays during the off season. Weekends, summer, and Chinese holidays are most likely select days. The Shanghai Disney Resort website has a calendar stating what type of ticket you need for the specific dates you want to visit. Shanghai Disneyland offers one- and two-day tickets.

A standard one-day ticket is ¥370.00 ($53.75) during a standard day and ¥499.00 ($72.49) during the select time. A standard two-day ticket is ¥825.00 ($119.82).

Child and senior tickets cost the same amount. A one-day child/senior ticket is ¥280.00 ($40.67) during a standard day and ¥375.00 ($54.47) during the select season. A two-day child/senior ticket is ¥710.00 ($103.12).

## Accommodations

As recently as twenty years ago, it was common to discover that hotels in mainland China still used straw mattresses.

Security and service were noticeably lacking, and Western travelers were often uncomfortable and confused. These "good old days" were highly overrated. Times have changed, and travelers are glad that they have. Today, you'll find thousands of hotels in Shanghai with every level of price and quality.

### Disney Hotels

Location, location, location. Shanghai is similar to Tokyo in that every type of hotel is available. However, unlike Tokyo, there aren't any non-Disney hotels adjacent to the resort's property. There is one big advantage to choosing a Disney hotel in Shanghai, and it's entirely location.

Guests of Shanghai Disneyland's two hotels, on some infrequent days, have access to Wishing Star Park one hour prior to the general public. This free park is an area of grass and walkways that straddles Wishing Star Lake in front of Shanghai Disneyland. It's a nice place to stroll, but that's about it. Understandably, early access—if it's even available during your stay—is not a huge benefit.

Besides the fact that both hotels are brand-spanking new, there are no other special perks for choosing a Disney hotel. That leaves us with location, and it's not to be ignored. As the area around Shanghai Disneyland is developed, things will certainly change. However, right now, if you want convenient access to Mickey's newest kingdom, a Disney hotel is by far your best option.

### Shanghai Disneyland Hotel

Shanghai Disneyland's flagship hotel is beautiful but different from the other flagships around the globe. Disney has finally made a departure from the Victorian-style theming reflective of Main Street, USA. Since this park lacks Main Street, Shanghai Disneyland Hotel's theme is art deco. If you've sailed on the Disney Dream, then this hotel will look familiar.

After entering a soaring lobby with an incredible sculpture, guests can explore well-manicured grounds. There is both ferry and bus service to Shanghai Disneyland, although I really enjoyed the ten-minute walk around Wishing Star Lake. As you walk, you'll cross a most unique glass bridge that I can't get enough of. Just remember, this hotel is quite secure. You must have an active room key to enter and exit the grounds.

There are three restaurants. **Lumiere's** is a buffet with character dining for breakfast, lunch, and dinner. The hotel's upscale restaurant is on the top floor and is called **Aurora** (like the princess). **Ballet Café** on the third-floor lobby level offers quick-service options and excellent pastries. Next door to this café, you'll find **Bacchus Lounge**. This *Fantasia*-themed bar is a great place to get an evening drink. I had the most unique martini I've ever seen here; it had a fresh flower floating in it.

The rooms are nice but nothing spectacular. Most have two beds and a cute child's bed that pulls out from underneath the television. This small mattress reveals an adorable painting of sleeping Mickey Mouse when you use it. Everything is immaculate with all the amenities you'll find at most Asian hotels, including slippers and robes. (Next to one of the beds is a phone. Behind this phone is a bronze decoration that looks out of place. Press this bronze circle, and you'll have a private fireworks display above your head.) However, you should note that like most hotels in China, the walls are thin. You will hear noises from the rooms next to you, and there is really no escaping this at Shanghai Disney Resort. I'm a light sleeper, and I've found that a white noise app on my phone works wonders.

Speaking of fireworks, there is a real advantage to securing a room with a theme-park view. These rooms are more expensive, but the view on the other side of the hotel is terrible. Park-view rooms face Wishing Star Lake with an incredible panorama of Enchanted Storybook Castle, TRON, and other brilliantly lit buildings. At night, these rooms have the best view of Shanghai Disneyland's fireworks.

There is a floor of club rooms that serve a fantastic breakfast and afternoon tea. I've noticed that these Magic Kingdom Club rooms are not all that more expensive than standard rooms; it may be worth it to save some money on meals. Plus, guests on the club floor can attend a nightly bedtime story where Mickey himself makes an appearance and poses for photographs in his pajamas!

**King Triton's Pool** is a small but nice place to swim. It's indoors, and there is no outdoor option here. Don't select this hotel for the pool as it's not all that great. In addition to the pool, there is a full fitness facility and a nice gift shop.

With the exception of location, the best aspect of Shanghai Disneyland Hotel is, by far, the amazing service. I'd rate it right up there with the Disney hotels in Tokyo. There are some incredibly professional and courteous cast members at this place, and I hope that trend will continue. Expect to pay ¥1,650.00 ($238.31) for a standard room on a weekday and ¥3,100.00 ($447.55) for a club room on a Saturday night. Rates during Chinese New Year will be substantially higher.

### Toy Story Hotel

The budget-friendly option on this property is the Toy Story Hotel. It's larger than Shanghai Disneyland Hotel, and you'll notice it as a large glass structure with clouds painted on it. This hotel is supposedly closer to the park, but I found that the walking path meanders and takes quite a while. It's better to use the complimentary and quick bus service from this location.

Standard is the word I use to describe Toy Story Hotel. The rooms are standard, and none have views that are all that great. Most have two beds and are immaculately clean. Again, the walls are thin, and light sleepers will want to keep that in mind.

One thing that's not standard here is the pool. There isn't one! I find this shocking and believe many guests do as well.

**Sunny Side Café** is a large quick-service restaurant on the main floor of the hotel. It offers a nice selection and carries its theme well. (Sunny Side is the name of the nursery school from *Toy Story 3*. In my opinion, it's the best movie Pixar has ever released.) There are about a million tables here surrounded by lots of art of the Toy Story franchise. Next to the café, **Sunny Side Market** offers grab-and-go food and beverages.

Like everywhere at Shanghai Disney Resort, service at this hotel is extraordinary. Even though it's cheaper than the resort's other option, you'll still receive top service from friendly cast members. Expect to pay ¥850.00 ($122.72) for a weekday and ¥1,450.00 ($209.34) for a Saturday night.

You can tell that I'm not overly excited about the Toy Story Hotel. It's no surprise that Shanghai Disneyland Hotel is much better. However, if that property is not an option for you, Toy Story Hotel is certainly better than staying far away from the park.

### Non-Disney Hotels

Shanghai is a large city full of all types of hotels. But when you think of Shanghai Disneyland's hotel situation, it is more like Florida and less like the other Disney resorts. In other words, location is a huge advantage for staying in one of the two Disney hotels.

With that said, the main business district of Shanghai is accessible by taxi and train. While the train will require two transfers and can be extremely crowded, taxis are inexpensive and abundant; just be sure to always secure a registered cab from an established taxi line. Regardless of your method, you should allow an hour to travel between the resort and downtown Shanghai.

Massive skyscraper hotels fill the central area of the city. You'll find all the major brands, and you may be surprised at how affordable the rooms can be. Do your homework and research rates online. You will also want to utilize tripadvisor.com as you research non-Disney accommodations.

Heading the opposite direction from Shanghai Disney Resort, there are a large number of hotels in the vicinity of Pudong International Airport. Again, you'll find all the major brands. A cab from this area to Shanghai Disneyland will take around twenty-five minutes. There is train service, but it will require two transfers on three lines for about an hour. If you're taking taxis, airport hotels are much closer, but they come without the excitement of Shanghai.

I'm often asked about travel insurance and whether it's necessary. Well, the answer depends upon the circumstances surrounding your travel plans. Travel insurance is no different than any other kind of insurance: you'll weigh your amount of risk against the cost of the premium to determine if you need it.

First, determine the amount of your trip that is not refundable if you need to cancel. If you're driving to Disneyland and are staying at a cancelable Fairfield Inn, travel insurance will not be worth the cost. In this scenario, your risk of loss is extremely low. However, if you are flying to Orlando and have booked a Walt Disney World Vacation Package, then your amount of loss is considerably greater. In this scenario, travel insurance is highly recommended.

When considering the true amount of risk, remember that not all costs are directly apparent in the price of your trip. For example, most US citizens who travel abroad do not have medical coverage through their domestic insurers. Travel insurance is a necessity in this case. A minor eye infection or bout of food poisoning could cost a substantial amount of money in a foreign country.

When booking a package at either Disneyland or Walt Disney World, you'll be given a chance to purchase Disney insurance. This is the most convenient way to access travel insurance because it will be included in the price of your package. However, only travel components purchased directly from Disney will be covered by the insurance. If you book your own airfare, then the Disney insurance will cover your resort expenses but not any portion of your transportation.

There are several companies that offer travel insurance. It's quite easy to find out online what your premium will cost. You just need to provide the company with your travel dates, ages of those traveling, cost of trip, and the destination. Most travel insurance companies will give you a few options at a variety of premiums. A cheaper premium will include less medical coverage and a cap on the amount of trip cancelation you can receive. A higher premium will provide more medical coverage, a full refund of the trip, and compensation for lost luggage. Again, do your homework.

After decades of traveling on my own and arranging travel for students, I can confidently recommend Allianz Travel Insurance. I don't receive any sort of benefit for recommending this company; I've just had positive experiences working with them. I've navigated many policies and even a few claims with Allianz, and they've always been easy to work with.

▲ ▲ ▲

## Shanghai Disneyland

Congratulations! You've made it to Mickey's brand-new home in the East. Whether you've arrived by train, bus, or foot, you're standing on the shore of Wishing Star Lake. The whistle you hear is coming from a glorious fountain of Mickey Mouse as Steamboat Willie. Everything is new and exciting. At Shanghai Disneyland, you don't need to wait to get a glimpse of the castle. It's so large you can see it from a distance. We'll talk more about that later.

Take some time to appreciate what's happening here in Shanghai. This tightly controlled government has formed a partnership with a cartoon mouse to bring joy and laughter to its people. Walt said that America's greatest export is happiness. Here, you can see how correct he was.

Pass through bag check and security. Across a small plaza, you'll find the main gates, where your ticket will be scanned. Curiously, ahead of you is a train station with no train! It's a nod to the nostalgia of Walt's first park in California. Go ahead and pass under the station and into the world's first Main Street fit for a mouse, duck, dog, and all their colorful friends. Welcome to Mickey Avenue.

**Mickey Avenue**

Some Disney purists bemoan the loss of Main Street and can't accept Mickey Avenue. I love it! The interior of the buildings contain the largest shops in the park. But the exteriors are full of amazing details that will make most Disney fans' heads explode. The amount of creativity on Mickey Avenue is astounding.

Each faux storefront on the avenue is a salute to the early short films of Walt Disney's career. There's a music shop themed to the *Silly Symphonies,* a flower shop paying homage to *Flowers and Trees,* and the Big Bad Wolf's Demolition Company. These are scattered among salutes to Mickey and all his many friends. Minnie has a candy shop here. Donald sells ice cream, gelato, and waffles. Scrooge McDuck operates the bank. (I'm sure he doesn't give the best interest rates, so it's best not to invest.) Mickey Avenue is the epitome of fantasy realness.

Like Main Street, USA, Mickey Avenue doesn't contain any of the major attractions. It serves as a way to welcome you to the park and to provide a place to get a souvenir when you're ready to leave. Take a lot of time and explore every last inch of this wonderful land.

### Mickey's Film Festival

This is your chance to see inside the large theater where *The Lion King* Broadway show occurs. During the days when the production show is off, guests can wander into the theater to watch thirty minutes of classic Mickey Mouse shorts. The film festival is scheduled, and the times are listed in the Times Guide. The theater is beautiful and worth a look if you have the time.

### Shops of Mickey Avenue

Mickey Avenue is the shopping hub of Shanghai Disneyland. **Avenue M Arcade** is the largest store in the park with all the themed merchandise you'd expect. The candy store is called **Sweethearts Confectionery** and is just as cute as it sounds. Among other shops is **Whistle Stop Shop,** home for Garden of the Twelve Friends merchandise (the only place outside Minnesota with Babe the Blue Ox key chains).

*Dining in Mickey Avenue*

**Mickey & Pals Market Café:** A large quick-service café with lots of intricate theming. There are mostly Chinese dishes here. Even if you don't dine at Mickey & Pals, you should step inside to have a look around. One of the several dining rooms is themed to the Three Caballeros (I love them).

**Il Paparino:** Donald Duck runs this establishment that sells ice cream and character-shaped waffles.

**Chip & Dale's Treehouse Treats:** Quick-service snacks are offered along the avenue in this small kiosk.

**Remy's Patisserie:** Remy, the rat chef from *Ratatouille*, operates the best patisserie this side of Paris. It's incredible with quick-service pastries, cakes, cookies, and lots of other wonderful things. This establishment offers the only food available when Mickey Avenue opens in the morning.

Dreamlly's Disney Direction

Immediately after Shanghai Disneyland's opening, there were several media reports about poor behavior from the mainland Chinese guests. These reports detailed children defecating on the sidewalks, people spitting, line cutting, and unruliness in theaters. While I've seen these kinds of things in Chinese cities, I have not observed any of this behavior at Shanghai Disney Resort. In fact, I find that the typical guest of this park is better behaved than guests at Hong Kong Disneyland. Heck, I've seen much worse behavior in the American parks.

Yes, personal space is an issue for those of us from the United States. You will notice that people tend to stand much closer to you than you'd like. Just remember that space is limited in this extremely crowded country. All park maps and guides list lots of reminders for guests to follow the rules. Donald's nephews seem to be the poster kids for good (or bad) behavior as their pictures accompany reminders of how to stand in line. Pumba is often depicted with a warning not to sit on a rope as you wait for a parade or show.

Overall, the people of mainland China are charming and love to laugh. They love to attempt English and strive to provide a positive image. I've nothing but good things to say about the Chinese guests and cast members of Shanghai Disney Resort.

▲ ▲ ▲

### Gardens of Imagination

Instead of an open hub that connects the park's other lands, Shanghai Disneyland's center contains its own land. Gardens of Imagination is a first for Disney. It's beautifully landscaped with lots of meandering paths. Among the paths, you'll find several attractions. Mostly,

Gardens of Imagination is where you want to be to get that perfect photograph of Enchanted Storybook Castle.

### Garden of the Twelve Friends

I can't get enough of the Garden of the Twelve Friends. It's a fine example of Disney's use of local culture. Most people know that Chinese New Year celebrates the transition of one animal symbol on the Chinese zodiac to the next. There are twelve animals. Here at Shanghai Disneyland, each animal is represented in the garden by a Disney character. Incredibly detailed mosaics depict the animal characters surrounded by flowers and trees.

- Rat—Remy from *Ratatouille*
- Ox—Babe the Blue Ox from *Paul Bunyan*
- Tiger—Tigger from *The Many Adventures of Winnie the Pooh*
- Rabbit—Thumper from *Bambi*
- Dragon—Mushu from *Milan*
- Snake—Kaa from *The Jungle Book*
- Horse—Maximus from *Tangled*
- Sheep—Jolly Holiday Lambs from *Mary Poppins*
- Monkey—Abu from *Aladdin*
- Rooster—Alan-A-Dale from *Robin Hood*
- Dog—Pluto (Mickey's dog)
- Pig—Hamm from *Toy Story*

During the first week of January 2017, roosters could be seen in decorations all over the park. I'm sure Pluto is quite excited that he'll be celebrated for a whole year in 2018. (The rooster, Alan-A-Dale, is probably the least-known Disney character on the list. Oh, well, sorry 2017.)

### Dumbo the Flying Elephant

Here is the only place where you can fly around on Dumbo in front of the castle instead of behind it. While the location is different, the ride is the same, although Shanghai's version has more Dumbos.

### Fantasia Carousel

This carousel is themed after the Beethoven's Sixth Symphony scene of *Fantasia*. It's actually more interesting to watch than to ride. There are lots of small details around the carousel that can be spotted as it rotates. However, the line to ride is always long as the Chinese guests consider it iconic for some reason. Also, the ride's duration is by far the shortest I've ever experienced for a carousel—under one minute.

### Marvel Universe

I know what you're thinking: this attraction doesn't really fit into Gardens of Imagination. If it helps any, it's sort of on the Tomorrowland side of the gardens. Perhaps the imagineers plan to turn this pavilion into something else if the Marvel franchises lose their popularity in China. But since the Marvel movies continue to do very well in this country, expect Marvel Universe to stick around for a while.

The Marvel Universe pavilion is mainly a place where you can meet your favorite Marvel heroes. There are some nice costume and prop displays from the films to look at while you wait. Shanghai Disneyland's photopass people are well trained and will use your phone to take a few photos if you like.

### Meet Mickey

Inside this facility, you can, of course, meet the guy who's running the whole operation. Even though he's quite busy overseeing this brand-new park, he'll take some time to greet you and pose for photographs. Mickey Mouse is one of the few older Disney characters that is well known in China. There can be long lines to meet him on a busy day.

### Golden Fairytale Fanfare

Shanghai Disneyland is the first Disney park to have a versatile and technologically advanced stage directly in front of the castle. The stage is able to drop below ground level and rise above the crowd for better viewing. This means that the cast of the show can enter and exit on multiple levels without blocking access to the castle itself. (In Florida, the castle is off limits during shows because the performers use it to make their entrances.)

Golden Fairytale Fanfare is a fantastic show that utilizes this advanced stage. You'll see it all here: singing, dancing, beautiful costumes, sets, and pyrotechnics.

I'm happy to announce that one of the favorites, Merida from *Brave*, is heavily featured with her own song. She even rides around on a horse!

Not only is the stage better designed here, but the place for guests to watch the show is much improved. Instead of audience members just standing around on the flat central hub, Shanghai Disneyland has an area of graduated incline with support railings for the crowds to utilize. It's too bad that the other parks won't be able to have this feature unless they dig a big hole in front of their castles. Just enjoy the castle show in Shanghai and be thankful that you can actually see over the guy in front of you who just put his kid on his shoulders.

### Melody Garden and Tai Chi with ~~Characters~~ Donald

The ancient movements of tai chi are beautiful to watch when performed by experts all over China. They are not quite as beautiful when performed by Chip and Dale. Several times each day, this short tai chi show occurs near the Dumbo ride at a place called **Melody Garden.** A tai chi master attempts to teach the crowd while he's constantly interrupted by the mischievous chipmunks. Donald Duck arrives and tries to help, but, of course, things seem to get a little worse.

Even though it's not very educational, this short show is entertaining. The start times for these performances are not listed in the Times Guide; there is a sign near the Melody Garden where Tai Chi with ~~Characters~~ Donald times are listed.

### Shops of Gardens of Imagination

**Marvel Mementos,** inside Marvel Universe, offers gifts for heroes and heroes for gifts. **Casey Jr. Trinket Train** and **Scuttle's Shiny Things** are two kiosks with small gifts outside in the gardens.

### Dining in Gardens of Imagination

**Picnic Basket:** Quick-service place for a smoked duck leg.

**Timothy's Treats:** Dumbo's mouse pal cooks American hot dogs inside this kiosk.

**Wandering Moon Teahouse:** A large quick-service restaurant in a stunning Chinese building, Wandering Moon offers Chinese food. Even if you don't eat here, the building makes for an excellent photograph.

## Tomorrowland

Finally, there is a Disney park that puts the tomorrow in Tomorrowland. While the other locations utilize a retro-future theme, the wide, curving walkways of faux stone in Shanghai are a better prediction of what tomorrow may look like. However, this comes with a cost: Shanghai's Tomorrowland risks becoming outdated quickly. Enjoy this multitiered land for now and let the imagineers worry about tomorrow. I love the multiple levels here as they help me to feel like I'm lost in a cosmopolitan future metropolis.

### Buzz Lightyear Planet Rescue

*Fastpass* A similar version to the others around the globe. This is the only ride at Shanghai Disneyland where guests attempt to rack up a high score.

### Jet Packs

Shanghai Disneyland's version of the Astro Orbiter is better than the others. Instead of riding around in an elevated rocket, here, riders are suspended on jet packs. Your feet will dangle as you rotate, and you can control the height of your ascent. This orbiter is much more futuristic than its retro cousins around the globe.

### Star Wars Launch Bay

This is the best place on the planet to meet the *Star Wars* characters, not just because it's well themed but also because there are no lines! For some reason, *Star Wars* doesn't resonate with the Chinese in the same way that it has with other countries. I walked in and saw Darth Vader pacing in his area with nobody in line. It was weird. I, of course, went up to him. To my dismay, he only spoke Mandarin. It was terrifying! I also met Kylo Ren and the droids I'd been looking for. All kidding aside, this was one of the most unforgettable experiences I've ever had inside a theme park. And I have the pictures to prove it.

My experience at Star Wars Launch Bay shows that at theme parks, it's not always the large rides that create the best memories. Often, it's these unexpected interactions that make the Disney parks worthy of my time and money.

### Stitch Encounter

Stitch appears and entertains guests in Mandarin. Often you don't need to understand the language to be entertained in a theme park. But here, you'll be bored if you don't speak Mandarin. You might be bored even if you do speak Mandarin.

### TRON Lightcycle Power Run

*Fastpass* Disclaimer: I loved both of the *TRON* films. Some others did not. But no matter how you feel about the movies, this ride is incredible. Here is another attraction that is difficult to explain. It must be experienced.

Basically, you'll sit on a lightcycle and careen through TRON's virtual world. But there's nothing virtual about it: you really will sit on a lightcycle and careen through the world of TRON. Yes, you must straddle the cycle and bend over the handlebars. A back brace will keep you safely in place (I hope). This has to be the most unique rider position for a roller coaster on the entire planet.

After you're all settled in on the bike, you'll blast off as this attraction is a launch coaster. There are both indoor and outdoor sections of track. You won't be able to catch your breath as the lights fly past you. Speaking of lights, TRON at night isn't all that different for the riders. But nonriders will be amazed at the lighting on this attraction. It looks so much like the movie.

A couple of things to note: Larger guests will not be able to ride. Others with disabilities may also find the experience difficult. You must be able to maintain the hunched-over position for the duration of the ride. Also, the front row of most coasters usually offers a different experience. Nowhere is that truer than here. Because you're riding headfirst, the front row of TRON is absolutely terrifying. My husband and I were put in the front row on our first ride. I don't really remember much of it. (In fact, after our ride, we went to look at the ride photos to see how goofy we appeared. My husband pointed us out on the screen, but upon further inspection, it was a photo of two old Chinese women. This ride rattled both of our brains!)

### TRON Realm, Chevrolet Digital Challenge

Next door to the ride, this space showcases several interactive displays where guests can experiment with the world of motion. I didn't find it all that exciting, but those into video games might want to spend some time here. Look in the lower right corner of each display to switch the language from Mandarin to English.

### Baymax Super Exercise Expo

Baymax is that giant white puffy guy from *Big Hero 6*. If you've seen the film, you know that Baymax is concerned about your health. That's why he wants to make sure that you get plenty of exercise and eat right. During this show, Baymax leads the crowd in a round of exercises. Don't worry—the whole thing is a cleverly disguised dance. You won't learn any new techniques for your gym back home, but you will have a lot of fun watching Baymax as he tries to bend and jump along to the beat. In the winter, you won't work up much of sweat. In the Shanghai summer, you will need an intravenous saline drip when the show is over.

### Club Destin-E at Tomorrowland

Club Destin-E is a nightly dance party that's held on the same stage as Baymax's exercise instructions. The music is loud, and tons of lights are all around. An age-appropriate DJ manages the whole experience. No matter their language and politics, all people like a good street party.

### Shops of Tomorrowland

**Intergalactic Imports** is the main shop in this land. *TRON*-themed merchandise is found at **Power Supply**, and *Star Wars* fans will want to head for **Imperial Trading Station.**

### Dining in Tomorrowland

**Spiral Snacks:** This cart offers Shanghai street food; it's quick service.

**Stargazer Grill:** A very large quick-service café, Stargazer Grill is the most American restaurant in the park.

### Fantasyland

This is not your grandma's Fantasyland. It's not even your mother's Fantasyland. You won't find the quaint European-village feel that dominates all of the other lands of this name around the globe. Instead, Shanghai Disneyland's realm of fantasy rests around a lagoon and other open areas. There is lots of room for expansion here, and it will be exciting to watch.

Disney, with its vast resources, is the king of research. Market testing is a cornerstone of Disney's park-planning process. They must have discovered that the Chinese wouldn't require the iconic dark rides based on classic Disney film. The planners must have also learned that table-service restaurants were not something the Chinese would patronize while in a theme park. Consequently, there are only two iconic dark rides here—Peter Pan and Winnie the Pooh—and Fantasyland contains the only table-service restaurant in the entire park. Again, there is only one restaurant inside Shanghai Disneyland where wait staff is employed: Royal Banquet Hall.

Here, Fantasyland is more of a modern fantasy than it is a nostalgic nod to the royal days. Shanghai Disneyland is definitely embracing a progressive view: prince and princesses are not required to have a fantasy, just dreams and a touch of magic.

### Enchanted Storybook Castle

One princess wasn't going to cut it here. The expectations for this park were high. The imagineers needed to use everything they could dream of, and they dreamed of an enormous castle where all stories could come to life. This is Enchanted Storybook Castle, the first Disney castle that's not dedicated to a specific princess.

Enchanted Storybook Castle is the largest Disney castle on the planet, both in height and volume. It stands 196.8 feet (sixty meters) tall and holds three attractions, a couple shops, and a cavernous restaurant.

The main hall on ground level features the four seasons, each represented by a different princess via beautiful mosaics. Tiana (*The Princess and the Frog*) represents spring. Both Anna and her sister, Elsa (*Frozen*), represent summer. Just checking to see that you're with me. Of course, Anna and Elsa represent winter. Rapunzel (*Tangled*) is for summer, and Merida (*Brave*) is fall.

There is a lot of symbolism all over the castle, and I've been told that you really have to be Chinese to understand much of it. That's fine with me because I love discovering new things each time I look at it. On the very top of the castle sits a peony made of solid gold. The peony is a symbol of China and is often referred to as the flower of riches and honor.

Overall, Enchanted Storybook Castle is absolutely stunning. It can be seen for miles around, especially when it's lit in all the glory of nighttime. It's probably the first Disney castle that's completely functional as well as beautiful.

### Disney Princesses at Enchanted Storybook Castle

This is the only place on the planet where you can meet a famous Disney princess inside the castle without paying for dinner. Look for signs aside the castle that state which princesses are currently greeting guests.

Meeting a princess at Shanghai Disneyland is a charming experience. The setting was designed specifically for this, and you'll be impressed by the opulent décor. Except for Mulan, most of the princesses here speak

English, although the language of Disney is fairly universal, and you'll have a worthwhile experience regardless of dialect.

### *"Once Upon a Time" Adventure*

This walk-through attraction is located completely inside Enchanted Storybook Castle. Historically, Disney imagineers despise walk-through attractions because there is so little control of the experience. Some guests linger around and cause back-ups for those who want to get on with it. However, technology has finally caught up. "Once Upon a Time" proves that walk-through attractions can be a fantastic use of your precious theme-park time.

Basically, you'll walk through the story of Snow White. But there's nothing really basic about the experience here. Everything interacts. When you wave at a squirrel, he'll wave back. If you don't wave, he'll jump up and down until you decide to give him some attention. This is just one example of the many surprises you'll find inside. The technology controls the flow. When things stop being interesting, that's the time to move on.

Just like the Snow White rides at the other parks, the Evil Queen changes into the old hag before your eyes. This is the only part of the attraction that may scare younger, and older, guests. Also, word has gotten around, and the Chinese guests are quite curious about this specific experience. Expect a line.

### Voyage to the Crystal Grotto

Voyage to the Crystal Grotto is sort of the second generation of the Storybook Land Canal Boats from Anaheim and Paris. You'll sit in a boat with others and float through some of the more iconic moments from Disney films.

Again, technology has caught up with this ride. The boats are timed so that when you reach a vignette, it will come to life. Beautiful fountains spring forth and highlight the scenes. The figures themselves also move when your boat is near. Speakers inside each vessel are synced to play the appropriate climatic music.

This is the second attraction that occurs, at least partly, inside Enchanted Storybook Castle. You'll sail through gigantic doors that magically open into the basement of the castle. There are some cool lighting effects inside, and you will eventually discover the Crystal Grotto.

### Seven Dwarfs Mine Train

*Fastpass* This family coaster is a replica of the version in Florida. Guests will swing in their mine cars as they're sent careening through the workplace of the seven dwarfs. Lines are always extremely long for this ride, even on days when the park isn't crowded. Get a Fastpass early in the day to avoid the queue.

### Peter Pan's Flight

*Fastpass* Here is another fine example of technology giving new life to an icon. This is the best version of Peter Pan's Flight on the planet.

Similar to the others, you'll sit in a pirate galleon that's sent soaring through the Darling home, above London, and past the second star to the right. Then you'll enter Neverland, and things will get interesting. While at the other parks the galleons are attached to a track, here they are independent. Your small ship can move quickly through fast sections and slow down for dramatic effect. Your vessel can move up and down as it turns to direct your focus on the scenes. You'll even splash down in the Neverland Sea (don't worry—it's simulated water, and you won't get wet).

But that's not all. You'll get to fly around Captain Hook's ship to see what's been happening behind that large sail all these years. Some purists will be quite upset at all this new-fangled ride technology that the kids have these days. Fortunately, they can still enjoy the iconic Peter Pan's Flight in other places. In my book, some things do improve with the times.

### The Many Adventures of Winnie the Pooh
*Fastpass* Unfortunately, this version of Winnie the Pooh is not like Tokyo's trackless ride. Here, you'll ride in hunny pots through scenes of the Hundred Acre Wood. Shanghai's version of this ride is quite similar to the ones in the United States except for a pretty neat water effect during the finale.

### Hunny Pot Spin
The Mad Hatter isn't the only person who wants you to vomit all over Fantasyland. Instead of teacups, Shanghai

offers hunny pots that spin. Rabbit would never ride this, and neither will I.

### Alice in Wonderland Maze

I'm not a huge fan of *Alice in Wonderland*; neither the animated classic nor the modern live-action film does much for me. I also find that most theme-park mazes are tedious. So I was quite surprised to discover how much I liked this maze in Shanghai. It's probably because this attraction is less of a maze and more of an exploration area.

You'll enter Wonderland and wander around mani-cured gardens, sculpted caves, and lots of beautiful flowers. There are surprises everywhere in the form of steampunk animals. You will encounter the Queen of Hearts (from the live-action film), and, of course, the maze ends with the iconic tea party scene from the ani-mated version.

### Frozen: A Sing-a-Long Celebration

This show is exactly like the version at Disney's Hollywood Studios in Florida. Well, with one really big change: it's in Mandarin. You probably won't be able to understand any of the dialogue, and following the bouncing ball is pretty much impossible. Still, I really enjoy hearing these wonderful songs in another language.

The performers sing all the songs live. I can't stress enough how glad I am that Disney is committed to live music, even here at this modern park. We, all of us, get so little live music in our daily routines, and it's refreshing to witness talented people who are not on television or the Internet.

Oh, one more thing; Elsa shows up, and it snows.

### Shops of Fantasyland

Many of Fantasyland's attractions contain their own gift shops. These shops are generally smaller and offer attraction-specific merchandise. The largest store in this land is **Mickey & Minnie's Mercantile.** This place is for general Shanghai Disneyland items. Inside Enchanted Storybook Castle is **Bibbidi Bobbidi Boutique,** where guests can get all made up like a princess. There is also a glass shop in the castle.

### Dining in Fantasyland

**Fairy Godmother's Cupboard:** A quick-service kiosk for pizza.

**Celebration Café:** This odd quick-service café is almost in Tomorrowland. A collection of windows serve pizza and rice bowls to a large outdoor seating area.

**Pinocchio Village Kitchen:** Just as he does around the globe, Pinocchio operates this Italian Alps-themed quick-service restaurant. There are pizza and noodles here.

**Merlin's Magic Recipe:** The world's first wizard, Merlin, offers steamed buns from this kiosk. There are several tables nearby for eating. This small place has quickly become my favorite place for a quick meal. The buns are both sweet and savory.

**Royal Banquet Hall:** Inside Enchanted Storybook Castle, Royal Banquet Hall is the only table-service restaurant in the park. It's simply stunning. The rooms are themed to the various Disney princesses. Ask for a tour when you've finished eating; they are proud to show you around. As you dine, Mickey, Donald, Minnie, and Daisy will greet you while wearing their most regal attire. If the park isn't crowded, you can walk right in. If you anticipate that you'll be at the park on a crowded day, you can make reservations by calling the number on the website. The operators I've spoken with have always had excellent English skills. Currently, there is no way to make an online reservation.

**Tangled Tree Tavern:** This quick-service tavern is themed like the one in the film, minus the show-tune-crooning thugs. Inside, you can order fish and chips, chicken, and Mongolian beef. However, all the seating is outdoors. Look for Maximus's hoof prints near the entrance.

**Troubadour Treats:** Another quick-service place for rice bowls.

Yes, Shanghai Disneyland's Enchanted Storybook Castle is amazing. But other Disney parks need not have castle envy. Each version around the world is special in its own way.

**Sleeping Beauty Castle, Disneyland:** Walt's original castle that built an empire. Its graceful design and subtle colors inspired all the other Disney castles around the world.

**Cinderella Castle, Magic Kingdom:** The tall gothic structure that's the most photographed building in the world. For many Americans, this is the Disney castle of their dreams.

**Cinderella Castle, Tokyo Disneyland:** The castle that rises above the Pacific. This will always be the first international castle; it's a symbol of partnership.

**Le Château de la Belle au Bois Dormant, Disneyland Paris:** The most visually appealing of Disney's castles. It's pure fantasy, and that's what we came for.

**Sleeping Beauty Castle, Hong Kong Disneyland:** Walt's original design but in an exotic atmosphere. It's the only castle where nature is a prominent feature. Even though this structure is being completely remodeled in appearance, the castle's spectacular natural setting is sure to remain the focus of its design.

**Enchanted Storybook Castle, Shanghai Disneyland:** A castle of form and function. It's a castle of big dreams for a big country.

▲ ▲ ▲

**Treasure Cove**
Shanghai Disneyland's Adventureland is so large that it's been split into two different lands, each with its own name.

This first piece, Treasure Cove, is where you'll discover the world of pirates and other maritime misadventures. Almost entirely devoted to the Pirates of the Caribbean franchise, Treasure Cove makes the perfect transition from Fantasyland to the more exotic Adventure Isle.

### Explorer Canoes

Treasure Cove and Adventure Isle sit along the shore of a rather large lagoon. Similar to the canoes around Tom Sawyer Island in California and Tokyo, guests in Shanghai board vessels and float around the lagoon. Each guest is given and paddle, and you will need to help propel the canoe with the assistance of a cast member.

### Pirates of the Caribbean: Battle for the Sunken Treasure

If the imagineers ever attempted to completely change Pirates of the Caribbean in either Florida or California, the outcome would be mayhem. Both Main Streets would be littered with the bodies of nostalgic fans who no longer had a purpose in life. Sure, changes have occurred to this iconic ride over the years, but the basic concept has remained the same. Here in China, Disney was free to do something completely new—and did they ever!

When this attraction opened along with Shanghai Disneyland in June 2016, there were many positive reviews. More than once, I saw theme-park experts state that it's the best dark ride on the entire planet. After riding it once, and then again, and then again, and so on, I completely agree.

Like the other pirate rides around the globe, guests board small boats that float through a canal. That's where the similarities end. Here in Shanghai, the boats are actually sophisticated ride vehicles; it just looks like they're floating in water. Because a mechanism completely controls their motion, these boats can move forward, backward, and side to side. They can float slowly through a tranquil moment and speed rapidly through a thunderstorm.

All around you, Disney has everything they've learned on display. You'll see audio-animatronics, projections, and intricate sets. Full IMAX screens are used for some unbelievable effects. Your boat will plummet to the bottom of the sea, where you'll glide among shipwrecks. You'll get caught in a pirate battle as you float between two massive ships. You'll even get sucked through a hole in a ship to explore the interior.

Pirates of the Caribbean: Battle for the Sunken Treasure is the closest you will ever come to walking into a movie. Sixty years ago, Walt loved the concept that guests could ride the Jungle Cruise and pretend that they were in a nature documentary. I can't imagine what he would say about Pirates of the Caribbean at Shanghai Disneyland. More than likely, he'd just want to ride it again and again. You will too.

### Shipwreck Shore & Siren's Revenge

These two attractions are similar in that guests can explore each one on their own. Shanghai Disneyland has quite a few of these explore-at-will areas. All of them are good places to go if you're sick of lines and want to see intricate theming.

Shipwreck Shore is exactly what it sounds like. Here, you can explore broken pieces of a ship that's been washed ashore. This experience is mainly for the younger set and includes several interactive water features.

Siren's Revenge is an entire pirate ship moored and ready for explorers of all ages. There's a lot happening on the ship; it's packed with interactive games, gadgets, and just general pirate stuff. There are some great views of Treasure Cove from the upper deck of Siren's Revenge.

### Eye of the Storm: Captain Jack's Stunt Spectacular

This popular show takes place inside a fantastic theater near the back of the park. Because Captain Jack Sparrow is well liked in China, there are almost always long lines to get into performances here. Plan to arrive early as the theater can fill quickly.

The show itself is just OK for non-Mandarin speakers. There is a lot of dialogue, but the Mandarin speakers seem to love it. Expect a fair amount of swashbuckling and sword play. Also expect a large amount of hijinks.

Go here and to the Tarzan show nearby to escape unpleasant weather or to rest your feet. Neither performance will change your life, but they are enjoyable nonetheless.

### Shops of Treasure Cove

All the merchandise in Treasure Cove is about being calm, well-mannered, and sober. Of course not! This is pirate territory, and **Doubloon Market** sells everything you could ever want to look like one.

### Dining in Treasure Cove

**Barbossa's Bounty:** This quick-service restaurant offers Asian food and the best atmosphere of any quick theme-park café on the planet. You can sit inside the Pirates of the Caribbean while you dine without paying table-service prices!

**Pintel & Ragetti's Grub to Grab:** A quick-service place with some fine bratwurst.

**The Snackin' Kraken:** This kraken offers quick-service snacks that change regularly.

**Tortuga Treats:** Here is where everyone is getting that turkey leg you see them walking around with.

## Adventure Isle

Shanghai Disneyland's second piece of Adventureland is where you'll find all the nonpirate stuff. This is sort of the Tarzan's jungle part of the park. You'll know you're in the right place when you see an enormous mountain with a cascading waterfall towering above you. After the castle, this mountain is the second-highest point in the park, but it is actually the tallest mountain in Pudong.

### Camp Discovery

Camp Discovery is a mini land inside Adventure Isle that comprises three attractions. I've fallen in love with Camp Discovery, and I hope you will too.

First, the **Excavation Site** is a place for younger guests to burn off some energy. It's themed like an archeological dig. There's nothing fancy or technological here, but it's a nice place to rest while the toddlers explore.

Second, the **Vista Trail** is an explore-on-your-own adventure. There are many paths to take, and I haven't seen them all; you can spend hours on these trails. You'll get to journey behind towering waterfalls and through mysterious caves. There are no right or wrong ways to do this exploration.

Lastly, the **Challenge Trails** are a rope course on steroids. You'll be efficiently fit with a safety harness from well-trained cast members. Then you'll choose one of three challenge courses. Each of them is unique with its own merits, but none will disappoint. I'm partial to the first course on your right as it utilizes the greatest number of obstacles. Your harness is attached to a rail that leads you through the course. You'll balance on logs, step on narrow bridges made of rope, and cling to the side of caverns. You'll be completely safe at all times; no prior experience is necessary. The design of the overhead rails allows plenty of opportunities for others to pass you should you need to take a break.

The scenery on the Challenge Trails is extraordinary. You'll see the same waterfalls and caverns as the Vista Trail but from a higher vantage point. Consequently, you don't want to try these trails if you're too scared of heights. When you get to the upper levels, there are a few places where you can see the skyline of Shanghai in the distance (if the smog isn't too bad). I never thought I'd enjoy getting exercise, but I sure do love it on the Challenge Trails. If there was one of these in my neighborhood, I'd be in much better shape.

There are free lockers located at the entrance to the Challenge Trails. You're not allowed to bring anything with you on the course and cast members will make sure you follow that rule.

### Happy Circle

Happy Circle is a really nice character meet-and-greet location near Camp Discovery. It's well organized, and the lines move quickly. I met Officer Judy and Nick from *Zootopia* here.

### Roaring Rapids

*Fastpass* This attraction is, sort of, Shanghai Disneyland's answer to Splash Mountain. You'll see this attraction as it towers over most of the park in the form of a large mountain and cascading waterfall. The mountain is incredible and worth a look even if you don't ride.

You will get wet on Roaring Rapids. You will probably get soaked. Guests are loaded in a raft and sent on a journey to Field Camp Beta. But, of course, in true Disney fashion, something goes horribly wrong. Your raft encounters a fallen tree and is sent down an unexplored stream.

As the ride continues, your raft meets a gigantic Chinese monster called a q'aráq. You're then hurled into a whirlpool and through several geysers. It's not as scary as it sounds, and all the theming is incredibly well done. However, lines can be extremely long, especially when the unbearable Shanghai humidity is present. Also of note, Roaring Rapids was closed for most of the 2016–2017 winter season. I would expect the same to happen each year as it does get quite chilly in this part of China.

### Soaring Over the Horizon

*Fastpass* Here at Shanghai Disneyland, Soaring Over the Horizon is the same attraction from California and Florida. Guests sit in a simulated hang glider and soar over the world's landmarks courtesy of a large IMAX screen. You'll smell the smells and feel the wind as you do in the United States. The only real difference is that this version ends with a flight over Shanghai.

This is the attraction that most of the Chinese guests will not miss. Consequently, lines will be hours long. If you must ride it here, get a Fastpass as soon as the park opens. If you've been on Soaring at another park, then skip this attraction here. Your time is too precious to wait in this line.

### Tarzan: Call of the Jungle

Tarzan: Call of the Jungle is a theatrical experience that occurs several times each day in Adventure Isle. It's in Mandarin, but there's not much dialogue, and non-Mandarin speakers won't have a problem. The show tells the story of Tarzan that most Westerners are familiar with.

The theater for this production is immense, and the audience sits around the action. There are a lot of acrobatics presented in the form of performers wearing creepy monkey costumes.

The performance times are listed in the Times Guide. There are strict warnings that the doors to the theater will close fifteen minutes prior to show time. I found this wasn't true, and people are seated up until show time. However, even on days of low park attendance, the show fills quickly.

### Shops of Adventure Isle
**Laughing Monkey Traders** and **Rainbow Frog Trinkets** offer animal-themed safari merchandise.

### Dining in Adventure Isle
**Piranha Bites:** One of the healthier options in the park, this quick-service place offers wraps.

**Tribal Table:** This larger quick-service restaurant sells rotisserie chicken and beef.

Shanghai is an incredibly large city. Here's how it stacks up against the other Disney locations:

- Anaheim—population 345,012 (Los Angeles metro area—13.2 million)
- Orlando metro area—population 2.1 million
- Tokyo metro area—population 36.92 million
- Paris metro area—population 12.4 million
- Hong Kong—population 7.22 million
- Shanghai metro area—population 34.0 million

It's interesting to note that without Disney, the populations of these cities would probably remain the same... well, except for Orlando. Without the theme-park industry, central Florida would still be swamps and farmland. It blows my mind to think of the impact that one decision had on a single location.

▲ ▲ ▲

**Parades, Evening Shows, and Special Events**
*Ignite the Dream—A Nighttime Spectacular of Magic and Light*
Fireworks were invented in China. It's ironic that all of the Asian parks have lackluster firework displays. Even brand-new Shanghai Disneyland can't compare to the awesome fireworks displays of the United States and Paris.

Occurring nightly, this show uses projections on the castle along with the fireworks. Part of the problem is that it relies too much on the projections and not enough on the fireworks. Still, it's better than nothing, and the show makes a nice way to end your day.

You'll need to show up at least an hour before if you want to stand in a prime spot directly in front of the castle. Otherwise, you can find good places throughout Gardens of Imagination and Mickey Avenue. If you're inside Shanghai Disneyland Hotel, the terrace outside the lobby is a good place to be. You'll see all of the fireworks and some of the castle projections from here.

### Mickey's Storybook Express

Currently, the only parade at Shanghai Disneyland is each afternoon's presentation of Mickey's Storybook Express. This parade will occur either once or twice depending on park attendance. The route is indicated on park maps. This is the longest parade route in all of Disney.

The parade itself is just OK. Four floats carrying the Disney characters make their way through the park. The first float, with Mickey and Donald, is themed to a train. After that, the theme gets lost. See this parade if it's convenient; otherwise, don't waste your time.

This park is begging for a nighttime parade. Hopefully the imagineers are listening.

### Chinese New Year

The largest celebration of the year at Shanghai Disneyland is Chinese New Year. The dates for this holiday change from year to year. Do not travel to China during the week of the actual holiday—you won't like it. Everything is unbelievably crowded. However, you can experience the park's Chinese New Year offerings starting about a month before the holiday.

Special decorations are all over the hotels and park. The decorations all celebrate whatever animal is that year's feature. I will never forget that 2017 is the year of the rooster because I saw them absolutely everywhere. Pluto is looking forward to 2018, when he will be the main attraction during the year of the dog.

The background music for the entrance plaza, Mickey Avenue, and Gardens of Imagination changes from Disney favorites to a wonderful selection of traditional Chinese melodies. As a Westerner, I don't get to hear this kind of music often, and I appreciated the atmosphere it provides.

Every afternoon during this time of year, Chinese New Year is celebrated with a dragon procession on Mickey Avenue. The Disney characters will don their traditional Chinese garb, and dancers will appear with a large Chinese dragon. This show is choreographed to music with all dialogue in Mandarin. Donald is somehow in charge of the event, though I'm not sure what he was attempting to arrange. Regardless, the whole thing is beautiful, and it's a great example of discovering authentic traditional ritual mixed with modern theme-park culture.

*Dreamlly's*
*Disney*
*Direction*

There are approximately 1,955 blogs devoted to various Disney topics. This is in addition to more vlogs and forums than there are spots on Cruella's new coat. However, the great majority of these online resources focus on the U.S. locations. Less than a handful of sites are available in English about the international Disney resorts.

My favorite of these sources is disneytouristblog.com. This site, and its accompanying social media counterparts, offers comprehensive information about the worldwide Disney Parks. Sarah and Tom Bricker, the authors of the blog, are so adorable that they may be animatronic. (I haven't met them and cannot confirm this. Although, they seem to eat a lot—so they might be human.) Putting their adorableness aside, disneytouristblog.com is updated constantly with news and trip reports. All that eating is to your benefit as they post reviews of Disney restaurants around the globe. In addition, Tom is a superb photographer. His photos are a great way to indulge your vicarious Disney life.

Whatever you do to gain information for your travels, enjoy the pre-trip planning process. In my former life as a Study Abroad coordinator, I encountered several studies that reinforced the benefits of planning a journey. In fact, more dopamine is released while reading about your upcoming destination than is released during the actual journey! Since the planning and dreaming stage of travel is this important, these studies conclude that several smaller vacations offer a greater health benefit than one long one.

Because you bought this book, even without leaving home you're experiencing the benefits of travel. (By the way, thank you for your purchase—I've already spent the proceeds on a Country Bear Jamboree coffee mug.) Use this book and sites like disneytouristblog.com to further inspire your dreams and travel goals.

▲ ▲ ▲

## Disneytown

Disneytown is Shanghai Disneyland's version of Downtown Disney. It's a collection of shops and restaurants that opened along with the park in June of 2016. There are several entrances into the large area, and no admission is required. However, unlike Wishing Star Park, Disneytown is considered private property, and guests must adhere to the same rules that they would inside Shanghai Disneyland. Near the rear of Disneytown, there is an entrance into the park, and guests can exit Shanghai Disneyland through Disneytown as well.

Disneytown is divided into five districts. **Marketplace** is where you'll find the enormous World of Disney. Here you can purchase most of the Shanghai Disneyland merchandise that you'll see in the park. World of Disney is surrounded by several other stores offering specialized Disney items including the Spoonful of Sugar candy shop. In addition to the Disney offerings, Marketplace includes a bakery, Starbuck's, and a couple other small cafés. There is a Lego Store, Swatch, Build-A-Bear, and several other brand-name shops.

**Broadway Boulevard** only contains one restaurant, Blue Frog Bar & Grill. The rest of this district is devoted to higher-end shopping. You'll find UGG, Coterie, and a few others.

**Broadway Plaza** is the area right around the massive Walt Disney Grand Theatre. Currently, this theater is home to the Mandarin version of the Broadway hit *The Lion King*. It's easy to purchase tickets for this show online in English. However, unless you speak Mandarin, "hakuna matata" will be the only phrase you'll understand. Across the plaza from the theater, you'll find the Cheesecake Factory; it's the largest restaurant at Disneytown. Wolfgang Puck operates a small restaurant nearby as well.

Most of the Asian cuisine is found in **Spice Alley**. There are no shops here, but you'll find food from all over the continent. Among the restaurants are a Japanese noodle café called Ippudo and Coconut Paradise, a Thai restaurant.

The last district of Disneytown is built atop a pier that juts into Wishing Star Lake. **Lakeshore** contains the large Boathouse, an upscale restaurant direct from Disney Springs in Florida. Several other shops and restaurants complete the district.

The hours for Disneytown vary, and you can find them online. I've noticed that, in general, Disneytown opens around 11:00 a.m. and closes an hour after Shanghai Disneyland closes. Since there is only one table-service restaurant inside the park, Disneytown may be your best bet for a nice evening dinner.

## Wishing Star Park

Wishing Star Park is a large public park that wraps around one side of Wishing Star Lake. Mainly, it's used as a promenade to connect the Disneyland Metro Station to the park. It also connects the Shanghai Disneyland Hotel to the park. There are some well-maintained paths and lots of landscaping. Two unique bridges inside the park cross portions of the lake.

There is no admission required to explore the park, and it's open to the public. However, Wishing Star Park's hours are strictly enforced. Often, it's not open that much longer in the day than Shanghai Disneyland.

Security around Wishing Star Park is tight. Everyone needs to enter and exit through gates that are always staffed. If you wish to use the park, be prepared to explain your purpose and destination. Guests of Shanghai Disneyland Hotel may have to show a room key. I don't think those in charge are opposed to the public spending some quality time in this park. I think they just don't want all of Shanghai doing it at the same time.

Perhaps your philosophy isn't leading you in the direction of a Disney park right now. There's nothing wrong with that—but don't give up entirely on theme parks. Here are a few alternatives for you to consider on your travels.

- **Dollywood—Pigeon Forge, Tennessee** (alternative for Walt Disney World). Nestled in the foothills of the incredibly beautiful Great Smoky Mountains lies Dolly Parton's fantasy realness. Just like with its namesake, there is a lot going on here—and it's not all about country music. Dollywood park boasts a large collection of award-winning roller coasters. This park, by far, offers the most live entertainment of any theme park on the planet. The food is outstanding. Next door, Dollywood's Splash Country is one of the top three water parks in the nation according to *Amusement Today* magazine. There is also a full-service hotel on the property, Dollywood's DreamMore Resort, that rivals Disney's hotels. I love Dollywood so much that I wrote a whole book about it—*2016 Dollywood and Beyond: A Theme Park Lover's Guide.*
- **Knott's Berry Farm—Buena Park, California** (alternative for Disneyland). Just a stone's throw from Disneyland is one of the first theme parks in the country. Seriously, from certain top floors of the Disneyland Hotel, you can see Knott's Berry

Farm better than you can see Disneyland itself. Knott's boasts coasters, shows, and one of the best kids' lands in the country: Camp Snoopy. There is also Soak City Water Park, a hotel, and a historical recreation of Independence Hall.

- **Europa Park—Rust, Germany** (alternative for Disneyland Paris). This awesome park has a monorail, pirate ride, space-themed coaster, and a mouse for a mascot. However, don't think of it as a rip-off of Disney; it's all so well done that it stands on its own. Ed Euromaus (probably a *very* distant cousin of Mickey) welcomes you to this park, where each land is a different country. Ireland is an adorable children's area, and Iceland contains the best coasters on the continent. Located on the Rhine River, you can have a croissant in the fake France-land and see the real France from the top of the observation tower. There are several hotels on the property for all budgets.

- **Ocean Park—Hong Kong, China** (alternative for Hong Kong Disneyland and Shanghai Disneyland). Located on the south shore of Hong Kong Island, Ocean Park is a combination of the San Diego Zoo, Sea World, and Six Flags. The park has pandas. You can watch playful beluga whales and see the gorgeous scenery from the top of a coaster. They also have several pandas. There is a fantastic penguin-themed restaurant where you can observe real penguins as you dine. Oh, did I mention that they have pandas? You can't go all the way to China and not see pandas! (Sorry, that was one of those "must-do" statements that I said I wouldn't make. Of course you can go to China and not see a panda—there are plenty of other things to visit.) This enormous park is extremely clean and easy to get to via a direct bus from Hong Kong Central Station.

- **Fuji-Q Highland—Fujiyoshida, Japan** (alternative for Tokyo Disneyland). In a country where even gas stations each have their own mascots, it often feels like Japan is just one huge theme park. It's no exaggeration that there are theme parks around every corner. Fuji-Q Highland stands out due to its gorgeous location at the bottom of Mount Fuji. This park boasts some of the world's fastest coasters and a Thomas the Tank Engine Land. To be honest, nothing can even begin to compare with the amazing Tokyo Disney Resort. But if you are in Japan and your plans don't include Tokyo, this park may be a good alternative.

▲ ▲ ▲

## Area Sights outside Disney

It can be easy to get to the other tourist sights in Shanghai. It can also be quite difficult. Everything depends upon the type and time of day. The Shanghai Metro system is easy to access from Shanghai Disney Resort, but it can be extremely crowded during most of the work week. I don't just mean crowded in a New York City sense. I mean unpleasantly packed with many bodies pressed against yours. Taxis are a good alternative because they are fairly cheap. However, traffic congestion can add to your fare considerably. Just remember to always take an official taxi from a hotel taxi line and never go with any driver who approaches you on the street.

### The Bund

This is Shanghai's top tourist draw, and there are always lots of crowds here. The Bund is an area on the Huangpu River where you can see the entire city skyline before you. It's an amazing view, to say the least, and your photographs will reflect that. However, if it is at all smoggy—and it often is—wait until evening to visit the Bund. At night, all the city lights cut through the smog and provide a much better sight.

### Shanghai World Financial Center

This is the tallest building in Shanghai; it's the one that looks like a giant bottle opener. Shanghai World Financial Center is not the tallest building in the world, but it does offer the highest observatory on the planet. On the very top is Sky Walk. Here you can walk across a glass bridge and marvel at the city below you.

### Oriental Pearl TV Tower

The Oriental Pearl is probably the most recognizable symbol of Shanghai. It's the tall tower with the various pink spheres that you've seen on television. You can get a great photo of it from the Bund. There is an observation deck at the top, but only go if the weather is clear.

### Nanjing Road

Bring all your extra yuan and wander through this shopper's paradise. Nanjing Road is the commercial center of Shanghai—and of the entire country. There's a lot of neon here, and visiting at night provides a sight to behold. You can truly experience the mixture of East and West as you pass traditional Chinese shops existing with American brand names. Needless to say, there are also many restaurants in the area.

### Yuyuan Garden

Shanghai's version of Central Park is the Yuyuan Garden. Initially designed to be the park for a single Ming-dynasty ruler, the garden is now a playground for all of Shanghai. Yuyuan is actually a collection of several gardens, playgrounds, parks, monuments, and memorials. If you visit, give yourself enough time to leisurely stroll and enjoy all the traditional Chinese architecture. However, do not go to Yuyuan Garden during a public holiday; everyone else in China will already be there.

**Dreamlly's Disney Direction**

Both Disneyland Resort and Walt Disney World Resort are crowded during American holidays. For example, on Christmas Day and the Fourth of July, you can expect wall to wall people. However, you'll still be able to get around the resorts fairly easily, and you'll surely find some fun things to do.

Holidays are not the same in Asia. This is one continent that takes its holidays seriously. The Disney parks in Tokyo, Hong Kong, and Shanghai are not pleasant places to be during a public holiday. Going to a theme park on your day off is a big part of the Chinese and Japanese lifestyles. Not only will the parks be packed, but all the infrastructure leading to the parks will be unbearable. Use Google to determine when Asian public holidays are to occur, and avoid these dates.

# 8

## The Rest of the World

### Disney Cruise Line

THIS BOOK IS about traveling the world with a focus on Disney. No book on the subject would be complete without mentioning the presence of the worldwide Disney Cruise Line. With departures from multiple continents and many cities, Disney Cruise Line offers travelers another way to experience Disney while seeing the world.

A cruise vacation isn't for everyone, but you may not know that until you try it. Gone are the days of *The Love Boat*, and thank goodness for that! No longer is cruising for lecherous people and those who care more about baked Alaska than actual Alaska. I'm a world traveler and a former director of international programs for a university; I'm not ashamed to state that I enjoy cruise vacations.

Even those who have cruised before with negative results may want to give Disney Cruise Line a try. I've been on several different lines, and nobody does it like Disney. There are no casinos and ridiculous sex-themed contests. You won't see people who are so drunk they can't find their staterooms. Taking a Disney cruise is like visiting a Disney park that's gently gliding over blue water on the way to an exotic port.

Disney began to have a presence on the ocean as early as 1985. Premier Cruise Line, which went bankrupt in 2000, included Disney characters on some of their ships. Premier also offered cruise, hotel, and theme-park packages in Florida. You may even remember seeing ads for something called the Big Red Boat; that was one of Premier's ships.

Believe it or not, Premier and Disney even leased a private island way before anyone else had thought of it. Treasure Cay was located in the far eastern Bahamas. Premier would dock its ship there and guests could experience a wonderful pirate-themed buffet on the island. But in 1993, Premier ended its relationship with Disney to focus on other itineraries. Treasure Cay sat vacant for a long time and was recently converted into a luxury golf resort (its land was never owned by Disney).

It took less than a year for Mickey to decide that maybe he needed his own cruise line so that he could do things differently. Disney Cruise Line was formed on May 3, 1994. The new line commissioned its first two vessels in 1995. Disney Cruise Line's official business name is Magical Cruise Company Limited.

In 1996, Disney purchased an entire island named Gorda Cay. Imagineers spent the next two years transforming it into a private oasis for their passengers. Disney renamed the island Castaway Cay.

The first Disney Cruise Line voyage took place on July 30, 1998. The Disney Magic was the first ship completed. The Disney Wonder joined the line in August of 1999. The two ships are similar but not identical. Several interior areas are themed differently.

The Disney Dream began to sail in 2011, soon followed by the Disney Fantasy in 2012. Two more ships are scheduled to be ready in 2021 and 2023. (These ships have not been named yet, but they will be larger than the Disney Dream and Disney Fantasy.)

Pros of a Cruise Vacation:

- You don't have to unpack more than once as your hotel travels with you.
- Cruises are normally all-inclusive. This means that you don't have to open your wallet once your vacation starts unless you want to.

- You can completely relax and let someone else do all the planning, even at an international destination.
- You never have to worry about the safety of your hotel's neighborhood.
- All the traveling occurs while you sleep, and you won't waste time getting from place to place.
- Even in Europe, you can get as much ice as you want for your soda.

Cons of a Cruise Vacation:

- You won't get to enjoy the nightlife in the town you explored during the day.
- Cruise excursions can be expensive and crowded.
- Seasickness can be a problem if you are prone to it.
- You must adhere to a strict schedule as the ship will not wait for you.
- You may get annoyed by all the extra things, which cost money, constantly being offered to you.

▲ ▲ ▲

**Travel Knowledge**
*Booking and Cost*
Disney cruises can be booked over the phone or at disney-cruise.disney.go.com. It's extremely difficult to estimate how much a cruise will cost because there are so many variables. Longer cruises cost more than shorter ones,

larger cabins cost more than smaller ones, and four people will cost more than two. None of this will surprise you.

However, you may be surprised to learn that the time of your cruise can change the price considerably. Much more on Disney Cruise Line than other companies, sailings that occur when school is not in session will be higher. Cruises over Christmas vacation and the summer can be four times as much as cruises during the fall. Spring is another time when prices are higher but not quite as high as summer.

The popularity of your specific itinerary also impacts the price of a cruise. Cruises of the Norwegian fjords are more expensive than those of the Baltic Sea, even though they are the same duration and both occur during the summer. Generally speaking, cruises of the Bahamas and Caribbean are always cheaper because there is enough supply to decrease the demand.

If your plans are flexible, don't rule out a repositioning cruise. These itineraries are considerably less expensive because they occur at odd times. Also, families don't generally like to end at a different port than where they began. In late spring, the Disney Magic makes her way from Florida to Copenhagen with a stop in New York City. It's not nearly as expensive as you might imagine to cross the Atlantic; school is in session, and most families can't afford the time to spend two weeks getting to Europe. During the same time of year, the Disney Wonder leaves Florida for Vancouver. She travels through the Panama Canal and stops in San Diego and San Francisco. The five-night voyage from San Diego to Vancouver is an exceptional deal that I've sailed on before (and you can easily combine it with a few days at Disneyland).

Currently, the Disney Dream and Disney Fantasy do not reposition; they stay off the Florida coast the entire year. However, that may change when the two new ships come onboard sometime around 2020.

### Documents

Regardless of your cruise itinerary, you will need a passport, even if you are a US citizen. United States law prohibits a cruise ship (from any company) to travel without at least one international port. (That's why all cruises of the Californian coast make a stop at the horrible eyesore that is Ensenada, Mexico. Mexico has some spectacular ports; Ensenada is not one of them.) It's possible to travel to some Caribbean countries with just a US driver's license and a birth certificate. However, it can be cumbersome. Just do yourself a favor and get a passport.

Disney will let you know at time of booking if you need any other type of special visa for your journey. Right now, the only place Disney sails where you may need a visa is St. Petersburg, Russia. (Those partaking in a Disney excursion do not need a visa to enter Russia. Passengers who depart the ship and want to travel on their own will need Russian visas.)

In addition to obtaining a passport, another favor you can do yourself is to arrive at the port one day in advance. The ship will leave at 4:00 p.m. on your day of departure. Disney has extraordinary customer service, but they cannot change time to accommodate your delayed flight. Things happen. Arrive a day early and relax at a cheap hotel. I've heard too many horror stories of those who missed cruises due to travel delays.

In related news, you may want to consider travel insurance when you book your cruise. You can purchase this insurance directly from Disney Cruise Line. This insurance will compensate you for cancelation and/or delay. On the Disney Cruise Line, there are absolutely no refunds ninety days from departure. Insurance will offer some nice peace of mind for a nominal fee. Just remember, insurance purchased through Disney will only cover those items on your reservation. If you buy your own airfare, Disney insurance will not cover it.

### Arrival

No matter the departure port, Disney offers ground transportation from the nearest airport to the ship. These transfers can be purchased at the same time that you book your cruise. They will even accommodate your desire to arrive a day early. This will be the easiest option to get from plane to ship, especially in a city that you're not familiar with. Of course, it's usually less expensive to make your own way to the ship.

Disney's home port of Port Canaveral, Florida, is beautiful and well maintained. It's an easy forty-five-minute drove from Orlando International to the port. Disney offers transfers in themed buses that are a lot of fun. You can also combine a cruise with a few days at Walt Disney World Resort. Disney will arrange your transportation from there as well.

The other ports around the world will have ground transportation, but that transportation will not be Disney themed. It will still be reliable and convenient. Generally, the more Disney cruises that leave from a port, the more themed that port's facilities will be. Port Canaveral is all Disney all the time because Disney Cruise Lines is always there. The other sometimes Disney home ports are Miami, Galveston, Vancouver, Copenhagen, Barcelona, and New York City. Any other city will be a one-off departure port and will not be themed.

### Embarkation

If you've been on another company and still have nightmares about getting on the ship, just forget all of that. I've traveled on several cruise lines, and none of them come even close to the level of service found with Disney Cruise Lines. You're going to pay more for a Disney cruise, and that increase in price will be apparent when you see how many more cast members Disney is able to employee. Because they have more people, they can move passengers quickly and efficiently. Unlike with other companies, you will not have to wait in order in a gated cattle pen before you board.

Three months before your cruse, you'll complete an online check-in procedure. This is when you'll pay your final balance and confirm that all your arrangements are correct. You'll also choose a port arrival time. On the day of your departure, just arrive at the port during your arrival window. You'll check in and receive your room key (which is also your boarding pass and charge card during the cruise). You'll also get a boarding number; just check one of the monitors and board the ship with your number is posted. If you've arrived during your arrival window, you won't have to wait long to board the ship.

**Dreamlly's Disney Direction**

Remember when I said to vacation the way you want? That's especially good advice when it comes to cruising. Don't let others tell you what you must and must not experience.

You'll see all sorts of promotional cruise videos of passengers partying all night in dark nightclubs. If this is for you, great. Go ahead and boogie oogie oogie till you just can't boogie no more. But don't feel bad if you just want to go to bed at 9:00 p.m. and let the ship gently rock you to sleep. It's OK to eat every meal at the buffet and skip the dining rooms. I've known people who have had a fantastic cruise by ordering room service and never leaving their rooms. What may be a waste of money to some may be heaven to others.

On a Disney cruise, you can plan to do as little or as much as you want. Port excursions are available to book when you complete your online check-in. Disney will make sure you are well aware of the options. They make a bit of money off these things and don't want you to forget about them.

Just like in a good Disney film, always let your heart be your guide. One time, my husband and I were on a Disney cruise of the Baltic Sea. We had stopped in Tallinn, Estonia. During the morning, we got off the ship and explored this beautiful town on our own. We had a guided museum excursion booked for the afternoon. However, when we were in the middle of Tallinn, we found a charming square where a music festival was occurring. A full orchestra was playing selections from *The Phantom of the Opera* when we walked passed. Our hearts told us to sit at a café and spend the afternoon enjoying coffee and music. Yep, we had already paid for the excursion and couldn't cancel. There's no doubt that we wasted some money. But that afternoon wasn't just the highlight of the cruise—it was also one of my fondest memories ever. All these years later, when I need to visit my happy place, I remember that square in Tallinn, the coffee, and the orchestra. I realize this paragraph makes me sound pretentious, but I won't apologize, and I sincerely hope you will also have a fond memory to be pretentious over. Let your heart be your guide, and the memories will surely follow.

▲ ▲ ▲

# Ships
## Disney Magic

- First sailed in 1998
- 964 feet (294 meters) in length
- eleven decks
- twenty-seven hundred passengers
- 945 crew members
- 875 staterooms
- Foghorn plays "When You Wish Upon a Star"
- Godmother: Patricia Disney (wife of Walt's nephew Roy)
- Atrium statue: Mickey Mouse as helmsman
- Art on the ship's bow: Sorcerer Mickey
- Art on the ship's aft: Goofy

The first of Disney's ships, Disney Magic is decorated in an art deco–style. It's a beautiful ship with an open staircase in the lobby underneath a colorful chandelier.

There are three dining rooms that passengers rotate through during the cruise. The wait staff rotates as well so that passengers can count on getting the same service each night. **Lumiere's** is a princess-themed elegant dining room, **Carioca's** has a Brazilian theme, and **Animator's Palate** is an interactive third dining room. There is a buffet called **Cabanas**. For an additional fee, passengers can book a special meal at **Palo**, the ship's specialty dining room.

The big production shows on the Disney Magic are *Twice Charmed: An Original Twist on the Cinderella Story*, *Tangled: The Musical*, and *Disney Dreams: an Enchanted Classic*.

Disney Magic spends the winter in the Caribbean. In May, the ship sails up the East Coast to New York City. By June, Disney Magic has crossed the Atlantic and arrives at its summer home in Copenhagen. From there, the ship offers cruises of the Baltic Sea and Norwegian fjords. The Disney Magic heads back from Europe in late September. The ship spends a month in New York City offering cruises of Canada and then returns to Florida in time for winter.

**Disney Wonder**

- First sailed in 1999
- 964 feet (294 meters) in length
- eleven decks
- twenty-four hundred passengers
- 945 crew members
- 875 staterooms
- Foghorn plays "When You Wish Upon a Star"
- Godmother: Tinkerbell
- Atrium statue: Ariel
- Art on ship's bow: Mickey as Steamboat Willie
- Art on ship's aft: Donald and his nephews

The Disney Wonder is a sister ship to the Disney Magic. It's decorated in the art-nouveau style.

The dining rooms on Disney Wonder include a princess-themed room called **Triton's**, the New Orleans-themed **Tiana's Place,** and **Animator's Palate.** This ship still features the original version of Animator's Palate, where the dining room begins in black and white and colorizes itself during the meal. **Beach Blanket Buffet** is the ship's buffet. **Palo**, again offered for an extra charge, is present on one of the top decks.

The big productions shows on the Disney Wonder are *Frozen: A Musical Spectacular, Disney Dreams: An Enchanted Classic,* and *The Golden Mickeys.*

Disney Wonder spends the winter in the Caribbean. In early May, the ship sails through the Panama Canal and docks in San Diego. From there, Disney Wonder offers a few cruises of the Mexican Riviera. By June, the ship has moved to its summer home in Vancouver. Disney Wonder offers cruises to Alaska all summer long before returning to Florida via the Panama Canal in the fall.

**Disney Dream**

- First sailed in 2011
- 1,114.7 feet (339.8 meters) in length
- sixteen decks
- four thousand passengers
- 1,458 crew members
- 1,250 staterooms
- Foghorn plays several songs including "Be Our Guest"

- Godmother: Jennifer Hudson
- Atrium statue: Donald Duck as admiral
- Art on ship's bow: Mickey as captain
- Art on ship's aft: Sorcerer Mickey with brooms

The Disney Dream is Disney's first larger ship. The lobby atrium and chandelier are considerably larger than those on the previous two ships. Similar to Disney Magic, the decor is art deco.

The princess-themed dining room on the Disney Dream is **Royal Palace. Enchanted Garden** is an elegant dining room themed to the gardens of Versailles. The lights slowly change while you eat to give the illusion of the setting sun. The third dining room is **Animator's Palate. Cabanas** is the buffet. Disney Dream offers two premier dining rooms for an extra charge: **Palo** and **Remy.**

The big-production shows on the Disney Dream are *The Golden Mickeys, Disney's Believe,* and *Villains Tonight.* Starting in November of 2017, *Villians Tonight* will be replaced with a new live-action musical based on *Beauty and the Beast.*

The Disney Dream spends the entire year sailing from Port Canaveral in Florida. Normally, the ship rotates between three- and four-night sailings to the Bahamas with a stop at Castaway Cay.

**Disney Fantasy**

- First sailed in 2012
- 1,114.8 feet (339.8 meters) in length

- sixteen decks
- four thousand passengers
- 1,458 crew members
- 1,250 staterooms
- Foghorn plays several songs including "A Dream Is a Wish Your Heart Makes"
- Godmother: Mariah Carey
- Atrium statue: Minnie as French mademoiselle
- Art on ship's bow: Sorcerer Mickey
- Art on ship's aft: Dumbo and Timothy Mouse

The Disney Fantasy is a sister ship to the Disney Dream, but Disney Fantasy has art-nouveau decor. It's barely longer than the Disney Dream, just a few inches, but it's enough to make it Disney's largest ship to date.

On this ship, **Animator's Palate** includes an interactive show where passengers draw figures that are then animated on giant screens. The princess-themed dining room is called **Royal Court**, and **Enchanted Garden** is the third venue for dinner. **Cabanas** is once again the buffet. The Disney Fantasy also offers both **Palo** and **Remy** for an extra fee.

The big-production shows on the Disney Fantasy are *Disney's Believe, Disney's Aladdin: A Musical Spectacular,* and *Disney Wishes.*

Like her sister, the Disney Fantasy spends the entire year departing from Florida. However, most of this ship's journeys are seven-night cruises a bit deeper into the Caribbean.

Apps aren't just for theme parks anymore. The Disney Cruise app can be a handy tool to use during your cruise. However, make sure to download the app before you board.

On the ship, check that your phone is set to airplane mode (unless you want a nice surprise on your phone bill when you return home). Then connect to the ship's Wi-Fi signal. You won't be able to use this signal to access the Internet, but you can use the Disney Cruise app all you want for free.

The app will always have the most current schedule of the ship's events. There are also interactive maps that make finding your way a bit easier. However, the best feature is the ability to text with other app users. After you accept a friend request, you can send messages as much as you want for free. It's quite nice to be able to let your family and friends know where you are. The app has lots of fun Disney emojis that you can share. Hopefully you won't need to use the seasick Mickey!

▲ ▲ ▲

**Cruise Knowledge**
*Dining*
Dining is always an event on a Disney cruise. Disney invented the concept of rotational dining. Each night,

you'll dine in a different themed room. However, your wait staff will rotate with you for each night of your cruise. This means that you'll get the same excellent service from those you recognize.

**Animator's Palate** is Disney Cruise Line's signature experience. It's done a little differently on each ship, but expect some type of show while you dine.

Room service is complimentary on Disney Cruise Line. And, most importantly, Disney is the only cruise line that offers complimentary soft drinks, coffee, and tea to all passengers.

Each ship offers a buffet on one of the top decks. The buffet is always open for breakfast and lunch. You can eat in the buffet for dinner if you want a change from the more upscale dining rooms.

One or two specialty restaurants are available on each ship. These are available for a surcharge in the range of $50 to $100 per person.

### *Clothing/Attire*

Your destination will dictate the kind of clothing you'll need for most of your journey. You'll wear shorts and T-shirts for most of your cruise to the Bahamas, but you'll need jeans and sweatshirts in Alaska and the Baltic Sea.

One of the great things about a Disney Cruise is that dinner can be, to a certain extent, any way you want it. You won't see shorts and T-shirts in the dining rooms, but pretty much anything else will work. Some families will go all out and don formal dresses and suits. Others will dress more casually with dress pants and shirts. You will see people in jeans and button-down shirts as well.

On Disney Dream and Disney Fantasy, the specialty restaurant Remy has a dress code. You'll need semiformal attire to dine here.

What's with all the crap on stateroom doors? Well, this isn't your grandparents' *Love Boat*. Many passengers on a Disney cruise are full-on Disney fanatics, and they are not ashamed of it. As you walk the halls, you'll see all sorts of magnetic designs applied to stateroom doors. Some people are quite creative, and a stroll through each corridor is as thrilling as window shopping on Fifth Avenue during Christmas.

You'll also see homemade pouches hanging beside some of the doors. These are called "fish extenders." Each stateroom has a small metal fish fixed aside the door. Cruise staff uses these fish to clip any notices or messages for your cabin. But some passengers use the fish to hang pouches—hence the term "fish extender."

Before your cruise, you can visit disboards.com and sign up for your journey's fish-extender list. This means that you'll bring a small gift for everyone else on the list, and they'll bring one for you. Sometime during the cruise, you'll visit all the other cabins on your list and leave a small gift in their extenders. You'll find small surprises in your own extender from time to time.

Passengers use all sorts of items for their gifts. Pencils, stickers, postcards from home, and key chains are common, but some people get very creative. I've found that I have enough stuff in my life, so I generally don't participate with fish extenders anymore. However, once in a while, someone will suggest that instead of gifts, an exchange of recipes would be nice. In this case, I always participate. I love getting favorite recipes from around the world.

▲ ▲ ▲

### Shows

Disney Cruise Lines does shows well—very well, in fact! While cruising, expect a Broadway-caliber experience with amazing sets, fantastic costumes, and live music. Peter Pan and Mary Poppins will fly through the air, even during rough seas. Each cruise includes three big-production shows. On other nights, Disney brings onboard various magicians and comedians.

There is always one themed night on each Disney cruise. You'll know which theme you're getting when you book your cruise. The themes include pirate night, *Frozen*, or *Star Wars*. On a themed night, the dining rooms have a special menu. There will also be an evening deck party that includes fireworks. Disney is currently the only cruise line in the world that has the ability to launch fireworks at sea.

### Character Greetings

There are lots of characters on each ship. You'll get a schedule each night detailing where the specific characters will be during the next day. You can use your own camera or have a Disney photographer snap a few pictures. One of the big advantages of being on a Disney cruise is that there are far fewer people in character meeting lines than there are in the theme parks. Take advantage of the short lines onboard and get some excellent photos.

Some of the more popular characters, like the famous sisters from *Frozen*, require a reservation to meet them on a Disney ship. You can reserve these experiences online when you check in for your cruise.

### Shutters Photography

There are several thousand photo opportunities on each Disney cruise. They range from photos with characters, to candid snapshots, to formal portraits. Disney photographers and their expensive cameras are available everywhere to take your photo. However, they are also happy to take a shot with your own camera as well. Photos taken by ship photographers can be viewed on screens in the Shutters Photo Gallery. You can purchase the photos individually or as part of a package.

### Activities for Those Who Are Kids at Heart

A Disney cruise is not just for kids. I've been on many cruises with no children and have always had a great time. Each ship features a nightclub area that's large and fantastically themed.

On the Disney Dream and Disney Fantasy, you can have a martini in a lounge that overlooks Paris. Just wait a few minutes and suddenly you're overlooking Hong Kong. Even the art on the walls and the music overhead change to reflect whatever city is being portrayed behind the bar. The Skyline Bar is a relaxing marvel that is seldom busy.

Each ship features some sort of large dance club, a sports bar, a piano lounge, and a lounge with views of the ocean. Each ship also has a spa and an adults-only pool area.

Ironically, the best Disney Cruise feature for adults is all the kids' activities. Kids are so busy on a Disney ship that adults never have to deal with unruly youngsters running around. (See below.)

### Kids' Clubs

I've been on other cruise lines that have been overrun by kids. This is because there isn't any place for kids to be on their ships. You will never have to worry about kids getting out of control on a Disney cruise.

Each ship features several clubs for different aged kids. The clubs are a private space where parents can drop off their kids for all sorts of entertainment. Cast members are numerous and well trained to make sure the kids are involved and occupied. When I've sailed with kids, I hardly ever see them after they've been introduced to their clubs, although cast members will always make sure that your kids are at your table for dinner.

The kids' clubs are open until 1:00 a.m. The younger clubs offer story and calm bedtime activities. The tween and teen clubs offer full-on dance parties with smoothies and organized mixers.

All of this is complimentary for passengers. I know that a Disney cruise is a bit more expensive than other lines. That's mostly because they offer so many organized activities for kids. Even when I'm traveling without kids, I don't mind paying extra to give kids these unforgettable experiences.

### 1820 Society

No, contrary to its name, this is not a club for very old people who want to sit around and drink mulled wine from snifters in front of fireplaces. It's always been difficult for those aged eighteen to twenty to find interesting activities on a cruise ship. They are too old for the teen club and too young to drink inside the nightclubs. The 1820 Society is Disney's clubs for these folks.

Disney is quite strict about the age requirement, so I have no direct knowledge of what exactly occurs. However, I've been told there are a lot of activities that focus on gathering with food and beverages. There are cooking classes, coffee tastings, game nights, and satellite viewing of sporting events from around the world.

### Castaway Cay

Disney Cruise Line is the only cruise company in the world to have a private island that doesn't require tendering. This means that the ship can dock right on the island, and passengers can walk on and off as they please.

Castaway Cay is gorgeous. There are all sorts of excursions you can take on the island, or you can just sleep underneath an umbrella. There is a large family beach near the ship and a private beach for adults on the other side of the island.

There's lots to do on Castaway Cay. You can rent a bike and spend the day exploring the island. You can get snorkel gear and try to spot all sorts of objects that Mickey Mouse hid under the waves. There is parasailing, kayaking, hiking, and a stingray experience.

The same cast members that staff the kids' clubs on the ship will be available in special places on the island to provide activities. There is always a dance party in the afternoon.

While on the island, you'll eat at **Cookie's Barbeque.** There are soft drinks and ice cream available all day.

Some of the special adventures require a separate fee, but the beaches and all the food are included with your cruise fare. Castaway Cay is not its own country. (Wouldn't it be cool if it was?) The island is in the Commonwealth of the Bahamas. Consequently, you will need a government-issued photo ID in order to visit. Castaway Cay has its own post office with special stamps and postmarks, but they only take cash.

*Holidays*

The Disney cruise ships don't have to be jealous of the theme parks when it comes to the holidays. That same seasonal Disney magic transforms the ships into floating celebrations.

During September and October, **Halloween on the High Seas** is celebrated on the Disney Dream and Disney Fantasy in the Caribbean. There are special shows, trick-or-treating, decorations, and Halloween-inspired menus.

During November and December, most of the Disney ships offer **Disney's Merrytime Cruise.** (It's a pun on the word "maritime." It took me a while to get it too.) During these cruises, there are special holiday shows, tons of decorations, and a Christmas tree-lighting ceremony. The characters don their holiday finest, and the ship's bakers create enormous gingerbread houses for you to photograph. And, to the amazement of many, Disney magic can make it snow on Castaway Cay!

You will know if you're going to be on one of these holiday cruises when you make your booking. Any holiday celebration will be directly reflected on the cruise itinerary. Just know that during both of these special cruises, it's easy to avoid the celebrations and still have a normal cruise (well, as normal as sailing over the ocean with a giant mouse and a temperamental duck can be).

*Disembarkation*

Ending your vacation is never fun. It's even worse when you have to literally wave good-bye to characters you've known your whole life. Disney Cruise Line makes it a little better by providing all their guests a full plated breakfast on the morning of departure.

Despite being one of the most powerful corporations in the world, Disney has no control over passport control and customs. Regardless of whatever country you're entering, be patient and follow all directions. Also, do not use any electronics in a customs area as they can be confiscated. I've seen this happen more than once.

After clearing customs, Disney will once again handle your transportation to your next destination if you've chosen that option. If not, there are taxis available outside every port in the world. Uber is also an option in most ports. Regardless of how you depart, cherish your memories and revisit your household budget so you can travel again.

## Disney's Aulani Resort

Disney owns property all over the globe. The Disney Vacation Club operates resorts on the Florida coast and at Hilton Head, South Carolina. These are smaller properties that still offer the amazing Disney customer service.

However, there is one last comprehensive Disney destination to speak of. It's the fabulous Aulani: A Disney Resort and Spa. Aulani is located on the Hawaiian island of Oahu. It opened in 2011.

When designing and constructing the property, Disney purposefully wanted it to be big on the Hawaiian and small on the Disney. And it succeeds in a spectacular fashion.

"Aulani" is a Hawaiian word that means "a place that speaks with deep messages." As soon as you enter the soaring lobby, you'll encounter Hawaiian culture like no place else on the island. I visited the resort once with friends who live on the island. They were a bit skeptical of Disney's presence in Hawaii, but once we walked around, they immediately saw how Hawaiian everything was. You cannot turn a corner without seeing some form of Hawaiian music, art, or history.

While staying at the resort, you can sit and listen to native Hawaiian storytellers. There are also ukulele lessons and lei making. There's a hang-out for teens and yoga for adults. The resort offers a luau at night.

The pool complex at Aulani is arguably the best in the entire state. The pool alone is eighty-two hundred square feet (760 square meters). But that's not all. Aulani has its own lazy river, water slides, and an artificial snorkeling lagoon. All of this is surrounded by gorgeous lava rocks, waterfalls, and more flowers than you could ever imagine.

Aulani has direct access to the ocean. There is a nice beach that's actually part of a lagoon. Consequently, the seas are seldom rough here, and swimming is safer. But the beach is not as beautiful as others on the island. You're probably trading the beach for a much better pool—a trade most families might make that other travelers may reject.

The resort is part Disney Vacation Club (timeshare) and part regular hotel. There are many different types of rooms to choose from. A standard room with two beds and no view begins around $250. Rooms with multiple bedrooms and ocean views will cost considerably more money.

If there is any downside to Aulani, it's the location. Aulani is in Ko Olina, twenty miles west of Honolulu International Airport in the opposite direction of Waikiki. It may surprise you to learn that traffic is a nightmare on Oahu. It's much worse than Los Angeles! Those who love the kitschy fun of Waikiki will not want to stay at Aulani. For me, a perfect stay in Hawaii would be four nights on Waikiki and three nights at Aulani.

Dreamlly's Disney Direction

Even though Aulani is decidedly Hawaiian with minimal Disney influence, there are still a few Disney characters that make appearances. You can check the resort schedule to find out where and when to have your photo taken with Mickey Mouse or Donald Duck in their Hawaiian finest. (Donald wears a Hawaiian shirt—still no pants!—except when he goes surfing. Then he wears swim trunks and no shirt. Go figure.)

Regardless of where you are when you meet them, the characters greet guests for thirty minutes. Cast members are excellent at stopping guests from getting in line if they won't have a chance to get a photograph before the character has to depart. Disney adheres to strict guidelines as to how long a character can interact. It can get warm for Minnie and Daisy in all those clothes, and they need to take a break.

There are other rules that need to be followed as well. Remember, there is only one Mickey Mouse. When Mickey is in a parade, he's not going to be able to pose for your photograph on Main Street. Yes, adults, I know what you're thinking. But protecting the integrity of the characters is Disney's number-one goal. There is, after all, only one Mickey Mouse.

# 9

<hr>

# Disney Difference and Time to Go!

## What's a Disney Park?

I'VE USED THE term "Disney park" a lot in this book. It's my hope that as you've read, you've also gained some insight into what that term means. Typically, an amusement park contains lots of thrill rides without themed lands and back stories. A theme park is a place that tells stories through the use of themed architecture, employee uniforms, and food. However, a Disney park has evolved into something different.

Universal Studios Orlando is great. Both of their parks include highly themed lands with some fantastic attractions. One evening, I was waiting for my food at a quick-service café. I asked the employee behind the counter how her day was going.

"It's been long," she said, "but I get to go home soon."

Now, I don't begrudge her. Most likely her day had been long and like all other people at work, she was happy to be going home soon. But you would never hear that answer from a Disney cast member. Even if they have also had long days, Disney cast members will always show positive attitudes. Don't get the idea that Disney brainwashes their employees. Disney is, however, great at teaching their cast members to respect their guests' vacations. One reason I love Disney parks is because I can go there and forget the world for a bit. I can forget that some people aren't happy. At Disney, I know that the cast members understand and respect my decision to forget reality in their park.

I love Dolly Parton's Dollywood in Pigeon Forge, Tennessee. It's a fantastic theme park with lots of things to do for all ages. Christmas at Dollywood has no comparison on this planet; it's an unbelievable display of spirit. I love Dollywood so much that I wrote a book about it. But one day, my husband and I were walking through the park, and he pointed out a custodian emptying the trash in jeans and a T-shirt.

"Why do the maintenance workers here dress like that? Shouldn't they wear a uniform?" he asked me.

Then, later in the day, we saw a woman wearing a poodle skirt working at a shop in the Craftsman's Valley land of the park. Most likely, she was an employee from the Jukebox Junction land who had been asked to fill in for someone in Craftsman's Valley. My husband commented that this type of thing would never happen at Disneyland. He said that you'd never see a cowboy working in Tomorrowland.

He was right. I explained to him that this was one reason Dollywood costs less to visit each day. It's still a great park, but it's not able to operate on the same level as a Disney park, and I wouldn't want it to. I love Dollywood because it's Dollywood. Turning Dollywood into a Disney park would also take away some of the unique charm that envelops its Smoky Mountain environment.

But it's not just that Disney uses the right costumes in the right lands; it's also that these costumes are each intricately designed. The shoes and socks will be coordinated with belts and hats. No button will be missing. Disney cast members are always clean and wrinkle-free. And, for special events, the Disney costumes will change. A regular Frontierland cowgirl will become a Christmas cowgirl when Mickey's Christmas Party starts at 7:00 p.m. Belle may don her poor Provençal blue dress during the day and change into her gold ball gown at night. A Disney park is all about detail. These details are not held to the same standard in other parks.

I was at a park in a country outside the United States; I won't name it because it wasn't that great. In the kids' land, there was a character dressed as a hippopotamus walking around and posing for photographs. This hippopotamus was cutely outfitted in a floral dress and a big straw hat. She was quite adorable. Then some crass male visitor walked up to her and grabbed her butt. She pushed him away and went on with her business. There was nobody around to help her. I can tell you that if anyone ever grabbed a Disney character by the butt, there would be an instant reaction—and it would not turn out well for the crass visitor.

I've seen empty beverage containers floating in ponds at theme parks around the globe. It's not a huge deal, but the sight does make me grimace. I don't worry about seeing litter at a Disney park because it's simply not tolerated.

I've encountered theme-park employees who clearly had no training and were unable to perform their duties. That's not going to happen at a Disney park either. Disney's famous cast-member training, Disney University, is the ideal for customer-service training in the world. In addition, Disney's long tradition of promoting from within provides large incentives that encourage cast members to always give 100 percent.

Yes, Disney makes mistakes, and when they do, they also make headlines. Because of the company's popularity and reputation, the media loves to promote negative Disney news because those headlines sell more papers. I've found that negative Disney moments are few and far between. Reporters rarely print Disney's side of the story, nor do they follow up with Disney's plans to rectify a negative situation.

It's not that I will only go to a Disney park. But when I go elsewhere, I travel with different expectations. I love the Disney parks because I know I can rely on my high expectations. I know that they will be immaculately clean, friendly, themed, organized, diverse, bright, educational, inclusive, happy, safe, innovative, entertaining, thrilling, and—most of all—magical.

## Time to Go!

Travel is an integral part of the human experience. I can't think of a better gift you could give your family. I know it's the best gift you can give yourself. I hope you've enjoyed reading about Disney's kingdoms around the globe. But even if you didn't, I still hope you travel. Regardless of what you learned from this book, here are the four most important things to remember:

1. Theme parks are awesome, and Disney parks put the "awe" in "awesome."
2. Travel does not have to be expensive if you do your homework.
3. Travel the way you want to.
4. Always see the world through the eyes of a kid.

In the great theme park of life, I hope you spend a lot more time on the attractions and a lot less time waiting in line. Now, go!

# INDEX

[Note: The term "Disney's" has been omitted for the purpose of this index. For example, Disney's Contemporary Resort is listed as Contemporary Resort.]

# INDEX

# INDEX

# INDEX

# INDEX

# INDEX

# INDEX